Dramatic Dialogue

Dramatic Dialogue

The duologue of personal encounter

Andrew K. Kennedy

Cambridge University Press

Cambridge

London   New York   New Rochelle
Melbourne   Sydney

Published by the Press Syndicate of the University of Cambridge
The Pitt Building, Trumpington Street, Cambridge CB2 1RP
32 East 57th Street, New York, NY 10022, USA
296 Beaconsfield Parade, Middle Park, Melbourne 3206, Australia

First published 1983

Printed in Great Britain
at the University Press, Cambridge

Library of Congress catalogue card number: 82–4257

British Library Cataloguing in Publication Data
Kennedy, Andrew K.
Dramatic dialogue.
1. Dialogue   2. Drama
I. Title
808.2   PN1551
ISBN 0 521 24620 2 hard covers
ISBN 0 521 28845 2 paperback

WP

Contents

Acknowledgements   p. vii

Introduction   1

1   The duologue of recognition in Greek tragedy   34

2   Duologues of transformation in Shakespeare   62

3   The combat of wit   106

4   The confessional duologue from Ibsen to Albee   167

5   Duologues of isolation : towards verbal games   198

6   The impersonal/personal duologue from
    Brecht to Shepard   234

Notes   257

Index   275

Acknowledgements

The best part of the work on this book was carried out in the stimulating quiet of the Institute for Advanced Studies in the Humanities, University of Edinburgh (1977) and at Clare Hall, Cambridge (1979–80) where I was Visiting Fellow. A generous grant from the Norwegian Research Council for Science and the Humanities – Norges Almenvitenskapelige Forskningsråd – enabled me to make good use of the leave of absence granted to me by the University of Bergen.

Two shorter sections were first published in the *Yearbook of English Studies*, 9, Theatrical Literature Special Number (1979) and in *Contemporary Approaches to Ibsen*, 4 (Oslo, 1979) and draft papers covering some of the ground were read at the 14th F.I.L.L.M. Congress, Aix-en-Provence, 1978, and at the British Comparative Literature Association's Conference at the University of Kent at Canterbury, 1980.

Sections of the manuscript were read by Peter Bilton, Jean Chothia, Christopher Gillie, Peter Holland, John Northam and Leo Salingar, whose specialist knowledge and personal interest were greatly valued by me. While there is not much in the book that is strictly linguistic, I have gained fresh understanding from the work of David Crystal and from conversations about 'conversation' with Rukmini Bhaya, Gillian Brown, Nils-Erik Enkvist and Roman Jakobson. Richard Holton Pierce kindly read the chapter on Greek tragedy at proof stage.

Introduction

1. Concepts of dialogue

On the face of it, 'dialogue' is a transparent term, without marked ambiguity or haziness, and, what is more, without marked contradiction between the popular and the critical denotations of the word. Ordinary usage overlaps at several points with the (all too few) useful definitions offered by theorists of drama. I myself have been able to assess everyday usage by noting the response of all kinds of people to the word 'dialogue' over a certain period of time: always, some idea of conversation is at once understood or implied; it tends to have, further, a connotation of 'serious talking' rather than of 'chat', of something relatively sustained, with attempts at bridging gaps in understanding between opposed or contending parties. The growing currency of the word 'dialogue' with some such connotation – as testing and clarifying the conflict of values, standpoints, 'worlds', among opponents – underlines the general sense of dialogue as a *significant* human activity. It also seems to be understood that 'dialogue' is primarily a *verbal* activity. Paying attention to the choice of words, by speaker and listener as partners, is a prime rule of this particular 'language game' – whatever the degree of attention paid to posture, gesture, facial expression, movement, pauses and silences, or other para-linguistic clues to meaning. But those who reflect on 'dialogue' are generally aware that an exchange between speakers is more than an exchange of speeches; *what* is being said must be heard with or against *how* it is being said, what style of speech, what tone, tempo and so on. It would seem that – in a persona-ridden and word-devaluing culture – people retain a good deal of trust in signals exchanged in dialogue: perceiving and assessing character, motivation, attitude, degree of conviction and feeling; in short, all that makes for total communication. General ideas concerning the 'rules' or the 'art' of

1

conversation tend to persist – ideas that significantly overlap with a philosophical/linguistic definition of conversation as essentially co-operative and logic-guided.

Despite the spread of the word 'dialogue' into areas of everyday communication, the unique distinctness of *dramatic* dialogue is immediately understood: written for the stage, overheard by a member of the audience who does not participate through replying, interrupting, counteracting, as he might participate in a conversation. It is probable that children acquire an early aptitude for miming or at least responding to the 'doubleness' of stage dialogue – from Punch and Judy on, it is like talk/it is not 'real' talk – as part of the general aptitude for grasping fictional–theatrical experience. If that is so, we have here another 'competence' (language learning being the primary one) which has a direct, intuitive ground. Though simple in origin, the experience of mimed dialogue has a complexity that may seem to require several disciplines to account for; dramatic criticism proper needs to be informed by linguistics, the psychology of playing, and the semiotics of the theatre in the first place. But in all our theorising we need to keep in mind that universal-seeming faculty for direct, intuitive response to dramatic dialogue.

Let us take Francis Bacon's counsel and 'cut off infinity of inquiry' by concentrating on a limited number of concepts of dialogue – those most directly bearing on the intimate duologue, the main focus of this study. The governing concept for all dramatic dialogue is *verbal interaction*. That may sound like a tautology, yet among the very few studies of dramatic dialogue (and most general studies of drama neglect dialogue in any case),[1] little is said concerning the interpersonal exchange of speech – as distinct from the study of individual character, dramatic form and genre, or the features of a particular verbal style, imagery, word-play. The word 'dialogue' itself carries with it a fuller etymological connotation than is generally recognised; even those who have a sound enough grasp of the concept 'dialogue' seem to think that the word must mean two (*di*) people talking. However felicitous such a restricted meaning would, in one respect, be for a study concentrating on the duologue, we need to recall the very much richer network of ideas behind *dialogos* (from *dialegomai* =to converse, a compound of *dia* =. . . through, and *logos*). Any concept of dialogue needs to recapture at least an echo of the Greek significance of *logos* – one of the keywords of Western culture, connecting word and meaning, language and reality (later enriched by Christian and neo-Platonic mysticism, the opposition of words/Word, the incarnation declared in 'In the beginning was the Word'). Not everyone can, or wants to, reach the mystical dimension of language or go all the way with Martin Buber's concept of dialogue as deep communion, springing from a meeting of persons, in an I–Thou relationship directly experienced.[2] We need only retain our awareness of dialogue as a search for significance and as a flexible state of being-with-others through speech.[3] Aristotle, hardly a mystic, first stressed the significance of dialogue as an element of drama; though the 'plot is the first principle', the dialogue has a unique function which cannot be replaced by other dramatic elements: 'For what were the business of a speaker, if the thought were revealed quite apart from what he says?' However, the *Poetics* has been rather over-exposed in criticism since the Renaissance (from Castelvetro and Hédélin to our own primers), so much so that Aristotle is now often held responsible for any verbal (or over-verbal) concept of drama – the polar opposite of Artaud.[4] It may be more challenging to take a leap in time and examine the central concept of dialogue offered by Peter Szondi in his *Theorie des modernen dramas*.[5] The context of this study (not well enough known in England though a classic of criticism on the Continent) is post-Renaissance drama seen as a *pure* form of drama. In that drama interpersonal relations have a unique role in defining and reflecting the condition of man –man in the sphere of 'between': between other people, between conflicting states of being (two compound words in the German text underline the relatedness of persons in drama, of man as 'fellow human being' – *Mitmensch* – and the relatedness of persons, through acts of decision, to the surrounding world – *Mitwelt*). Such a person-centred concept of drama excludes everything else: 'the unspeakable . . . and the closed soul, as well as ideas that had become alienated from the personal; above all, the world of objects, beyond expression, except in so far as they enter interpersonal relations' (p. 14). Dramatic dialogue then becomes the most significant vehicle of the interpersonal world. (The German word *zwischenmenschlich*, literally 'interhuman', is at once more concrete and more richly associative: 'The verbal medium of man's interpersonal world [is] the dialogue.' 'Das

3

sprachliche Medium dieser zwischenmenschlichen Welt aber war das Dialog', pp. 14–15).

In Renaissance drama (admittedly defined by Szondi through an arbitrary concept of pure or absolute form) dialogue becomes, perhaps for the first time in history, the unique element in the texture of the drama. The prologue, the chorus, the epilogue, have all been set aside. Then dialogue attains a supreme place in the hierarchy of dramatic elements, mirroring interpersonal relations – its proper sphere.

Such a concept of drama strongly emphasises what can only be called the absence of the dramatist from his text: the author does not speak, only the characters. The dramatist does not address the audience directly. (Szondi's view resembles the eloquent definition of Stephen Dedalus in Joyce's *A Portrait of the Artist as a Young Man*, where the god-like dramatist remains 'within or behind or beyond or above his handiwork, invisible, refined out of existence, indifferent, paring his fingernails'.)[6] It follows that the words of the dialogue have the feel of being spoken 'out of the situation enacted, and remain within it'. And, in a further development of the argument, drama is seen as 'primary', and dramatic dialogue as 'original' in the sense that it is non-derivative – not a quotation or variation.

The interpersonal concept of dialogue can be taken as a fruitful starting point, for it illuminates the essential link between the *relational and stylistic* features of all dialogue (even though Szondi himself neglects language). It is illuminating, further, to have a strong concept of dialogue – one that sees in dialogue a central and controlling element rather than something secondary, or, worse, decorative and incidental.

Such a view does not commit us to Szondi's doctrine of the pure, absolutely 'closed' and dialogue-centred dramatic form (which is, in my view, too dependent on Hegelian aesthetics as well as on Brecht's polemical arguments against Aristotelian ideas of drama). When drama is approached with such purist *a priori* concepts, no niche is found for Shakespeare's multi-dimensional theatre: for types of play that work through multiple mirrors of genre, perspective and dialogue. Yet what we need is a full spectrum of drama, which can accommodate all the traditional modes of dialogue (starting with the Greeks, and with Shakespeare central), and which can then accommodate experi-

4

ment and mutation – new modes of dialogue being created in our own time. Modes of dialogue vary so much: their structures and textures suffer a 'sea-change', with the changes of period and genre, changes in the language of the community and in that of the individual dramatist. Nevertheless, they all have an interpersonal function and significance. For wherever there is exchange of dramatic speech, an exchange of persons – of values, attitudes, 'worlds' – as well as of structures and styles takes place.

A strong concept of dialogue does not, further, commit us to a doctrine of verbalism or literary supremacy. In this study at least the total sign language of a play – its visual/auditive/tactile effects in performance, the dependence of the lines on acting styles, on the voice, the tones and intonations of the actor – will always be taken into account. Our method leans towards the study of the text as we can only focus on one object at a time; but performance values are constantly kept in mind: *seen* in the text, and, wherever possible, seen and heard in the theatre. A study of dialogue as verbal interaction – both existential and stylistic – can only benefit from any study of the non-verbal elements of drama which illuminates the total sign system of the theatre. It is rewarding to return to the work of the Prague school of semioticians, especially Honzl and Veltruský, and to contemporary scholars as varied in approach as John Russell Brown, J. L. Styan, Keir Elam, Umberto Eco, Tadeusz Kowzan and others.[7] As for the 'quarrel' with the post-Artaud defenders of *anti*-verbal theatre (happening, physical action, improvisation, collage, neo-Dada randomness and orgiastic sounds), it need not concern us in this place.

It is more important to grasp that whenever a play has dialogue written into its text (and not just stage directions, or pages with acoustic possibilities calling for noises, cries, whispers and breathing) the proper limits of dialogue become manifest. For the resources of dialogue are not infinite. They may seem so only if viewed ahistorically and unpractically, with the whole 'imaginary museum' of drama in mind, rather than the particular struggle for expressive and actable dialogue in one particular playtext. Placed between the rhythmic incantation of 'music' and the raw energies of everyday 'conversation' – those polar opposites and inseparably paired twins – dialogue may approximate, but never become, either music or conversation.

'Music' has been placed in scare quotes here, because we are not concerned with music proper in interplay with dialogue proper (the power of song or of the occasional instrument as a stage effect – as in Shakespeare and Brecht) nor with the relation between libretto and score in an opera. That direct kind of interplay requires fine artistic balance from the dramatist, and a fine critical balance in our response; but it presents no special problem in a poetics of dialogue. By contrast, the dream of a musicalised language, a language of sounds, of incantation beyond persons (and beyond 'sense'), does present a problem. Nietzsche was among the first who, still under the hypnotic influence of Wagner, declared that 'tragedy, being a product of the spirit of music, must surely perish by the destruction of that spirit'. 'Music' is 'in the highest degree a universal language' identified with the chorus, the source of pure Dionysiac power, with dithyrambic dance and orgiastic abandon. Dialogue then in effect becomes the enemy of that power, the instrusion of an optimistic Socratic dialectic, dealing in mere ideas and images. If music 'beholds the world of the stage at once infinitely expanded and illuminated from within', then 'what analogue could the verbal poet possibly furnish?'[8]

The nearest parallel to Nietzsche's dream-language in our time is probably the recurrent dream of a language of pure sounds (whether a sublime incantation or a cacophony is not the issue): some language that will free the performers from the intolerable curse of words embedded in syntax, semantic context, and the human struggle for verbal interaction. The babel-language made up of 'pure sound' – not corresponding to any known spoken language – might be one example.[9]

The critical doctrine that regards a play as a continuous 'dramatic poem' may seem a long way from the polar extreme of 'music' *instead of* dialogue. Yet there is a built-in bias against dialogue in the 'dramatic-poem' approach. L. C. Knights – whose famous 'How Many Children had Lady Macbeth?' (1933) marked a healthy corrective to the excesses of character study in Shakespeare criticism – hardly ever quotes dialogue (and then he discusses its impersonality, its function as choric commentary).[10] Shakespeare criticism is rich in studies that concentrate on themes, on keywords, or symbols and imagery, the 'plums in the plum pudding' of dialogue, while disregarding the full texture of the dialogue (its syntax and rhythm, its overall design and its theatricality). When dialogue is discussed at all – as a concept – it tends to get fused with other modes of dramatic speech – the monologue, the set speech, the ritual or group dialogue. Thus Bertram Joseph in *Elizabethan Acting* states: 'it does not matter whether [Shakespeare] has used speeches that can be interpreted as dialogue, "mental" or "verbal" soliloquy, or the kind of monologue known as "direct address" '.[11] In this approach – what I call the hyper-rhetorical fallacy – the healthy attempt to correct a reductive, naturalistic reading of poetic drama, ends with concepts of dialogue pointing to declamation or verbal music.

At the opposite pole from 'music' we find the idea of dialogue as conversation. It might be expected that an interpersonal concept of dialogue would be hospitable to a conversational model; yet I would rather dwell on the distinction between conversation and dialogue – as concept and as practice – than run the risk of blurring the two or, worse still, equating them. The two words had best be kept distinct, with the symbiotic connection between them understood. Apart from casual usage, one keeps finding instances of otherwise precise criticism using the two terms interchangeably. Auerbach points to 'the conversation between the two sisters' in *The Antigone* and to 'a conversation between Prince Henry [and Poins]'[12] and Northrop Frye defines drama as 'a mimesis of dialogue or conversation'.[13] Frye's 'or' is not illuminating, and one is tempted to split it into either/or. We then have two competing definitions: *either* 'drama is a mimesis of dialogue' (a strongly dialogue-centred definition of drama) *or* 'dialogue is a mimesis of conversation'. The latter would commit us only to the view that all dialogue mimes conversation in some respects, but not in others; and we are still left with the task of briefly rethinking 'mimesis' in this matter of *writing dialogue* with conversation in mind (in the mind of the dramatist, writing *between* the world of speakers 'out there' and the performing speakers on stage).

What all interpersonal dialogue mimes is the essential question–answer structure of all conversation – the inescapable need to address and, at some point, respond to another speaker. (We can postpone dealing with the complexities of silence and partial monologue, of Gaev in *The Cherry Orchard* addressing the bookcase and Kaspar – the autistic youth in Handke's *Kaspar* –

speaking his one and only sentence to a chair or a table or a broom.) The mimesis of conversational structure, as distinct from its exact verbal texture, may seem obvious enough; yet certain critical practices and controversies have always tended to obscure it. The tendency to think of dramatic *speech* – of the dramatist writing speech, and of this or that character speaking more or less in isolation – tends to disconnect speaker from speaker, and diminish the interactive function, the fully 'dialogical' language of encounter. (Even Romeo and Juliet, Antony and Cleopatra, and other paired protagonists tend to find themselves in separate compartments of critical description.)[14] The other tendency is to confuse the question of mimesis (miming the interactive structure of conversation) with the long, in itself significant, debate on the role of naturalistic speech in post-Ibsen drama. As one who has at times been distracted by one or another of these critical tendencies, I may be allowed to report a certain sense of *eureka* on rediscovering the concept of interactive structure – within which dramatic dialogue does 'imitate' conversation – without being committed to tape-recording fidelity or verisimilitude in verbal texture.

All types of dramatic dialogue – all kinds of shaping and verbal texture, from stichomythia through blank verse to naturalistic prose – are embraced and illuminated by the interactive concept. Further, wherever we find a dislocation in the personal encounter, we recognise some of the features of mannerist and parodic dialogue – a derangement of relationship as well as of language.

The relationship between two (or more) speakers *as* speakers – the way they interrelate, dominate or balance one another's speech and the way they exchange value-carrying lumps of language – is in itself a dramatic/theatrical act. (One may note in passing that patterns of verbal exchange are interesting even in languages one does not understand.) The broad audio-visual posture of speakers confronting one another – asking, asserting, promising and so on, within the whole 'speech act' – often arrests and demands attention as much as the speech that is individually 'characteristic' for a character. Individual speech is often secondary in dialogue written in a univocal or standard language: in the Greek stichomythia and in naturalistic prose dialogue, especially that based on the standard speech of the urban middle class. In all drama differences in social role colour the mode of self-expression as well as the mode of address, and thus the interplay of speech styles in an encounter. Prince Hamlet, flooded by 'whirling' speech (and in danger of losing his identity through the chameleon-poet's sudden shifts of style) confronts Horatio, a 'normal' speaker (limited by his role, as the confidant of a prince, to almost self-cancelling spareness in his responses).[15]

While we shall keep, for good reasons, strictly to the study of dialogue in dramatic texts, it is reassuring to know that several directions in linguistics are now concerned with the study of ordinary conversation. It is part of a significant general movement away from the analysis of linguistic structures (for example, the sentence-based paradigm of language in Chomsky and transformation grammar) towards the study of linguistic process or, as Nils Enkvist put it: from the motorway of strict syntax to the scenic road of interactive linguistics. On this wider conceptual map, discourse analysis has a clear bearing on the study of dialogue; while the very names given by Austin and other philosophers to 'the speech act' and to 'performative' utterances point to their relevance to both conversation and to dramatic/theatrical performance.[16] All such concepts focus on what is happening in verbal interaction, on language that functions interpersonally. One may single out H. P. Grice's 'Logic and Conversation' (1975) which establishes a 'co-operative principle' for 'normal' conversation: 'our talk exchanges do not normally consist of disconnected remarks, and would not be rational if they did. They are characteristically, to some degree at least, co-operative efforts; and each participant recognises in them, to some extent, a common purpose or set of purposes, or at least a mutually accepted direction.'[17] One notes that the very idea of an end (*telos*) and the notion of 'logic' takes us back to something that is implied in *dialogos*. At the same time, as might be expected from such a hyper-rational approach to conversation, the maxims of co-operation (useful post-Kantian categories covering the Quantity, Quality, Relation and Manner of what is being said) ask us to be, respectively: informative, truthful, relevant and unambiguous. So the co-operative principle – a philosopher's norm for valid conversation in our society – would strongly mark the presence of any irony and of any such figures of speech as metaphor, meiosis and hyperbole. Would not, in the light of such criteria, much dramatic dialogue sound non-co-operative?

Probably. But one is thankful for a normative principle of conversation, which may enable us to gauge the 'angle of deviation' in any particular dialogue from that ideal or hypothetical colloquy: where speakers are said to be exchanging words (information, appeals, values) in a 'logic' of full co-operation.

The 'mimetic pull' towards conversation is an element in all dialogue – from the Greeks to our own time – for what is actually spoken in the world is a kind of speech-energy that keeps revitalising dramatic dialogue. Total abstraction – as we said concerning 'music' – remains an unattainable aim; nor is it, I think, much to be desired. I would still affirm that 'the dramatist cannot wholly lose touch with everyday speech without sterility'.[18] But, having said that, it seems clear that the uses of a 'conversational model' in the study of dramatic dialogue are relatively limited. The limits are implicit in what might be called the cardinal features of dramatic dialogue, which make it distinct and unique:

(1) The cumulative dialogue. Behind the immediate dialogue sequence lies the totality of the play and its language: the gradual build-up of action, the whole network of motifs, phrases, words repeated till they become keywords – in short, the complex overall dialogue 'behind' each particular dialogue. (It may be objected that the dialogue of an opening scene can hardly be thus underpinned by further dialogue sequences. However, the best opening dialogue – take *Hamlet* again – usually communicates a pressure that anticipates the 'cumulative dialogue', and is presumably written with that in mind: the art of 'coding' dialogue.)

(2) Counter-speech, or the counterpointing of verbal styles whereby the speakers talk to each other in sharply opposed or 'orchestrated' speech-styles: distinct in quantity, shape, texture, and so on.

(3) Acting and reading signals. The audience is being allowed to 'overhear' the dialogue, and in so doing is responding to all the signals written into the play-language. ('Cumulative dialogue' and 'counter-speech' contribute to that system of outward-directed communication.) Even the most participatory (empathy-driven) spectator or reader will enjoy the benefits of 'aesthetic distance': he or she does not have the role of an interlocutor in conversation, or that of a listener silently nodding or shaking his or her head by way of active response, or even the role of one eavesdropping behind the door. The dialogue is written for – and

spoken from within – this or that genre and speech convention; it is only 'possible' within an aesthetic/dramatic/theatrical context. That is why a dramatic performance can be regarded as a very special 'speech act' where the arrow that links Speaker 1 and Speaker 2 is always directed outwards to the anonymous and non-conversational auditor/spectator. Even the simplest diagram for dramatic dialogue will be triangular:

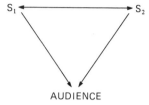

The three features summarised – 'cumulative dialogue', 'counter-speech' and 'acting signals' – all combine (and can, of course, only be separated for the purpose of critical discussion) to mark dramatic dialogue as a different order of discourse from ordinary conversation. Without saying any more on this point here,[19] I would appeal once more to experience and experiment. At one time we are engaged in a personal conversation that seems to us – in the act – richly expressive (carrying the 'voice of true feeling' or strong argument); then we listen to some banal-seeming dialogue, say, the opening sequence of Pinter's *The Birthday Party*. We may find a paradox: the diminishment of the experienced 'rich' conversation and the enhancement of that 'banal' dialogue (in the context of the whole play-language, especially in performance). Reflecting on that paradox will give us some insight into the 'peculiarities' – the complex shaping and texturing – of dramatic dialogue.

2. Structures and textures

'Structure' is the most over-used (often abused) critical term of our time, so that it becomes a debased or useless currency unless its specific sense in one context is made clear and then kept faith with. For the purposes of this study 'structure' is to retain some of its more robust connotations as a building or construction metaphor – pointing to the broader architectonic or compositional frame of dialogue – especially to the balance of speakers, the genre-guided choices of style and interactive coherence. The best word for this idea of structure may be 'shaping'; my own preference for that word stems both from its visual clarity and from the 'doing' element in shaping, as a verbal noun, suggesting the Coleridgean 'shaping imagination' at work in the dialogue (an integral element in the total design of the play).

'Texture' is clear in general use, but it too lacks precision as a critical term. In ordinary language one can say that a certain animal 'can feel the texture as well as the shape of a branch' – and the distinction is at once clear. The *Concise Oxford Dictionary*'s first entry under 'texture' is: 'arrangement of small constituent parts, perceived structure (of skin, rock, soil, organic tissue, literary work, etc.)'. At first sight, 'perceived structure' looks disappointingly tautological (texture = structure); yet it is clear that what is meant is small-scale or micro-structure, like the roughness/smoothness, etc., of rock or organic tissue; and, by analogy, in the literary work, stylistic features, verbal devices of many kinds, beginning with patterns of syntax and rhythm, vocabulary and sound, and leading to the perception of verbal mode and tone, precise subtleties. Such a distinction between structure (shaping) for the compositional frame of dialogue, and texture (the verbal varieties and complexities of individual speech) would suit us well – provided these terms are taken as mere tools of discussion and not as 'things in themselves', reified entities. What Whitehead called 'the fallacy of misplaced concreteness' is the particular danger of all general criticism; and in this instance, we are dealing with features that are interlinked – and often inseparable – aspects within the flow of dramatic dialogue.

(a) *Balance and dominance*

'Balance' is probably the most palpable, physical structural element: it can be seen on the printed page at a glance, and felt upon our pulses in the theatre. For in the interaction of two (or more) speakers the dominance of one over the other, or their equilibrium (exact, approximate, shifting or see-sawing) is immediately perceived in reading and performance. So immediate is our perception that it is often transparent – looked through as an almost invisible 'code' which we seldom take the trouble to interpret.[20] Yet the balance of speakers does provide, in a particular exchange or in a sequence of exchanges, the frame of interaction, while implicitly embodying something essential in the inner relationship of the speakers. One of the most immediate *given* features of stichomythic dialogue in Greek drama is the symmetry between speakers: the regularly recurrent line-by-line exchanges build a dialogue sequence somewhat in the way the columns in the collonade of a Greek temple form an overall design through repetition and regularity. (Coleridge called Greek tragedy 'statuesque'.) Though our detailed study will show that the formal fixity of Greek dialogue is compatible with a fine variety of types of encounter and texture, the face-to-face equivalence does remain unvaried. There is nothing quite like it in later European drama; nothing as sustained and universal. But the stichomythic balance does remain a paradigm for all kinds of symmetry or full equilibrium in dialogue: in 'flyting' (a regular duel of dirt, abuse and obscenity in the slanging-matches of the medieval Moralities); in the formal lament of the earlier plays of Shakespeare (the Queen, the Duchess and the Children in *Richard III*, 2. 2; the comic lament of the lovers in *A Midsummer Night's Dream*, 1. 1); in the repartee of the wit-combat (to be studied in full); even in the music-hall patter of Didi and Gogo in *Waiting for Godot*.

The hyper-dominant speaker is an obvious structural device with growing psychological interest. In its primitive form – as in Marlowe's *Tamburlaine* – it is simply an assertion of hubris through language, as well as by other means: he who dominates the stage is dominant; the universe of other speakers can be more or less excluded by the conquering hero of the tirade, whose speeches are still striving after language infinite. This kind of super-speechmanship was already parodied, with consummate control, by Jonson in the hubristic hyperbole given to characters like Sir Epicure Mammon; the eloquent logorrhoea of such a speech-maker is seen as an exploitable 'folly'. In modern drama we get subtle versions of the speech-dominant person: John Gabriel Borkman, the bankrupt banker as self-styled Titan, lapses, in the final scene of Ibsen's play, into a dominant quasi-monologist addressing not the woman who had loved him (and who is talking to him) but the hidden powers of the mines in the hills. Strindberg's would-be dominant speakers – the Captain in *The Father*, or Hummel in *The Ghost Sonata* – ultimately expose their vulnerability in their speech excess; in *The Stronger* (1899),

Mrs X confronts her completely silent companion, Mrs Y, with wave upon wave of patronising statements and anxious questions, yet she fails to obtain the expected benefits of self-assurance from out-talking her partner. In later drama, the incongruity of a fragile character attempting to dominate the dialogue – the universe of other speakers – through his own speech-making propensities, has become a recurrent focal point in dramatic construction: the Father in *Six Characters in Seach of an Author* trying to compensate, in a luxury of solos, for the poverty of his fixed dialogue; Hamm rehearsing his stories and warming-up for his last soliloquy in *Endgame*; Osborne's ego-centric heroes (Jimmy Porter naively presented through robust improvisations, and Bill Maitland in *Inadmissible Evidence* as a conscious victim of the tirade that isolates). Pinter repeatedly creates patterns of dominance through speech, most successfully in *The Caretaker*, where the highly controlled yet mannered bravura speeches of Mick significantly contrast – over every inch of the battle for territory – with the fumbling colloquial speech of the tramp Davies and the pathological 'poor' speech of his brother Aston. In sum, the dynamic balance, or imbalance, of speech between speakers is always significant and often offers a key to interpreting the more subtle forms of interaction between characters who have entered a (shared or contested) territory of exchange within a certain structure of dialogue.

(b) *Modes and moods*

Genre conventions control all levels of dialogue, its overall structure as well as its texture. 'Genre' is, however, a particularly unstable critical term; at one time over-defined and normative if not prescriptive (in the Aristotelian poetics and its neo-classical elaborations, especially on tragedy); at other times, as in the modern era, genre concepts get so blurred that they seem irrelevant to the perception of new modes of style – especially when innovation is stressed above all. This is not the place to try and disentangle at any length the uses and abuses of genre in criticism; so I will merely summarise my own approach to genre in so far as I think it illuminates the study of dialogue. All drama is, in one sense, a vast gallery of play-*types* on permanent show: the application of Malraux's *musée imaginaire* to the theatre. But genre concepts, so far from being 'strong' (i.e. stable from period to period and definable with rigorous rules) or an example of essentialist form (with invariable characteristics that constitute the 'essence' of this or that genre) are better thought of as 'family resemblances' free from the tyranny of the family. Such a Wittgensteinian concept underlies the approach of Morris Weitz in *Hamlet and the Philosophy of Literary Criticism.*[21] With such an approach, 'genre' seems still to be a valuable critical shorthand: it clarifies the discussion and grouping of all classical and neo-classical plays; it enables us to discuss the multiple style and imaginative genre-shifts in Shakespeare within a shared frame of reference; and, finally, it alerts us to every kind of continuity as well as mutation and innovation in the text of a new play. Genre guides our perception of verbal echoes, of parody and pastiche, quotation or allusion – in short, variations leaning on, and against, a type of play already understood by the literary/theatrical community. (Arguably, *Endgame* can only be understood by an audience or readers who have grasped the form and vision of traditional tragedy.)[22]

Bearing all this in mind, concepts of genre and dialogue are nearly always interdependent. Often the opening lines of a first scene define the mode of the whole play: the first sixty lines of dialogue in *Hamlet* (to 'This bodes some strange eruption of our state') immediately evoke a world wholly different from that conjured up by the opening slanging-match of *The Alchemist* (from 'Believ't, I will. / Thy worst. I fart at thee' to Subtle's roaring refusal to talk softly in line 60). The Shakespearian combat of wit only 'makes sense' within the conventions of the love-game comedy; and a critic who responds to that duologue of wit romantically (like Quiller-Couch) or with a metaphysical earnestness more appropriate to absurdist drama (like Terence Eagleton) can hardly endure, let alone do justice to, the dialogue of wit. (See chapter 3, pp. 109–11.)

Genre concepts, as already suggested, are as useful in illuminating subtle shifts of dialogue within a particular form as in showing correspondence between form and verbal style. Thus an alert reading of dialogue in Euripides can reconstruct the shift from mythic (Aeschylean) and personal (Sophoclean) to a dialectical and often parodic mode of dialogue in tragedy – a shift in thought, feeling, structure and texture. Again, if we had never heard of certain problems of genre – tragi-comedy in

Shakespeare, or 'romantic comedy', or modern 'dark comedy' –
we would have to invent some provisional generic term to point
to quite distinct tonalities of dialogue in, for example, *Measure for
Measure*, *The Tempest* and *The Cherry Orchard*.

New modes of dialogue explore new moods of *speech*. The
kinship between the two words is indicative.[23] It may well be that
we cannot read – and cannot see in the theatre – any new play
without making some kind of genre judgement about it, however
tentatively. From the first exchange on, the dialogue itself often
prompts us to see the play as having a 'family resemblance' to a
certain genre. Our experience of a new play is sharpened by this
or that provisional genre concept: a working hypothesis to be
confirmed or disconfirmed in the course of reading or seeing the
whole play. For example, I first observed certain recurrent 'comedy of manners' features in the dialogue of later Pinter plays,
especially in *Old Times*; I was already interested in what looked
like a new mannerist mode of dialogue; at a certain point I
lightly coined a phrase – 'comedy of mannerism' – which acted as
a home-made genre term and which then helped to sharpen my
awareness of several quite specific devices in Pinter's dialogue
(see chapter 5).

(c) *Coherence*

The extent to which speakers within any dialogue exchange are
'attuned' to one another can vary enormously – from complete
co-operation at one pole to systematic derangement at the other.
Linguistically – for we can postpone the personal level, the exchange of values, for the moment – those engaged in dialogue
may 'speak the same language' or may enter a world of babel;
and there are any number of theatrical possibilities between these
two extremes. The term 'coherence' is used here to denote this
aspect of dialogue both on the level of interactive responses, or
'turns', between two or more characters, and on the level of
verbal texture. The formal symmetry of Greek dialogue exem-
plifies a highly 'coherent' question-and-response frame and language; and, at the other pole, we may place any attempt to give
dialogue the *semblance* of completely spontaneous improvisation
– for example the talk of the 'real' people in Pirandello's *Each in his
Own Way* (1924), or in Jack Gelber's *The Connection* (1959). In
Greek drama the convention of the stichomythia frames every

dialogue exchange without exception; and in the improvisatory theatre 'the illusion of reality' is carried so far as to suggest that certain characters in the play-within-the-play (the stage audience, the acted non-actors) speak like the actual audience, their dialogue is *our* conversation. (That kind of carefully scripted spontaneity raises different questions from the dramatic use of unscripted improvisation, 'happenings' or tape recordings.) It should be illuminating to contrast critically the differences in dialogue coherence in Racine/Shakespeare and Ibsen/Chekhov, showing the respective importance of 'logic' and 'flow' in their dialogue. In a play like *Ghosts* the dialogue (for instance, in the exchanges between Mrs Alving and Pastor Manders) is often so tightly organised that it strikes many readers and audiences as over-rational or over-expository, translating intimate emotion into a dialectic of beliefs; by contrast, a play like *The Cherry Orchard* mimes the fluidity – the spontaneity – of live conversation, with unpredictable responses, interruptions and fade-outs, which make the shape of the dialogue contingent, and its lines 'curved' rather than 'straight'. (The idea of 'spontaneity' is, admittedly, itself borrowed from a certain socially coloured ideal of conversation – that of the parlour and of the playground. Other social and contextual codes would contain the flow of talk – through a particularly dominant, order-imposing speaker, or a pre-arranged educational, forensic, ritualistic framework – the 'holy ground'.)

Dialogue coherence varies greatly in different modes of drama; yet it is difficult to think of any pre-modern dialogue that does *not* aim at coherence in structure (interchange, co-operation between speakers) and mostly in texture as well (naturalness of utterance, or else clarity in poetic diction). This may sound a large claim, and it is easy to think of traditional exceptions by pointing to inarticulate dialogue involving characters like Cassandra in the *Agamemnon*, and quite a gallery of characters in Shakespeare (led by Hamlet), Webster, Jonson and other dramatists. However, what is interesting when one returns to any of those 'classics of dislocation' in dialogue is that there are signals that point to the madness of the speaker – as speaking through 'divine frenzy' or under the cover of an 'antic disposition' and so on. The deviant or non-coherent stretch of dialogue itself is carefully placed within the coherence of the cumulative dialogue

17

of the whole play. Moreover, the audience/reader is, so to speak, made to stand outside the zone of non-coherence: it is Clytemnestra and the chorus who find the silence, the cries, the cryptic–apocalyptic allusions of Cassandra incomprehensible, so that *they* cannot enter into a dialogue with her; the privileged reader and listener (who knows the myth of the *Oresteia* and sees Cassandra suffering the speech-curse of Apollo) *follows* the drift of her raving; the dislocated medium is the clear message. Comparably, it is Polonius, Rosencrantz and Guildenstern, and the King who are, in turn, puzzled – drawn into a non-cohering dialogue – by Hamlet's riddling speech and 'antic disposition'; the reader/audience has been cued: we follow the mocking wit, the luminous if oblique intelligence, and the zig-zag lines of dialogue whose opaqueness is clear. (Clear to the young and non-specialist audience, not just to the good student who has read all the glossaries in the major editions.)

The first play that presents deliberately non-coherent frames of dialogue is probably Büchner's *Woyzeck* (1836). (We cannot be sure: the text's fragmentariness is partly due to its being an unfinished work.) Yet *Woyzeck* still has a coherent psychological frame which demonstrates the victim–hero's disintegration, precipitated by the dialogue thrust upon him by his interrogators. It is then only in recent drama, above all in Pinter, that non-coherence is made pervasive in several new ways. First, large sections of a play, if not the total play-language, are made up of dialogue sequences that do not, locally, 'cohere'. Secondly, the cumulative dialogue is itself systematically deranged, so that it has to be put together (the jigsaw-puzzle analogy) by the alert audience and reader, retrospectively – out of shifting patterns of open-ended 'talking'. Thirdly, the dialogue never resolves (is not intended to verify) the built-in ambiguities of particular exchanges. This verbal instability underlies the 'unverifiability' of states of being – the relation of the past to the present, of fantasy to actuality, of the smoke-screen of words to truth-telling (see section 3). It is often said that non-coherence in Pinter's dialogues mimes the conversation of everyday life, paralleling *its* dislocations, ungrammaticality, and idiomatic idiocy. My own view is different: deliberate patterns of non-coherence ('systematic derangement') in both the structure and texture of the dialogue create a highly style-conscious, mannerist, theatre *of* language. Further, non-cohering dialogue often makes itself its own subject so as to exhibit the cliché-ridden automatism of talk (Ionesco's *The Bald Prima Donna*), or the failures of language, suspended between autistic babble and the crippling stereotypes of the tribe (as in Peter Handke's *Kaspar*). But at that point questions of coherence become inseparable from questions of social value (what is 'communication' in a community?); and from questions of health or pathology in speech (can dialogue be kept distinct from the interior monologue of the solitary mind?).

3. The interchange of values

As our study of dramatic dialogue is primarily concerned with the speech of interaction (as distinct from the individual speech style of characters, or choric speech) we shall concentrate on the dialogue of personal encounter. The full dramatic and theatrical context of a play can often only develop and crystallise through scenes of 'close encounter' – the concentration and dynamics of interchange, a kind of verbal osmosis. (A felicitous ambiguity in the word 'plot' points to the broad 'intrigue' of the whole play as well as to private, conspiratorial secrecy: the external action – the murder of Clytemnestra or King Duncan, the 'ennobling' of a small town community in western Norway – may be rooted in, enacted through, the subtle and intimate interaction of two persons.) Most interactive dialogue embodies a transference of values, which amounts to a transformation of the speakers. Those who *have* exchanged values are no longer the same persons as those who entered into that dialogue. The disintegration of Othello – the change from self-possession to total moral chaos through a central duologue with Iago – is a paradigm, however exceptional in intensity.

The interchange of values implies an exchange of 'worlds' (still the best term in English to cover *vision du monde* or *Weltanschaung*: belief, vision and ideology overlapping). Values bring conflict or union, sympathy or alienation, confession or concealment, and many other modes of relationship in flux; only immobility or stasis may have to be excluded. Not even Beckett has succeeded in creating static dialogue, though his plays attempt to mime the paradox of Zeno's arrow: unmoving movement.

While the concern with values does seem to be inseparable

from the study of dialogue, it does raise certain problems, especially in demarcating our critical territory. For a value-system can only be grasped fully in its social/cultural contexts (norms of relationship, totems and taboos): the pressure behind both the psychological subtext and the theatrical convention of a particular play. These enormous territories invite potentially infinite study. As it is, these contexts are behind this study of dialogue: they come into the foreground mostly in shorter introductory sections to this or that period or mode of dialogue; they will tend to remain in the background, implicit in the discussion of actual exchanges in dialogue. The play-language embodies values, which are part of our primary reading; the outer contexts are 'readings' (further measurements) to guide our understanding of the historical change of values. The dialogue of lovers' wit, for example, makes much better sense when we have accurate readings for the word 'wit' and the mutations of sensibility in the seventeenth century (see chapter 3).

But: 'We are in fact more concerned with the relationship between men and values in themselves than with the discussion of how and why, in terms of psychological and sociological conditioning, men have come to adopt these values. From an existential perspective, in other words, not the *why* but the *what* is important: which purpose? which values implied in that purpose? what sort of commitment to the values involved?' Daniel Haakonsen's approach to an 'existential' study of Ibsen,[24] may well define our approach to studying the interchange of values. However, as we connect the relational/existential and the theatrical/stylistic aspects of dialogue, we must go on asking '*how?*': how is this or that particular value being spoken, being exchanged?

Values embodied in a particular dramatic encounter often reflect a clear strategy of presentation – the dramatist's poetics. In some cases, especially in modernist and post-modernist drama, we can hardly ignore whatever is relevant to dialogue in a dramatist's 'manifesto' – Brecht on *Verfremdung* (distancing) or Beckett on the art of impotence, or Pinter on the 'univerifiability' of motives. That does not mean that we must innocently fall into the much-dreaded 'intentionalist fallacy'. The overall verbal style of a dramatist, where it tallies with a known idea of theatre and language, offers the clearest guide to our reading and hearing of any particular sequence of dialogue. Values of personal relationship and textures of dramatic style remain inseparable within each dramatist's peculiar genius in writing dialogue.

As it is impossible to offer a survey of the many different kinds of value discussed throughout the book, I shall focus on a cluster of values that control further values, both relationally and structurally. For the interchange of values is the emotional mould of dialogue.

(a) *Sympathy and alienation*

The flow of sympathy governs dialogue (did not Lawrence say it governed our lives?) in an immediate and palpable way. It governs the distance between the speakers (both physical and spiritual), the rise in intensity, the move towards intimacy in speech, the disclosure of personal experience in confessional situations. From the *Electra* of Sophocles to Racine, Ibsen, Chekhov and O'Neill, many major plays have at least one intimate encounter at their very centre. The move towards that degree of sympathy which can only be called love or communion is often the climax or peripety in the structure of a play. And some major plays – *Antony and Cleopatra* and *Rosmersholm* most memorably – enact all the fluctuations of relationship, the sudden hostility and distrust no less than the love (*eros* and *agape*) in a series of cumulatively intensified duologues. Certain emotional turning points (Cleopatra calling out 'pardon!' to Antony after she had betrayed him at sea; Rebecca's destructively cleansing confession of her past passion for Rosmer) are among the supreme exchanges of all drama. As several of these patterns of dialogue are to be traced in detail later (chapters 2 and 4 especially), we need to attend here only to a general question. Do we not find in the recent, or 'postmodern', development of drama – with the rise of predominantly mannerist and parodic dialogue – a growing exclusion of dramatic exchange through sympathy (as distinct from verbally alienating modes)? Of Pinter at least it may be said that all encounters in his plays (excepting Aston's early sympathy for Davies, the tramp, in *The Caretaker*) are fuelled by paranoid distrust and unpredictable bursts of malice. What in all the traditional types of drama was only *one* mode of (alienated) encounter within the dialectic of relationships that makes up a whole play – or a dramatically motivated estrangement within the decline or ruin of one particular relationship – has become dominant. No doubt the energies of misanthropy are richly productive (we think of Iago's role in the dialogue of *Othello*) and entire plays *can* be constructed out of predominant patterns of alienation. But a question of value judgement remains: not so much 'is it too negative?' (the common reader's question) or 'is it unrepresentative?' (in its portrayal of 'dehumanised' human relationships, the classical Marxist objection), but to what extent can dialogue 'do without' the interplay of sympathy *and* alienation? Does not the interchange of personal values require polarities of emotion?

(b) *Sincerity and dissembling*

The love-test in the opening scene of *King Lear* is, among other things, a dramatic opposition of two modes of speaking – one natural and spare, by the wholly sincere Cordelia; the other, florid and hyperbolic, by the totally hypocritical Regan and Goneril. It may serve as a paradigm for a recurrent problem of dialogue, where 'value' and 'style' are inseparably connected. The opposition of values in *King Lear* is completely transparent to the audience, in keeping with the allegorical or parable-like simplicity of the opening scene. Sometimes even in Shakespeare, only context and choric commentary or, as in Iago, self-confessing soliloquy, can reveal the lack of sincerity; hence the Elizabethan fascination with the 'smiling villain' and mere appearance in speech, as in all else. However, what is being said in an interchange among friends (Hamlet and Horatio as the confidant – see chapter 2) can usually be trusted: what is mutual and spoken with confessional integrity is 'underwritten' by the language of the speakers. 'Natural language' – which in this study always includes the interactive frame of question-and-answer as well as the texture of the dialogue – would seem to be one of the recurrent criteria for recognising sincerity of utterance. From Sophocles to Chekhov, the confessional scenes – the scenes of self-disclosure – are always free from ostentatious rhetoric or style-consciously mannerist speech. (Yet in this area local judgements often have to be made with particular alertness, especially in distinguishing true rhetoric from false rhetoric in Elizabethan tragedy. In Jonsonian comedy linguistic excess – hubristic hyperboles, jargon-mongering and false rhetoric – is used satirically.)

The problem of rhetoric ('false' or 'true') is only one example of the general problem of sincerity in theatre language. The very word 'theatrical' has a set of connotations that range from mildly pejorative notions of exaggeration to the recurrent purist and puritan 'anti-theatrical prejudice'[25] against characters acting and speaking in socially or psychically 'abnormal' ways. Ostentation and hypocrisy are suspect (the word *hypocrates* once meant actor).

If we accept and even celebrate the human, and linguistic, release offered by the theatre, we still remain aware of the artistic paradoxes of language in the theatre: its artifice of spontaneity, its rhetoric of naturalness, its often grandiloquent simplicity. Such paradoxes go with all kinds of ambivalence, including ambivalence of motive for saying something, for a character speaking *like that*. 'Sincerity' can seldom be taken for granted in dramatic dialogue. However, in pre-modern drama, sincerity in speech (or its lack) can nearly always be directly discerned by the audience or established in the course of the play, through proper attention to the play-language, the interplay of speakers. Wit, for example, is an unstable and ambivalent instrument in human/dramatic relationship – shifting from genuine communication to the deliberate ironies of the verbal smoke-screen; just as it can shift from sympathetic wit ('love-wit') to alienated or alienating wit ('out-witting' and 'in-wit'). The wit of Rosalind is wholly sincere but still a language of disguise; the wit of the Jonsonian master-wit is the dissembler's linguistic weapon to undo the speakers of folly; and the wit of the Restoration Wit is, usually, a battle between what Congreve himself defined as true and false wit. (See chapter 3.)

If sincerity – direct, truthful utterance – is often considered an unwitty virtue, few would question the central significance of sincerity in some two centuries of European drama: roughly, from Lessing to O'Neill, with certain individual contemporary dramatists like Tennessee Williams and Wesker still writing in the line of truth-structured dialogue. In this very large body of drama the truth-telling urge, and a 'natural language' in the dialogue, are nearly always inseparable. As early as Lessing 'both the affectation of elaborate formality and the uncontrolled, spontaneous outbursts of passion, as well as the coarse and uneducated speech of the lower classes' are to be avoided, to give a moderate tone of dialogue (the middle-class values).[26] The urgencies of the Romantic and later existentialist world-views tended to intensify the personal significance of 'the true voice of feeling'. (The new and central significance of sincerity is such that there is a change not just in degree but in kind – a shift to 'authenticity' in Lionel Trilling's strong sense.)[27] One could take almost any Ibsen playtext and read 'out of it' the essential pressures of truth-seeking and self-revelation. A reader who knew nothing about Kierkegaard's existential absolutes (in terms of personal commitment and 'purity of heart') would still see that in plays like *Ghosts* and *Rosmersholm* the search for some final, true and sincere, disclosure provides the essential structure of dialogue. The old tragic pattern, which can be seen as a relentless drive towards the discovery of 'the truth' (*Oedipus Rex*), is retranslated into a series of personal duologues – concerning what really happened in a particular personal relationship – expressed in natural(istic) idiom.

It is only to be expected that such an insistence on sincerity of speech – as an aspect of 'reality' – would produce a consistent awareness of its opposite: pretence, false ideas, 'ghosts', saving lies, mendacity, illusion. At the same time, the ambiguities of 'self' and 'identity' were being explored, through new techniques of dialogue, by Ibsen, Strindberg and Chekhov (all writing with the enormous artistic advantage of a pre-Freudian generation: exploring psychological ambivalence without the clutter of a semi-scientific framework). The borderline between 'reality' and 'fantasy' in dialogue was beginning to get blurred in the late plays of Ibsen: Hilda Wangel's erotic power over her Master Builder lies partly in the way her speech mixes memory and desire (unverifiable memory and limitless desire). From Strindberg's *Ghost Sonata* on, statements in dialogue are often indistinguishable from sudden gratuitous utterance, subjective compulsion; and in Pirandello the 'theatre of illusion' is itself used to point to the existential illusion that characterises all action and consciousness. The old multiple vision of Renaissance drama – with its multiple planes of reality and internal mirrors – gives way to a built-in relativism of values: personal dialogue is always burdened with a dubious, barely testable, 'sincerity' of utterance. From there it is only another jump to the wholesale use of some 'principle of unverifiability' as the governing principle of dialogue – the merging of reality and fantasy, of past and present states, the blurring of the speakers' identity (see chapter 5). At that point 'sincerity' becomes a virtually useless term since it can no longer be perceived or scaled in dialogue. It is replaced by the self-sustaining interest, for a metropolitan audience (often unsure of its own values but fascinated by the patterns of uncertainty and sudden shifts of attitude and language), of ambiguity itself. At that point a dialogue of verbal games – with hints of relationship gathered from guesses out of puzzling speech-clues – opens up the prospect that all dramatic speech is heard as evasion, or dissembling.

(c) Taboos

ALCESTE: Let men behave like men; let them display
    Their inmost hearts in everything they say
PHILINTE: In certain cases it would be uncouth
    And most absurd to speak the naked truth.
             (Molière: *Le Misanthrope*, translated by
           Richard Wilbur, London, 1955; opening scene.)

Philinte expresses the all-but-universal need for a taboo on what can be said, socially/personally and stylistically, in a given dialogue within a given dramatic convention. This is a vast and complex subject, and all one can do here is to offer a few pointers to its direct relevance to dialogue study. Clearly, what is left unspoken – and what is felt to be unspeakable – varies from period to period, and is usually implicit rather than 'advertised' in the text of the dialogue. A good deal of what we now call subtext (best understood as a director's term, as Stanislavski meant it, and especially needed to interpret the often cryptic, oblique or understated communicative language of naturalistic dialogue) is made up of taboos. A famous example is Rebecca's inability, and that of Ibsen behind her, to bring into the open, even in her most intensely self-revealing confession to Rosmer, her horror of a possible incestuous relationship with her father. Indeed, a good deal of the intensity of the dialogue springs from its roundabout and indirect 'unspeakability' (often missed by audience and readers), which alerted Freud to the presence of a powerful repressed emotion.[28] What strikes the student of the theatre, however, is that no such taboo existed in certain other periods, within other theatrical conventions. The incest committed by Oedipus is, indeed, seen as a monstrous *hamartia* which pollutes the land of Thebes and, when found out, makes Oedipus blind himself; but the whole play is so structured that the 'unspeakable' is finally declared, brought into the open. Jacobean drama, among the freest in the expressible range of emotion, allowed John Ford to write amorous dialogue for brother and sister in '*Tis a Pity She's a Whore*. Neo-classicism – which could not accept the total lack of 'poetic justice' in the murder of Cordelia, and which objected to the word 'grunt' spoken by a prince – inevitably excluded an enormous range of utterance in the name of strict decorum. The Romantics may have aspired to restore the emotional and stylistic freedom of the Renaissance – as in Shelley's *The Cenci*, another drama of incest – but they could not overcome their own limitations, and the social taboos of the age. Taking a leap, one can say that it is only quite recently – in England paralleled by the lifting of censorship – that, potentially at least, no particular subject, emotion, mode of dialogue, is 'taboo'. Those who have lived through this festival of release may well have lived through a genuine revolution in sensibility. A good short social history of the contemporary theatre could be written by recapturing the breaking of this or that taboo: from Eliza Doolittle's short 'not bloody likely' to, say, the male members of the family in *The Homecoming* talking of their share in their brother's wife, the queen-whore of the household. The dialogue of that particular play gains its power from a certain obliqueness and ambiguity, coupled with the probable fact that sharing the wife of one's brother is not yet a universal custom in our society. In other words, the dialogue seems to thrive on an outer social and inner stylistic resistance – in the form of a dialogue that 'defamiliarises' what is being said. The lifting of all taboos – for example the sudden flood of four-letter words, or the total readiness of men and women to discuss intimate details of their sexual experiences – probably deprives a whole area of dialogue of a great deal of potential dramatic power. When characters say things too easily to one another – with the casual facility of the dialogue of Etherege or Noel Coward brought to the expression of fully personal experience – dialogue is impoverished. It is certain that a hesitant awareness of inner and/or outer taboo – from the duologues of Orestes and Electra to the love duet of Masha and Vershinin in *Three Sisters*, act two – is an enriching ingredient in interpersonal dialogue.

26

4. The functions of the duologue

It is often the mark of greatness in a play that it orchestrates a rich variety of speech-modes: juxtapositions of monologue, duologue, and group dialogue with a possible range from the trio and the quartet to the dialogue of the extended family. Further, the choric or the epic cast can fill the stage with a pool of speech. The interplay between many modes of speech is itself a source of dramatic interest and delight in plays that excel in the art of 'polyphony' – a texture that works like a musical score (e.g. *A Midsummer Night's Dream* or *The Cherry Orchard*). And even where we are dealing with more limited and 'homophonic' plays, the whole play-language must be attended to, since any unit or detail makes full sense only when it is heard to resonate against the total text. It is not, then, the purpose of this study to single out the duologue so as to give it a privileged status in a hierarchy of dialogue modes. The two major reasons for concentrating on the duologue involve strategies of economy: (1) the duologue is a prominent mode of dialogue from Sophocles to Beckett, which can be studied historically, with the comparative criticism of texts in a clear context, attending to both changes and continuities, to the local features and to the poetics of dialogue. (2) The duologue can be seen as the kind of concentrated dialogue structure that most often enacts an encounter – a crisis or an exchange of values – wherein relationship and language are fused and transformed.

Oscar Wilde attempted to improve on a cliché ('two is company and three is none') with the aphorism: 'in marriage three is company and two is none'. That is a witty way of advertising the advantages of the triangle – especially for marital comedy and farce. Most great comedies do set their *couples* in a verbal dance at the centre of a merry *group* (*Much Ado about Nothing* is the best example), yet the witty combat of the couple often remains at the centre of the stage. It is tragedy that most often is structured around the interaction of two interlocked protagonists (the 'agonist' and the antagonist, or the accomplices, or the lovers). Often their duologues become pivotal: a duality of worlds moving through sympathy towards union, or else through conflict towards disintegration, destructive 'doubleness' (in the sinister sense of 'double' in *Macbeth*). From Orestes and Electra to Hamm and Clov, the paired yet estranged counterparts speak to each other through paired voices: voices theatrically embodied in 'the antiphonal effects of two main vocabularies, strengthened by diversity of manner, costume, placing on the stage'.[29]

The relational and the stylistic opposition is, here too, often fused. In the duologues of Greek tragedy, given the symmetry of structure and rhythm in stichomythia, the individual voice and idiom may seem to be suppressed; yet voices and values (Creon and Antigone, the sisters Electra and Chrysothemis in Sophocles, and the Euripidean Orestes and Electra) come into collision through the use of opposed keywords. They are paired through a dualistic dialectic:

ANTIGONE: I cannot share in hatred, but in love.
CREON: Then go down there, if you must love, and love
the dead.

And that confrontation between love and death (*eros* and *thanatos*) is the central conflict of the *Antigone*. The ceremonial frame of the stichomythia moulds the dialogue with exceptional formality but does not freeze it. (Comparable formality can be found in the couplet responses in early Shakespeare, in the sonnet duologue of the first encounter of Romeo and Juliet, and, with tact and variation, in Racine.) However, in Shakespeare, in mature Renaissance drama generally, the duologue acquires a new fullness both in the possibilities of relationship ('the principles of growth and change in human relations' in which Muriel Brandbrook sees Shakespeare's 'esemplastic power')[30] and in the possibilities of dramatic speech *in* dialogue. Then relationship and language fuse in a total interplay. The pivotal relationships (the ebb and flow of love, the powers of verbal poisoning and seduction) are enacted in what is perceived as a wholly new dialogue – one created by and for each occasion, each crisis. Then human transformations are fully embodied in verbal transformations: the structure and texture of the dialogue itself changes with the speakers. If the stichomythia can be compared to a strict verse form, then the dialogue of mature Shakespearian tragedy (as early as *Romeo and Juliet* in some respects) is like an 'organic poem', shaped by the fleeting emotion and the demands of the dramatic moment: two voices being modulated, given precise tones, by the mimetic imagination. The well-known progression of Shakespeare's dramatic language towards an approximation of speech rhythms (the relaxation of verse form, through all the phases of development)[31] contributes to the growing dominance of 'natural' speakers in duologue. Complex interactive relationships are enacted through 'coherent' question and answer, challenge and response; dislocations of the frame of dialogue, of syntax or vocabulary – the marks of mannerist texture – are relatively rare and specialised style-markers for a character and situation (like Hamlet's 'antic speech').

In naturalistic prose drama, beginning with Ibsen, both the scope and the language of the duologue will at first seem limited in comparison with Renaissance drama. However, in Ibsen and later in O'Neill, the duologue often achieves a pivotal place in the structure of this or that playtext – *Rosmersholm* or *Long Day's Journey into Night* – which may well be regarded as unique. The emotional pressure springs from an existential need to 'confess' – face-to-face in a truth-seeking trial, a private inquisition, between two people. This type of confessional duologue is charged with the pursuit of complete 'authenticity' in the modern sense, stronger than 'sincerity', as Lionel Trilling has argued. The simplified naturalistic language itself is turned into a principle of purity, capable of a quiet intensity, a verbal power built up through the exchange of images and keywords. The language itself helps to authenticate or 'verify' the truth of experience disclosed in confidential and confessional encounters. For such communication the 'natural language' of the naturalistic duologue is the most appropriate vehicle.

It is arguable that the duologue becomes less central – as well as quite different in texture and values – in several major modes of post-naturalistic drama. A simplified but still usable map of modern drama would place epic and absurd theatre at opposite poles: each in its own way a mode of 'anti-drama', reacting against the dialogue-centred drama (which Brecht called 'dramatic', and which Szondi considered a kind of absolute form). As early as Chekhov, within the subtly scored group dialogue where characters interact obliquely and often speak in fragments, the duologue becomes rarer and less central (and, compared with Ibsen, it also develops a non-logic in conversation). Brecht's epic theatre presses all dialogue – which is only part of the choric/epic montage – towards impersonality. The duologue is much diminished (though it was present in Brecht's early plays, especially in the desperate verbal duel between Shlink and Garga in *In the*

Jungle of the Cities (1921–4)). Yet in the mature parable plays – *The Good Woman of Setzuan* (1938–42) and *The Caucasian Chalk Circle* (1943–5) – the duologue re-emerges as a vehicle of 'almost personal' encounter within the framework of folk art. Ceremonial *and* personal attitudes, gestures and speech-styles interact within the betrothal duologue of Grusha and Simon.

By contrast, wherever the theatre attempts to embody visions of solipsism – from Strindberg's *Ghost Sonata* (1907) – the function of the duologue is 'smothered in surmise' even where it retains the semblance of talk between two stage figures. Sudden ellipsis or mutation hurl the speakers through time and consciousness, blurring the boundaries of their own identity. At that point the duologue may become no more than a still-convenient unit in the playtext, holding together the parallel or criss-crossing lines of a dual monologue. (This mode of non-interactive, *as if* duologue eventually came to be directly dramatised, for instance in Pinter's *Landscape*, (1968).) The dislocation of verbal interaction is often inseparably linked with modes of speech which are textured with a complexity that is consciously non-natural and non-personal: mannerist, when playing intricate verbal games; parodic when playing variations on former texts, theatres, languages. Yet the dissolution of the duologue opens up the way to new kinds of dramatic dialogue.

If we can speak of a dissolution, at what point does the duologue cease to be what its name claims to be (dual) and become reabsorbed in choric speech ('music') or suffer itself to be recognised as 'mere' monologue? The best answer would seem to be the common-sense one: wherever there is only one 'dramatis persona', lines for one actor to speak, one voice (as in Beckett's *Not I* (1973), which embodies the solipsistic monologue of the Mouth – its agony of lost dialogue – archetypally).[32] But there are shades and in-between stages. Just as in Greek drama it is sometimes impossible to 'distil' the duologue out of the surrounding chorus, since it is an integral part of it (as in the sustained ritual lament for Agamemnon, the *commos*, in *The Libation Bearers (Choephori)* of Aeschylus) and just as in Shakespeare the duologue may be meta-personal, purely formal/figurative (like the antiphonal songs of the Owl and the Cuckoo in the finale of *Love's Labour's Lost*) so, in modern and late-modernist drama, there are some teasing instances of dialogue that are *less* than interpersonal. We reach the mutations of the double monologue and the solitary duet. Gaev addressing the bookcase in *The Cherry Orchard* is followed by a long line of speakers in a void (or by voices of the divided self); Kaspar the autistic youth in Handke's *Kaspar*, repeats one sentence, the only one he knows, to chair, table, and broom, and to any other object that he may expect to answer. But, starkly, the objects refuse to answer; and the person who keeps up that mode of address is at risk: in, or moving towards, a state of isolation or dehumanisation. The voice that splits itself into two ('then babble, babble, words, like the solitary child who turns himself into children, two three . . .')[33] can be interesting psychologically as well as vocally. But if the speech remains univocal – to be spoken by one actor, with whatever variations of style and inflection – it is not a duologue. In Beckett's *Krapp's Last Tape* the solipsistic voices of two identities (with an age gap of thirty years) are so consummately patterned that what we hear is the interaction of two monologues. I once suggested that this should be heard as solo dialogue;[34] but I would now stress the crucial 'peculiarity' of an old man listening to the mechanically recorded voices of his younger selves – mostly in silence. True, he does record his present self and voice ('Just been listening to that stupid bastard I took myself for thirty years ago') and in so doing is uttering a response. But the canned old self is, alas, in no position to answer back; the tape does not offer an exchange of voices, such as we find in the lyric convention of the Dialogue of the Soul (where two inner voices dispute each other in the live tension of time still being lived). Krapp is celebrating – in a rapture of distress – the near-perfection of stasis in his present state. Meanwhile, all the 'characters' in his diminished saga are frozen in the lyric narrative of the recording (the girl in the punt had become a figure from the Grecian Urn of Keats). There is, then, no place for Krapp in any interpersonal duologue. (Nor do the two voices of Shen Te in Brecht's *The Good Woman of Setzuan* – her gentle exploitable female voice giving way to the harsh, economy-conscious male gutterals of Shui Ta – amount to a duologue.) In late-modernist drama, monologue and duologue have become fluid and interchangeable in several respects, but the common-sense criterion of distinguishing speech for one speaker/actor from speech for two, can be applied to all dramatic contexts. One may compare the modern split monologue with the Elizabethan convention of the soliloquy, for both are capable of subtle interiorisation, split states of being and voices. Hamlet's cross-examination of himself ('am I a coward? who calls me villain . . .?', a question that Hamlet does attempt to answer, in his own manner) does not break the formal frame of speech *as* soliloquy.

Focussing on the study of the fully interpersonal duologue is not intended to see that particular mode of dialogue in isolation. On the contrary, the attempt must be made, as already suggested, to reconstruct the 'cumulative dialogue' into which every particular exchange enters as a current in a circuit. In Greek tragedy the 'duo' and the chorus are formally inseparable, in keeping with the gradual emergence of dialogue out of the matrix of the chorus: first one actor answering the chorus, then another, and finally (introduced by Sophocles) the third actor. (It is worth recalling that the Greek name of the actor originally meant the *answerer*.) Readers of Greek drama – though not the spectators – sometimes forget that every duologue took place in the physical presence of the chorus; thus Euripides makes his Orestes almost comically self-conscious about the eavesdropping chorus of Argive peasant women overhearing his plot. The formal tie between chorus and protagonist was imitated by Eliot in *Murder in the Cathedral* (along with other Aeschylean elements) so that Thomas Becket's sudden revelation ('Now is my way clear') can only be grasped if the audience 'extrapolates' a hidden dialogue between Thomas and a chorus of women of Canterbury. More generally, it may be said that all the great duologues of Renaissance drama make full sense only by seeing their connection with something like a chorus of bystanders, eavesdroppers and commentators. The love-duets of Romeo and Juliet must be heard against the criss-crossing dialogue of the whole market-place of Verona, and, quite specifically, against Juliet's dialogue with the Nurse and Romeo's dialogue with Mercutio and the Friar. In comedy, the combat of wit is like the figure-dancing of one couple in the midst of a whole dancing school of 'wits': Beatrice and Benedick, for example, are parasitical, in their own fine witcombats, on the goads and prompters, respectively Margaret and Ursula, and Leonato, Claudio and Don Pedro.

In short, the choric and epic context of a play – from Aeschylus to Brecht and the Brechtians – is heard around, and often be-

tween, the lines of the duologue. The precarious borderline between interior monologue and monologue-dominated dialogue
has already been touched on, and we drew a sharp common-
sense line of demarcation based on the number of speaking
voices/actors involved in the play. Yet we need to bear in mind
constantly that all human speech – and the monologue exem-
plifies this – calls out for response, for dialogue. Isolated speech is
a form of existential and linguistic suffering which only dialogue
can cure. There exist playtexts that have directly dramatised this
aspect of the human predicament. In *Hughie*, O'Neill makes a
taciturn but not speechless hotel clerk attend, naturalistically, to
the needs of Erie in his search for euphoric talk in a terror of
solitude. Cocteau uses what may appear as a cliché to dramatise a
solitary woman's one-sided telephone conversation with the
lover who will not answer. And the Winnie of Beckett's *Happy
Days* cannot reach her bitterly ironic 'happiness' until her cheer-
fully macabre longing for her decrepit partner on the sand-
mound terminates in her calling out his name, and her call is
answered:

WINNIE: [at the end of a very long monologue] Out of your poor old
wits, Willie?
WILLIE: (*just audible*) Win.
Pause. WINNIE's *eyes front. Happy expression appears, grows.*
WINNIE: Win! (*Pause.*) Oh this *is* a happy day, this will have been
another happy day! (*Pause.*) After all. (*Pause.*) So far.
Pause.

A one-syllable response may be a poor thing, but it is his own,
and now her own: her name has been called; the endless
monologue is not, after all, being spoken in a totally uninhabited
and voiceless desert. Of such a delicate response a duologue may
be made.

1 The duologue of recognition in Greek tragedy*

1.

The study of dialogue has had a modest place in the vast critical literature on Greek tragedy.[1] The chorus has a primacy in Greek drama in terms of origin (without question) and in terms of imaginative impact (seldom questioned). Historically, dialogue emerges only gradually as first one actor began to 'answer' the chorus; then Aeschylus developed the art of two actors speaking in 'character', changing from declamatory or narrative monologue to interpersonal dialogue; finally Sophocles introduced the third actor, each actor playing more than one role. Metaphorically, the lines of the dialogue are rivers flowing into and out of the ocean of the chorus (especially in Aeschylus). Functionally, dialogue may be compared to the recitative against the aria in an oratorio: 'the recitative corresponds, roughly, to the spoken iambics, the aria to the sung lyrics'.[2] It is thus impossible to contemplate, let alone study, an aspect of Greek dramatic dialogue without reconsidering its place in the overall design of tragedy. We must understand the limits of the first dialogue proper in European drama in order to appreciate its power.

The physical presence and dimensions of the Greek theatre alone tell us that it was intended for a performance that gave the orchestra, where the chorus danced and sang, a central place. The dancing and singing chorus and the speaking actors shared that dancing floor. Although we cannot know what the original wooden theatres, where the great tragedies were performed, looked like, it is legitimate to picture their plan by analogy with the surviving theatres.[3] In these the stage seems modest in relation to the orchestra, especially when viewed from the higher rows of the auditorium, taking in the entire theatre, and around it the natural amphitheatre formed by the splendour of the landscape, the whole panorama. The immense scale of that theatre,

34

its openness to sky and earth, its openness to the gods: the altar stone in the centre of the orchestra and the recurrent 'descent' of this or that deity into the performance itself; the hieratic and ritualistic functions of the whole festival; the large and multi-layered audience; the masked and buskined actors; all these point to a theatre art with larger-than-life symbols and signs. Personality, in the sense of individual character, is subordinate in such a system of art. One would expect the broad features of speech – rhythmic, syntactic, and rhetorical – to be predominant; and one would *not* look for emphasis on individual speech – dialect and idiolect, the nuances and idiosyncracies of self-expression – in the dialogue. In such a theatre the characters *as speakers* are not emphatically differentiated; we expect them to converge in *how* they express themselves even if *what* they express brings them into fundamental conflict. The dialogue may embody a dialectic of opposed values, without a corresponding opposition of language (although our own concepts of language leave little room for a completely neutral style in personal encounter).

The classic debating points on the major differences between Greek and Shakespearian/modern tragedy have a direct bearing on what may be seen as the attenuated role of dialogue in the former. Coleridge in his famous essay 'Greek Drama and Shakespeare's Drama' (1813)[4] said that the productions of the Greeks were 'statuesque', while those of the moderns are picturesque; these are wide umbrella terms, yet 'statuesque' does aptly suggest the frieze-like, carefully carved, symmetrical and relatively static quality of much dialogue in Greek tragedy. Coleridge also stresses the significance of a shift of interest in Shakespeare from plot to character: 'the interest in the plot is always in fact on account of the characters, not *vice versa*'. The Greeks, as every schoolboy used to know, from Aristotle's *Poetics*, put plot (*mythos*) before character (*ethe*) and, by implication, before language (*lexis*) and thought (*dianoia*): but 'most important of all is the structure of incidents. For Tragedy is an imitation, not of men, but of an action . . .'[5]

This structure-before-character concept of tragedy contributes to the attenuated function of the dialogue of personal encounter in Greek tragedy, even though dialogue usually occurs in episodes crucial to the action, in moments of crisis. Newcomers to

Greek tragedy often miss attributes like psychological complexity and inwardness in the speeches of the protagonists; and Greek scholars confirm the absence of a 'self-analytical, self-exploring mode of language'.[6] This, one assumes, was no problem whatever for the Greeks, but can certainly trouble readers and spectators who have a Shakespearian or modern sense of the tragic in and through dialogue. Kierkegaard probed this question in 'The Ancient Tragical Motif as Reflected in the Modern' (1843), starting from the Aristotelian stress on characters 'for the sake of the action', but placing the problem of dialogue in his own, speculative context – the limited degree of suffering and action that dialogue in Greek tragedy *can* express, given its relatively limited function:

> Here one readily notices a divergence from modern tragedy. The peculiarity of ancient tragedy is that the action is not only the result of the character, that the action is not reflected sufficiently into the subject, but that the action itself has a relative addition of suffering. *Hence the ancient tragedy has not developed the dialogue to the point of exhaustive reflection, so that everything is absorbed in it*; it has in the monologue and the chorus exactly the factors supplemental to dialogue. Whether the chorus approaches nearer the epic substantiality or the lyric exaltation, it thus still indicates, as it were, the more which will not be absorbed in the individuality; the monologue again is more the lyric concentration and has the more which will not be absorbed in action and situation. In ancient tragedy the action itself has an epic moment in it, it is as much event as action.[7] (Emphasis added.)

By contrast, Kierkegaard goes on:

> the modern tragic hero is subjectively reflected in himself . . . We are interested in a certain definite moment of his life, considered as his own deed. Because of this tragedy can be *exhaustively represented in situation and dialogue*, since nothing of the more immediate is left behind. Hence, modern tragedy has no epic foreground, no epic heritage.[8]

Kierkegaard's speculative criticism is especially interesting to us for the way it connects dramatic value and function: what is being expressed (out of the tragic character's suffering or consciousness) with how it is being expressed (through chorus, monologue, or through the dialogue). The claim he makes in contrasting ancient and modern tragedy ('modern', years before the appearance of Ibsen!) cannot be tested in short space; this whole study may contribute to testing the validity of that leap in comparative criticism. Even so, Kierkegaard seems accurate enough in hitting a dramatic target within his far-ranging speculative perspective. For Greek drama (viewed from a nineteenth-century perspective) must have seemed unique in *not* centering the dramatic action – the verbal interaction between the characters – in the dialogue. It may at once be objected that in Shakespeare, too, dialogue is dependent on, imaginatively parasitical on, choric speech: not the formal chorus, but the set speeches of this or that 'spokesman', or the long narrative/speculative set speeches of almost any character (Ophelia *on* Hamlet, the Queen *on* Ophelia), on top of the soliloquy. However, a substantial difference in kind and degree remains; for the dialogue of the great Shakespearian tragedies is not encircled or about to be engulfed by choral/lyric/epic verbal tides. One has to look further ahead, to the late-modern drama Kierkegaard could not have dreamt of, to see the re-emergence in drama of a dialogue which, once more, does not 'absorb everything' – all the suffering and action. The epic drama of Brecht reduces the inwardness and subjectivity of dialogue; hyper-naturalist drama minimises its expressive explicitness; and Beckett and absurdist drama dislocate (or lyricise) the connection between character and dialogue. But even with that expanded perspective in mind, Kierkegaard's remarks make sense, and illuminate the limitations of the *structure* of dialogue in Greek drama. (We can postpone discussing the texture for the moment.)

Aeschylean tragedy is, clearly, the least dialogue-centred type of Greek drama known to us. It has often been said that in Aeschylus we can see – or reconstruct – the primitive ritual and the primitive drama that had no actors, or only one actor. But leaving speculations about the origins of Greek dialogue aside,[9] it must be clear to every reader of the *Oresteia* (written in full maturity, after the 'invention' of the third actor by Sophocles) that here dialogue, in any interpersonal and interactive sense, is only just beginning to emerge. The reader and spectator is almost submerged in 'the sea' of the lyric/mythic odes: the chorus of the *Agamemnon* with its richly metaphoric language.[10] Nearly half the length of that play is made up of alternations between a single speaker: in turn the Watchman, Clytemnestra, the Herald,

Clytemnestra again, the Herald again – and the choral songs –
The Parodos, and the Stasima. Agamemnon himself speaks many
lines in isolation on his first entry; and the long silent presence
of Cassandra, followed by her cry before she finally speaks – in
rhapsodic verse 'beyond' the personal – is probably the most
unforgettable example of speech 'beyond' dialogue. Again and
again characters address the chorus, or directly the audience, and
not one another. Clytemnestra does not address the Chorus at
all; and Aegisthus in his first speech is speaking to 'no one' –
except the audience. As Kitto noted: 'one often has the impression that [the characters of Aeschylus] are speaking to each other
over a distance of fifteen or twenty yards, not of five or ten feet, as
on our stage; often, that they are not speaking to each other at
all, but straight at the audience.'[11] Thus, even if speech in dialogue is marked out as a *speech* rhythm from the sung *dance*
rhythm of the chorus, the actors/speakers remain figures within
the larger dance.

The contemporary reader or spectator (with all the critical noise
aroused by our so-called non-communication still ringing in his
or her ears) may be pardoned for provisionally concluding, on
returning to *The Libation Bearers*, that Electra and Orestes cannot
communicate with each other except through the mediation of
the chorus. Their face-to-face dialogue is, as we shall see, minimal (lines 212–24 to 263). Their mutual participation in the communal lament and invocation around the tomb of Agamemnon
(the *commos*) is much more substantial. A brief extract will point to
the physical and aesthetic distance in their mode of address:

ELECTRA: You tell of how my father was murdered. Meanwhile I
      stood apart, dishonoured, nothing worth,
      in the dark corner, as you would kennel a vicious dog,
      and burst in an outrush of tears, that came that day
      where smiles would not, and hid the streaming of my grief.
      Hear such, and carve the letters of it in your heart
CHORUS: Let words such as these
      drip deep in your ears, but on a quiet heart.
      So far all stands as it stands;
      what is to come, yourself burn to know.
      You must be heard, win no ground, to win home.
ORESTES: I speak to you. Be with those you love, my father.
ELECTRA: And I, all in my tears, ask with him.

                                   (lines 445–57)

Over and above the fusion of the personal voices of Electra

and Orestes with the voices of the Chorus, in metre and rhythm, there is this strange separateness of the close speakers. 'You tell of how my father was murdered' is addressed by Electra to the Chorus; meanwhile she is exempt, for the duration of the *commos*, from speaking directly to Orestes in person. The Chorus does indeed address Orestes with the terrible directness of the interpreter turned witness: 'Let words such as these / drip deep in *your* ears . . . *yourself* burn to know. / *You* must be heard.' But in the next speeches of the protagonists the new personal connection is all but disconnected: 'I speak to *you*' is addressed to the father in his tomb; 'And I . . . ask with *him*' speaks of the brother in his presence as though he were still absent, in the third person of obsessive memory and commemoration. In that long and centrally placed invocation (over 200 lines, lines 306–513) Electra and Orestes, reunited in love and murderous plotting, do not address each other at all. Their speech enters a ritual circle beyond the intimate, the personal, removed from direct exchange. This degree of impersonality remains even if we accept that the ritual incantation depicts the inner struggle of Orestes, emerging from despair to new resolve.[12]

We find the same degree of abstraction when we turn to the almost invariable line-for-line structure and language of Greek dramatic dialogue, the *stichomythia* ('dialogue in alternate lines, employed in sharp disputation, and characterised by antithesis and rhetorical repetition or taking up of opponent's words'. *Shorter Oxford Dictionary*). Stichomythia is an almost impersonal mode for personal encounter, though this will have to be qualified when we come to Sophocles. In a powerful one-sentence comparison Auerbach suggests that in the Gospels, in the scene of Peter's denial of Christ, 'the dramatic tension of the moment when the actors stand face to face has been given a silence and immediacy compared with which the dialogue (stichomithy) of antique tragedy appears highly stylised'.[13] Although Auerbach does not discuss Greek tragedy (only the wholly expressed, uniformly objective 'foregrounding' of the Homeric style) it is clear from the context that he finds in the Gospel dialogue the open, risky, random quality of the unexpected speaker saying something 'here and now'. By contrast, the highly stylised stichomythia eliminates that randomness, imposes a rational ordering and proportioning (Coleridge's 'statuesque').

The Greek scholars seem to make a habit of stressing the limitations of stichomythic dialogue. George Thompson writes rather condescendingly of the 'severely formal character' of stichomythia: 'to our ears the effect is often incongruous or even absurd, as for example at the crisis of the *Agamemnon*; and if the Athenians accepted it, it was mainly, we must suppose, because it was a fundamental, and therefore primitive, feature of the convention'. The notion of 'primitive', a word that tends to put us on guard, is supported by a hypothesis of literary anthropology: the dialogue of Greek tragedy may *derive* from the riddle of ritual and folklore. There is evidence to suggest that 'in Greece, as in other parts of the world, the custom of asking riddles was derived from catechism in the secrets of initiation, the purpose being to test the novice's knowledge of the mystical symbols. It is possible therefore, since so much in Greek tragedy goes back to initiation, that the *stichomythia* are a vestige of such catechisms; and it is easy to see how the identification of the god might be used as a means of expounding those symbols in the course of a ritual drama.'[14] An argument from 'origins' is no substitute for seeing what goes on in the text, and Thompson's comments on the language of Greek dialogue sound rather like Darwin sniffing at primitive man as naked barbarians (in *The Descent of Man*). Other statements include:

> In dialogue exchanges, no matter how banal or momentous the question, a whole line and no more than a line must be spoken. The constant presence of the chorus impeded the development of secret intrigue and inhibited the presentation of violent action.[15]
>
> (Lesky, *Greek Tragedy*, p. vii)

Lesky also refers his readers to A. E. Housman's parody of Greek drama.

> Recurrent stiffness is found also in the alternate lines of a stichomythia. The characters ask questions so obvious that we are at times inclined to find subtle reasons for their being asked at all. This is not so; the dramatist apparently prefers this, to us, quite unnecessary explicitness.[16]
>
> (Grube, *Drama of Euripides*, p. 28)

> Stichomythia – a form of dialogue that recurs in every play as regularly as versicles and responses in Christian liturgical services. It seems relatively natural to us when it is used for the

quick verbal exchanges of persons quarrelling with each other or plotting eagerly together. But even here the *undeviating regularity of the one line at a time*, continued sometimes for forty lines or more without a break, is *impossible in real life* or *in any drama that aims at producing the illusion of real life.* And further, stichomythia is often used where such exchanges would not, in real life, occur at all, but one person would speak continuously, and the other either listen in silence or at most interpose a brief ejaculation now and then.

(Greenwood, *Euripidean Tragedy*, p. 129. Emphasis added.)

One is grateful for the definition given, and yet one wonders how presuppositions taken from the 'illusionist theatre' of modern drama have crept into the judgement. Why assume that the Greek dramatists aimed at 'producing the illusion of real life': a more or less naturalistic surface with heterogeneous modes and tones? I think we should assume from the start that Greek drama was a drama of *convention* throughout – 'statuesque' or highly stylised – and that its interest in personal exchange had certain strictly defined limits. Even so, the dialogue is much more varied than has so far been suggested.

There remains the question of performance, the way dialogue was spoken, a very tricky subject that could only be settled finally if some archaeological windfall brought us a Greek commentary on the subject – an embryonic tape recording. In *Euripidean Tragedy*, Greenwood says:

We do not know if the actor changed or tried to change his voice with his part: there is nothing to show that he did, or that his doing so would not have been thought as absurd an innovation as the rags of Telephus. The poet's diction is the same for man and woman, for young and old, for free man and slave: why should the actor's voice not be the same also?

(pp. 127–8)

Against such a hypothetical argument, one can only pit one's disbelief in total human monotony wherever two (or more) speakers clash. Performances of Greek tragedy, whether in classical or modern Greek, have – like performances in other languages – adopted a richer vocal range. A typical experience is this: the supposed stiffness of the verse (iambic trimeter) exchanges gives way to a question-and-answer that has its own urgency and tension – accompanied by changes of tone, by gesture, and posture, including approach and retreat, as the distance between speaker and speaker is dictated by the dialogue. A certain symmetry, the regular recurrence of the line-by-line pattern, can of course be heard. But the moment there are two actors on stage – two distinct human voices, modes of being and breathing – the lines seem to acquire a varying weight: word clusters are grouped so that they do not seem to be of equal length, let alone texture. It is a duet, not a 'monotone' shared monologue that is heard.[17]

The function of the duologue in the structure of Greek tragedy seems to be significant and multiple – going far beyond the 'quarrelling and plotting' suggested by Greenwood. The rapidity and symmetry of question-and-answer does, naturally, lend itself to debate, to 'flyting', as we know well enough from its uses in Elizabethan drama (often to humorous effect as in *A Midsummer Night's Dream* – e.g. 2. 2. 49–52). But the moment one begins to reflect on it, the personal stichomythic confrontation of two characters will be seen as placed in a crucial episode, at a point of crisis. The dialogue of Agamemnon and Clytemnestra (*Agamemnon*, lines 931–43) is, no doubt, a quarrel, but what a quarrel: a concentrated battle of wills ending with the returning king's fatal submission to her possibly demonic pleas for generous yielding. And the spare opening lines of this, admittedly 'non-poetic', exchange immediately show the dramatic strength of symmetry:

CLYTEMNESTRA: Yet tell me this one thing, and do not cross my will.
AGAMEMNON: My will is mine. I shall not make it soft for you.

The opposition of the repeated keyword 'will', coupled with the clash of assertive personal pronouns, constitutes a miniature dramatic conflict in itself. Such conflct of wills can become highly charged with personal feeling and poetic concentration within the antiphonal dialogue:

ELECTRA: Yes; but how am I given an answer to my prayers?
ORESTES: Look at me. Look for no one closer to you than I.
(Aeschylus: *The Libation Bearers*, lines 218–19)

Or, with a variation: one line answered by two lines at the end of the stichomythic exchange:

ANTIGONE: I cannot share in hatred, but in love.
CREON: Then go down there, if you must love, and love
the dead. No woman rules me while I live.
(Sophocles: *Antigone*, lines 523–5)

And again:

CREON: You'll never marry her this side of death.
HAEMON: Then, if she dies, she does not die alone.

> (*Antigone*, lines 750–1; E. F. Watling translation)

Such exchanges have a cumulative power in the total episode, they bring the speakers to a kind of vertigo over the abyss. It is the confrontation of two kinds of 'right', the famous Hegelian essence of tragedy, in a non-meeting of minds. It does make sense to say that the stichomythia is hyper-explicit, for it epitomises a personal situation in an impersonal way. It gives, one might say, the equation of a relationship (but then, for the Greeks, poetry and mathematics must have been nearer than for most of us). It does not, however, make sense to say or suggest that such encounters are superficial or perfunctory. A fuller account would have to trace the great duologues of dilemma and change-of-mind, for example, Agamemnon's enforced choice between two kinds of total commitment (to his beloved daughter and to the Greek army) in the *Iphigenia at Aulis* of Euripides. In his dire dilemma Agamemnon has to confront one by one: his brother and chief ally Menelaus, in a quarrel over loyalty; his wife Clytemnestra, first unsuspecting, then in a frenzy of grief and anger; and, in between these two encounters with his wife, comes the painful duologue with the daughter he loves but whom he cannot now save from the trap-like consequences of his own consenting to her cruel, priest-dictated sacrifice. The confrontation of values, the psychological focus, and the subtle modulation of voices – especially in the magnificent duologue between father and daughter (see also p. 56 below) – foreshadow the crisis dialogue of later European drama, in Racine and Ibsen.

2.

To see the resources of the dialogue in Greek tragedy, within its built-in limitations, we may now turn to a comparison of the central recognition episodes in the three *Electra* plays. The survival of three tragedies using the same myth is unique, and so is our opportunity to scale differences in dialogue against differences in vision and underlying conception among three 'competing' dramatists: Aeschylus in the *The Libation Bearers*, Sophocles and Euripides each in his own *Electra*. (Since scholars have been unable to settle conclusively the chronology of the second and third *Electra* tragedies, and since interesting speculations can be based on the interplay between these two plays, whichever came first, I shall keep to the order just given.)[18] The three tragedies differ in certain immediately recognisable and significant ways, both in structure and vision, creating different contexts for the Orestes–Electra duologues.

The Libation Bearers of Aeschylus must be read and interpreted as an integral part of the Oresteia trilogy: mythopoeic throughout, with a sustained vision of cosmic justice being gradually worked out under the guidance of a newly-envisioned Zeus and the new justice of the *polis* of Athens. The matricide committed by Orestes and Electra is central in that cosmic/politic design; it is inescapably tragic: justly ordained by Apollo, yet justly bringing torment on Orestes from the Furies. However, the actual relationship of Orestes and Electra – in personal, let alone psychological terms – is of limited interest in the tragedy; they are figures in the design, agents and sufferers in their world's general agony that works towards justice (*diké*). Nevertheless, two powerful voices are embodied in that brief duet of the children of Agamemnon which precedes the communal lament.

Sophocles offers a paradox – an almost impersonal conception of the myth, of matricide – which ends by leaving the protagonists fully personal, at all events more fully personal than either in Aeschylus or in Euripides. This *Electra* is very much a 'dramatist's drama', without a palpable bias or ideological standpoint: it shows and presents, does not tell and judge; the myth is drained of its darker chthonic power; the Chorus (the women of Mycenae) is capable of mediocre, play-safe commentary, and it brings the play to an end with an abrupt and unearned celebration of the house of Atreus. Yet, at the core of the play, Orestes and Electra briefly enact a relationship of discovery and love – in a brief and intense duologue of personal encounter.

Euripides comes nearest to the parodic dramatist we know so well from modern drama, who can create variations of both myth and form – demythologise and 'make it new' – through a critical re-vision of earlier plays. His parody of the particular dramatic convention of Recognition – mockery of matching locks of hair and footprints, as used in Aeschylus – is only a minor instance of the post-mythic conception. Such a parodic conception recasts the structure and language of previous tragedy, with a partial dislocation of relationship in personal encounter. Even though Euripides does conceive character in psychological terms, his Electra and Orestes may appear to us as relatively depersonalised figures: reservoirs of 'psyche', of contagious fears and obsessions. They are matched in intensity of feeling, yet evade one another in dialogue.

We shall now contrast the three significant variations in the dialogue of recognition. In Aeschylus, as already suggested, the brief duologue of Orestes and Electra is overshadowed (some might say eclipsed) by the tremendous lyric intensity of the ritual incantation which they share with the Chorus (the *commos*). Moreover, what is being transacted by the speakers does not amount to a crisis; it is not structured as a palpable turning point, a felt peripeteia, as is the duologue of Clytemnestra and Agamemnon, which ends with the king treading on the purple tapestry in the false humility of his hubris. All that seems to 'happen' in the brief duet is that Orestes reveals himself, gradually, indirectly, almost circuitously, to Electra (lines 212–28):

ORESTES: Pray for what is to come, and tell the gods that they
　　　　　have brought your former prayers to pass. Pray for success.
ELECTRA: Upon what ground? What have I won yet from the gods?
ORESTES: You have come in sight of all you long since prayed to see.
ELECTRA: How did you know what man was subject of my prayer?
ORESTES: I know about Orestes, how he stirred your heart.
ELECTRA: Yes; but how am I given an answer to my prayers?
ORESTES: Look at me. Look for no one closer to you than I.
ELECTRA: Is this some net of treachery, friend, you catch me in?
ORESTES: Then I must be contriving plots against myself.
ELECTRA: It is your pleasure to laugh at my unhappiness.
ORESTES: I only mock my own then, if I laugh at you.
ELECTRA: Are you really Orestes? Can I call you by that name?
ORESTES: You see my actual self and are slow to learn. And yet
　　　　　you saw this strand of hair I cut in sight of grief
　　　　　and shuddered with excitement, for you thought you saw
　　　　　me, and again when you were measuring my tracks . . .

It is a *personal* recognition, though the external tokens – strand of hair and so on – are stressed by Orestes in his speech immediately after the line-by-line duologue. Electra's catechism of doubting questions explores the reality still to be tested, to be proved – her relationship to this stranger/brother. The testing is charged with reciprocal emotion, moving from quiet, still sceptical wonder, towards affirmation. In the longer speech that follows (not quoted here) Electra's response reaches ecstasy: 'O bright beloved presence, you bring back four lives to me' (line 238: the four lives are the four loves, of father, mother, sister and brother, now centred in Orestes). In just thirteen lines of dialogue the protagonists ascend the steps of a transformation. The symmetry of question-and-answer corresponds to those steps: the gradual self-revelation of Orestes eliciting a gradual, tentative acceptance from Electra. Each paired stichomythic exchange is an existential gain; each groping exchange is underpinned by the firm precision of stylistic formality. (A formality still found in early Shakespeare; see the study of the exchange of lines from a sonnet between Romeo and Juliet in the next chapter.) There is a tension across the stichomythic exchange as well as within each line:

ELECTRA: It is your pleasure to laugh at my unhappiness.
ORESTES: I only mock my own then, if I laugh at you.
ELECTRA: Are you really Orestes? Can I call you by that name?

Lines like these should be heard with the intonational patterns fully articulated; then, even though the rhythmic, quantitative values of the original are lost, the crescendo of emotion will be transmitted. Given their full tonal value, the lines work towards a tremendous release, the release of tension amounting to a temporary shift into something not far from the motif of reunion in comedy, as the disguise is shed, and a new emotion is carried by the positively charged values within pairs of opposites: *pleasure*/unhappiness; mock/*laugh*. The separated brother and sister then enact a brief ceremony of reunion in their longer speeches (lines 225–45), before Orestes turns from Electra and apostrophises Zeus. At that point the Chorus re-enters the dialogue, preparing the full incantation. Electra 'vanishes' from the text of the tragedy after that incantation, to the almost certain puzzlement of anyone who has not grasped the degree of mythic ritualisation in Aeschylus. Even so, Orestes and Electra have their moment of dialogue.

In the *Electra* of Sophocles the encounter between Orestes and Electra is postponed to the final third of the tragedy. Structurally, this makes their encounter a direct conspiratorial preparation for the murder of their mother (nowhere else so emphatically placed and presenting Electra as ruthless and vindictive). Nevertheless, the poetic emphasis seems to shift from 'conspiracy' towards 'reunion in love'; that at least seems to be the most compelling reading of their sustained duologue (lines 1174–227, followed by longer lyric exchanges after the intervention of the Chorus, lines 1232–363). These sequences are so rich and concentrated that only a longer study could do justice to them; here only selective quotation, bearing on our context, can be given. In the moment of encountering his sister, Orestes experiences and expresses a personal and linguistic perplexity, as if entering a rite of passage into an authentic meeting:

Ah!   What shall I say? What words can I use, perplexed?
        I am no longer master of my tongue.

(lines 1174–5)

Something of the 'tremendousness' of this utterance survives in almost every translation, though we need the larger context to re-experience that *awe* fully. In the ensuing duologue their exchanges lead directly to intuitive sympathy, a sharing of Electra's suffering; at the same time, this directness is also indirect, for its function is to delay the brother–sister recognition as in some ritual of teasing (almost fifty lines). It is probable that no modern audience can now recover the emotion that must have accompanied the performance of such a delayed Recognition scene. One suspects that for the Greeks this convention fused the delights of 'suspense' with the Elizabethan delight in disguise and its inevitable tangles of non-recognition. In other words, it is a 'structure of emotion' preparing release and ecstasy. Certainly many of the paired exchanges are best seen as stylised transmitters of compassion (i.e. partial, undeclared love):

⎧ ELECTRA: Why do you look at me so, sir? Why lament?
⎩ ORESTES: How little then I knew of my own sorrows!

⎧ ORESTES: So great, so sore, I see your sufferings.
⎩ ELECTRA: It's little of my suffering that you see.

⎧ ORESTES: Poor girl! When I look at you, how I pity you.
⎪ ELECTRA: Then you are the only one that ever pitied me.
⎨ ORESTES: Yes. I alone came here and felt your pain.
⎩ ELECTRA: You haven't come as, in some way, our kinsman?

(from lines 1184–202)

47

These stylised exchanges do not come across as 'statuesque', or else the statues are coming to life, as in those Greek myths which have haunted European drama (Pygmalion–Galatea). There is even an element of sheer spontaneity in these exchanges: the kind of formal semi-intimacy often found in the folk-tale, something Brecht tried to re-create in plays like the *Caucasian Chalk Circle*, in the stiff courtesy of the soldier wooing Gruscha. The use of the formal 'sir', by sister to brother, is an obvious pronoun irony, preparing for the celebration of the rediscovered 'Thou'. The repetition of keywords with a negative charge (lament/sorrow, pity/pain) patterns the dark emotions into a play-like ritual, carried by the waves of half-recognition expressed by the speakers, and supported by the irony of audience participation in Orestes playing a non-self-revelation. The general effect is that of a light beat under the communication of 'heavy matters', accentuated, as always, by the stichomythic repetitions.

The formality of that 'frame of utterance' counterpoints what is being said: all that talk of Electra's suffering as the central 'point of conversation' – what might threaten excess of *pathos* with a flow of self-indulgence – marks the exchange of sympathy around which the new relationship grows and crystallises. It is that growth of sympathy (shared suffering) which prepares the way for the full duologue of recognition. And we note the skill with which Sophocles – and he alone among the three tragedians – lightly turns, in the course of the dialogue, a matter of external plot (Orestes pretending to be the bearer of an urn containing his own ashes) into something internal and personal, the pivot of personal recognition:

ORESTES: No body of Orestes – except in fiction.
ELECTRA: Where is the poor boy buried then?
ORESTES: Nowhere.
        There is no grave for living men.
ELECTRA: How, boy,
        What do you mean?
ORESTES: Nothing that is untrue.
ELECTRA: Is he alive then?
ORESTES: Yes, if I am living.
ELECTRA: And are you he?
ORESTES: Look at this signet ring
        that was our father's, and know if I speak true.

ELECTRA: O happiest light!
ORESTES: Happiest I say, too.
ELECTRA: Voice, have you come?
ORESTES: Hear it from no other voice.
ELECTRA: Do my arms hold you?
ORESTES: Never again to part.

(lines 1217–26)

The immediate effect is that of intense personal emotion expressed in a natural language – supported by the whole context as well as by the inner movement of the duologue. The broken lines of stichomythia suggest a conversational pattern; yet it is carefully shaped, with an expressive parallelism, through Orestes echoing keywords in Electra's speech (the translations vary: 'happiest' occurs in the Greek text, and so does 'hold' or embrace). The simple vocabulary, the absence of 'poetic words', adds to the sense of both essential and spare utterance in the dialogue (comparable to the recognition of Cordelia by Lear in the last act of *King Lear*).

This reading is reassuringly supported by F. R. Earp's painstaking stylistic study of the language of Sophocles, showing that in the *Electra* (though another passage is used for close reading) 'the language is simple and direct . . . and the structure of the sentences limpid and natural'.[19] With some qualification, this applies to much of the language of Sophocles in the later plays; and all good translations preserve this diction, at once so intense and natural.

The quiet intimate duologue just quoted soon gives way to the richer, more metaphorical, lyric strophes and longer speeches which Orestes and Electra exchange – prompted by the Chorus (lines 1231–321). But this lyric encounter is not orchestrated in the Aeschylean manner (in the fullness of the *commos*, see above); the full expression of feeling is still muted and then checked by a built-in urging of silence:

ELECTRA: Child of the body that I loved best, at last you have come,
         you have come, you have found, you have known those
             you yearned for.
ORESTES: Yes, I have come.
         But bide your time in silence.
ELECTRA: Why?
ORESTES: Silence is better that none inside may hear.

(lines 1232–7)

The conspiratorial reason for silence is plain enough; but then it is not in the least like the melodramatic silence which immediate plotting might demand and instantly impose – it answers a personal and stylistic need as well. The intimate duologue is sustained, surges on to celebrate the abundance of things to be spoken *about* by the celebrants – and then checks its own 'grace abounding' by asking for silence once more:

ELECTRA: You have awakened my sorrow no cloud can dim,
        no expiation can wash away,
        no forgetfulness overcome,
        no measure can fit,
        in all its frightfulness.
ORESTES: I know that too. But when you may speak freely,
        then is the time to remember what was done.
ELECTRA: Every moment, every moment of all time
        would fit justly for my complaints.
        For hardly now are my lips free of restraint.
ORESTES: And I agree. Therefore, hold fast your freedom.
ELECTRA: By doing what?
ORESTES: Where there is no occasion,
        do not choose to talk too much.
ELECTRA: Who could find a fit bargain
        of words for that silence,
        now you have appeared?
        Past hope, past calculation,
        I see you.
ORESTES: You see when the Gods moved me to come.
ELECTRA: You tell me then of a grace surpassing
        what I knew before, if in very truth
        the Gods have given you to this house.
        This I count an action divine.

                          (lines 1246–70)

And still the flood of Electra's emotion – her abundant speech – is unchecked. The pattern cannot be missed: Orestes is given the role of the restraining and restrained lover against Electra's role of barely controlled utterance in passion (in the sense that includes suffering). Orestes would limit 'the frame of utterance'. Another bout of stichomythia might well suffice for him: 'spare me all superfluity of speech' (line 1288); 'tell me what we need for the present moment' (line 1293). By contrast, Electra insists on 'superfluity' of speech, and on the present disclosure of the pent-up emotions of the past, before the present, which includes attending to the murder of Clytemnestra, can be attended to. We have in this duologue perhaps the first fully personalised encounter in European drama.

Euripides veers away from the fully personal – certainly the intimate and the tender, brother–sister relationship – in the Electra–Orestes duologues of his version of the myth. At first sight this is surprising, because, on several levels, the *Electra* of Euripides carries one stage further the man-centred 'realism' of Sophocles: probing inner states of mind – motives and values, doubt against certainty, *before* the act of matricide – as well as the general human 'rationale' behind the terror of action. On reflection, however, we can see that there is no contradiction: a degree of analytic thrust, combined with experimentation in tragic design, goes with a diminished use for character-as-person and speech-in-character. There is a certain drive towards abstraction in Euripides, towards foregrounding the dialectic in dialogue. For Euripides 'saw tragic ἁμαρτία and tragic action not as part of the character of the individual, but, in a more abstract way, as a disastrous element in our common human nature which leads to suffering, in which the guilty person may share or not'.[20] (One recalls the way in which Strindberg, in comparison with Ibsen, moved towards *both* greater subjectivity *and* abstraction in form and dialogue through simultaneous psychological and formal heightening.) Moreover, as already suggested, Euripides is playing a parodic variation on earlier Electra plays, certainly on Aeschylus, and possibly on Sophocles as well: this *Electra* is a style-conscious and mutated form of tragedy, which Kitto groups with 'melodramas'.[21] The dialogue within that form often sounds non-tragic, and sometimes comic; it is a language that has a critique of its tragic modality written into it – 'modern', if we do not push the analogy too far. (It is not surprising that the Royal Shakespeare Theatre should have chosen Euripides as the pivot of its racy and sceptical modernisation of the Trojan War cycle of plays in *The Greeks*, in early 1980.)

Euripides may well be considered a conscious 'demythologiser', and as such a sceptical questioner of tragic vision and tragic form. What is surprising is that his radical experimentation in myth and form has no counterpart in his attitude to the language of dialogue. The prosaic quality of his language was already the subject of parody in *The Frogs* of Aristophanes. And contemporary Greek scholarship confirms, what intuitive judgement affirms, that Euripides moves away from the marked personal accents in the dialogue of Sophocles towards rhetorical speech that tends to have a standard accent for all the characters. In short, while Sophocles in his later plays, including the *Electra*, worked with and for a personalised 'natural language', Euripides seems detached from persons and less interested in differentiating his dialogue in terms of individual speech style, idiom and usage.[22]

The domestic setting in which we find Electra in the opening of the Euripides play, the cottage of 'poor Electra's' poor husband, immediately announces an oblique, newly envisioned presentation. Electra looks and sounds 'low' – in situation, in appearance, and in spirits. Her first words to the unrecognised Orestes express desperate fear (heightened by flinching, then kneeling): 'Do not kill me' and 'Get out; don't touch.' Gesture and speech at once reveal the wounded human being we call the neurotic personality. That does seem to be the key to the Euripidean Electra, and to her first encounter with Orestes (accompanied by the silent Pylades). Their first duologue (lines 220–89) has some aspects of the Sophoclean confessional with its exchange of sympathy:

ELECTRA: I think you see me. First, my body wasted and dry.
ORESTES: Sadness has wasted you so greatly I could weep.
ELECTRA: Next, my head razor-cropped like a victim of the Scythians.
ORESTES: Your brother's life and father's death both bite at your
           heart.
ELECTRA: Alas, what else have I? I have no other loves.
ORESTES: You grieve me. Whom do you think your brother loves but
           you?

(lines 239–44)

But neither the sharp physical detail ('my head razor-cropped like a victim of the Scythians') nor the self-advertised isolation ('I have no other loves') is there in Sophocles. Here Electra is eager to display, as it were, the stigmata of her martyrdom. In the Sophocles play nearly all Electra's 'misery' statements are prompted by the questions Orestes puts to her. In the Euripidean duologue Electra becomes, in the opening sequence at least, the dominant speaker – through intensity of feeling (her self-pity) as well as through taking the initiative in the dialogue: asking the questions (lines 225, 229, 233, 235, 237) and projecting her vision into the vision the still unrecognised Orestes *might* have of her: 'I think you see me. First, my body wasted and dry.' A conscious rhetoric of grief and grievances is being exploited here; the duologue is a profane ritual lament.

After this high-toned opening, Euripides abruptly changes key, and the rest of the duologue is a long (emotionally ambivalent) cross-examination of Electra by Orestes. Within the ironic situation of a prolonged non-recognition between brother and sister, as Orestes will not reveal himself, the very length – over thirty lines – of this catechismic duologue has a certain air of parody about it. (No doubt more so for the modern reader; not for nothing did Joyce use circumstantial catechismic questioning as a form of parody in *Ulysses*.) The plot-directed probing tends towards something like prying, as Orestes wishes to ascertain the exact how and why of Electra's virginity, why has she not been touched by her low-class husband, out of respect or disdain, etc.:

ORESTES: A vow of chastity? or he finds you unattractive?
ELECTRA: He finds it attractive not to insult my royal blood.
ORESTES: How could he not be pleased at marrying so well?
ELECTRA: He judges the man who gave me had no right to, stranger.

(lines 256–9)

But this 'stranger' goes on to ask 'personal questions' – and in the process transforms a potentially intimate duologue into a somewhat furtive inquest. After what looks like a slip of the tongue as Orestes briefly assumes the role of Orestes ('*we* must pay' the husband well for his decent attitude), he continues the cross-examination: 'was Clytemnestra calm?' 'What was in Aegisthus' mind?' . . . Does he know you are a virgin?' 'These women listening as we talk are friends of yours?' (If not friends, the question comes a little late, after their eavesdropping to over fifty lines of dialogue.) One cannot be sure of how to interpret this style of talk. But it is legitimate to suppose that Orestes is deliberately prolonging and partially evading – through his mask of impersonality, his early 'Prufrock stance' – the overwhelming questions that might commit him. As it is, his terror-driven questions skirt tragic irrevocability through the answer given by his 'totalitarian' sister:

ORESTES: Mother and lover both? Are you bold for that killing?
ELECTRA: Mother by the same axe that cut Father to ruin.

(lines 278–9)

The first duologue may, indeed, be deliberately wordy and circumlocutory – making the most of the stichomythic drill. That would be in keeping with the later portrayal of Orestes as the doubting and reluctant follower of Apollo's oracle (the command to kill his mother). If so, this type of Euripidean dialogue could be an early example of presenting a character whose 'torrent of words' hides uncertainty: his probing an attempt to evade full encounter. The Recognition does *not* take place here; it does not even arise from the first duologue, which is deflected by the semi-comic interruption of the returning farmer husband. The husband is at first suspicious, then effusively hospitable, towards 'the friends of Orestes', prompting a gauche and platitudinous, tension-dissipating commentary from Orestes on the noble manners of this humble man.

It may well be that Euripides invented an early form of the 'comic relief', that favourite standby of the old schoolmaster commenting on Shakespearian tragedy. The structure that effectively postpones the Recognition scene (the second duologue) includes the first choral ode – 'O glorious ships who sailed across to Troy once' – whose lyricism seems less action-directed than are the myths retold in the choral songs of Aeschylus. After the incantation of the Chorus (Nereids bearing the shield of Achilles with its multitude of images sufficient to fill a shorter classical dictionary), the Old Man enters. It is here that the parodic element is strongest. For the Old Man, who had once 'nursed and helped' the infant Orestes, suspects that he had already returned incognito; so the tell-tale tokens – lock of hair, footprint and a piece of weaving – are enumerated one-by-one, only to be scorned by Electra. When Orestes re-enters, the Old Man first stares at Orestes ('Why do you stare at me like a man who squints at the bright stamp of a coin?' askes Orestes, line 558) and then begins to walk round and round the familiar stranger, scrutinising him intently ('why does he walk round me in circles?') until he finally identifies Orestes. This thoroughly external recognition recalls the great Homeric scene when Odysseus' scar is recognised by the old housekeeper Euryclea in Book 19 of the *Odyssey*: 'The scar above his eye where once he slipped and drew blood' (Old Man, lines 573–4). Within such a triangular episode – as a frame of action – the Old Man, as agent and go-between, palpably contributes to the near-comic distancing of Orestes and Electra from each other. Finally a brief, bare and seemingly perfunctory personal duologue is allowed to take place (before the dialogue proceeds, at roughly ten times the length of the intimate encounter, to plot the technicalities of the double murder):

OLD MAN: The scar above his eye where once he slipped and drew
      blood as he helped you chase a fawn in your father's court.
ELECTRA: I see the mark of a fall, but – I cannot believe –
OLD MAN: How long will you stand, hold yourself back from his
      arms and love?
ELECTRA: I will not any longer, for my heart has trust
      in the token you show.
                        O Brother so delayed by time,
      I hold you against hope –
ORESTES: Time hid you long from me.
ELECTRA: I never promised myself –
ORESTES: I had abandoned hope.
ELECTRA: And are you he?
ORESTES: I am, your sole defender and friend.
      Now if I catch the prey for which I cast my net
ELECTRA: I trust you and trust in you. Never believe in god
      again if evil can still triumph over good.
                            (lines 573–84)

In comparison with Sophocles the emotion expressed in this Recognition scene – supposedly in loving reunion of brother and sister – is minimal. That some suppression of emotion is being 'foregrounded' here is clear from the way the dialogue develops: Orestes abruptly, and with conventional social rhetoric, puts an end to the personal exchange: 'Enough. I find sweet pleasure in embrace and welcome,/but . . .' (line 596); and he proceeds to ask the Old Man for advice on the best way to approach murder. But what is happening *within* that strange laconic duologue? Has Euripides, who has invented so much in terms of dramatic psychology and language, also invented the subtext? Is there supposed to be more emotion here than words can express – an early instance of the unspoken or the unsaid? Is it the stammer of ecstasy at mutual recognition? Or is it, on the contrary, the pain of an inhibited, or a spoilt Recognition scene that is being dramatised in the dialogue? For both speakers have fears, causes to fear. In the language of our own time, and that of Philip Vellacott:

> Orestes is consciously reluctant to be recognized because he
> sees all too clearly the inevitable consequence; and Electra is
> unconsciously reluctant to recognize him because, having for
> so long nursed the grievance of his failure to appear, she cannot
> bear to see the grievance removed. This tragic-comic situation
> explains the slowness of the recognition, the nervously foolish
> remarks of both brother and sister, and the perfunctory ex-
> change of endearments that follow.[23]

It seems to me more likely that this duologue deliberately
hardens the focus and the feeling of the encounter between
brother and sister. Such a reading would be in keeping with the
later shift to a semi-personal dialectical debate, over the terrible
issue of matricide, between the two protagonists; the exchange
of fully personal emotion is postponed until the final, grief-
stricken scene of separation.

The semi-personal dialogue goes with the explicit exchange of
low-keyed emotions rather than with a subtext of subtly implicit
and 'unconscious' emotions. 'Unconscious' is, in any case, a risky
word to apply to the dialogue of Greek tragedy. Vellacott's point
on Electra's unconscious clinging to her grievance against her
brother sounds somewhat too post-Freudian for interpreting
even such an eminently pre-Freudian dramatist as Euripides:
inventor of the 'Electra complex', first demonstrator of the narcissistic element in the melancholia of mourning, in the incurable
distress of the father-fixated virgin. However, a subtext of repressed fears is at least more plausible than one of suppressed joy
– more Euripidean and more actable. In performance all that has
to be conveyed is the reluctant embrace and the less than full
voice: in this imperfect reunion of brother and sister 'the rapture
of the moment is distinctly modified'.[24] My other reason for not
wanting to make too much of a verbal and psychological subtext
is that Euripides is perfectly capable of controlling the nature and
extent of emotion suppressed, and signalling the 'unspoken' to
the audience. There is, for example, the duologue between Agamemnon and Iphigenia, where the tormented and guilt-ridden
father cannot respond (and is shown to be unable to 'speak the
truth') to the joy at reunion expressed by his daughter, who is
wholly unaware that her father is plotting to sacrifice her
(*Iphigenia at Aulis*, lines 640–75). Why then should Euripides, in
the more consummately organised tragic structure of the *Electra*,
omit such signals for the unexpressed?

The deliberate shift of focus towards a 'dialectical' interaction –
including but transcending the personal – becomes clear when
we look at the Electra–Orestes duologues that follow this
strangely minimal Recognition scene. In the brief 'plotting' exchanges (between the second choral ode, lines 647–8; 668–70;
and 685–94) as well as in the last sustained stichomythia just
before the entrance of Clytemnestra (lines 962–87), Electra is
presented as the goad of Orestes – who is still doubting, still
divided. Electra has now recovered the obsessive intensity of
feeling shown earlier in her grief speeches; she appeals to
Orestes in such a way as to undermine his self-respect, his sense
of manliness *if* he should hesitate (anticipating Lady Macbeth
here): she first threatens suicide if he should fail, and then, in
effect, challenges her brother to 'be a man':

ELECTRA: And if Orestes in his struggle falls to death
      I too am dead, let them no longer say I live,
      for I will stab my belly with a two-edged sword.
    . . .
                    If you die
      triumph will shift to desolation.
ORESTES: I understand you.
ELECTRA: Make yourself fit man for the hour.

                              (from lines 686–94)

The keyword is 'man', however difficult to render this idiom of
the line:

      πρὸς τάδ ἄνδρα γίγνεσθαι σε χρή.
      Wherefore must thou play the man.[25]

The next duologue is intense, but in quite a different way from
the Orestes–Electra encounters in Aeschylus or Sophocles. Clytemnestra can be seen approaching, enticed by a ruse to Electra's
dwelling place:

ORESTES: What – what is our action now toward Mother? Do we kill?
ELECTRA: Don't tell me pity catches you at the sight of her.
ORESTES: O god!
      How can I kill her when she brought me up and bore me?
ELECTRA: Kill her just the way she killed my father. And yours.
ORESTES: O Phoebus, your holy word was brute and ignorant.
ELECTRA: Where Apollo is ignorant shall men be wise?
ORESTES: He said to kill my mother, whom I must not kill.
ELECTRA: Nothing will hurt you. You are only avenging Father.
ORESTES: As matricide I must stand trial. I was clean before.

ELECTRA: Not clean before the gods, if you neglect your father.
ORESTES: I know – but will I not be judged for killing Mother?
ELECTRA: And will you not be judged for quitting Father's service?
ORESTES: A polluted demon spoke it in the shape of god –
ELECTRA: Throned on the holy tripod? I shall not believe you.
ORESTES: And I shall not believe those oracles were pure.
ELECTRA: You may not play the coward now and fall to weakness.

(lines 967–82)

The intensity springs from the way diametrically opposed personal attitudes – tentative/questioning/sceptical against inflexible/fixed-in-one-faith – get fused with the contending ideologies. Thus the question-and-answer dialogue is used to test the 'will' – the inner being and commitment – of Orestes; but it is also used to act out the battle over the gods (Apollo versus a polluted demon) within and behind the human contestants. That is what makes it a true dialectic, and one can understand why Nietzsche thought fit to compare the Euripidean to the Socratic dialectic. It is the chain of argument and counter-argument, working towards resolution – which makes the whole duologue a compressed drama in itself. It can be epitomised in exchanges like:

ORESTES: O Phoebus, your holy word was brute and ignorant.
ELECTRA: Where Apollo is ignorant, shall man be wise?

(lines 971–2)

The stichomythia, as we have seen (pp. 39–43 above) is particularly fitted for this kind of almost epigrammatic opposition of key statements in the rapid thrust of point-counterpoint. To modern ears the exchanges may seem too rapid or pat – as if a major confessional with profound emotional undertones were enacted in jangling neo-classical couplets. But for Euripides (and presumably for the Greeks) the general ideas were as interesting as their embodiment in individual minds: the language of statement was valid as lyrical evocation. And, above all, he wanted to explore, with the clarity of a diagnostician, the conditions under which a state of mind is changed, changed utterly (*metanoia*). The duologue is to illuminate a problem: what kind of mental condition can lead brother and sister together to kill their mother? For given that matricide cannot be accepted by the Orestes of Euripides as divinely sanctioned, and cannot be seen in the context of the whole play as socially or personally 'normal', the interchange of 'thoughts' about the murder in this duologue is presented as a pathology (the *logos* of disease) rather than as *pathos* (felt suffering).

The bold collision of pathological ideas in the confrontation of brother and sister may seem to lack the fullness of tragic feeling and the verbal complexity, which we find in the central duologues of later drama. Nietzsche, we recall, found the Dionysiac, and the Wagnerian, tragic release in the chorus; by contrast, the dialectic of the dialogue, especially in Euripides, dealt in mere ideas and images, in limited and inadequate ways.[26] Modern audiences and readers may not share Nietzsche's view; but they may still expect emotional and verbal complexity in the dialogue of personal encounter and crisis. Since the Renaissance, various kinds of complexity enrich the texture of personal dialogue: the exchange of emotionally-charged metaphors fusing with the exchange of ideas (Shakespeare); or keywords carrying the full pressure of personal significance as they are transferred from speaker to speaker (Ibsen); or else a texture of ambiguity for speakers groping 'in a mist' both existentially and linguistically (Beckett and others). Yet the diagnostic spareness and clarity of the debating duologue in Euripides, which allows Electra to invade the mental territory of Orestes, has its own kind of transforming power.

Moreover, Euripides can and does change the mode of dialogue immediately after the murder of Clytemnestra. Only then does Euripides allow a fully personal emotion between Electra and Orestes: intense and shared tragic guilt over the act that cannot be undone, in a lyrical (no longer stichomythic) duologue:

ORESTES: O Earth and Zeus who watch all work
   men do, look at this work of blood
   and corruption, two bodies in death
   lying battered among the dirt
   under my hands, only to pay
   for my pain.
ELECTRA: Weep greatly for me, my brother, I am guilty.
   A girl flaming in hurt I marched against
    the mother who bore me.
CHORUS: Weep for destiny; destiny yours
   to mother unforgettable wrath,
   to suffer unforgettable pain
   beyond pain at your children's hands.
   You paid for their father's death as the law asks.

ORESTES: Phoebus, you hymned the law in black
    melody, but the deed has shone
    white as a scar. You granted us rest
    as murderers, rest to leave the land
    of Greece. But where else can I go?
    What state, host, god-fearing man
    will look steady upon my face,
        who killed my mother?

                                  (lines 1177–97)

Here the personal grief, the personal address – 'Weep greatly
for me, my brother' – is inseparable from the grief addressed to
the chthonic and Olympian powers (to Earth and Zeus, and
Phoebus Apollo) directly apostrophised in the opening and concluding strophe. The personal-within-the communal, dialogue
within a mode of ritual lament, is restored by Euripides with great
local power. Divinity is evoked just before the parodic *deus-ex-
machina* appearance of the demythologised commentator-god
Castor: 'As for Phoebus, Phoebus – yet he is my lord, silence. He
knows the truth but his oracles were lies' (lines 1245–6). It is a
deliberate ideological assault on the mythic conception of the
older, Aeschylean tragedy. That in turn is counteracted in yet
another shift to the personal and lyric: the separation dialogue of
Electra and Orestes in the final sequence of the tragedy. The grief
of parting, of anticipated exile, of alien and alienating states, is
there poignantly evoked. Euripides who seemed to show so little
'interest' in conveying the emotion of Recognition, is – unlike
Aeschylus and Sophocles – concerned with the emotion of un-
fulfilled relationship, physical and spiritual exile, and total separation:

ELECTRA: I shall never more walk in the light of your eye.
ORESTES: Now is the last I can hear your voice.

                                  (lines 1332–3)

This final encounter is much more personal than the catastrophe in Aeschylus, the torture of Orestes by the extra-personal
Eumenides, and in Sophocles, where the interaction between
protagonists fades out in a muted catastrophe, as Aegisthus is
trapped. The dialectical dialogue has become intimate – a subtle
internal shift which should warn us off classifying the Euripidean, or any other, mode of dialogue too firmly. Yet, provided
we do not turn our findings into a schematic diagram, it may be

concluded that the three *Electra* plays do illuminate three different ways of staging tragic dialogue: the mythic/archetypal; the 'dramatistic' and personal; and the parodic/dialectical (grounded in 'inner drama'). The three types of dialogue correspond, always within the stichomythic frame, to three different types of dramatic language: respectively, tending towards the ritualistic (communal), the conversational (speech-in-character), and the rhetorical (forensic, tending to speech-beyond-character). The three modes are like paradigms that point to recurrent patterns, recognisable across the varieties and the mixing of styles, in all the periods of Western drama.

2   *Duologues of transformation in Shakespeare**

1.

Shakespearian tragedy, and Elizabethan tragedy generally, is character-centred in a complex and new way, as Coleridge first noted when he contrasted it with the plot-centred structure of Greek tragedy.[1] With the shift to a new type of tragedy, the interactive dialogue of dramatis personae acquires a new significance. Scenes of personal encounter – confession, love, temptation, antagonism – become pivotal to the action and the meaning of the whole play. This can be said even though Shakespeare's dramatic language is still often choric: characters do not always speak 'in character',[2] and the spokesman, the chorus-like character, recurs to express universal insight in a language drawn from the common pool of blank verse (for example, the Gentleman in *King Lear* 3.1 who draws a parallel between the fury in the King's 'little world of man' and the fury of the elements). And even though the soliloquy is a powerful convention in several major tragedies – from direct address to subtle self-examination – it completes the total meaning of the play without overshadowing or engulfing the dialogue, as the Greek chorus does, especially in Aeschylus.

The language of the dialogue becomes more and more personal, an imitation (in the sense of imaginative counterpart not in the sense of reproduction) of the spontaneity of ordinary speech. Thought itself becomes personal, 'grows out of the speaker's immediate situation and remains connected with it', as Auerbach, in another memorable contrast with Greek tragedy, remarked.[3] What the speakers say goes beyond any speech that might be predicted from the preceding action, from the logic of relationships or from the formal and rhetorical conventions of the dialogue. Such a dialogue 'flows' far beyond the confines, the symmetries, of repartee and stichomythia. We are dealing, then, with a new kind of creative unpredictability in the modes of dramatic dialogue. The relational and verbal energies of dialogue are in constant interplay; a rich fusion is achieved that can hardly be summarised. All one can say, by way of introduction, is that this new kind of dialogue is often an agent of transformation: the speakers change with and through the changes in their mode of speaking. Much of this can be seen in a study of dialogue at its most personal – the duologue.

The interactive flexibility of the dialogue is carried by a speech-based dramatic speech. Although dialogue in Shakespeare has not been adequately studied,[4] there is a wide enough consensus on one aspect of dialogue: the development of Shakespeare's dramatic verse from the stiffer kind of rhetorical conventions towards: 'the uninhibited exchange of speech and counter-speech' (Franz); towards 'colloquial emphases and prose order' (Rylands) and the extension of *the line* as unit to give 'the effect of conversation' (Simpson). The famous run-on line and the corresponding freedom of syntax and rhythm, vocabulary and idiom, become vehicles of a fully interactive dialogue. An 'artificially natural' language makes the audience attend to character and situation (Kermode). A poetic mimesis of the 'turns' of question-and-answer creates the tempi and the tones of individual voices speaking under pressure: antiphonal or counterpointed voices. Words dictated by the urgencies of interaction may be idiomatic, or 'unpoetic' or nonce words, or verbal noises:

HORATIO: 'Twere to consider it too curiously, to consider it so.
HAMLET: No, faith, not a jot, but to follow him thither with modesty
      enough, and likelihood to lead it: as thus
(Hamlet, 5. 1. 200ff)

or:

OTHELLO: What? What?
IAGO: Lie –
OTHELLO: With her?
IAGO: With her, on her; what you will.
OTHELLO: Lie with her! lie on her! – . . .
      Pish! Noses, ears, and lips. Is't possible? – Confess?
(Othello, 4. 1. 34ff)

This is not to put the emphasis on early naturalistic elements in Shakespearian dialogue, merely to point to a dramatic possibility hardly present in any drama before mature

63

Shakespeare – not in Greek tragedy, not in the Moralities, nor in the Tudor drama, nor in Marlowe, nor in early Shakespeare where the stichomythia recurs, as in the exchanges between Richard and Elizabeth in *Richard III* (4.4). The shifts of style from the sonnet-dialogue to the relatively conversational exchanges in *Romeo and Juliet* are an early example of internal change, of a search for new modes of dialogue within one play. The extent of the external, historical style-shift can be illustrated economically by setting side by side the recognition encounter between Lear and Cordelia in the original *King Leir* and the corresponding scene in Shakespeare:

CORDELIA: But looke, deare father, looke behold and see
      Thy louing daughter speaketh vnto thee.   *(She kneeles.*
LEIR: O, stand thou vp, it is my part to kneele,
      And aske forgiuenesse for my former faults.   *(he kneeles.*
CORDELIA: O, if you wish I should inioy my breath,
      Deare father rise, or I receiue my death.   *(he riseth.*
LEIR: Then I will rise, to satisfy your mind,
      But kneele againe, til pardon be resigned.   *(he kneeles.*
CORDELIA: I pardon you: the word beseemes not me:
      But I do say so, for to ease your knee.
      You gaue me life, you were the cause that I
      Am what I am, who else had neuer bin.
LEIR: But you gaue life to me and to my friend,
      Whose dayes had else, had an vntimely end.
CORDELIA: You brought me vp, when as I was but young,
      And far vnable for to helpe my selfe.
LEIR: I cast thee forth, when as thou wast but young,
      And far vnable for to helpe thy selfe.
CORDELIA: God, world and nature say I do you wrong,
      That can indure to see you kneele so long.
    (From *The True Chronicle History of King Leir* (sixteenth century),
                                     scene 24)
CORDELIA: O! look upon me, Sir,
      And hold your hand in benediction o'er me.
      No, Sir, you must not *kneel*.
LEAR: Pray, do not mock me:
      I am a very foolish fond old man,
      Fourscore and upward, not an hour more or less;
      And, to deal plainly,
      I fear I am not in my perfect mind.
      Methinks I should know you and know this man;
      Yet I am doubtful: for I am mainly ignorant
      What place this is, and all the skill I have
      Remembers not these garments; nor I know not

> Where I did lodge last night. Do not laugh at me;
> For, as I am a man, I think this lady
> To be my child Cordelia.
> CORDELIA: And so I am, I am.
> LEAR: Be your tears wet? Yes, faith. I pray, weep not:
> If you have poison for me, I will drink it.
> I know you do not love me; for your sisters
> Have, as I do remember, done me wrong:
> You have some cause, they have not.
> CORDELIA: No cause, no cause.
> LEAR: Am I in France?
> KENT: In your own kingdom, Sir.
> LEAR: Do not abuse me.

(*King Lear*, 4. 7. 57ff. Emphasis added.)

The essential features of the style-shifts in dialogue from the chronicle to the Shakespearian tragedy leap to the eye and the ear at once: the change from the symmetry of a heavily rhymed framework to the boldly unpredictable yet simple opposition of two speakers, two worlds, presences, voices. The actional/visual pattern changes with the rhetorical pattern: from the bathos of over-emphasis (the repeated kneeling and rising, for instance, goes on for some forty lines after our extract) to the single focus on the image of the broken old man kneeling and being bidden not to kneel, once only, by the compassionate figure of his daughter. Interaction between these two is subtle in the Shakespearian duologue. The stages of Lear's partial recovery, partial recognition, are marked in the text, from 'I think this *lady*' to 'To be my *child* Cordelia', and yet the tone and gesture of the actors is needed to re-create the transformation. The dialogue can be enacted in several ways, but in any performance the breathtaking verbal and vocal opposition between Lear and Cordelia will remain: for instance, the transition from Lear's long hesitant speech to Cordelia's monosyllabic 'unpoetic words' – 'And so I am, I am' – rising out of silence and pain. The stages of emotional transformation are enacted in and through the dialogue. Shelley called *King Lear* 'the most perfect specimen of dramatic poetry';[5] and here we see the achievement of a dialogue that is poetic through being colloquially dramatic, not through richly imagistic language.

Within the many different kinds of dialogue the intimate personal duologue acquires in Shakespearian tragedy a range, a flexibility and a significance of its own. We tend to think of the tragic hero as being linguistically as well as psychically isolated; and this is true of Hamlet throughout much of the play he moves in (the exception, his confessional duologue with Horatio, is the starting point in our study). In all the other major tragedies pivotal duologues between paired characters are a dominant structure. Dual worlds are drawn into the interactive encounter of the speakers, moving towards communion or relentless collision, through dual modes of being and speech. In certain kinds of antagonistic duologue – as in the temptation scenes in *Macbeth* and *Othello* – Shakespeare seems to be anticipating what in our own time has been called a 'theatre of language': the enactment of profound psychological change working at the level of language through the urgency and 'magical' power of the dialogue itself. A kind of 'transvaluation of values' through dialogue can take place; and in the systematic derangement of Othello we witness what may be the first example of verbal contagion in drama – breakdown induced through words alone. Though we shall always bear in mind the whole play (the performance values across several planes of action and speech) it is only through detailed attention to the shifts of relationship *and* style in intimate encounter that we can perceive the complex dualities of the duologue in Shakespeare.

2.

In the duologue of Hamlet and Horatio we find an unparalleled early example of a confessional dialogue that is also 'natural' speech, neither mannered nor parodic.[6] The existential and stylistic simplicity of their exchanges are two aspects of an integrated relationship. The duologues themselves form something like a focus and a resting place amid the welter of ambivalent encounters between Hamlet and the other characters – including the histrionic dialogue with the Queen (3.4). Relatively unobtrusive in their seeming neutrality of speech, these duologues yet embody significant functions and values.

The relationship of the friends is, from the start, a unique kind of interaction. Along a line whose opposite poles are marked by full intimacy and public formality, this friendship moves towards intimacy; yet it falls short of the intensely personal and often symbiotic interaction between Shakespeare's lovers and paired antagonists. From the start Horatio is singled out by Hamlet as the 'good friend' who can be trusted and who, as a fellow-student, can be talked to in a tone of light seriousness, with a degree of outspokenness that is the prelude to confessional disclosure (1. 2. 168–82). Though Hamlet's first confidence, the assumption of 'antic disposition' after his encounter with the Ghost, is shared by two other witnesses (also called 'friends' at one point, 1. 5. 140), Horatio becomes the only confidant in the disclosure of Hamlet's later intentions and hidden action: the king-catching design behind the play-within-the-play, and the return to England from Claudius's murderous trap (in the prose letter). Paralleling these confessions of relatively external intrigue, there is a movement towards inward self-disclosure in a more intense mode and with an appropriate shift to 'thou' in the 'passion's slave' speech (3. 2. 60–72), in the graveyard and in the final scenes. Despite such intensification, the confessional duologues remain marked by the laconic passivity of Horatio as interlocutor; and the structure of the dialogue – and with it the emotional and verbal pressure – is kept within the limits of decorum, at several removes from Hamlet's propensity towards 'wild and whirling words'.

In a critical study of modern drama written as early as 1909, Lukács pointed to the significant absence of the confidant(e) in the isolated situations in which the protagonists of the new drama find themselves. This loss can be appreciated in full only if we grasp the role of the confidant in the old drama as going far beyond a mere convention, as symbol of a universal emotion:

> The emotion for which they stood could only have been one of the absolute possibility of understanding. If we consider the most complex of these relationships, the one closest to our own emotion, we will see that the functioning of Horatio vis-à-vis Hamlet only confirms that no discord of spirits did or could exist between them; all Hamlet's actions and all his motives are rightly regarded and valued by Horatio, in their original sense. What one says to the other is understood and felt as the other understood and felt. Hamlet – remarkable as this may sound – is thus not alone. When he dies he does so with the sure knowledge that a man lives in whom his own spirit is mirrored, pure, without the distortion of incomprehension.[7]

Lukács's comment gains its own pressure – and what may now appear as a degree of idealisation in stressing absolute understanding between hero and confidant – from our knowledge of absence or dislocation in relationship in modern drama. It does not seem likely that an Elizabethan audience would have responded in quite that way. And even today an audience may well find nothing to remark on in the 'understanding' between Hamlet and Horatio, either as a mirror of real-life communication or as a dramatic convention. I recall how little attention we used to pay to these exchanges, at a time when every word in Hamlet's soliloquies was remembered by heart and scrutinised. The isolation of Hamlet was what one responded to most strongly in first reading the play in adolescence; and a certain line of criticism, from Coleridge's stress on Hamlet's inwardness, his 'enormous, intellectual activity' to L. C. Knights's censure of Hamlet's self-centredness,[8] confirmed one's experience of the play as one wherein the individual consciousness of uncertainty, disintegration and death is primary. Readings of the play as a theatrical structure, as ritual, or as a sophisticated and complex version of the Elizabethan revenge tragedy, offer a healthy corrective to a wholly Hamlet-centred reading of *Hamlet*. But, in any context, Hamlet's key relationships may still be seen as histrionic, self and word-conscious, as in Hamlet's crucial encounters with Ophelia and his mother, or parodic, with Polonius, Rosencrantz and Guildenstern, and Osric, the butts of Hamlet's personal and linguistic satire. Riddling and ambivalent language-consciousness seems to engulf the dialogue embodying all these relationships. And then an imaginative effort is needed just to see and hear in the Hamlet–Horatio duologues an approximation to 'normality' – some norm of communicative dialogue that includes direct self-revelation to another person, in counterpoint *against* the modes of dislocated ('out of joint') encounter and language.

The passivity of Horatio presents something of a problem, because existentially the modern reader would expect a greater degree of participation from a friend, and dramatically the self-effacing voice (especially against Hamlet's genius for self-dramatisation) risks being perceived as banal. In the study already quoted Lukács says that Horatio's whole personality is fulfilled in his relationship to Hamlet (as is Kent's in his relationship to Lear); this view is based on the larger argument that in the old drama the subservient character (the servant, the confidant, etc.),[9] reflecting the old order of society, could interact with others and fulfil his personality through gestures, and formal relations. However interesting as a comment on the social and psychological significance of the confidant's role in general, there is more to Horatio's presence in *Hamlet* than formal relations. From the start Shakespeare fused the role of the confidant with that of the spokesman, who is given lines of great beauty and chorus-like universality. In the opening act, it is Horatio who gives voice to the world's general anxiety felt in Elsinore, 'This bodes some strange eruption to our state' (1. 1. 60) invoking the Roman moon before the murder of Julius Caesar 'sick almost to doomsday with eclipse' (line 125). In the fourth act Horatio briefly appears as attendant to the Queen, and is made to remark on the danger of not speaking to Ophelia. And most prominently in the final scene, Horatio, as he obeys Hamlet's dying injunction 'Absent thee from felicity awhile . . . To tell my story', becomes the survivor / witness whose words promise a form of absolute authenticity: 'so shall you hear . . . all this can I / Truly deliver'. While this extension of Horatio's role is clearly in keeping with Shakespeare's tendency to make minor characters act as spokesmen / chorus – and to distribute fine lines from the common pool of blank verse among them – the larger role enhances the stature of the confidant/friend and, as it were, underwrites his trustworthiness in dialogue.

For the sake of clarity I shall group the confessional duologues of Hamlet and Horatio into: (1) the prologue (the two platform scenes, scenes 2 and 4); (2) the full confessional duologue (3.2); and (3) the epilogue (the churchyard and final scenes).

The first exchange of the prologue gains immediate intimacy from the direct juxtaposition of the Hamlet–Horatio dialogue and Hamlet's own soliloquy: as if Horatio's greeting of Hamlet answered Hamlet's 'But break my heart, for I must hold my tongue', and prefigured the one kind of communication where silence/soliloquy, the concealment of grief, is no longer an absolute need.[10] The immediate recognition and explicit naming of the 'good friend' and the light seriousness of this exchange has already been mentioned; it must be further noted that the duologue is embedded in group dialogue (with Barnardo as silent bystander and Marcellus an occasional interjector, on the naturalistic/ theatrical level anxious not to be excluded). The tone of confidentiality is rapidly established (lines 160ff), and at once modulates into an exchange concerning the apparition, releasing Horatio's eye-witness account and making possible Hamlet's intense cross-examination of Horatio (lines 213ff). This twenty-line catechism is the kind of dialogue that is barely perceived as a significant theatrical and stylistic structure, in performance or even in reading, such is its transparency. Nevertheless, in the context of the play, it establishes a unique kind of dialogue. It is, first of all, not merely expository in the rudimentary sense of using Horatio to provide necessary information about the Ghost to the audience. Rather, the dialogue enacts a process of exploration and discovery, of urgent truth-seeking within an undistorted communicative framework, precise question-and-answer:

HAMLET: What, looked he frowningly?
HORATIO: A countenance more in sorrow than in anger.
HAMLET: Pale, or red?
HORATIO: Nay, very pale.
HAMLET: And fixed his eyes upon you?
HORATIO: Most constantly.
HAMLET: I would I had been there.
HORATIO: It would have much amazed you.

Although this dialogue is not intimately personal, only intimate trust makes it possible. And although the verse leans on plain prose – the lines are irregular, the short lines completing one another, the vocabulary and rhythm being simpler than in Hamlet's 'antic' prose speeches – the urgency of inquiry gives it dramatic intensity. There remains the paradox that in the Hamlet world the 'natural' exchange is eccentric (not central). The alternative mode of self-expression, apart from the soliloquy, being mannered dialogue:

HAMLET: Do you see yonder cloud that's almost in shape of a camel?
POLONIUS: By th' mass and 'tis, like a camel indeed.
HAMLET: Methinks it is like a weasel.
POLONIUS: It is backed like a weasel.
HAMLET: Or, like a whale?
POLONIUS: Very like a whale.

(3. 2. 377ff)

The semblance of coherent question-and-answer is kept here; but what is said mocks the possibility of dialogue, since 'the truth-seeking urge', the cogency behind question-and-answer becomes a canter, a verbal game.

Or we have this:

QUEEN: Come, come, you answer with an idle tongue.
HAMLET: Go, go, you answer with a wicked tongue.

(3. 4. 11ff)

where the frame, the crude symmetry of a mocking stichomythia, seems to introduce the tone of pathological theatricality
in Hamlet's encounter with his mother. The uniqueness of the
Hamlet–Horatio dialogue is explicitly underlined by the action of
the cellarage scene, where Horatio protests against Hamlet's
manic and evasive outburst: 'These are but wild and whirling
words, my lord' (1. 5. 133). Horatio's objection is at once personal
and stylistic. Hamlet's ranting evasions break the trust established, a trust which the code of friendship would seem to require, and Hamlet feels obliged to apologise and 'explain': 'For
your desire to know what is between us / O'ermaster't as you
may'; and they break the linguistic rules of conversation too.
The rest of that scene is a masterful theatrical enactment of the
shift away from the norms of 'natural' dialogue: the mock-ritual
of Hamlet's swearing his friends to secrecy, and the excited and
ambivalent assumption of 'antic disposition'.

The full confessional duologue opens, without any interaction
between Hamlet and Horatio in the long intervening scenes, and
with an abrupt directness:

HAMLET: Horatio, thou art e'en as just a man
        As e'er my conversation coped withal.
HORATIO: O, my dear lord, –
HAMLET: Nay, do not think I flatter
    . . .
                Dost thou hear?
    Since my dear soul was mistress of her choice,
    And could of men distinguish her election,
    Sh'hath sealed thee for herself, for thou hast been
    As one in suff'ring all that suffers nothing
    . . .
                    give me that man
    That is not passion's slave, and I will wear him
    In my heart's core, ay in my heart of heart,
    As I do thee. Something too much of this –
    There is a play to-night before the king . . .

(3. 2. 52ff)

The pronoun shift to 'thou' is the clear signal for intimacy;

from now on Hamlet addresses his friend in the second person for the rest of the play, except for the curiously functional and mid-conversational opening of the final scene: 'So much for this, Sir, now shall you see the other –', followed by another 'Sir' before Hamlet reverts to 'thou' (line 27). It follows from the hierarchic Elizabethan social code that Horatio cannot be fully reciprocal, and must continue to address Hamlet with unobtrusive formality – 'You'; 'my lord'; 'good my lord' – throughout. This sample of social grammar in Shakespeare is in keeping with Horatio's relative intellectual and emotional passivity in relation to Hamlet. At the same time, Hamlet clearly sees in Horatio the only person in his world who can be addressed intimately, 'as just a man / As e'er my conversation coped withal' – the unusual phrase pointing precisely to the significance of this rare 'conversation': fully felt and confessional, not a verbal game, not 'antic', not pathologically histrionic. The word 'just' – almost what we mean by 'well-adjusted' – is the keyword expressing love (*philia*) towards the one person who is not 'passion's slave': not subject, as Hamlet is, to the fluctuations of intense, ambivalent, and threatening emotions. Indirectly, the speech is 'an important piece of self-criticism', in Dover Wilson's words;[11] and the indirect, non-introspective, self-revelation makes it a particularly interesting device as dramatic speech. The dialogue frame, the occasion of addressing another person, an interlocutor who is immediately present in the speaker's words, who is the ostensible object and subject of the speech – all that is distinct from any soliloquy.[12] If we add to this the consideration that the soliloquy was doomed to exhaustion as a dramatic convention after the seventeenth century – though it came to new life in opera and music drama and perhaps in monodrama from Goethe's *Proserpina* to Beckett's *Not I* – then the confessional duologue will be seen to have a special importance within the specific forms of dramatic dialogue.

But, it may be asked, is there not something peculiar about this dialogue frame – its being a 'frame', precisely. Hamlet dominates; he 'confesses' more than Horatio (and the audience) is prepared for; the speech is, as a declaration of love and high esteem, more personal than anything the role of the convention makes one expect. (One cannot think of Juliet speaking to the Nurse in the language of such intimate emotion, nor does

Racine's Phèdre address her nurse / confidante Oenone with such feeling for her person even though *what* she confesses, her love of Hyppolite, is the central emotion of the tragedy.) Moreover, on the naive level of action as intrigue it is not 'necessary' for Hamlet to lead up to his request – 'observe my uncle', be my fellow-witness, be my trusted accomplice – with such a confession. Despite all this, Horatio remains passive and laconic: he is given one quick, conventionally modest phrase, and a concluding phrase, a promise to do as he is bidden:

> Well, my lord,
> If a' [The King] steal aught the whilst this play is playing
> And 'scape detecting, I will pay the theft.
>
> (3. 2. 85ff)

Horatio's bland wit and matter-of-fact acceptance ends this duologue. Shakespeare does not attempt to intensify Horatio's degree of participation in Hamlet's emotional world or to transpose his self-detached, 'neutral' style into a more intense key. The confidant(e) convention remains at several removes from the duologue of lovers and paired characters; it is also more protagonist-centred than the naturalistic confessional duologue in Ibsen and O'Neill.

The relative detachment and neutral style of Horatio's responses is significantly varied in the final act. The responses are still laconic, giving Horatio the role of the good listener, with prompt and sympathetic answers, but falling short of full intellectual and emotional participation. In the graveyard scene Horatio's terse rejoinders express a state of mind that seems immune from the infection of Hamlet's death-conscious wit. But now these responses gain greater intrinsic interest; they form an integral part of the dialogue (are not mere props, mere stooge-talk), acting as an essential counterpoint to Hamlet's prose speeches. The question-and-answer sequences interlock, cogently, responsibly:

HAMLET: [on the skull of the imagined lawyer]
Is this the fine of his fines, and the recovery of his recoveries, to have his fine pate full of dirt? will his vouchers vouch him no more of his purchases, and double ones too, than the length and breadth of a pair of indentures? the very conveyances of his

lands will scarcely lie in his box, and must th'inheritor himself
have no more, ha?
HORATIO: Not a jot more, my lord.
HAMLET: Is not parchment made of sheep-skins?
HORATIO: Ay, my lord, and of calves'-skins too.
HAMLET: They are sheep and calves which seek assurance in that.

(5. 1. 102ff)

On the level of interaction Horatio's matter-of-fact voice acts
as a distancing device for the intensity of Hamlet's death-
consciousness. The logic of this counter-voice leads to the best-
known exchange of all:

HAMLET: Why, may not imagination trace the noble dust of Alexander,
till 'a find it stopping a bung-hole?
HORATIO: 'Twere to consider too curiously, to consider so.
HAMLET: No, faith, not a jot, but follow him thither with modesty
enough . . .

(5. 1. 198ff)

A monologue on death could hardly have achieved this effect.
The compressed dialectic of this dialogue – the interruption, the
immediate presence of an opposed state of 'considering' – ends
by adding to the intense irony of Hamlet's death-consciousness.

The final scene confirms the importance of the confessional
duologue. After participating in the parodic onslaught on Osric
('Is't not possible to understand in another tongue?' 5. 2. 126) in
keeping with his role as a focus of linguistic naturalness, Horatio
becomes a more active counter-voice to Hamlet in the poignant
duologue just before the duel. His controlled tone, which might
be expected to be in tune with the Stoic/Christian resignation in
Hamlet's final state of mind, is actually raised against the overt
fatalism which is part of that complex and much-discussed 'readiness'. In rapid succession Horatio warns Hamlet that he will lose,
objects to Hamlet's dismissal of his own premonitions and then
openly counsels: 'If your mind dislike any thing, obey it.' The
open sympathy which was there from the start, now comes near
to imaginative empathy. The neutral tone does not express neutrality but concern; the confidant's role has grown into that of
the participant. No doubt Shakespeare is preparing the audience
for the catastrophe: for Horatio's presence at Hamlet's death, his
function as survivor, witness and self-denying spokesman, and
for the intensification of catharsis through the many lines of tragic

pathos spoken in the context of the final elegiac duologue (lines 330–59). But the Hamlet–Horatio duologues become interactive and reciprocal well before the ritualised ending.

3.

We may approach the duologue of paired protagonists in Shakespearian tragedy with certain generic expectations: they are compressed units integral to a larger structure of action, the carriers of irrevocable encounter, both psychologically and stylistically complex. Yet, in text and in performance, in significant detail, the contrasts seem to me to be more interesting than the correspondences. The pattern of verbal interaction in this or that duologue is governed by several contexts of which the *type* of play we are dealing with (early or mature tragedy, lyric or epic-related, *Romeo and Juliet* or *Antony and Cleopatra*) is only one. On the one hand, there are significant variations in the structure and texture of duologues within the same play (as in either of the plays just mentioned). On the other hand, plays studied in contrast illuminate differences in the emotional pattern of a dramatic relationship, which underlie the verbal pattern. The duologue of young lovers with their harmonising antiphons has quite a different pattern from the wrangling rhetoric of lovers in decline; and both together may be seen more sharply when contrasted with the fully dualistic duologue of antagonists, Iago and Othello for example. The selection and the grouping of plays in this section – not strictly chronological though aware of Shakespeare's stylistic development – is designed to highlight such contrasts and to connect the existential and verbal elements of interaction in duologue.

So intense are the main duologues of *Romeo and Juliet* in their lyricism that they seem to 'carry' the action of the play. Yet there are only three key duologues: the first encounter (1.5), the balcony scene (2.2) and the antiphonal verse of the wedding-night (3.5). The unique emotional and verbal world of these love duets has to be established in the first three acts before Shakespeare – as if realising that such intensity might not be sustained beyond the nuptial scene – separates the lovers and silences their duologue. Moreover, the intimate yet complex lyricism of the duologues has to work against strongly counterpointed styles: the jejune

Petrarchan poesy out of which Romeo is to grow, as well as the public rhetoric and declamation, with a goodly admixture of punning bawdy from the Nurse and Mercutio ('Prick love for pricking, and you beat it down').

The shared and sacramental sonnet of the first encounter takes up barely one minute of action time; yet it is enough to transform the action and transpose the play into a new key. Just as, theatrically, the encounter takes place in a corner of the festive house (possibly speaking against the muted music and the voices of the masked revellers), so the sonnet has to create verbal space for itself against brawling voices – with Tybalt's choleric rhetoric still ringing in our ears. It is a 'privileged moment', which starts the process of felt excess whereby a tale of two houses (which might have been an epic or chronicle running on for generations, material for five acts of feuding) modulates into the compression peculiar to tragic encounter. From now on the action is invaded by inwardness, yet oppressed by the sense of time as the lovers' enemy. And the style-conscious lyricism is transformed into dialogue proper:

ROMEO: (*takes Juliet's hand*). If I profane with my unworthiest hand
This holy shrine, the gentle pain is this:
My lips, two blushing pilgrims, ready stand
To smooth that rough touch with a tender kiss.
JULIET: Good pilgrim, you do wrong your hand too much,
Which mannerly devotion shows in this:
For saints have hands that pilgrims' hands do touch,
And palm to palm is holy palmers' kiss.
ROMEO: Have not saints lips, and holy palmers too?
JULIET: Ay, pilgrim, lips that they must use in prayer.
ROMEO: O then, dear saint, let lips do what hands do,
They pray: grant thou, lest faith turn to despair.
JULIET: Saints do not move, though grant for prayers' sake.
ROMEO: Then move not, while my prayer's effect I take.
[End of sonnet]
Thus from my lips by thine my sin is purged.

(*Kissing her*)

JULIET: Then have my lips the sin that they have took.
ROMEO: Sin from my lips? O trespass sweetly urged!
Give me my sin again. (*Kissing her*)
JULIET: You kiss by th' book.

(1. 5. 97–110ff)

I would put the stress on dialogue both naively and critically. Naively, in performance the uninstructed audience can barely hear the sonnet as sonnet, or even as a distinct verbal sequence, so seamlessly is it woven into the texture of the climactic lines which follow the final couplet (lines 107–10). Critically, it seems a mistake to put too much emphasis on the sonnet as lyric. In *Elizabethan Acting*,[13] Bertram Joseph expounds the art of performing verse – as singers sing operatic arias. In his otherwise justified eagerness to refute the naturalistic fallacy in approaching Shakespeare's dramatic verse, Joseph says, concerning the first encounter of Romeo and Juliet: 'If these [lines] are *primarily* imagined as representing dialogue which could be exchanged between a pair of romantic lovers, each inspired to heights of poetry, the scene cannot achieve its full effect. For these lines are written in the form of a sonnet, and no attempt at representing the dialogue must be allowed to prevent this particular arrangement of sounds and rhythms reacting upon the audience.' (Emphasis added.) I do not know what 'primarily' means in this context. The sonnet may be primary, as a literary form and texture; but it is certainly to be exchanged 'between a pair of romantic lovers'. The lyrical expressiveness, the figures, the rhymes, the rhythm of the sonnet are all integrated in the dialogue. One is aware of the interaction of speakers at all levels: for example, the pilgrim conceit is initiated and enacted by Romeo (dressed as a palmer), and is then developed and shared, carried from mouth to mouth. Joseph himself offers a fine analysis of the sonnet (pp. 128–9) which shows how the lines are shared by the lovers: the first two quatrains equally, the next one dominated by Romeo (giving him two extra lines in all), whilst each has one line in the couplet. The sharing of the lines, and of the rhyme-scheme, is interaction: Juliet in turn half-withdrawing, half-granting, and finally suggesting both attitudes in one line: 'Saints do not move, though grant for prayers' sake.' The qualification is sufficient to embolden Romeo to close the sonnet on a kiss. There is a gradual intensification that is fully dramatic; the climax, Juliet's rapt protest at the second kiss ('You kiss by th' book') taking the sonnet world, and its rhyme, outside the sonnet form. The compressed lyricism enters the playtext in full, and will be allowed to spill over, so to speak, into the more open texture of the subsequent duologues.

Moreover, the sonnet conceits are free from mannerist tricks of speech. There is a clearly structured, in itself dramatically

gradual, development of a dominant image-cluster – shrine, pilgrim, devotion, palmer, palm – which fuses feeling and thought.
It is clear, and performable (though complex enough to yield
pages of meta-text if it were transcribed in full, in the manner of
Roman Jakobson).[14] The rhythm, though it is not that of colloquial
speech, is far from declamatory. By contrast, when Shakespeare
dramatises the love-sick Romeo he deliberately piles up oxy-
morons in 'a parody of the language of the sonneteers':[15]

> Why, then, O brawling love, O loving hate,
> O any thing, of nothing first create!
> O heavy lightness, serious vanity,
> Misshapen chaos of well-seeming forms,
> Feather of lead, bright smoke, cold fire, sick health . . .
>
> (1. 1. 175ff)

Appropriately enough, such lines are not to be spoken to the
beloved. They are spoken 'to' the absent one, Rosaline, whose
function is to keep out of reach of love's dialogue. The poetaster
language is for the patient minor confidant, Benvolio, and for
Mercutio who, like a tired critic, expects Romeo to continue in the
tired old style of *amour-passion*: 'Now is he for the numbers
Petrarch flowed in' (as late as 2. 4. 38). The audience overhears all
this and can judge the 'shift of style' towards greater maturity in
Romeo's speech.

The balcony and the wedding-night duologues – both
played on the upper stage or balcony – are justly so famous that
detailed discussion and quotation is not needed for a few essential points to be made. What stands out with a clarity that each re-
reading and performance reinforces, is the perfect artifice of
spontaneity in these duologues. The intensity of the first encounter is not diminished, rather carried further; yet the duologues
break out of the strict formal frame of the sonnet duologue towards a progression in emotional maturity, directness, and an
intense yet natural – not naturalistic – speech, as Eliot noted in
'Poetry and Drama': 'The stiffness, the artificiality, the poetic
decoration, of his early verse has finally given place to a simplifi-
cation, to a language of natural speech, and this language of
conversation again raised to great poetry which is essentially
dramatic: for the scene has a structure of which each line is an
essential part.'[16]

For though the first encounter had conveyed a sincere experience, the sonnet duologue expresses the verbal equivalent of the masked ball: there *is* a distancing. The lovers could still, hypothetically, withdraw from commitment, their exchange might be only a privileged moment. Their insecurity in the opening of the balcony scene – and the need to say it again – is then both universally and locally the right tone. And the dramatic device of making Romeo overhear the love confession that is 'meant to be' a soliloquy is an ingenious extension of the love duologue. This alone makes it possible to circumvent, at one and the same time, the Elizabethan social taboo on the girl taking the initiative in her confession of love – 'Fain would I dwell on form – fain, fain deny / what I have spoke' (lines 88–9) – and the potential bathos of a second 'first encounter'. (The anxiety felt over breaking the taboo would probably have been a long and central speech in Racine; and a naturalistic dramatist might retranslate what was spoken eloquently, in disguise at night, into a suitable language of the day, with all the pauses, hesitations, and repeated replay desired.) Shakespeare's solo-into-duet device (2. 2. 1–60) modulates into an equally masterly lopsided dialogue: Juliet's spare statements of practical concern for Romeo's physical survival provoke the latter's return to a series of passionate declarations. This asymmetrical sequence (lines 61–84) also creates the illusion that Juliet is, after all, as 'strange' as the social code requires, for wanting to know precisely 'by whose direction' Romeo found the orchard is a little low-keyed, coming between Romeo's ardent hyperboles of love. Juliet's own passionate speech ('My bounty is as boundless as the sea . . .') is delayed; it is released, with full dramatic effect, by the simple yet dangerous exchange:

ROMEO: O wilt thou leave me so unsatisfied?
JULIET: What satisfaction canst thou have tonight?
ROMEO: Th'exchange of thy love's faithful vow for mine.
JULIET: I gave thee mine before thou didst request it;
    And yet I would it were to give again.
ROMEO: Wouldst thou withdraw it? For what purpose, love?

(2. 2. 25ff)

After Juliet's passionate speech, the duologue itself ends in a wave-like rhythm (the Nurse's interruptions, Juliet's double withdrawal and return), counterpointing the prolongation of speech with a naturalness 'as boundless as the sea'. The lovers' physical distance from one another at once justifies and intensifies the lingering returns – and innovations – of the duologue. Their words alone enact an irrevocable and tragic commitment, with the playful abandon of love's comedy.

Taken together with the wedding-night encounter,[17] the major duologues of *Romeo and Juliet* embody a transformation of experience in a changing dramatic language. Just as the protagonists are maturing, with the irruption of tragedy, the language of love is becoming flexible and mutual: the lyrical becomes dramatic, the exchange of vows corresponds to exchanged rhythms and ways of speaking.

Antony and Cleopatra is so open in its structure that one line of criticism rightly stresses its distinctness: its lack of the compression of tragedy, its free flow of time and space, 'its strung-out sequence of events', with traces of 'continuous staging',[18] its large-scale themes of empire, with Antony as 'emperor' of a hemisphere, its authentically Roman 'arms and men' tonality. The eight encounters of the lovers, who are seldom alone, are seen as a microcosm by Shakespeare and the audience; the vast frame of action is, among other things, an ironic counterpoint to passion's claim to a love-centred universe. Nevertheless, there *is* dramatic compression within the epic play, and it is provided by the duologues of Antony and Cleopatra.

This compression comes, however, from the repetitions or variations in the duels of passion; there is no true progression, peripety or crucial recognition. And the rhythm of emotion is marked by the constant see-sawing of duality: sublimation and carnality, romantic rhetoric and plain speech as direct physical gesture ('The nobleness of life is to do thus' 1. 1. 36) or else essential emotion compressed into one or two words ('Pardon, pardon' 3. 2. 68).

Structurally, the duologues enact the lovers' duality and come in pairs. The expression of passionate antipathies becomes as crucial as the affirmations of love; the sexual strife, though several removes from the modern kind (the Strindbergian inferno of neurosis) is charged with ambivalence, play-acting, and 'negative repulsions [that] can serve to hold the mutual pair together as firmly as positive attractions'.[19] The two duologues of the prologue (1.1 and 1.3) can be seen as paired or as sections of a continuous, but interrupted, encounter: to-and-fro-ing between polarities. The initial antiphonal incantation on love (1. 1. 14–17) leads straight to the first wrangling match, which is carried over into Cleopatra's wholly dominant mockery of Antony (1. 3. 13–41), and gradually muted, through the stages of dispute over Fulvia's death and Antony's supposed play-acting, to the final play of tenderness in parting. The long absence of Antony in Rome (approximately an hour and twenty minutes of playing time during which the relationship is imaginatively re-created for the audience through Cleopatra's replay of vicarious love-scenes) naturally silences direct exchange. When the duologues are re-sumed with full intensity, after Antony's fatal decision to return to Cleopatra, they enact a cycle of emotion around the two sea battles of Actium and Alexandria, made 'traumatic' by Cleo-patra's double betrayal (3.11 and 13; 4.8 and 12). The Actium duologues are a counterpoint of grief/forgiveness followed by fury/reconciliation. The Alexandria duologues contrast a brief paean of victory with Antony's second and murderous fit of fury, at once reduced and magnified into an unanswerable monologue by Cleopatra's exit. With all their internal variations, the two pairs of duologues come near to duplicating the shifts of emotion. This is due partly to Shakespeare's reliance on Plutarch's chroni-cle; but North's Plutarch has no dialogue for the protagonists, and Daniel's *Cleopatra* (1594) has no Antony, while its dialogue is in rather stilted quatrains. The duologues are Shakespeare's own invention, then; and the duality is something we recognise from the sonnet cycles, with their opposition of 'high love' and 'low love'. The duologues are unique in the great tragedies. The redoubling seems significant in itself: do they not suggest some-thing endlessly spiralling and equivocal – 'double, double' – as the essence of passion's duologues? The pathos of the *Liebestod* duet in act four, and Cleopatra's solo apotheosis of the dead Antony, do not cancel out the direct enactment of vacillation and alienation, through encounter, in the central duologues.

Stylistically, the duologues offer 'polyphonic' contrasts, as if miming the famed 'infinite variety' of Cleopatra herself, her fluctuations of emotion reflected in constantly changing modes of speech. This does not mean that Cleopatra as it were dictates the duologues, for the shifting weight of the couple's disequilibrium in the way they interact – various kinds of assymetry in which either Cleopatra or Antony is in turn the dominant speaker – is an essential feature of the duologues. Only rarely, as in the opening antiphony, is there emotional and stylistic equilibrium:

CLEOPATRA: If it be love indeed, tell me how much.
ANTONY: There's beggary in the love that can be reckoned.
CLEOPATRA: I'll set a bourn how far to be beloved.
ANTONY: Then must thou needs find out new heaven, new earth.

These lines precisely balance the element of ceremony and self-performance in the lovers' mutual celebration of love. The intrinsic balance of the stichomythia underscores the brief episode of classically matched speakers. Even the raillery – the bids in the auction of love's measure – is decorous play. (It is also a stylistic reminder and remainder of the early plays and the major comedies of love.) It is important to recall how consciously this encounter is staged, following the chorus-like satirical portrait of Antony as 'a strumpet's fool' by Philo: 'Look where they come.' Discussing this opening exchange, in *Drama in Performance*,[20] Raymond Williams argues that 'this is not ordinary dramatic dialogue . . . The question and answer, the balancing single lines, are as formal as a song, and in performance are given their full emphasis: a momentarily isolated pattern that creates a whole feeling. It is, in a sense, a deliberate emphasis of stillness.' This is true, though it needs to be qualified (as we qualified Joseph's view of the sonnet encounter in *Romeo and Juliet*), for the formal patterning is still dialogue. It is distinct from any set speech *about* the pair, it embodies *their* interaction and hints at *their* inwardness in this halcyon phase. And as the duologue turns into wrangling, what Williams calls a marked 'break in the verbal music' is really the first style-shift into the language of combat, with its rise and fall of 'high' and 'low' styles, hyperbole and natural speech-as-gesture (usually erotic):

ANTONY: Let Rome in Tiber melt, and the wide arch
    Of the ranged empire fall! Here is my space.
    Kingdoms are clay: our dungy earth alike
    Feeds beast as man: the nobleness of life
    Is to do thus;
                [. . .]   (*Embracing*)
CLEOPATRA: Excellent falsehood.
    Why did he marry Fulvia, and not love her?
    I'll seem the fool I am not; Antony
    Will be himself.

                                  (1. 1. 33ff)

Embracing yet speaking to the lover in the third person – this foreshadows a pattern that is worked out, with variations, in the prolonged duologue of combat already summarised, with Cleopatra alternately plaintive, ironic, pettish and conciliatory (1.3).

We turn to the supreme economy of the first duologue after Actium (3.11). It will be recalled that this duologue is doubly delayed or prepared: first by Antony's virtual monologues of ignominy and shame ('I have fled myself, and have instructed cowards / To run and show their shoulders') and then by the physical distance that separates, on stage, the emotionally prostrate Antony from the insecure Cleopatra. In a supreme effect of visual theatre it is suggested that Antony cannot see Cleopatra who shares his space and is approaching. And when he comes to realise her presence (roused by Eros: 'Sir, the Queen'), his short speech is a dignified and even tender lament, without a trace of the later fury, countered by Cleopatra asking for forgiveness; an interaction that is sustained with simple yet astonishing modulations:

ANTONY: O, wither has thou led me, Egypt? See
How I convey my shame out of thine eyes
By looking back what I have left behind
'Stroyed in dishonour.
CLEOPATRA: O my lord, my lord,
Forgive my fearful sails! I little thought
You would have followed.
ANTONY: Egypt, thou knew'st too well
My heart was to thy rudder tied by th'strings,
And thou shouldst tow me after . . .
CLEOPATRA: O, my pardon!
ANTONY: Now I must
To the young, and send humble treaties, dodge
And palter in the shift of lowness, who
With half the bulk o' th'world played as I pleased,
Making and marring fortunes. You did know
How much you were my conqueror, and that
My sword, made weak by my affection, would
Obey it on all cause.
CLEOPATRA: Pardon, pardon!
ANTONY: Fall not a tear, I say; one of them rates
All that is won and lost. Give me a kiss;
Even this repays me. We sent our schoolmaster:
Is 'a come back? Love, I am full of lead.

(3. 11. 51ff)

The depth of feeling that runs across this exchange, intensified by each successive 'pardon', can perhaps only be fully realised in performance. But even a glance at the printed page will show the simplicity of the design which is meant to convert the speakers to sincere utterance. In that moment, in that encounter, the 'dissembling' elements of the wrangling rhetoric gradually fall away, and the reduced lovers say what they feel, and are enabled to declare and share the loss they have inflicted on each other. There is a broad contrast: Antony's rhetoric is answered by Cleopatra's spare speech with its moving, unpredictable, crescendo of 'Pardon!'. Yet, in this instance, Antony's rhetoric is itself spare, its nautical images are exact, barely metaphorical, as if miming both his infatuation and his rout at sea: 'My heart was to thy *rudder* tied by th'strings / And thou shouldst *tow* me after.' Again, the lament over his fall is equally precise and mimetic: '. . . dodge / And palter in the shift of lowness'; and precise description is qualitatively worlds apart from histrionic rhetoric with its fighting terms of guilt and recrimination. Moreover, the reproach turns, on the second sentence of the second speech, into a new and more strongly felt affirmation of love: 'you did know how much you were my conqueror . . .' The feeling of a lament is partly carried by modal verbs and hypothetical statements (*would have* followed, *shouldst* tow, *would* obey). The response and counter-response then becomes, on the third 'pardon', a purgation of negatives, forgiveness and reconciliation fully embodied. It is a duologue of unique power in Shakespearian tragedy, indeed in all drama; for though the reconciliation of Lear and Cordelia could be evoked for its moving beauty, it has a completely different actional and symbolic significance, as well as style. Antony and Cleopatra's 'reconciliation' duologue enacts the transformation of carnal lovers from near-destruction to mutual self-renewal, in one brief exchange; and the words suffice to enact the transformation.

This duologue, together with the later cycles of duologue, give *Antony and Cleopatra*[21] a special place in Shakespearian tragedy: no other pair of protagonists is so essentially embodied in and through dialogue. Cleopatra never soliloquises, and Antony only for a few lines. In contrast to the recurrent isolation of the soliloquising tragic hero in *Hamlet*, *King Lear*, and even in *Othello* and *Macbeth*, in this play the fluctuations of passion are fully worked out in the concrete rhythms of full encounter and interactive dialogue.

4.

If we tried to place the duologue of intimate encounter on a sliding scale according to dramatic situation and style, then the sonnet encounter of Romeo and Juliet would be near one pole – there is dramatic unison, two-voices-in-one. (This particular dialogue is also highly formal in its lyrical stylisation; but, as the Ferdinand and Miranda wooing duologue in *The Tempest* (3.1) shows, unison can also be dramatised in an 'artificially natural' dialogue which tends to transparency, making the audience attend to character and situation and not to the imagery.)[22] The wooing duologue of Romeo and Juliet in the orchard scene moves from unison towards passionate/playful collision of two attitudes, two voices, even ways of speaking, distinct yet exchanged, miming 'conversation'. Further along the scale we may place the wrangling and asymmetrical 'bouts' of Antony and Cleopatra: their coupling duality, with all those complex changes of feeling and language. However, the Antony and Cleopatra duologues are, even at their most discordant, several removes from the duologue of tragic antagonists: where the duality itself provides the energy of interaction; where the language, the speaking voice, of one character, the open or hidden seducer, becomes the principal instrument in manipulating or destroying the answering partner. Then we have a full, as it were symbiotic, verbal interaction between two attitudes, two voices, speakers, whose very act of communing ends with the defeat of one. Then we have a transforming duologue that is fully *of*, and not only *in*, tragedy – annulling the dialogue of proper exchange.

In his study of 'The Jacobean Shakespeare', Maynard Mack discusses the function of duality in tragedy in its wider actional and metaphysical context. This context goes well beyond any particular dialogue to that dialectic of dramatic worlds and attitudes where feeling is counterpointed by detachment, tragic involvement by comedy or indifference – as in the famous counterpointed scenes of Hamlet and the gravedigger, Cleopatra and the clown. Paired voices enter drama for a number of excellent reasons:

They occur, partly, no doubt, because of their structural utility, the value of complementary personalities in a work of fiction being roughly analogous to the value of thesis and antithesis in a discursive work. Partly too, no doubt, because in stage performance, the antiphonal effects of the two main vocabularies, strengthened by diversity of manner, costume, placing on the stage, supply variety of mood and gratify the eye and ear. But these are *superficial considerations*. Perhaps we come to something more satisfactory when we consider that these two voices apparently answer to reverberations which reach far back in the human past. *Mutatis mutandis* Coriolanus and Menenius, Antony and Enobarbus, Macbeth and Lady Macbeth, Lear and his Fool, Othello and Iago, Brutus and Cassius, Romeo and Mercutio exhibit a kind of duality that is also exhibited in Oedipus and Jocasta (as well as Creon), Antigone and Ismene, Prometheus and Oceanus, Phaedra and her nurse – and also, in many instances in Greek tragedy, by the protagonist and the chorus.[23] (Emphasis added.)

It is strange that in Maynard Mack's hierarchy 'structural utility' and the 'antiphonal effects' of opposed voices and vocabularies should be '*superficial considerations*' compared with 'the reverberations which reach far back in the human past'. I should have thought that these are inseparable aspects, the body and the psyche of drama. However deep-rooted the cultural sources of our dual worlds, the duality *can* only be expressed in structured and antiphonal dialogue.

At this point we shall focus on the duality that marks *the duologue of antagonists*, whose opposed attitudes and voices interact at the centre of the tragic action. Maynard Mack himself points to the opposing voices in *Macbeth* and *Othello*, singling out the scene after the murder of Duncan as the most 'thrilling tragic counterpoint [ever] set down for the stage'. The dialogue embodies the opposition of Lady Macbeth's purely physical responses and Macbeth's metaphysical intuitions: 'his "noise" to her is just the owl screaming and the crickets' cry. The voice of one crying "sleep no more" is only his "brain-sickly fear". The blood on his hands is what "a little water clears us of" ', and so on.[24] Clearly, this fundamental opposition is *there*, in a signature of dual voices, from the start, from the moment of Macbeth's entry into Lady Macbeth's totalitarian world, bringing his own imaginative ambivalence. She has just summoned, in her sustained black incantation ('Come, you spirits') the forces of evil and darkness; but Macbeth confines himself to a laconic statement of facts:

MACBETH: My dearest love,
    Duncan comes here tonight..
LADY MACBETH: And when goes he hence?
MACBETH: Tomorrow, as he purposes.
LADY MACBETH: O! Never
    Shall sun that morrow see.

          (1. 5. 57ff)

This is followed by a nine-line speech which opens the process of persuasion/seduction by telling Macbeth how to 'look like the innocent flower' while 'this night's great business' (the thought of murder left unspoken) is to be put in *her* 'dispatch'. Soon, in the magical superimposition of her voice on the ambivalent/imaginative Macbeth in the crucial scene in the prologue to Duncan's murder (1.7), the pattern is elaborated. In the supreme economy of this encounter we find another paradigm of dialogue: a similar pattern of supreme verbal manipulation is enacted in the chronologically somewhat earlier *Othello*.

The word 'seduction' seems justified by Lady Macbeth's deliberate resort to the crudest tactics of persuasion, including sensuality and a grossly/subtly sensational language. (Verdi's simpler opera brings this into the foreground by making Lady Macbeth overtly seductive.)[25] But there is much else to note, clustering around the strategy and language:

MACBETH: . . .   (*Enter Lady Macbeth*)
          How now, what news?
LADY MACBETH: He has almost supped: why have you
    left the chamber?
MACBETH: Hath he asked for me?
LADY MACBETH: Know you not he has?
MACBETH: We will proceed no further in this business:
        He hath honoured me of late, and I have brought
        Golden opinions from all sorts of people,
        Which would be worn now in their newest gloss,
        Not cast aside so soon.
LADY MACBETH: Was the hope drunk
        Wherein you dressed yourself? hath it slept since?
        And wakes it now, to look so green and pale
        At what it did so freely? From this time
        Such I account thy love. Art thou afeard
        To be the same in thine own act and valour
        As thou art in desire? Wouldst thou have that
        Which thou esteem'st the ornament of life,
        And live a coward in thine own esteem,

Letting 'I dare not' wait upon 'I would',
Like the poor cat i'th'adage?
MACBETH: Prithee, peace:
I dare do all that may become a man;
Who dares do more, is none.
LADY MACBETH: What beast was't then
That made you break this enterprise to me?
When you durst do it, then you were a man;
And, to be more than what you were, you would
Be so much more the man.

Structurally, the most striking feature is the hammer-blow-like, inquisitorial succession of Lady Macbeth's questions, in speech after speech: 'why have you left the chamber?'; 'Was the hope drunk / Wherein you dressed yourself?' followed by four other questions, precise, intimately personal, minatory. After Macbeth's one perfectly controlled answer ('I dare do all that may become a man . . .'), the rhythm of 'What beast was it then . . .' lashes out with its extra strong stress, and the hissing sibilant after the tense i:, on *beast*, the keyword. The force with which this personal attack is uttered is enough to split Macbeth's insecure integrity. Or, to be more precise, the duality, the inner duologue in Macbeth's mind (seen most clearly in the monologue that immediately precedes this duologue) is swayed by the demonic single-mindedness of the other voice.

Within the inquisitorial frame, the energy of Lady Macbeth's questions leads the dance in this duologue; it seems inevitable that hers should be the dominant role, in length of speech and force of imagery too. (Macbeth's only speech of some length comes after the passage quoted, in his submission, lines 72–7.) The wordplay on 'man' is charged with tremendous emotional tension. It becomes the vehicle of Macbeth's undermining and change of mind. For in Macbeth's defence, 'I dare do all that may become a man', the connotation of man is, quite simply, human/ humane; but Lady Macbeth instantly converts this image into the subhuman ('beast'), and then, through a kind of incantation, opposes to it the power-laden mirage of becoming superhuman: 'And to be more than what you were you would / Be so much more the man.' Given the clear personal and sexual context, the bullying intimacy in Lady Macbeth's preceding speech ('From this time such I account thy love. Art thou afeard . . .') and given the ambiguous connotations of being a 'man', Lady Macbeth's lines insinuate, with spare brutality, that not to be 'manly' is not to be virile. At the same time, the 'supermanly' has undergone corruption into an image of dehumanised man. Such is the duplicity of a keyword used within a duologue shot through with the spirit of 'double, double'. Using the wider insights and imagery of the whole of *Macbeth*, in this duologue we see the single-minded voice of Lady Macbeth, which is subservient to the evil power of equivocation, triumph over the divided voices of Macbeth, through verbal power alone. Incantation is, dominant, certainly in the section quoted. In what follows (lines 6off) there is more rational, that is rationalising, argument whereby Lady Macbeth removes Macbeth's fear of 'consequence' by scheming to put the blame on Duncan's two chamberlains; but the turning point, the core of interaction and transformation, is within the compass of those few (quoted) exchanges in this most concentrated of duologues.

The central duologue of *Othello* is the most sustained example in all drama of an antagonist wholly subverting the mind of the protagonist through words alone. The crucial temptation scene (3.3) is structured around the sustained duologue of Othello and Iago. It has a continuous crescendo of exchanges, though subtly broken by episodes and interruptions: by Iago's calculatedly stage-managed exits and entrances; by Othello's own exit after his brief and barren duologue (within the duologue) with Desdemona (lines 278–88); by Iago's duologue with Emilia (lines 298–316) and his brief soliloquy; by the return of Othello, deformed and tormented (line 335). The pressure of interaction is intensified throughout the scene, moving from hints and guesses to grossly explicit disclosure. It is a special kind of verbal interaction where Iago's language itself becomes the instrument of torture and destruction: his syntax of unspoken thought, little asides, repetitions and questions; his hypnotic transference of disease through words that suggest states of disturbance (not only jealousy); his imagery of copulation which eventually compels Othello to enact in his mind the scene he is made to fear until he *can* 'behold her topped'. Iago's histrionic technique of interruptions, silences and gestures, ('And didst contract and purse thy brow together' 3. 3. 116), underscores his mastery of words which, in the end, corrupt the listener. In our own time this came to be recognised as 'brain-washing' or induced mental breakdown, the fully conscious manipulation of verbal power: 'I'll pour this pestilence into his ear' (2. 3. 356); 'The Moor already changes with my poison' (3. 3. 327).

In the present context, traditional debating points like the question of Iago's motivation need not be discussed. It is more important to note that Iago's method does become a self-reward-ing instrument of verbal torture. What can, after all, still be recognised as a species of 'conversation' is used, or rather abused, to break all the logical and human rules of the co-opera-tive principle that underlies sound conversational exchange;[26] and the seeming cogency of the dialogue frame becomes a dialec-tic of total subversion. The words of the agent–speaker work on the suffering and often reluctant interlocutor. Iago's purpose is, no doubt, to undermine Othello with economy; yet there is an element of intrinsic, moment-by-moment, verbal improvisation which has its own indulgence and sadism: it is not merely a means to an end, but an end in itself. In this it differs from Lady Macbeth's subversion of Macbeth, which can be conceived, as 'co-operative' from her possessed and possessive point-of-view. And if Lady Macbeth uses the conspiratorial duologue to tip Macbeth's inner dialogue a stage towards monomaniac single-ness, Iago succeeds by imposing on the single mind of Othello a duality he cannot endure. Iago's voice enters; and the new duality of Othello goes on playing and re-playing the two voices created by their duologue. In this respect, too, the duologue *is* the action, and the instrument of torture. Though relatively natural-istic as verbal torture (contrast the ritual torturing of the dying Bracciano in *The White Devil*, 5. 3. 130–78) Iago uses language magically. That is to say, the hidden power of speech is released through him in a fully actional and contagious way (a power also recognised in the speeches of Hitler). Usually, that power is found in long incantatory speeches; but Iago is, first and fore-most, the master of intimate encounter, dialogue in its most parasitical form.

Bearing in mind the whole duologue, I shall now turn, selec-tively, to two features of the dialogue most relevant to our pre-sent context: the abuse of the confessional duologue and the stages of verbal conjuration. The syntax of indirectness which Iago skilfully forces on Othello in his two opening gambits (lines

33–41 and 93–109) need not be discussed in detail for it is transparent both in reading and in performance:

OTHELLO: What dost thou think?
IAGO: Think, my lord?
OTHELLO: Think, my lord! Alas, thou echo'st me,
      As if there were some monster in thy thought
      Too hideous to be shown. Thou dost mean something
                                (3. 3. 107ff)

Iago's sinister technique of insinuation and evasion is underlined by the dialogue itself, as Othello's initial dis-ease deepens, and he protests against 'these stops of thine' and the 'close dilations' (delays, pauses) which in a *just* man are marks of suppressed truth. So right from the opening of the duologue the audience is alerted, by the style-markers of abuse, to the distortions of dialogue: we have here the polar opposite of the duologue of Hamlet and Horatio (the 'just man'). Only the framework of dialogue is kept; the seemingly solid structure of question-and-answer is a prop to confidentiality; so Othello can assume that he is being led, step-by-step, through the stages of self-disclosure, to Iago's hidden thought, *the* truth. A long sequence (over seventy lines up to line 166) is given over to a kind of anti-confessional duologue: it demonstrates the compulsiveness of 'unspoken thought' itself. Othello begins to be unhinged by verbal ambiguities which stir in him an immoderate desire to clarify, to know. Othello finds himself in the classic situation of the man roused to turbulance by a riddle: like Oedipus who threatens to kill the old shepherd to extort the destructive truth from him. And it is here, in this dislocation of communication itself, that Othello's torture begins. He is in the position of a supplicant, and Iago is, already, in the superior position of the oracle: his every word, every fragment, is eagerly awaited, brooded on, subjected to intense questioning (variations on 'What dost thou mean?'). The antagonist has taken over the management of the dialogue from the protagonist by posing as the bearer of hidden knowledge, as the true confessor:

      I confess, it is my nature's plague
      To spy into abuses, and oft my jealousy
      Shapes faults that are not –

So Othello allows himself to be drawn into the compulsiveness of an intimate confessional situation even before the personal core –

that other jealousy – is broached. Iago's style of dialogue is subtler than is, for example, the overt rhetoric of adulation in the speeches of Regan and Goneril, which fool the King in the opening scene of *King Lear*. In this first phase, the confessional duologue, so aptly mimed by Iago, must be seen to convince and convict Othello.

The next phase of the duologue (lines 167–279) might be expected to hinge on Iago passing from unspoken thought to direct accusation, as in the all-too-explicit, and seemingly climactic, line 'Look to your wife; observe her well with Cassio' (line 199) and in the brazen insinuation that it was *unnatural* for Desdemona 'not to affect' someone better matched in 'clime, complexion and degree' (line 232). But the dialogue does not crystallise in that firm way around a core of accusation; it swerves from specific question-and-answer, it slides away from anything resembling a testing, clarificatory and personal dialogue. The speakers do not match each other, and do not interlock 'empirically'. Instead, the systematic derangement of Othello continues through a method of verbal conjuration. It begins in the well-known speech 'O, beware, my lord, of jealousy', placed before any specific statement whatever, and wholly relying on emotive words to create in the mind of Othello the feeling for 'the green-eyed monster': it rehearses a new consciousness clustering around words like 'that cuckold'; it exactly prompts the state of being divided against oneself (later so fanatically feared and enacted by Othello) in the image of the split lover: 'who dotes, yet doubts'.

Just as significant for the abuse of dialogue are those neutral-seeming exchanges where the words remain functional and the rhetoric is replaced by rapid, minimal speech – half-lines:

IAGO: I see this hath a little dashed your spirits.
OTHELLO: Not a jot, not a jot.
IAGO: In faith, I fear it has.

(3. 3. 216ff)

and a little further on; the phrase 'You're moved' occuring twice in short space:

IAGO: My lord, I see you're moved.
OTHELLO: No, not much moved:
     I do not think but Desdemona's honest.
IAGO: Long live she so! and long live you to think so!

Such exchanges seem co-operative but they intensify the element of duplicity in the duologue. By concentrating on Othello's state of mind, questions concerning the issue of infidelity are evaded or postponed until they can no longer be examined with any degree of true attention. By naming Othello's disturbance ('dashed your spirits', 'you're moved') that disturbance is made worse and the sufferer's struggle to repress his symptoms of strain ('not a jot'; 'not much moved'), becomes acute and, in performance, visible and audible. Shakespeare has here created a pre-modern type of subtext: a dialogue where the tension is carried, partly *under* the words, gaining intensity in transit from one seemingly plain exchange to another.

In comparison, the technique of excitation through Iago's imagery of copulation is crudely direct. Following his re-entrance Othello is now prepared for this kind of verbal assault; he is vulnerable to anything Iago says, defenceless, just as there are no more antidotes to torment in Iago's famous aside.

> Look where he comes! Not poppy, nor mandragora,
> Nor all the drowsy syrups of the world,
> Shall ever medicine thee to that sweet sleep
> Which thou owest yesterday.
> OTHELLO: Ha! Ha! false to me?
>
> (lines 332ff)

Here the convention of the soliloquy and the more naturalistic device of 'talking to oneself' are fused; if only for the moment, all interaction is suspended. The next round of the duologue is started off by this juxtaposition of two monologuists (once more anticipating modern drama – see chapters 4 and 5). Othello's subsequent outburst against Iago and his move to throttle his torturer, is an attempt to silence that other voice by violence; but that voice is now internalised, and so Othello is trying to silence the duel of voices within himself when he turns on his antagonist:

> Villain be sure thou prove my love a whore;
> Be sure of it; give me the ocular proof;

From now on the provision of such 'ocular proof' is a leading thread in the duologue and the dramatic situation of the two speakers becomes that of conjuror/dupe (the tragic counterpart of the kind of verbal conjuring that provides for Jonson's heroes

93

the comically hyperbolic images they crave, for instance in *The Alchemist*). From now on, the magical use of language involves the instant supply of images simultaneously wanted and abhorred – a species of pornography. Iago only has to prompt:

> In sleep I heard him say 'Sweet Desdemona . . .'
> . . . then laid his leg
> Over my thigh, and sighed, and kissed, and then
> Cried 'Cursèd fate that gave thee to the Moor!'

OTHELLO: O monstrous! monstrous!
IAGO: Nay, this was but his dream.
OTHELLO: But this denoted a foregone conclusion . . .   (3. 3. 421ff)

From now on verbal conjuration is equated with reality; the balance between 'reality' and 'fantasy' is wholly tipped to the pole of fantasy. Words alone give 'proof'. The duologue enacts gestures that are – as perceived by the audience but not by Othello – wholly fictional and histrionic: the outburst of fustian rhetoric: 'O that the slave had forty thousand lives!'; 'O blood, blood, blood!'; the ritual swearing of vengeance in a sacred vow of 'engaged' words and the final imprecations: 'Damn her, lewd minx. O, damn her! damn her!' (The fantasy is fully acted out in the dialogue of the 'brothel scene', 4. 2.)

At this point the duologue is suspended. The next scene shows the pitiful distortions of non-communication in the one sustained duologue of Othello and Desdemona that might – but cannot – break the vicious circle of words breeding words. Like two talking automata Othello can only keep repeating 'handkerchief' and Desdemona can only talk of Cassio; and the two sets of parrot-speech interlock as if mocking the resources of dialogue – in keeping with a 'tragedy of incomprehension', wherein the passions and the will cut off characters from each other.

But, as if to suggest an on-going perpetual duologue, 4. 1 bursts on us with one of Shakespeare's characteristic style-markers for a 'continuous conversation':

IAGO: Will you think so?
OTHELLO: Think so, Iago!
IAGO: To kiss in private?
OTHELLO: An unauthorised kiss.
IAGO: Or to be naked with her friend in bed.

From this almost cinematic exchange, we quickly reach the further psychological and linguistic corruption of the already 'corrupt text' of the previous duologue: 'In sleep I heard him say' now becomes: '*If* I had said I had seen him do you wrong? Or hear him say –' (line 24):

OTHELLO: Hath he said anything?
IAGO: He hath, my lord; but, be you well assured,
        No more than he'll unswear.
OTHELLO: What hath he said?
IAGO: Faith, that he did – I know not what he did.
OTHELLO: What? What?
IAGO: Lie –
OTHELLO: With her?
IAGO: With her, on her; what you will.
OTHELLO: Lie with her! lie on her! – We say lie on her, when they belie
        her. – Lie with her! (. . .) It is not words that shakes me thus.
        Pish! Noses, ears, and lips. Is't possible? – Confess? Handker-
        chief? – O devil!

                                                (Falls into a trance)
                                                (4. 1. 29ff)

The disintegration of speech in dialogue is here fully embodied: in the breathless monosyllabic exchanges, fighting for
verbal space like animals jostling for territory; the heavy punning on 'lie' (with that play on prepositions), which, as Robert
Heilman has pointed out, is given an extra dimension of irony,
for Othello 'half-mad as he is, is toying, like a virtuoso in language, with the ambiguity of meaning in the phrase: the very
verbal play leads him to the doorstep of truth ["when they belie
her" = tell a lie on her]. What is more, Iago's own provocative
embellishment of his lie – "lie with her, lie on her" – has led his
victim to the point from which he might see truth.'[27] But the
formal lapse into fragmented prose – with its frenzied staccato
rhythm – marks the point where Iago's language has taken over
the duologue: 'it is not words . . .' mutters Othello; but it *is*: the
'noses, ears and lips' of his tormented fantasy spring from Iago's
words. And, as has been noted before, at this point the Iago style
so to speak swamps 'the Othello music'.[28] One speaker's
gradual degeneration in imitation of the other's speech has led to
this climax in verbal contamination – a fully parasitic form of
dialogue.

5.

The two duologues of Angelo and Isabella in *Measure for Measure* (2.2 and 2.4) enact a pattern of transformation different from that found in any of the tragedies. The judge as would-be seducer feels himself seduced by the pure speaker, while the potential victim remains immune from passion and passionate speech. This early example of 'a dialogue of the deaf' across formally dovetailing exchanges, must be in keeping with the genre-shift to tragi-comedy: the avoidance of tragedy partly through one character's potentially comic avoidance of verbal contagion. Even so the first duologue enacts a one-sided 'contagion', as Angelo is moved to incipient lust through Isabella's gradually intensified verbal solicitation (pleading for the life of her brother condemned to death for 'pre-marital sex', prompted by Lucio who is present throughout the interview). As Isabella's speech becomes more and more impassioned, it becomes the mediator of passion. Angelo's ambivalance is peculiar to dramatic language itself – the passion transmitted can 'float' in an unpredicted direction. And here the whole context is ambiguous: the formal intercourse between two people obsessed by chastity; they discuss a 'vice' and a 'fault' which they will not name but constantly imply, for themselves and for the audience. Isabella's stages of 'warming to the role of the advocate'[29] are at first matched only by the minimal verbal signs of Angelo's hidden transformation. In performance Isabella's speech would be accompanied by more and more *expressive* gesture, movement, and voice; Angelo might well remain stiff in posture, fixed and remote. But the stages of change are clear, from the early stylised detachment shared by Angelo and Isabella (provoking Lucio's aside to Isabella 'You are too cold', for the second time):

ISABELLA: Must he needs die?
ANGELO: Maiden, no remedy.
ISABELLA: Yes, I do think you might pardon him,
      And neither heaven nor man grieve at the mercy.
ANGELO: I will not do't.
ISABELLA: But can you, if you would?
ANGELO: Look, what I will not, that I cannot do.

(2. 2. 48ff)

From this long-distance fencing, Isabella gradually tries to personalise her plea, beginning with 'If he had been as you' to the first moment of intense emotion:[30]

ANGELO: . . . He must die tomorrow.
ISABELLA: Tomorrow? O, that's sudden.
        Spare him, spare him.
        He's not prepared for death . . .

                                    (2. 2. 82ff)

The direct personal appeal once made, the pressure is increased: it transforms the duologue, and with it Angelo. The personal pronouns (deixis) play a more and more prominent part in energising the encounter: 'So *you* must be the first that gives this sentence, and *he* that suffers.' The psychic and verbal space between the speakers is suddenly reduced, even if the physical distance remains. Isabella's satirical attack on the image of authority, in the magnificent 'angry ape' sequence, moves Angelo (even as he fights his being moved) with its rhetorical incantation. 'Why do you put *these sayings* upon me?' (line 132, emphasis added) is Angelo's weakening defence. The tolerable abstract argument on mercy and authority has become an intolerable quest for truth about himself:

ISABELLA: (. . .)   Go to your bosom,
        Knock there, and *ask your heart what it doth know*
        That's like my brother's fault. *If it confess*
        A natural guiltiness, such as is his.
        Let it not sound a thought upon *your tongue*
        Against my brother's life.
ANGELO: (*aside*)   She speaks, and 'tis such sense
        That my sense breeds with it. – Fare you well.

               (2. 2. 137ff. Emphasis added.)

This is the first turning point in the duologue: Isabella's insistence that the encounter should admit the emotional truth of Angelo's unadmitted position. (At this stage, he has not yet admitted his true feelings to himself.) There is now a pressure towards authentic, confessional communication: the legal/moral issue of Claudio's lust ('a natural guiltiness such as is his'), can now only be perceived through the urgency of personal utterance – intimacy, the 'tongue' obeying the 'heart'. Angelo's response, in the aside, exactly indicates what is taking place: under the 'sense' of the argument Angelo's 'sense' (sensuality) is being stirred; the Empsonian ambiguity would be clear to most audiences.[31] To the contemporary reader/audience the aside may seem superfluous, unlike the fine self-revealing soliloquy which concludes the scene. However, it is essential for Shakespeare's dramatic structure to leave Isabella linguistically as well as relationally innocent: she cannot be allowed to become aware of the ambiguities of impassioned persuasion.

The ambiguities of verbal interaction itself are further exploited in the second duologue (2.4) where Angelo and Isabella are alone: he fully conscious of the change in his condition but persisting in formal prevarication coupled with the heavy fiction of a 'suppos'd' person of power demanding 'the treasures of your body'; and she non-conscious, pursuing the natural art of non-comprehension until Angelo becomes grossly and threateningly direct.

One of the early exchanges, plain enough to the audience, has this pattern of ambivalent clarity:

ANGELO: Might there not be a charity in sin,
    To save this brother's life?
ISABELLA: Please you to do't,
    I'll take it as a peril to my soul,
    It is no sin at all, but charity.
ANGELO: Please you to do't, at peril of your soul,
    Were equal poise of sin and charity.
ISABELLA: That I do beg his life, if it be sin . . .

                                (2. 4. 63ff)

This symmetry of circumlocution might be sustained indefinitely, for Isabella remains deaf to Angelo's *double entendres*. She can echo syntax, rhythm and exact phrase ('Please you to do't . . .') untouched by its sense – as if repeating a catechism mechanically. The attempted duplicity is deflected by 'simplicity of speech'. The speakers' inability to dovetail, raises the emotional and verbal pressure; more precisely, Angelo has to turn on the 'volume' to make himself audible:

ANGELO: Nay, but hear me;
    Your sense pursues not mine: either you are ignorant,
    Or seem so, craftily; and that's not good.
ISABELLA: Let me be ignorant, and in nothing good
    But graciously to know I am no better

                                  (2. 4. 73ff)

and again:

ANGELO: But mark me –
            To be received plain, I'll speak more gross:
            Your brother is to die.
ISABELLA: So.
ANGELO: And his offence is so, as it appears,
            Accountant to the law upon that pain.
ISABELLA: True.

(2. 4. 81ff)

Angelo, deflected by Isabella's stark monosyllables, resorts to blatant propaganda speeches concerning the proxy seducer and the frailty of women. And still Isabella fails to respond 'in kind'. Finally, the direct address is attempted, the rhetoric of blackmail:

            let me be bold.
        I do arrest your words. Be that you are,
        That is a woman; if you be more, you're none.
        If you be one – as you are well express'd
        By all external warrants – show it now,
        By putting on the destin'd livery.
ISABELLA: I have no tongue but one; gentle my lord,
            Let me entreat you speak the former language.
ANGELO: Plainly conceive, I love you.
ISABELLA: My brother did love Juliet
            And you tell me he shall die for't.

(2. 4. 132ff)

Here the pattern of incomprehension itself is being stylised; that, surely, is the point of making Isabella reflect on her 'one tongue' and, implictly, on the duplicity of Angelo's language, at last perceived. It is as if Shakespeare wanted to demonstrate that 'purity of being' is inseparable from 'purity of diction'. One point of the whole second duologue may then be seen as a failed duologue of seduction: Angelo's words (unlike Iago's) fail to attain magical efficacy; Isabella cannot be drawn into the whirlpool of intimate exchanges – dominated by a dominant speaker. Words here are not indefinitely malleable, and the duologue is double not through shared duplicity but through the opposition of 'one tongue' to a double tongue. In effect Isabella is given the role of 'defender of the faith' in language, in a purified dialogue where statement and response, question-and-answer, are not supposed to break down the principles of co-operative communication.

The 'fair encounter of two most rare affections' in *The Tempest* (3.1) offers an illuminating contrast to the duologues of love and temptation in the tragedies and in *Measure for Measure*. Not only is there nothing of the fevered perplexities, the moods and style-shifts of *Antony and Cleopatra*, but there is no return to the verbal bounty within the 'boundless bounty' of young love in *Romeo and Juliet*, and no attempt at showing the couple's transformation from immaturity to fragile maturity. The innocence of Ferdinand and Miranda in their ritualised meeting, staged and supervised by Prospero, is of the emblematic kind that befits the masque-like genre of the play;[32] it is not static, but it is lifted out of the ordinary dynamics of action and speech by the unique stillness of structure and style. The language of the dialogue itself has something of that 'natural' or 'neutral' mode which we find in the Horatio–Hamlet duologues. But here there are two speakers who seem to be reaching for a pristine 'language of nature': some language that might have been spoken before the Fall, in the Edenic world repeatedly evoked in *The Tempest*.

Before discussing this peculiar artifice of naturalness, let us briefly recall the structure and movement of the duologue. We must bear in mind that Prospero is present throughout; what was intolerable spying and eavesdropping in Polonius is here presented as a benevolent function: the father/magician as the perfect audience, invisible but benignly participitory. He is the master of this particular ceremony, combining the skills of match-maker and stage-manager, author and director. Yet if the encounter is 'staged' within a frame, the illusion of love's speech in a spontaneous encounter remains.[33] Prospero's asides are spoken (lines 31 and 75) on a different level, 'under' the lovers' duologue, like a bass under a duet of tenor and soprano (though the operatic analogy is checked by one of the limitations of dramatic speech – the babel of simultaneous talk).

Three movements within the duologue re-create three stages of accelerated union: meeting, courtship and betrothal; the virginal passion of the lovers comes to control the language and meaning of the duologue.

The first sequence presents Miranda's caring fuss over the slaving Ferdinand: her compassionate speech makes her into a virtual accomplice of Ferdinand against Prospero, the otherwise unchallengeable perfect father figure:

MIRANDA: Alas, now pray you,
        Work not so hard: I would the lightning had
        Burnt up those logs that you are enjoined to pile:
        Pray, set it down, and rest you: when this burns,
        'Twill weep for having wearied you . . . My father
        Is hard at study; pray now, rest yourself –
        He's safe for these three hours.
FERDINAND: O most dear mistress,
        The sun will set before I shall discharge
        What I must strive to do.
MIRANDA: If you'll sit down,
        I'll bear your logs the while: pray give me that,
        I'll carry it to the pile.
FERDINAND: No, precious creature, –
        I had rather crack my sinews, break my back,
        Than you should such dishonour undergo,
        While I sit lazy by.
MIRANDA: It would become me
        As well as it does you; and I should do it
        With much more ease: for my good will is to it,
        And yours it is against.

                                                (3. 1. 15ff)

The dialogue here enacts, and should be seen to do so in
performance, the rhythm of not yet conscious pairing, with a
tussle of yes/no over the courtesies of offer and refusal. It is at
once a verbal dance – a tentative courting dance – and a rhythm of
work, those logs being lifted and set down to the counterpoint of
voices in the duet:

MIRANDA	FERDINAND
Pray set it down,	O most dear mistress . . .
pray now, rest yourself	I must strive to do.
If you'll sit down,	No, precious creature
I'll bear . . .	I had rather crack my
I'll carry . . .	sinews . . .

These and other lines activate the encounter, and should
rescue it from becoming just a tapestry of voices. The spare
imagery is enough to convey the intensity of caring. ('When this
[the wood] burns, 'Twill weep for having wearied you'.) The
language of the dialogue is musicalised by certain devices (internal rhymes like 'while' and 'pile' in Miranda's speech, and light
terminal rhymes – 'do it' / 'to it'). At the same time the feeling of
naturalness is sustained by the colloquial rhythm of short

sentences: 'My father is hard at study . . . He's safe for these three hours'; the simplicity of this speech acts as a counterpoint to all the other styles and voices in *The Tempest* – Prospero's rhetoric, Caliban's hybrid speech, and so on.

The longer sequence that follows enacts a competition in mutual admiration between Ferdinand and the 'admired Miranda'. The naive directness is offset by a quiet parody, a romance and not a satire-directed parody, of the usual catalogue of lovers' attributes in the sonneteering convention. ('Full many a lady / I have eyed with best regard . . .')

FERDINAND: But you, O you,
        So perfect, and so peerless, are created
        Of every creature's best.
MIRANDA: (. . .)   I would not wish
        Any companion in the world but you;
        Nor can imagination form a shape,
        Besides yourself, to like of.

(3. 1. 46ff)

No doubt the very absence of self-conscious irony – the combat of wit which we find in the major comedies of love – can make a modern audience miss the light style-conscious irony. Yet there is a doubleness in these speeches: they are newly minted for these new-born lovers; and they have verbal echoes of the 'high love' convention, quotations for the theatre, the audience.

By contrast, the final sequence of betrothal is reached through a brief confession of love which is without parallel in catching 'the true voice of feeling' – not passion – in the fullness of personal speech. This is the sequence that is broken, and sealed, by Prospero's blessing on the lovers' union:

MIRANDA: Do you love me?
FERDINAND: O heaven, O earth, bear witness to
        this sound,
        And crown what I profess with kind event
        If I speak true . . . If hollowly, invert
        What best is boded me to mischief . . . I,
        Beyond all limit of what else i'th' world,
        Do love, prize, honour you.
MIRANDA: I am a fool
        To weep at what I am glad of.
PROSPERO: Fair encounter
        Of two most rare affections: heavens rain grace
        On that which breeds between 'em!

FERDINAND: Wherefore weep you?
MIRANDA: At mine unworthiness, that dare not offer
          What I desire to give; and much less take
          What I shall die to want. . .

                                        (3. 1. 67ff)

Here purity of diction expresses all the paradoxes of the couple's emotion: life-giving sadness, humble forwardness, eager reticence. These two interact in direct question-and-answer. Admittedly there is a certain amount of 'riddling' in Miranda's speech, from the moving balanced cadences of 'At my unworthiness . . .' to the possible (Elizabethan) sexual pun of 'much less take / What I shall *die* to want.' Miranda herself calls this way of speaking 'trifling'; and our extract is followed by the curious image of concealed pregnancy – 'And all the more it seeks to hide itself / The bigger bulk it shows' – to express the swelling volume of her love for Ferdinand. (The image may not be 'in character', but it does tie up with the play's vision of marriage and natural fertility, and the later betrothal masque.)[34] What follows, the betrothal itself, has unparalleled directness; the distinct stylisation of a 'ceremony of innocence', with another quiet parody, this time parody of the marriage vow, that catechism for two:

          I am your wife, if you will marry me;
          If not, I'll die your maid; to be your fellow
          You may deny me, but I'll be your servant,
          Whether you will or no.
FERDINAND: (*kneeling*).
                    My mistress, – dearest!
          And I thus humble ever.
MIRANDA:
                    My husband then?
FERDINAND: Ay, with a heart as willing
          As bondage e'er of freedom: here's my hand.
MIRANDA: And mine, with my heart in't; and now farewell
          Till half an hour hence.   (3. 1. 83ff)

This naive duologue (though perfectly achieved) carries risks of distorted enactment and audience response. The distortions of critical response can be illustrated through two opposed evaluations:

(1) 'Of Miranda we may say that she possesses in herself all the ideal beauties that could be imagined by the greatest poet of any age or country . . .' (Coleridge, Lecture IX)[35]

(2) 'The figures, as realistic figures, are pallid in the extreme. They are the dullest *jeune premier* and *jeune première*. Ferdinand is a very ordinary nice young man; the insipid young chit of fifteen that Miranda is can hardly interest us on the page (however much she might stir us in real life or in the theatre).' (Bonamy Dobrée)[36]

There is no need to adjudicate between these two samples from the history of critical taste; each points to a specific risk in the reception of this encounter. Coleridge trumps the already idealised figure (prompted by 'so perfect and so peerless . . .') without regard to the playful undertone in the dialogue; Dobrée finds that idealisation itself 'insipid' and seems to hanker after 'realistic figures'. But what we find in this duologue is neither transcendental nor a bathos of flat speech in banal relationship. What we find is a new version of the dialogue of love encounter: discovery and disclosure through innocence, which connects with the reconciliation of parental enmities within the context of the whole play; and an appropriate language of unique simplicity. It can be compared to certain duologues of recognition in other romances, (e.g. Marina and her father in Pericles, 5. 1)[37] and perhaps to Mozart's *Zauberflöte*. As encounter it 'supplies all the action . . . simply to meet suffices'.[38] Yet there is interaction, and intensification. The experience of being drawn into full relationship through love is re-created for the audience, but gone is the rhetoric of ecstasy (*Romeo and Juliet*) and the rhetoric of wrangling eros (*Antony and Cleopatra*). Both would be inappropriate, for this is a dialogue purged of role-playing, self-dramatisation, histrionic self-consciousness.[39] The rapid succession of the stages of love – meeting, courtship, declaration, betrothal – has a dreamlike compression and fluidity. It is a dramatic fusion later developed by Strindberg, in the hyacinth room of *Ghost Sonata*, where fusion gives way to dissolution (see chapter 5). In a different context, comparing the late plays of Shakespeare to the post-Chekhov theatre, Anne Barton suggested that there is a 'distrust of dialogue' in *The Tempest*: an insistence upon the difficulty of communication [that] foreshadows the techniques of the modern theatre'.[40] This statement has been barely tested against the actual dialogue of *The Tempest*, and in the present reading of one duologue at least we find not distrust of, but the exploration of trust in and through, dialogue.

Here all is growth and relationship but without complex trans-formation of the speakers through their speech. Such unison in relationship – and its appropriate decorously natural language – has no exact counterpart in either tragedy or comedy. For 'such singleness of focus and such simplicity of expression'[41] would not be adequate for transforming conflict – for duplicity and dualism – in the duologues of tragedy. At the same time, the degree of personality – of personal interaction and emotion – sets *The Tempest* duologue in a world apart from the more impersonal verbal dance of the wit-combat in the comedies.

3   *The combat of wit**

1.

Our title may evoke an initial surprise; the two keywords have connotations that might exclude full dramatic interaction and the fullness of dialogue. For 'combat' sounds a good deal less than 'conflict'. It conjures up a cluster of cognate gaming and battling metaphors: skirmish, chase, set, bout, duel – versions of verbal ping-pong. Full human encounter, 'the principles of growth and change in human relations',[1] which Shakespeare's 'esemplastic power' embodied in the duologues of tragedy, is not expected to be within the range of combat – nor within the range of wit. Our proper generic expectations, of comic mode, mood and language, may get coupled with moral expectations of superficiality, if not triviality. For our notion of 'wit' has long ago acquired what C. S. Lewis called its 'dangerous sense': 'that sort of mental agility or gymnastic which uses language as the principal equipment of its gymnasium'.[2] This sense of wit has become dissociated from its original sense of a man's full intelligence or *ingenium*; and outside literary–critical circles it is seldom associated with the wit we find in Donne: the fusion of intelligence and imagination (the full sense of wit revived by Eliot and Leavis). More often wit is thought of as at best an ingenious, and at worst a laboured, stream of wordplay: 'clenches (puns), quibbles, gingles, and such like trifles',[3] repartee, mannerist fustian, verbal fancy (not imagination). The weaker points along the long line of wit from Lyly through Restoration Comedy to Wilde and Orton may be recalled. A purist or puritanical anti-wit bias may add its own distrust of verbal ostentation, self-pluming and 'artificiality'. Other notions of wit include what I shall call 'out-witting' (at the expense of other characters) or 'in-wit' (the flux of knowing and capping remarks). The full interaction of character, and the dovetailing of proper question-and-answer, has seldom been observed in witty dialogue.

Further limitations of the combat of wit may occur to those who come to it from within the world of comedy itself, its specific conventions and methods. For a start, it is possible to hold that *verbal* wit is not a central or indispensable element of comedy. Images from a silent film may flit across the silent cinema screen of the mind: perhaps the scene where Chaplin as the tramp in *City Lights* encounters the suicidal millionaire at the quayside, attempts to save him from the river, and in the attempt initiates a chain reaction where each character in turn falls in, climbs out, dragging the other with him. All this movement is accompanied by a language of gestures expressing a rapid shift of emotions ranging from total despair to exhilaration, rage and gratitude, all without a word being spoken: a comic encounter *has* taken place. In the theatre, even in highly verbal comedy, the visual or non-verbal sign will clinch the situation for us: Benedick and Beatrice, separately tricked into a 'mountain of affection' for each other, make faces and gestures as they overhear the tricksters. And their skirmishes of wit, which may seem 'wire-drawn on the page, become warmly humorous as each reacts to the other's slanders'[4] – reacts with face and body. Yet wit is no mere verbal excess, superadded to the physical gesture and movement of the comic rhythm. Wit itself creates a comic rhythm – a rhythm which cannot be 'translated' into anything else, and cannot be mimed by non-verbal action. In Shakespearian comedy wit participates fully in the mood of holiday release and misrule, as C. L. Barber reminds us in *Shakespeare's Festive Comedy*. Wit is often akin to physical interaction, a kind of verbal sex, as in the winking innuendos and *double entendres* of group wit in *Love's Labour's Lost*, 4. 1, where word licence mimes the act that is not acted out. The banter of Rosaline, Maria and Boyet playing a 'set' is 'like making love; each makes meaning out of what the other provides physically'.[5]

There is something limiting in a theory of comedy which has a lot to say on genre and plot but next to nothing on the dialogue. Northrop Frye, to give only one example, defines The New Comedy in such a way.[6] The New Comedy, the ancestral comic structure which leads to Shakespeare (in a romantic form) and to Jonson and Molière (in a realistic form), is seen to operate through a 'teleological' plot, within which the characters have only a plot-function. Comic language is barely mentioned, and wit not at all. Only in the Old Comedy (whose generic line Frye traces as far forward as Beckett) do we find an *agon* or contest which lends itself to black or absurd comedy, and which may be verbal, as in the parody of vaudeville dialogue in *Waiting for Godot*. What Frye omits or belittles in his conceptual map of comedy is our principal subject – verbal *agon*, witty combat.

Another preliminary question may be asked: is the witty duologue all that central in comedy? First of all, both in Shakespeare and in Jonson some of the wittiest speeches are uttered by bravura soloists, from Falstaff's set speeches on recruiting and on honour (1 *Henry IV*. 4. 2 and 5. 1), to the hyperbolic near-monologues of Sir Epicure Mammon or Volpone. The Clown and the Fool in Shakespeare are professionally witty; but a good deal of their wit is offered as a comic chorus, directly addressed to the audience, or (as in the exchange between Feste and Viola in the third act of *Twelfth Night*) so 'professional' and mannerist as to cease being a vehicle of personal encounter. Further, the witty dialogue of *the group* is often all-important in comedy; much of *Love's Labour's Lost* is scored like a verbal dance for interacting couples, with the dominant pair to be heard against the pattern of the octet; and in *A Midsummer Night's Dream* the quartet of lovers are not fully individualised, their voices form only one plane of action and dialogue, richly counterpointed by the other voice-clusters in the polyphony of the total play. Even in *Much Ado About Nothing*, where the fighting courtship of Beatrice and Benedick is central, the witty duels are concerted with their own witty monologues on the one hand, and the wit-baiting dialogue of their observers, Don Pedro, Claudio, Leonato, on the other.

In short, the witty duologue must be studied as it is read and heard: in the larger context of dialogue, the rich counterpoint of the whole play with its multiple modes of speech. Nevertheless, the comic duologue or duet (still to be defined) does function, in Shakespeare's comedies of courtship especially, as a pivot of action and wit. The witty couple interacts; their combat becomes a vehicle of change, maturing, and recognition, in a way that invites comparison with the tragic duologue. We may test for ourselves the soundness of Wylie Sypher's statement: 'the comic and the tragic heroes alike "learn through suffering", albeit suffering in comedy takes the form of humiliation, disappointment, or chagrin, instead of death'.[7]

Wit at its best embodies creative imagination – it can have the unexpectedness of metaphor and the thrust of Elizabethan rhetoric in its syntax and rhythm.[8] The wit that is fully relational is far more than an exchange of verbal floss. A form of verbal game people play, decorous and decorative, it may be; but it is also an expressive dramatic language that changes with the changing awareness of the comic speakers.

2. Love-wit in Shakespeare's comedy of courtship

The combat can be seen most clearly as a pattern of vital interaction, and the language of wit as a vehicle of transformation, in the wooing games of Shakespearian comedy. It may come as a real discovery to see the playful encounters of the witty couple as not just recreational but relational; and their patterned play-acting as mutual exploration under the verbal disguise – between the lines – of combative wit. The sense of rediscovery deepens with close reading: it is supported by each successful performance of the plays, and by a few critical studies, notably by David Lloyd Stevenson's *The Love-Game Comedy*. Our understanding of wit is further sharpened when we attend to the opposition: the general anti-wit bias, already adumbrated, and the bias against euphuistic wit in particular, in Shakespeare's comedies of love. A famous editor, Quiller-Couch, dismisses the wit-combat as 'absurd' in the pre-modern sense (nonsense); while a contemporary Marxist critic, Terence Eagleton, sees wit as 'absurd' in the modern sense (dislocation of meaning in a linguistic vacuum).

In his introduction to the old New Cambridge edition of *Much Ado About Nothing* Quiller-Couch has this to say on wit-combats:

> Our trouble (we suggest) with Benedick's and Beatrice's 'wit-combats' is rather a trouble with Shakespeare's 'wit' in general. These two, as practitioners eminent by tradition, have served as lightning-conductors for a censure which should more justly be spread over many plays – indeed over almost all the Comedies.
>
> If we could rid ourselves of idolatry and of cant when we talk about Shakespeare, we should probably admit that his *'wit' – the chop-logic of his fools, the sort of stuff that passes for court-conversation and repartee – is usually cheap, not seldom exasperating,* and at times . . . merely disgusting. He purveyed this stuff for his age; certainly not for all time: and the more accurately we detect it, to put it away, the more cleanly we get at his virtues (emphasis added).[9]

After suggesting that Shakespeare acted as an ambitious provincial youth in imitating the artificial euphuism then fashionable at Court, 'Q' denounces the lapse of court-talk into parody and bawdy. He goes on:

> Even when the chop-logic is innocent, as it is in the first Act of *As You Like It*, or merely silly, it belongs to a fashion; and if we are bored by it, we advance the business of criticism by announcing the stuff for rubbish.
>
> There is not a little of *this rubbish* in the earlier scenes of *Much Ado*. But when we have sifted it out and made allowance that Benedick and Beatrice are both *fencing in a mode, the revelation of their true hearts, each to each*, when a crowd has left the chapel, has an effect the more startling because it breaks and shines through this artificiality. Beatrice has shone through it already, in promise. 'You were born in a merry hour,' says Prince Pedro.
>
> 'No, sure, my lord, my mother cried – but then there was a star danced, and under that was I born.' – born to 'keep on the windy side of care,' she says, 'born to speak all mirth and no matter.' When it comes to the test, there is matter enough in her.

We can learn a good deal from this sample of anti-wit prejudice, if we note what is excluded, what celebrated. In his general comments on the wit-combat and on the euphuistic style, 'Q', as literary historian, gives the reader no sense of history. We need to be aware of the changing styles of wit from Lyly[10] to Shakespeare; from *Love's Labour's Lost* to *Much Ado*, euphuism is often playfully parodied in the wit-combat. Then 'Q', as stylist, fails to account for the style under examination – it is just broadly dismissed as artificial, or as 'this rubbish'. And as editor, he hardly stops to indicate *how* Benedick and Beatrice 'are both fencing in a mode', so eager is he to get to the emotion finally released: 'the revelation of their true hearts, each to each', quoting, as a single poetic line and not as dialogue, Beatrice's romantic-sounding: 'but then there was a star danced, and under that was I born.' In the history of critical taste on dialogue this judgement might be set alongside Arnold's judgement on the poetry of wit, regarding Dryden and Pope as less than poetry. (But Arnold was, after all, applying a clear criterion of Victorian 'high seriousness' to poetry, while 'Q' was trying to exclude wit from the *language of comedy*.) The underlying preference for 'natural' and 'noble' utterance – a preference we might share in a different context[11] – fails to see that the dramatist uses the wit-combat as a conspicuous theatrical language, a counterpoint to other modes of speaking: self-expressive rhetoric, the Petrarchan conceits of love, even 'the true voice of feeling'. The combat of wit is not designed to act as a direct dialogue for 'the revelation of their true hearts, each to each', but as an indirect, verbally self-distancing, mock-ritual of falling *towards* love.

If a late-romantic attitude to language undervalues the combat of wit, a post-modernist attitude to language over-interprets and so distorts it. Thus, Terence Eagleton, in 'Language and reality in *Twelfth Night*',[12] puts a high-toned epistemological gloss on a passage of Clown-speech. Without once mentioning the word 'wit', Eagleton proceeds from the well-known contemporary point of view that all 'reality' depends on language, on naming and communicating. At one point Eagleton quotes from the conversation between Viola and the Clown at the beginning of 3. 1, with a characteristic critical comment:

VIOLA: . . . they that dally nicely with words may quickly make them wanton.
CLOWN: I would, therefore, my sister had had no name sir.
VIOLA: Why, man?
CLOWN: Why, sir, her name's a word; and to dally with that word might make my sister wanton.

> Yet the power of language to shape reality to itself, a power which involves the absorption of reality into speech, highlights paradoxically the distance of language from reality: 'in my conscience, sir, I do not care for you. If that be to care for nothing, sir, I would it would make you invisible'. Language draws real substance into itself and becomes a self-contained, substitute reality confronting a nothing – the vacuum left by the reality it has assimilated. Because it confronts nothing, and nothing cannot be changed, it is impotent to affect it: the Clown's rejection of Viola as nothing cannot in fact make her invisible.

Well, this seems to be an instance of reading backwards from Beckett. Language as a 'substitute reality confronting a nothing' is an interesting concept and experience, but not in *this* context. What one can say, in this context, is that wit intensifies ambiguity to the point where the co-operative logic of conversation is shaken.[13] Even then we would have to take into account: (1) the clear structure of *Twelfth Night* with its appearance/reality perspectives grasped by the audience from the beginning of the play; (2) the Clown's role as professional word-monger and coiner, quibbler, equivocator. His quibbles, with all his functions as court jester, are a licence. (Carried to the extreme point, where reality is about to break down, we get Hamlet's 'antic disposition' speech; but even in *Hamlet* Shakespeare takes care to counterpoint a norm of 'natural speech' in Horatio.)[14] Clown-wit is, in any case, much more depersonalised than the relational wit of the mature comedies, Beatrice and Benedick, for example. It is a clear theatrical convention, and not a good instance of the world's general language sickness. Wit illuminates the parodoxes of reality and wit may act as a prism: an experiment with a verbal telescope or kaleidoscope. But in the total language of a comedy wit is firmly placed, still holding up (as if on Hamlet's advice to the players) the mirror to nature.

The combat of wit is, then, neither just 'cheap' and 'artificial' wordplay, nor a fall from linguistic grace. It is a vehicle of personal encounter. We shall be testing this assumption, and may begin our study of the values and styles that go with the play of wit, by taking a quick look at *The Taming of the Shrew*. This is in several ways an untypical comedy of love-combat: as genre it leans into farce which the modern, pro-feminist, reader and audience may experience as a cruel melodrama of male chauvinism; it is the only play where the man not only takes the initiative in the dance of wooing but proceeds to fearful male hegemony; and it is not a play most of us remember for its excellence of verbal wit. But it is an interesting starting point, chronology apart, for in this play the potentially tragic, farcical defeat of Kate the Shrew is accomplished through a *defeat of her wit*, through a banishing of wit itself as a vehicle of courting. Petruchio the Tamer starts by going through a form of mock-courtship (a strategy that mocks the Petrarchan pedestal for the Lady meek and gentle):

> For thou art pleasant, gamesome, passing courteous,
> But slow in speech . . . yet sweet as spring-time flowers.
> Thou canst not frown, thou canst not look askance,
> Nor bite the lip as angry wenches will,
> Nor hast thou pleasure to be cross in talk;
> But thou with mildness entertain'st thy wooers,
> With gentle conference, soft and affable . . .
>
> (2. 1. 239ff)

The real Kate is here being ironically inverted, in an attempt to *cure* her with an overdose of the manners most *unlike* her. But the wit-cure fails, as Kate and Petruchio between them turn a potential combat of wit into something else:

KATHARINE: Where did you study all this goodly speech?
PETRUCHIO: It is extempore, from my mother-wit.
KATHARINE: A witty mother! Witless else her son.
PETRUCHIO: Am I not wise?
KATHARINE: Yes, keep you warm.
PETRUCHIO: Marry, so I mean, sweet Katharine, in thy bed;
    And therefore, setting all this chat aside,
    Thus in plain terms: your father hath consented
    That you shall be my wife; your dowry 'greed on; and,
    will you, nill you, I will marry you. . .

                            (2. 1. 256ff)

We see here a change to more combat, less wit, after the first bout of wit seemed to promise a prolonged combat. (There is no parallel combat in the early comedies; *The Comedy of Errors* and *The Two Gentlemen of Verona*, have only non-central, incidental exchanges of wit.)[15] The bout ends abruptly: *setting all this chat aside*. And the precarious patterns of verbal wit in wooing give way to the brutal force of the arranged marriage. Petruchio resorts to a series of more or less physical shock tactics: Kate is deprived of her wedding feast and then rushed to a cold palace to be deprived of food, sleep, love and reason. It is the method of violent homeopathy, curing 'like with like' (PETER: 'He kills her in her own humour' 4. 1. 171). As in a circus ring, a series of taming-acts reduce Kate – she has been *out*-witted, reduced to a wit*less* state. Or should we see her state in a different light? Consider the scene where Kate seems to be reclaiming for herself the reciprocal rights of dialogue – in her pat repartees when Petruchio insists on calling the sun the moon, and regarding the universe as his private property:

PETRUCHIO: Good Lord, how bright and goodly shines the moon!
KATHARINE: The moon! The sun: it is not moonlight now.
PETRUCHIO: I say it is the moon that shines so bright.
KATHARINE: I know it is the sun that shines so bright.

There is a stalemate: Kate is not allowed to continue her journey to her father's house. But the stalemate is broken as Kate has the wit to say:

113

> Forward, I pray, since we have come so far,
> And be it moon, or sun, or what you please:
> And if you please to call it a rush-candle,
> Henceforth I vow it shall be so for me.
> PETRUCHIO: I say it is the moon.
> KATHARINE: I know it is the moon.
> PETRUCHIO: Nay, then you lie: it is the blesséd sun.
> KATHARINE: Then, God be blessed, it is the blesséd sun –
> But sun it is not when you say it is not;
> And the moon changes even as your mind:
> What you will have it named, even that it is,
> And so it shall be so, for Katharine.
>
> (4. 5. 2ff)

Kate is here, in some measure, out-witting Petruchio by her ironic over-agreement, her verbal over-kill ('call it a rush-candle'). The bout can be played wittily, tongue-in-the-cheek (and is said to have been so played by Peggy Ashcroft) even though it is a long way from the later freedom of wit in the exuberant and elaborate combat of Beatrice versus Benedick. But Shakespeare's tamed Kate has wit enough not to succumb to despair – unlike the Marowitz *Shrew*, where Kate is reduced to a gibbering victim of brain-washing at the hands of her sadistic torturer.[16] One of the senses of wit includes intelligent self-assertion, out-witting (as we shall see when we come to Jonson); and this kind of wit may protect the losing partner, in the combat turned into sex-war, from the totalitarian psyche – from the total fusion of reality and language:

> PETRUCHIO: Nay, then you lie: it is the blesséd sun.
> KATHARINE: Then, God be blessed, it is the blesséd sun.

That mock-catechism and mocking pseudo-rhyme (as moon/moon in the previous exchange) creates a well-tempered duet.

Love's Labour's Lost is not a duet but an elaborate verbal dance for four wooing couples who move in measure. Berowne and Rosaline stand out as the combative couple, with Berowne more vocal but only precariously predominant: he moves from the ironic commentator on love (wit observing folly) into the role of the vulnerably wit-forsaken fool of love. Corresponding to this shift of role – one of wit's characteristic transformations in Shakespeare's comedy of courtship – is his use of a mannerist or 'conceited'[17] language and his criticism of it: he 'plays a double game with language throughout; the same game that the author himself is playing'.[18] So the transformation of the Wit into the lover is paralleled by a purging of wit towards sincere, direct expression of feeling – 'the heart's still rhetoric' (2. 1. 228). The central irony is that 'the great Wit' is out-witted by the seemingly lesser wit of Rosaline, partly because she never loses her sense that the wooing is a mock-wooing, a 'merriment', and thus remains immune from the self-destructive element in passion. We have here an early dramatisation of the relational role of wit, its risky doubleness: those who play with the idea of love in free-flowing repartee are being drawn towards the discovery of feeling at the centre of all that talk. When excess of wit is pruned, the skirmishing pair (in this play only the men) find a language of confession and commitment.

The wit of Rosaline and her companions is not all that striking in its lines, its verbal texture – compared with the later Rosalind who teases Orlando into witty wooing, or the Beatrice who sets out to torment Benedick with her wit. But the ladies of France have the wit to mock their would-be lovers, and use wit as a prophylactic against love. For wit is passion's antidote. That much is claimed by Katharine, who contrasts Rosaline's nimble wit and her own sister's despair, for Cupid:

> [He] made her melancholy, sad and heavy –
> And so she died: had she been light, like you,
> Of such a merry, nimble, stirring spirit. . .
> She might ha' been a grandma ere she died.
>
> (5. 2. 14ff)

In any case, the four lords of Navarre, led by Berowne who has a reputation for 'merciless wit',[19] deserve counter-mockery for their own mockeries of love. For first they try and escape into an Elizabethan ivory tower of learning purged from female presence; they next lapse into barren sonneteering, sub-Petrarchan mannerism and love-letter conventionality; and finally, they fail to woo wittily, but come clumsily in Muscovite disguise, pouring solemn confessions of love into the wrong woman's ears. The whole comedy is so structured that such labours of love – which include the euphuism, the laboured conceits of love's language – are exposed. The finale is, logically, not the ceremony of betrothal which is the promise of comedy (Jack has not Jill), but the penance imposed after the feast of language – with Berowne sent into linguistic exile among the 'speechless sick'.

If the combat of wit between Berowne and Rosaline is less central and less rich than are the comparable wit-duets in the mature comedies, it is still fine in itself; and it is also a good starting point, a paradigm, for understanding all the comedies of courtship. In the theatre, as in reading, one has to make a conscious effort to see and hear this couple emerge from the carefully wrought dialogue of the group – the verbal dance patterned in a figure of eight. And that group dialogue is in turn counterpointed by the linguistic satire of the subplot: Armado's hyper-artificial speech, Holofernes' self-indulgent pedantry, and the other typical scraps from that 'feast of language'. But when we do focus we see the love-game of Berowne and Rosaline as a combat, an ambivalent exchange of different kinds of wit. Their first encounter has this movement:

BEROWNE: Did not I dance with you in Brabant once?
ROSALINE: Did not I dance with you in Brabant once?
BEROWNE: I know you did.
ROSALINE: How needless was it then
          To ask the question!
BEROWNE: You must not be so quick.
ROSALINE: 'Tis long because of you that spur me with such questions.
BEROWNE: Your wit's too hot, it speeds too fast, 'twill tire.
ROSALINE: Not till it leave the rider in the mire.

(2. 1. 112ff)

And so on, in briskly mannered, rhymed repartee, fencing and insults.[20] Berowne's conversational opening (a social cliché still very much with us, in rather less euphonious versions) is at once parried and parodied by Rosaline's repeating the question word for word: a bad rhyme and a hollow echo mock Berowne's phrasing, tone, gesture and amorous strategy. In two lines the stable question/answer norms of dialogue are being undercut; Berowne's question is at once downgraded from its hint of genuine evocation and upgraded from 'mere' conversation into combat. For the rhythms of 'Did I not dance with you in Brabant once?' might, if taken that way, move towards a felt exchange of memory. But that tone is not to be tolerated by a woman of wit responding to a man whom the context of the play (and the convention of wit behind the play) presents as a jester, courtly

116

mocker and dangerous Wit. Berowne does indeed display wit in the company of his learned peers in the male commune (as in his 'And I – Forsooth in love', soliloquy, 3. 1. 172) but *not* here, in direct confrontation with the lady of wit. 'I know you did' is plain, all too factual, with another hint of wishing to engage in the intimate remembrance of things past; 'you must not be so quick' is already a plea, while 'your wit's too hot' is a surrender – the skirmish was undesired, and defeat in it is feared. Berowne has risked exchanging love-wit for a not particularly witty language of direct personal encounter too early; and he cannot, at this stage, regain wit's initiative. His lines remain pale in this exchange, though amusing to the reader/audience responding to the pattern of the combat – displaying Berowne's partial impotence within a frame of mocking couplets:

BEROWNE: What time o' day?
ROSALINE: The hour that fools should ask.
BEROWNE: Now fair befall your mask!
ROSALINE: Fair fall the face it covers!
BEROWNE: And send you many lovers!
ROSALINE: Amen, so you be none.
BEROWNE: Nay, then will I be gone.

(2. 1. 120ff)

A later bout in the same scene (lines 178–92) is similar in texture, but more mannered, hovering between erotic ambiguity and emotional stalemate. And from this point on, the combat of wit between these two contestants is virtually suspended, or at least foreshortened. For two acts the sets of wit are for internal consumption only, inside each of the fenced-off camps: the chaste lords rehearsing the styles of falling in love, the ladies practising the language of love-defying wit. Some of these 'sets' are indulgent and relatively static (that is, not relational and not actional), as in the long punning and bawdy game of wit between the ladies, presided over by Boyet, the love-monger and wit-master of France; and turned from sexual innuendo into 'greasy talk' by Costard the clown. Too long to quote here (forty lines to the end of 4. 2), this wit-match is the kind that gave wit its bad name – the mere 'clenches' Dryden later disapproved of. It is wit breeding wit, the practically homosexual 'jangling' wit which the Princess in an earlier scene declared wasteful:

This civil war of wits were much better used
On Navarre and his book-men, for here 'tis abused.

(2. 1. 224f)

Nevertheless, the 'in-wit' thrives, in the absence of, and at the expense of, the would-be lovers. Its guiding principle is 'mock for mock', the training of female wit against the wit of the suitors, despised for their poetaster labours. What is unique in *Love's Labour's Lost* is the length of such 'unilateral' skirmishes, so that the directly relational male/female wit-combat is postponed. It may be said that in the Berowne–Rosaline combat only the fore-play (the scene quoted above) and the afterplay (5. 2 quoted below) is enacted. The first round of the combat is visual and physical rather than verbal – the Muscovite masquerade which gives the ladies of France the opportunity to win the first round by exposing the sheer inadequacy of the would-be lovers. (The scene is Shakespeare's version of the *Cosi fan tutte*-type comedy, with an ironic comment on the interchangeability of lovers.) The second round *is* verbal, combative and witty but surprisingly short and lean, considering the festive exuberance of verbal wit elsewhere in the play, and considering the prolonged torture of Berowne that Rosaline anticipates with relish ('That same Berowne I'll torture ere I'll go' 5. 2. 60). In the enacted encounter Rosaline addresses the Princess over Berowne's head, exposing the folly of the 'Muscovite' lords:

> They did not bless us with one happy word.
> I dare not call them fools; but this I think,
> When they are thirsty, fools would fain have drink.

This is too much for Berowne who intervenes, and succeeds in engaging Rosaline in at least one personal exchange, however tartly combative:

BEROWNE: This jest is dry to me. My gentle sweet,
      Your wit makes wise things foolish: when we greet,
      With eyes best seeing, heaven's fiery eye,
      By light we lose light; your capacity
      Is of that nature that to your huge store
      Wise things seem foolish and rich things but poor.
ROSALINE: This proves you wise and rich; for in my eye –
BEROWNE: I am a fool, and full of poverty.
ROSALINE: But that you take what doth to you belong,
      It were a fault to snatch words from my tongue.

BEROWNE: O, I am yours, and all that I possess.
ROSALINE: All the fool mine?
BEROWNE: I cannot give you less.

(5. 2. 370ff)

Clearly, this is wit's surrender to counter-wit. Berowne's 'My
gentle sweet' invocation resumes the 'heart's still rhetoric', rising
to a quite intensely felt figure on blinding love: 'by light we lose
light'. That leads to: 'your capacity is of that nature' – a hyperbole
with a rhythm of the early Shakespearian 'mighty line' designed
to convey – or rehearse – genuine emotion. From such intensities
Rosaline draws back, engaging Berowne is another bout; the
latter responds in form, but not in substance: in repartee *without*
attack, and in wit humbled to elegant submission. The combat
has given way to a confessional language: 'I am a fool. . .' 'I
cannot give you less.' The duet has two voices, Rosaline's line of
wit countered by Berowne's lyrical mode. The long final scene of
the play has more than five hundred lines to run, yet we are
already witnessing the purge of wit, in keeping with a modified,
counter-conventional comedy of courtship. The low-keyed duet
between Berowne and Rosaline leads straight to the penitential
tirade in which the defeated wit pleads, rather masochistically:

> Thrust thy sharp wit quite through my ignorance

and goes on to renounce his own language and style:

> O never will I trust to speeches penned,
> Not to the motion of a schoolboy's tongue [. . .]
> Nor woo in rhyme, like a blind harper's song!
> Taffeta phrases, silken terms precise,
> three-piled hyperpoles, spruce affectation,
> Figures pedantical –

(5. 2. 398ff)

undertaking to woo only 'in russet yeas and honest kersey
noes'.[21] But even this sudden linguistic conversion is not enough
for Rosaline, who sentences Berowne to a full year's abstinence
from the old wounding wit of courtship to learn another language:

> Visit the speechless sick, and still converse
> With groaning wretches; and your task shall be
> With all the fierce endeavour of your wit
> To enforce the painéd impotent to smile.

(5. 2. 847ff)

Berowne's new-style 'converse' is not in the play; like the prescribed year of penance it would be too long for a play. It cannot be accommodated within a comedy of wooing which, after all, thrives on the combat of wit. In this play wit ends by purging itself from the dialogue, but not before we have seen how it can release emotion, as ambivalent wooing stumbles on a 'pure' language of commitment. If wit is one of love's labours, it wins when it loses itself.

In the mature comedies of courtship[22] – *As You Like It* and *Much Ado About Nothing* – the wit-combat becomes central: the play revolves around the witty couple who are themselves agents and carriers of wit – Rosalind and Orlando as principal player and foil, Beatrice and Benedick as equal and interacting counterparts in wit. In each play entire scenes are sustained wit-combats, with ingenious variations. Further, the patterns of courting and contending reveal fully self-conscious characters, who develop through their wit-combats.

The partners are (with the exception of Orlando) also fully language-conscious speakers, who play witty variations on their own speech-styles. As D. L. Stevenson remarked on *As You Like It*: 'The witty skirmish between the wooer and his lady . . . is no longer a set tableau, but has become a way of revealing character.'[23] The convention of courtship, which Lyly devised, ceases to be merely conventional – it is itself used wittily; the exquisitely controlled dialogue exploits the pleasure of counterpointed emotional and stylistic postures: affected versus sincere, hyperbolic versus natural. At the same time verse is abandoned, along with the mannered rhyme, mock-rhyme, stichomythia and occasional tirade so characteristic of the early comedies; and a supple, varied, cadenced yet conversational (but not colloquial) prose becomes the texture of wit.[24] That prose may be derived from euphuism, but it is much more sophisticated and critical: a parodic language that can mock a conceit with a conceit, even as it mocks one mode of love within another mode. In keeping with all that, the wit-combat becomes fully dynamic and theatrical: movement and gesture are constantly scored into the lovers' duologues, so that the ideal reading should be accompanied by performance.

The wit-combats in these two plays are generated by two quite different patterns of comedy: wooing in disguise in *As You Like It*, and falling in love under the guise of constant and intense quarrelling in *Much Ado*. Concerning disguise as a comic situation much has been written, mostly on the ironies of bisexuality in boy-acting-girl-acting-boy. Even so, it is not usually realised that the witty situation has a tonal and linguistic counterpart.[25] For the dual role (switching from Rosalind to Ganymede the page-boy) goes with a dual voice. The lover's speech is given the freedom of ambivalence: it can rapidly switch from sincere to parodic utterance, from seeming commitment, to seeming mockery of love. If wooing is, in any case, a playful prelude to love's fulfilment (with changes of emotion and language as permissible as see-sawing in a public park), then wooing in disguise, with the codes and taboos of the social and the sex-role temporarily suspended, doubles the duplicity of courtship. This is not just a matter of being 'changeable, longing and liking, fantastical, apish, shallow, inconstant, full of tears, full of smiles; for every passion something and for no passion truly anything, as boys and women are for the most part cattle of this colour' (*As You Like It*, 3. 2. 400–4). It is finding the tonal variations *for* the various stages within the 'mad humour of love' – a shifting, often dual or multiple language. So, if the duologue of tragic antagonists (we think once more of *Macbeth* and *Othello*) often releases the doubleness within the protagonist, the duologue of the witcombat in *As You Like It* releases a comic doubleness through the verbal aspect of disguise: costume language giving way, at appropriate moments, to the felt language of the 'real' person.

Wit as a theatrical and verbal style proclaims itself, with explicit assurance before each of the crucial encounters (3. 2. 295–425 and 4. 1. 36–195). In the first Rosalind declares her strategy – her Ganymede costume, tone and histrionic stance – in an aside to Celia: 'I will speak to him *like a saucy lackey*, and under the habit *play the knave* with him' (lines 293–4, emphasis added). In the second encounter, Orlando enters with a somewhat pale version of the 'mighty line': 'Good day, and happiness, dear Rosalind!' – to be spurned by the departing Jaques in the role of stylistic critic: 'Nay then, God be wi' you, an you talk in blank verse.' The audience is being alerted; the natural vigour of Rosalind's mode of speech stands out by contrast. Her opening reproach to Orlando, in the manner of courtly love, is a style-signal to the audience that a certain language of love is to be both used and mocked:

> Why, how now, Orlando! where have you been all this while?
> You a Lover! An you serve me such another trick, never come in
> my sight more.
>
> (4. 1. 36ff)

It is the opening gambit in the prescribed love-cure, and in the art of deflating a certain emotional rhetoric through inflating it. The audience must hear the tone with the over-tone. At the same time, the conversational language of Rosalind's wit is to be heard against alternative literary languages of love: Petrarchan, euphuistic, rustic/pastoral. All these are bracketed and counter-pointed by the context of wit, sometimes explicitly, as when Rosalind 'debunks' Orlando's versifying (compare the parody of bad verse in *Love's Labour's Lost* and *Much Ado*): 'O most gentle pulpiter, what tedious homily of love have you wearied your parishioners withal' (3. 2. 155–6, lines spoken to Celia). Yet Rosalind's satirical stance does not prevent her from: (a) recognising the genuineness of Orlando's feelings between the lines of his effete poeticising; (b) enacting the role of the Lady in Courtly Love, and using the role-language with verbal relish. Rosalind is placed at the centre of a map of love's language. She is the norm, as Allan Rodway has argued:

> This is a comedy of human ecology, dealing with the balance of
> nature, and the need for common sense (in its primary meaning
> of a unifying quality). Of this Rosalind, not Touchstone, is the
> great exemplar . . . she is the norm, set in the middle of the
> spectrum of tonal values, midway between cynicism and pas-
> toralism. So she is given some of the liveliest prose in the lan-
> guage. (At the other extreme from her characteristic speech is
> the parody of pastoral verse given to Silvius and Phebe.)[26]

In her dual role, Rosalind can both feel and judge feeling, be natural and artificial in turn – be naturally artificial.

It is most often *outside* her encounters with Orlando – in teasing duologues with Celia, the cousin confidante – that Rosalind can confess her love directly: in the spirited canter about the absent lover (3. 4. 1–32), and in the famous sequence beginning with 'O coz, coz, coz . . . my pretty little coz, that thou didst know how many fathom deep I am in love!' (4. 1. 200–1). But in the present context, the indirect showing of sincere feeling is more interesting than the direct telling, especially as Rosalind's feeling is revealed through a dislocation of natural dialogue in her rapid-fire 'catechism':

ROSALIND: Alas the day, what shall I do with my doublet and hose? What did he when thou saw'st him? What said he? How looked he? Wherein went he? What makes he here? Did he ask for me? Where remains he? How parted he with thee? And when shalt thou see him again? Answer me in one word.
CELIA: You must borrow me Gargantua's mouth first: 'tis a word too great for any mouth of this age's size. To say ay and no to these particulars is more than to answer in a catechism.

(3. 2. 217ff)

Here Rosalind herself is the target of sympathetic satire – including a measure of dialogue parody. As a speaker she is carried away – 'unconscious' of the manner of her speech – and it is up to the audience to share Celia's mocking response. By contrast, in the direct encounters with Orlando it is Rosalind who becomes the observer and parodist, Orlando the target. It is still a sympathetic kind of satire (contrast Jonson), where the excesses of love-sickness are mocked by a character who is in love, but who remains detached to the extent of her wit. The total pattern of the duologue is that of a one-sided wit-combat, where Rosalind conducts, imposes tone and rhythm on, the seemingly unsuspecting and stylistically unconscious Orlando. Rosalind's wit, in preparation for the love-cure, converts a potential duologue of confession, heading towards sentimentality, into a vigorous semi-combat:

ROSALIND: There is a man haunts the forest, that abuses our young plants with carving 'Rosalind' on their barks; hangs odes upon hawthorns and elegies on brambles; all, forsooth, deifying the name of Rosalind: if I could meet that fancy-monger, I would give him some good counsel, for he seems to have the quotidian of love upon him.
ORLANDO: I am he that is so love-shaked. I pray you, tell me your remedy.
ROSALIND: There is none of my uncle's marks upon you: he taught me how to know a man in love; in which cage of rushes I am sure you are not prisoner.
ORLANDO: What were his marks?
ROSALIND: A lean cheek, which you have not: a blue eye and sunken, which you have not: an unquestionable spirit, which you

have not: a beard neglected, which you have not . . . but I
pardon you for that, for simply your having in beard is a
younger brother's revenue. Then your hose should be ungar-
tered, your bonnet unbanded, your sleeve unbuttoned, your
shoe untied, and everything about you demonstrating a care-
less desolation: but you are no such man; you are rather point-
device in your accoutrements, as loving yourself than seeming
the lover of any other.

ORLANDO: Fair youth, I would I could make thee believe I love.

ROSALIND: Me believe it! you may as soon make her that you love believe
it, which I warrant she is apter to do than to confess she does:
that is one of the points in the which women still give the lie to
their conciences. . .

(3. 2. 351ff)

What is most striking here is the gradual personalisation – the
dramatisation – of the I/You relationship, despite the double
distancing of disguise and verbal wit. For a start, the subject of
conversation is love itself, two removes from the opening
impersonal canter on Time (3. 2. 295–329), through the semi-
personal gambit of the 'religious uncle' who read Rosalind many
lectures on the folly of courtship. It is a simple strategy of moving
inwards. The corresponding stylistic strategy is to let Rosalind
make general statements that provoke the right kind of direct
questions from Orlando, forcing the potentially endless talk on
'the symptoms of love' into a declaration, shifting from 'I would
give him' to 'I am he.' From that decisive transition on, much of
the duologue hinges on the personal pronoun, reaching a climax
in 'I would I could make thee believe I love.' / 'Me believe it! you
may as soon. . . .' (We also note Orlando's shift to the familiar
'thee', a usage that has already been studied.)[27] In dramatic terms
the interlocutors are being drawn into intimacy, or conspiracy,
with one partner still kept in the dark. In linguistic terms the use
of the personal pronouns ('shifters' or 'deictics') gives a dynamic
quality to the speech (as Roman Jakobson would say).[28] However, as observed before, the comic disequilibrium between main
speaker/stooge still remains. Orlando is directed to ask the questions, and make the confessions desired by Rosalind: the naive
conversationalist[29] ('the fancy-monger', who in Jonson would be
the gull) is up against the wit-monger who controls both context
and text – through wit.

It is a centripetal kind of wit which will not allow the duologue
to drift back into impersonality through a general parody of love's

symptoms and conceits. Instead of the symmetry of duets (as in the *Dream*), there is a precarious imbalance between the speakers; and like the convention of disguise itself, the exchanges are always *at risk* of being uncovered. The shifts of tone, and the pauses between and within the speeches (those commas) become risky – as Rosalind's long and witty sally on the methodology of the love-cure modulates into her direct challenge:

ROSALIND: this way will I take upon me to wash your liver as clean as a sound sheep's heart, that there shall be not one spot of love in't.
ORLANDO: I would not be cured, youth.
ROSALIND: I would cure you, if you would but call me Rosalind, and come every day to my cote, and woo me.

(3. 2. 410ff)

Here the exchanges of wit are in danger of becoming an intimate avowal – Rosalind echoing Orlando's confessional mood and mode. In the full passage, Rosalind 'descends' to something like the direct language of courting from her earlier catalogue of euphuistic contradictions in love: 'for every passion something, and for no passion truly anything . . . would now like him, now loathe him; then entertain him, then forswear him; now weep for him, then spit at him'. But situational wit still keeps the exchange from losing its indirect and hypothetical playfulness: 'I would not be cured' / 'I would cure you' is conditional both gramatically and actionally. It is true enough, as Leggatt remarked on this exchange, that 'under the cover of attacking love [Rosalind] wishes to act out her own desires. She does not want Orlando to be cured, any more than he does himself.' And up to a point, Rosalind's last speech is, like Orlando's, 'simple and direct'.[30] But one can still hear the mocking overtone – first in the felicitous discord of the altered echo ('I would not be cured . . . I would cure you'), then in the sustained conditional, and finally in the use of the words that, especially when spoken with the right laughing tremolo, produce witty sounds: 'come every day to my cote, and woo me'. So language still holds courtship at bay.

The mock-wooing and the ambivalence of wit in love's language is fully exploited in the second full duologue of Rosalind and Orlando (4. 1. 30–193). Here is one exchange:

ROSALIND: Come, woo me, woo me; for now I am in a holiday humour and like enough to consent. . . . What would you say to me now, an I were your very very Rosalind?

ORLANDO: I would kiss before I spoke.

ROSALIND: Nay, you were better speak first, and when you were gravelled for lack of matter, you might take occasion to kiss: very good orators, when they are out, they will spit, and for lovers, lacking (God warr'nt us!) matter, the cleanliest shift is to kiss.

ORLANDO: How if the kiss be denied?

ROSALIND: Then she puts you to entreaty, and there begins new matter.

ORLANDO: Who could be out, being before his beloved mistress?

ROSALIND: Marry, that should you if I were your mistress, or I should think my honesty ranker than my wit.

The controlled exuberance of Rosalind's wit, gently out-witting Orlando with her quickening verbal game, speaks for itself – it is fluent, conversationally based and carefully cadenced. The exchange is about the importance of being witty *before* any approach to kissing: this simple late Elizabethan creed is more than anything else the main source of love-wit. The importance of long-delayed courting for comedy would be underwritten by the historians of love who, from de Rougemont to Foucault, claim that our ideas of sublimation, and our endless debating of love, are among the most potent aspects of love in the culture of the West. Though the sublimation of sexual passion is not usually discussed in the context of wit, there can be little doubt that the combat of wit needs such a creed. For as Rosalind makes plain, the strategy of wit includes the 'putting you to entreaty', to 'begin new matter', in a combat; in the interaction of verbal action; in a non-kissing verbal climax.

Yet the comedy must end with the union of the contending lovers, when wit is somewhat muted. In the comic catastrophe of *As You Like It* disguise and mock-wooing lead straight to the pageant of four assorted nuptials, presided over by Hymen. At that point the ceremony of the masque takes over from wit, but Rosalind is given the Epilogue, perhaps to reinforce the sense of play – theatrical wit – through a final speech from the most play-conscious and witty character.

Much Ado About Nothing is organised around the most sustained and brilliant wit-combat in Shakespeare's mature comedies. Formally the subplot, the verbal skirmishing of Beatrice and Benedick becomes central. It has no known source; it is bred by Shakespeare's imagination out of 'airy nothing': out of a witty modification of the love-game convention, where the couple's seeming antagonism replaces sexual disguise as the secret agent of true relationship. There is no longer a dominant wit; the witty couple is perfectly matched in its mutual opposition to getting matched. The misogamists – the self-proclaimed eternal bachelor and the systematically love-scorning spinster – engage in a series of interlocked encounters: in anti-wooing. A 'humour' in the individual character (misogamy) is *doubled* in relationship; the couple's mutual declarations of verbal independence of love constitute a kindred language of ambivalent (love/hate) wit. When wit as antidote-to-love is, by the end of the play, converted into an instrument of 'critical' love, no one is surprised – the plot is predictable, yet its verbal expression remains fresh to the end. It is a unique invention in comedy (though a clear precursor of the witty couple in Restoration Comedy, especially of Mirabell and Millamant in *The Way of the World*). The prose of the combative duologues keeps the feel of conversational spontaneity, as if the antagonistic couple were constantly improvising variations on *their* theme: their own opposition in true friendship (to echo Blake). Though the play as a whole makes ample use of 'a mannered, schematic [prose] rhetoric derived from euphuism', the couple uses the old language *playfully*, as Jonas Barish has argued:[31] 'the syntactic symmetry' of Beatrice and Benedick is free from the 'spiky rigidity' of Don John's stiff mannerist prose (also found in the speech of Leonato, Claudio and Don Pedro). The couple moves from a wit of 'disdain' towards a wit of authentic companionship and attachment.

The verbal wit is, further, completely integrated in the situational wit – no texture without structure, nothing superfluous or indulgent in the wit-combats. The combats are precisely placed and surprisingly economic (surprising for those who expect wit to produce patterns of superabundant verbosity) within a teleological design: from the prologue-like first scene to the confessed lovers' wit in the final scene. Coleridge took *Much Ado* as a starting point for his celebrated statement that in Shakespeare 'the plot interests us on account of the characters, not vice versa'.[32] But Coleridge had oversimplified the comedic plot/character relationship in this instance (as John Palmer also argued),[33] and I think it is impossible to evaluate – and enjoy – the wit-combats fully without becoming aware of their exact place in the subtle design. Paradoxically, it is just when we focus sharply on the 'frontal' duologues of Beatrice and Benedick that we become fully aware of the web of indirect dialogue woven around their direct interaction: their obsessive talking about each other behind each other's backs, and the self-expressive monologues, which make up the full pattern of combat. The duologues proper are pivotal, but they depend on that opera of soloists and ensembles, with rapid changes of tone.

That larger structure of dialogue is complex; all we can do here is to recall it. The prologue to the combat (1. 1. 28–90) is not just expository – hinting that Beatrice may have been disappointed in Benedick as a lover since he 'had challenged Cupid at the flight' (1. 1. 37; 2. 1. 259–62). It is also a shadow wit-combat: Beatrice has begun fencing with her absent opponent while the audience is being offered a neat breviary on the meanings of wit:

LEONATO: There is a kind of merry war betwixt Signior Benedick and her. They never meet but there's a *skirmish of wit* between them.
BEATRICE: Alas, he gets nothing by that. In our last conflict, four of his *five wits* went halting off, and now is the whole man governed with one –so that if he have *wit* enough to keep himself warm, let him bear it for a difference between himself and his horse, for it is all the wealth that he hath left to be known a reasonable creature.

(1. 1. 57ff. Emphasis added.)

This exchange gets laughter from a contemporary audience which need not know that the unforced pun on 'wit'/'wits' includes a shift of meaning to wit 1 (as *ingenium*, intelligence, five wits) from wit 2 (exercise of verbal ingenuity). *Much Ado* is one of the texts that marks the point of transition from the old to the new meaning – and its double use.[34] The 'skirmish of wit' between Beatrice and Benedick is being advertised in advance of actual combat. We may then expect it to work on two levels: as one intelligence pitting itself against another both fearing the loss of four, or all five, wits – in love, the tester of wit; and as one self-conscious wit facing another – with turns of phrase, figures, questions, rejoinders as verbal weapons. The two levels must be fused in proper reading and performance: the surface exchanges of wit are fuelled by intelligences, and even by passions (Beatrice's 'disdain' or 'fury' and Benedick's hurt male vanity). The strength of those negative feelings – the force of 'war' – should be felt in and under the wit.[35]

The shadow-combat of the prologue (longer and just as wittily abusive as the direct encounter) precedes the first combat proper ('I wonder that you will still be talking, Signior Benedick – nobody marks you.' lines 112–13); and this direct combat is soon followed by Benedick's general attack on love (in the 'I will live a bachelor' dialogue with Claudio and Don Pedro, 1. 1. 221–72). This trio of wit scenes creates a perfect comedic pattern: the direct combat is advertised and underscored by the shadow-combats. And then the duologue proper gains an extra comic intensity from the confrontation, the unleashing of two wits separately itching to get at one another (though they later proclaim their desire not to encounter, not to speak to one another). The second combat (2. 1. 114–42) – the duologue exchanged at the festive revels where a quartet of masked couples engage in teasing talk – is relatively tame in wit. The mask convention curbs Benedick's appetite for repartee and he has to fall back on a self-cancelling, third-person speech-role: 'When I know the gentleman [Benedick himself, whose wit has been belittled] I'll tell him what you say.' In this short scene Beatrice has a monopoly of wit; offering wounding insults as her wit attacks his wit: 'None but libertines delight in him, and the commendation is not in his wit, but in his villainy.' But the larger context heightens the wit-effect of this mini-combat, first through Beatrice's anti-husband sallies (in the preceding conversation with Leonato, 2. 1. 1–76): 'Would it not grieve a woman to be overmastered by a piece of valiant dust?'; and then through Benedick's short monologue following the masked duet: 'But that my Lady Beatrice should know me and not know me. The prince's fool! ha . . .' (2. 1. 188–9) underlining the hurt inflicted on Benedick's wit by the temporarily superior wit of Beatrice. Within minutes that short monologue leads to Benedick's most sustained comic tirade against Beatrice (2. 1. 222–43): 'She speaks poniards, and every word stabs: if her breath were as terrible as her terminations, there were no living near her, she would infect to the north star. I would not marry her. . .' In a fine ironic variation on the theme of verbal combat, the opponent attacked is not yet present; her absence is filled with obsessive talk about not wanting to talk about her ('Come talk not of her.'); and when she finally does enter, Benedick refuses to address her, goes on railing at her as if she were still absent ('I cannot endure my Lady Tongue'), and departs without any direct exchange. Thus is a comedy of absence and evasion turned into combat – it goes on all the time, overflows into the space left by the absent opponent, and permeates most of the dialogue in the play.

The placing of the third duologue is a triumph of comedic construction: coming at the end of a sustained scene (2. 3) that builds up to this wooing at cross-purposes: Benedick's deluded and loving *entente* checked by Beatrice's churlish *mésentente*. The tricking of Benedick (in the orchard, overhearing rumours of Beatrice's love) is the actional centre of the scene, midway between Benedick's two monologues of wit: the first totally against love and marriage ('But till all graces be in one woman, one woman shall not come in my grace'); the second totally reversing his marital ideology through the invention of a new logic ('No – the world must be peopled. When I said I would die a bachelor, I did not think I should live till I were married'). The cumulative comic energy of these two monologues, in circuit with the 'tricking', then fuels the short duologue at the end of the act. This is not particularly sparkling in texture: a simple *dialogue des sourdes*, wherein Benedick's infatuation converts Beatrice's plain sarcasms into amorous 'double meaning'. (With the audience laughing at the blunder, the lack of wit.) Benedick's first groping towards sympathy temporarily disarms his wit; his share in the combat is defused.

The fourth duologue (4. 1. 254–334) is long-delayed, until Beatrice in turn has been tricked into reciprocal love for Benedick (with the busy intrigue of act 3 intervening: the Hero–Claudio plot entangling Dogberry, in a broad comedy of 'witlessness', of maladroit action and malapropism, to counterpoint the conscious generators of wit). At that point there is a further variation in the wit-combat: sincere declarations of love 'brake' the wit, and the sombre plot intrudes as Beatrice commands Benedick to kill his former friend, as the price of love: 'Kill Claudio'.

Further variations are played out in the two duologues of the last act (5. 2 and 5. 4), where a dialogue of newly found love is written into the old wit-combat, as we shall see. The placing of the first one seems unusual for it follows an 'unnecessary' combat of wit between Benedick and Margaret, Hero's gentlewoman (bawdy, punning and indulgent) and Benedick's inability to find rhymes for a love poem (he can only find 'lady' for 'baby', etc.). If this is not mere padding, a farcical episode, then it works like parodic counterpoint: Margaret's low wit, and Benedick's doggerel contrasting with the superior love-wit of Beatrice and Benedick. As for the final duologue, the placing is traditional: the festive group dialogue embraces the final exchanges of the lovers in nuptial release. But this couple remains witty to the end: the celebration of love's triumph tempered by the self-possession of wit.

In my reading of the comedic structure much of the highly patterned wit is found outside the duologues proper. The language of the direct/personal exchanges between Beatrice and Benedick is often furthest from euphuistic formality: it often approximates the conversational, miming spontaneity and enacting the surprise of a genuine encounter.[36] I have traced the relational transformation – from antagonism into wittily conditional love – through the progression of combats; it remains to look at the changes of tone in the texture of wit.

The combative wit is at its most war-like, appropriately enough, in the first encounter:

BEATRICE: I wonder that you will still be talking Signior Benedick – nobody marks you.
BENEDICK: What, my dear Lady Disdain! are you yet living?
BEATRICE: Is it possible Disdain should die, while she hath such meet food to feed it as Signior Benedick? Courtesy itself must convert to disdain, if you come in her presence.
BENEDICK: Then is courtesy a turn-coat. But it is certain I am loved of all ladies, only you excepted: and I would I could find in my heart that I had not a hard heart, for truly I love none.
BEATRICE: A dear happiness to women – they would else have been troubled with a pernicious suitor. I thank God and my cold blood, I am of your humour for that. I had rather hear my dog bark at a crow than a man swear he loves me.
BENEDICK: God keep your ladyship still in that mind, so some gentleman or other shall 'scape a predestinate scratched face.
BEATRICE: Scratching could not make it worse, an 'twere such a face as yours were.
BENEDICK: Well, you are a rare parrot-teacher.

BEATRICE: A bird of my tongue is better than a beast of yours.
BENEDICK: I would my horse had the speed of your tongue, and so good a
        continuer. But keep your way a God's name – I have
        done.
BEATRICE: You always end with a jade's trick. I know you of old.

                          (1. 1. 111ff)

The repartee is clearly kept going by a fit exchange of abuse – the
pattern we recognise from medieval 'flyting' to the invective of
the two vagabonds in *Waiting for Godot* (where the ultimate abuse
is 'crritic!'). The exchange of abuse is funny, but it may seem a
mild form of wit. Shaw grumbled:

> Paraphrase the encounters of Benedick and Beatrice in the style
> of a bluebook . . . it will become apparent to the most infatuated
> Shakespearean that they contain at best nothing out of the
> common in thought or wit, and at worst a good deal of vulgar
> naughtiness. Paraphrase Goethe, Wagner, or Ibsen in the same
> way, and you will find original observation, subtle thought,
> wide comprehension. . . . Not until the Shakespearean music is
> added by replacing the paraphrase with the original lines does
> the enchantment begin.[37]

Now this 'paraphrasing' of wit is naive, as is the notion of 'Shakespearean music' (later called the 'grace and dignity of diction') as
something superadded – to translate into an elegant tiff what
might have been the scene when 'a flower-girl tells a coster to
hold his jaw', etc. What Shaw calls 'music' is the rhythm of witty
dialogue, inseparable from the clash of two attitudes/voices. It is
no longer a style-consciously euphuistic rhythm; it mimes, as
already stated, the teasing/contrary quality of much combative
conversation. The comic tension of that conversational wit works
in two ways: (1) across the speakers:

> nobody marks you / What, my Dear Lady Disdain!
> for truly I love none / A dear happiness to women
> a predestinate scratched face / Scratching could not make it
> worse
> a rare parrot-teacher / A bird of my tongue is better than . . .

where repartee uses the ordinary pattern of 'counter-bidding'
and 'out-bidding' by taking either the sense (first two exchanges)
or the keyword (the third and fourth exchanges) into a 'doubly
redoubled' twist. At the same time we have (2) the comic tension
of the syntax *within* each speaker's speech: the exclamations, the
questions, the imperatives and personal invocations. I think

there is not one neutral statement in this duologue, i.e. not personalised by pronouns and directly addressed to the opponent. Contrast this with the invective levelled by Beatrice against Benedick in his absence – 'a very valiant trencherman' or 'a stuffed man' (1. 1. 48ff), and we can see the difference: the phrasing is funny in both encounters, but only the full combat releases the energies of a thrusting/questioning/commanding syntax. Further, the verbal fun springs not just from the balanced, antithetical cadences of the prose (for example Beatrice's 'I had rather hear my dog bark at a crow than a man swear he loves me'), but from the short, sharp, 'colourless', throw-away half-lines: 'nobody marks you' or 'Are you yet living?' – lines that depend for comic effect on their syntactic place (perfected by the actor's delivery). We need not conclude from this that the colloquial model is 'wittier' than the euphuistic one, merely that Shakespeare has mastered the verbal counterpoint that results from a criss-crossing of the two modes – and the *mixing* of styles is itself witty.

In that first encounter there is relatively little differentiation between the two speakers' attitudes, and they share the same tone of wit. It is that kind of dialogue that J. L. Styan called a *duet*, as distinct from a duologue (illustrating his point by quoting from the quarrelling couple's third encounter, 2. 3. 241–9):

> The characters of the prose duologues in the comedies are usually contrasted in their sex, but otherwise they share the given mood; this is true even of Beatrice and Benedick. Therefore, it is not inappropriate to think of such exchanges as duets. These display a special skill in verbal manipulation based upon the idiom of colloquial speech which can accommodate its own range of tone and tempo. A musical pattern is framed by the derision of Beatrice, who scarcely parries her lover's advances before she cuts them down:
>
> BEATRICE: Against my will I am sent to bid you come in to dinner.
> BENEDICK: Fair Beatrice, I thank you for your pains.
> BEATRICE: I took no more pains for those thanks than you take pains to thank me. If it had been painful, I would not have come.
> BENEDICK: You take pleasure then in the message.
> BEATRICE: Yea, just so much as you may take upon a knife's point, and choke a daw withal.
>
> (Styan, *Shakespeare's Stagecraft*, p. 178)[38]

Styan's distinction between duologue and duet is useful, though I am surprised by his choice of dialogue sample. But do Beatrice and Benedick 'share the given mood' in the exchange quoted? They are, clearly, at cross purposes emotionally, as we have seen. And with that relational discord goes a veritable collision of speaking styles: *his* humbled into sincerity and plain prose ('you take pleasure in the message'); *hers* still riding high on invective and verbal conceit ('Yea, just so much as you may take upon a knife's point and choke a daw withal') – a syntactic rhythm that ends with a 'lash in its tail'.

The opposition of voices and moods, is even clearer in the fourth ('Kill Claudio') duologue. Intensifying the divergence of speakers, Benedick's love is now crossed by the authentic fury of Beatrice:

BENEDICK: Come bid me do any thing for thee.
BEATRICE: Kill Claudio.
BENEDICK: Ha! not for the wide world.
BEATRICE: You kill me to deny it – farewell.
BENEDICK: Tarry sweet Beatrice.   *(he stays her*
BEATRICE: I am gone, though I am here – there is no love in you – nay I
        pray you let me go.
BENEDICK: Beatrice –
BEATRICE: In faith I will go.
BENEDICK: We'll be friends first.
BEATRICE: You dare easier be friends with me than fight with mine enemy.
BENEDICK: Is Claudio thine enemy?
BEATRICE: Is a' not approved in the height a villain, that hath slandered,
        scorned, dishonoured my kinswoman? O that I were a man!
        What, bear her in hand until they come to take hands, and then
        with public accusation, uncovered slander, unmitigated ran-
        cour – O God that I were a man! I would eat his heart in the
        market-place.
BENEDICK: Hear me Beatrice, –
BEATRICE: Talk with a man out at a window – a proper saying!
BENEDICK: Nay but Beatrice, –
BEATRICE: Sweet Hero, she is wronged, she is slandered, she is undone.
BENEDICK: Beat –
BEATRICE: Princes and counties! Surely a princely testimony, a goodly
        count, Count Comfect – a sweet gallant surely. O that I were a
        man for his sake! or that I had any friend would be a man for my
        sake! But manhood is melted into curtsies, valour into complé-
        ment, and men are only turned into tongue, and trim ones too:
        he is now as valiant as Hercules, that only tells a lie and swears
        it. . . . I cannot be a man with wishing, therefore I will die a
        woman with grieving.
BENEDICK: Tarry good Beatrice – by this hand I love thee.
BEATRICE: Use it for my love some other way than swearing by it.

                                      (4. 1. 287ff)

The divergence between the two speakers – disrupted by the intrusion of the sombre Claudio–Hero plot – seems so serious here that the wit gives way to naked combat. Apart from the irony of Beatrice's charges ('men are only turned into tongue', coming from 'my Lady Tongue'), and the comic pattern of interruptions (four times Benedick is prevented from having his say), the language of wit is spare in this exchange.

The tonal collisions of Beatrice and Benedick are newly attuned in the final duologues of act five. That much is appropriate enough: in keeping with the nuptial release of the comedic finale. However, the pending communion of this couple is in no way ritualised (as it is in *As You Like It* and the other comedies). By analogy with *Love's Labour's Lost*, or through assuming something like an archetypal convention, readers/critics might expect the wit to dwindle with the triumph of love's comedy. But the final pattern of wit is unique in *Much Ado*. The couple first engage in a genuine exploration of their state of loving. Wit – the light tone in declarations of love here – continues to offer the couple a kind of verbal screen to keep each other at the proper comic distance from ritual union:

BEATRICE: But for which of my good parts did you first suffer love for me?
BENEDICK: 'Suffer love!' a good epithet. I do suffer love indeed, for I love
thee against my will.
BEATRICE: In spite of your heart, I think. Alas, poor heart, if you spite it
for my sake, I will spite it for yours, for I will never love that
which my friend hates.
BENEDICK: Thou and I are too wise to woo peaceably.
BEATRICE: It appears not in this confession – there's not one wise man
among twenty that will praise himself.

(5. 2. 62ff)

In this delicately balanced exchange – wherein 'you' is converted into 'thou' – we have feeling and judgement, a kind of confessional duologue still within the frame of the wit-combat ('too wise to woo peaceably').

The pattern is further varied in the final exchange, in the public, festive scene. Here we have a new device – the opposition of half-lines – as if to demarcate the still contested bounds of love's territory:

BENEDICK: Do not you love me?
BEATRICE: Why, no; no more than reason.

(5. 4. 74ff)

The pattern is then echoed with the speakers reversed:

BEATRICE: Do not you love me?
BENEDICK: Troth, no, no more than reason.

The stubborn duality of this pair of lovers is mocked by the seeming unison in the 'almost/well-nigh' perfect symmetry of their exchanges (which recall the parodic stichomythia):

BENEDICK: They swore that you were almost sick for me.
BEATRICE: They swore that you were well-nigh dead for me.

This leads to the climax everybody remembers, the distancing lovers' vow to be imitated in the proviso-scene of Restoration Comedy (as in Congreve):

BENEDICK: Come, I will have thee; but by this light, I take thee for pity.
BEATRICE: I would not deny you; but, by this good day I yield upon
          great persuasion, and partly to save your life, for I was told you
          were in a consumption.

In this sequence, once more, the variations of mood and posture themselves become part of the wit. The to-and-fro-ing of sympathy and opposition between the would-be lovers has found its own expressive language; and the duologue of the wit-combat has matured into an instrument of self-discovery and shared, if embattled, exploration.

3. Out-witting in Jonson's major comedies

The dialogue of wit-combats could, in a direct if simplified line, be taken from Shakespeare straight to Restoration Comedy, say from Beatrice and Benedick to Congreve's Mirabell and Millamant. That line of development would leave Jonsonian comedy 'somewhat on one side',[39] as the combat in Jonson is both more realistically combative and less personal than in Shakespeare's comedies of courtship. An encounter in Jonson is usually a game in Volpone's punning sense, 'Methinks I lie, and draw – for an encounter' (*Volpone*, 3. 5. final line): a seduction, the master-wit swooping down on his prey. The duologue between the master-wit and his dupe may take many forms but hardly that of playful repartee and reciprocal verbal games, for there is no 'innocent' sparring couple driven by their mutual wit towards sympathy and nuptial union. The wit is antagonistic and underhand from the start. The linguistic texture of that wit may not strike the reader or the audience as 'witty' on the surface at all. There is little or no good-humoured swapping of epigrams, no delighted turning inside-out of one another's meaning and phrasing; instead, one speaker's speech-excess (deliberate and seductive jargon, hyperbole, ostentatious rhetoric) collides with the poor speech of another (the naive user of jargon, or the 'natural' speaker).

But it is just because wit in Jonson is a world apart from the other – more 'sympathetic' – wit-combat, both relationally and stylistically, that we need to look at it, briefly, at this point. We may bear in mind the supposition:[40] wit implies insincerity, de-personalisation or even alienation in relationship; and the language of wit is contra-natural as a vehicle of communication.

It must be said at once, that the opposition between wit in Shakespeare and in Jonson, though based on a fresh reading, is what we might expect from the traditional opposition of the two types of comedy. It is one of the rare examples in dramatic literature where a binary opposition really makes sense: 'the green world'/the city; romance/satire; all the world's a stage/ the world is vanity fair (or Bartholomew Fair); aristocratic role players/rogues and dupes. And so on. A few quotations may illustrate the critical consensus:

> Compared with the comedies of Shakespeare those of Ben Jonson are no laughing matter. A harsh ethic in them yokes punishment with derision; foibles are persecuted and vices flayed; the very simpletons are savaged for being what they are. The population he chooses for his comedies in part accounts for this: it is a congeries of cits, parvenus, mountebanks, cozeners, dupes, braggarts, bullies, and bitches. No one loves anyone.   (Coghill, 'Shakespearean comedy', p. 201)[41]

> Shakespeare, with a unifying and informing power, both harmonized and animated a society which he swayed by 'delight' and 'wonder', leaving no room for that critical detachment which Jonson in general required.
> (Bradbrook, *Elizabethan Comedy*, p. 94)

> Shakespeare seems to promote integration with nature, Jonson with society. In the one a *sharing* is offered, in the other a *warning*. Shakespeare relies not on one comic view, but on a comic sense of relativity. Consequently he creates characters whom one may laugh *with*, who are funny in themselves, like

Beatrice and Benedick, or Falstaff. In Jonson, the characters are to be laughed *at*, and are funny only as parts of an all-embracing design.

(Rodway, English Comedy, p. 98)

In all this we have a particularly clear shift to satirical City comedy, as the context for a shift in dialogue, essentially to a new type of exploitative wit. (We know from L. C. Knight's *Drama and Society in the Age of Jonson* that large-scale change – a shift to a more acquisitive, capital-accumulating society – was the macro-context for the change in Jacobean comedy.) We have already seen that the word 'wit' has at least a double, an often precariously overlapping meaning: that of general intelligence (*ingenium*) and that of verbal display (which C. S. Lewis called its 'dangerous sense'); and the two kinds of wit get fused in *Much Ado About Nothing* (written about the time the later, more frivolous, sense may have come into prominence). Now it would seem that the two senses and uses of wit also get fused in Jonsonian comedy, but with a shift to a new emphasis on 'scoring off', on 'one-up-manship' – nourished by the competitive and word-conscious metropolitan milieu of Jonson's London. It follows that the Jonsonian master-wit's speech will be an instrument of outwitting through various types of false wit, as we shall see. Leo Salingar, in his meticulous article, '"Wit" in Jacobean Comedy', reminds us that in Jonson the moral and social concern is inseparable from the literary and linguistic one. Jonson himself states in *Discoveries*: '*There cannot be one colour of the mind, another of wit, wheresoever manners and fashions are corrupted, language is.*'

Salingar's comment on this text sums up the context of wit in Jonson's dialogue:

> His great achievement as a comic playwright was to capture the effects of verve, acuteness and surprise striven after by practitioners of conversational wit within a strictly controlled and ironic, yet abundantly imaginative dialogue. But this meant that his own wit was embedded within his dialogue, not concentrated on the surface in a sparkling exchange of epigrams, as later in Restoration comedy; such a firework display would have been alien to his purpose.[42]

The corruption of wit, the abuses of language, become a dominant feature of dramatic encounter in three of Jonson's major comedies: *Volpone, The Alchemist* and *Epicoene, or The Silent*

Woman. It is not too much to say that Jonson is the first language-obsessed dramatist, creating a theatre of language in the precise sense (in which Jean Vannier and myself have used the term in relation to Beckett, Ionesco and Pinter): 'human relations at the level of language itself . . . a theatre of language where man's words are held up to us as a spectacle'.[43] Not until our own time has a dramatist explored, with such intensity, the 'absurdity' of human speech – in Jonson, its tendency to degenerate into cant and incantation, into a vehicle for creating a verbal fog between deceiving speaker and confused or equally deceiving listener. Paradoxically, this language mania, this recurrent dramatisation of elaborate speech, logorrhoea and jargon-folly, comes from a dramatist who can be represented as committed to 'natural language' (taking a roughly Baconian view of the dangers of verbal affectation). In the Prologue to *Every Man in His Humour* (1598) Jonson asked for 'deeds, and language, such as men do use', possibly with a hint of opposition to Shakespeare's comic language; and his critical aphorisms in *Timber, or Discoveries* include the creed 'Pure and neat Language I love, yet plaine and customary.' Further, it can be shown that Jonson's English was essentially 'native' (that is, he was not 'a learned plagiary of all the ancients' at the expense of the 'native springs of his vitality', as Dryden thought); and much of his linguistic usage – derisive compounds, alliterative jingles, and easy flow of words – was near enough to popular speech.[44] However, the tension between 'natural' and 'mannered' speech in Jonson is complex. Eliot was the first to argue that Jonson's language, based on Marlowe's rhetoric, often appears to us as 'forced and flagitious bombast'; yet, when the full design of Jonsonian comedy is grasped, we experience an 'effect not of verbosity, but of bold, even shocking directness'.[45] The design being satirical, it delightedly *cherishes* the exposure of the vices of speech; and the ambivalent artistic love-hate for the satirised types of language only enhances the potency of Jonson's dialogue. The whole tension or paradox just discussed can be summed up as 'the decorum of fools' speech, which lies in misuse of language'.[46]

The combat of out-witting in Jonson is, then, nearly always generated between speakers who are speaking past each other in a hyper-histrionic lingo to display their verbal potency and gain possession of – to ravish – their listeners. The master-wit (Volpone and Mosca, Subtle and Face) assumes a costume speech, a borrowed language, with the ease of an accomplished actor and ironist. Linguistically, though not morally, the irony of the Jonsonian impostor is greater than that of an Iago; for Iago's duplicity consists in drawing his antagonist into a complicity of shared feelings and language; whereas the Jonsonian impostor attempts to gain power over his dupe through a speech that is not intended to be understood and shared (*The Alchemist*), or a speech that is overtly intended to overwhelm from the start (Volpone wooing Celia). Moreover, the Jonsonian impostor is nearly always an excessive speaker, a bravura speaker. As Alexander Sackton observes in *Rhetoric as a Dramatic Language in Ben Jonson*, Jonson, like Shakespeare, uses disguise, 'but it is often *disguise of speech* which would be apparent to any free intelligence. The language of Mosca, Subtle and Face is made obviously rhetorical to the audience; its falseness would be obvious to their dupes if they were not blinded by avarice, or pride, or ambition.'[47] The argument goes on to contrast *As You Like It* (dependent on isolated ironic scenes which exploit the convention of disguise) with *The Alchemist* and its all-embracing linguistic irony. It seems to me the most interesting and central point of Sackton's book that in Jonson the misuses of language – false rhetoric, hyperbole, jargon – become a fully dramatic and interactive (as distinct from a merely rhetorical or satirical) language.

Characters interact upon one another in a pattern of out-witting where the master-wit tries to get the better of his victim by out-talking him or her. The clash of character may take the form of a verbal battle, a competition of virtuoso speakers. In a miniature form the battle is present in the lusty exchange of invectives (a version of the medieval 'flyting') in the opening scene of *The Alchemist*, including this little fugue:

SUBTLE:		Cheater.
FACE:	Bawd.	
SUBTLE:	Cow-herd.	
FACE:		Conjurer.
SUBTLE:		Cut-purse.
FACE:		Witch.

(1. 1. 106–7. Note Jonson's vigorous
cutting-up of one pentametric blank verse line.)

While this is colourful – and there are much more elaborate types of insult being hurled at each other by the quarrelling impostors in this scene – it is a rather modest example of the speech-battle. The masterpieces of linguistic cunning are to be found in the great jargon-contests of the same play: when the practised deceiver and the deceived apprentice, Subtle and Mammon, exchange the same learned alchemical terminology; when two jargons confront each other's 'wordscreen' in a babel of incomprehension (Subtle and the Anabaptists). One would like to return to those scenes, but in our present context detailed attention will be given instead to the most personal kind of encounter to be found in Jonson's impersonal theatre – the attempted seduction. We may start with Volpone, where the overweening 'wit' of the seducer fails to win over Celia (willingly prostituted by her old and impotent husband Corvino as the price for a legacy) whose innocence – and natural language – remain undented by Volpone's sensual hyperboles.

Although the encounter is quite long (127 verse lines of duologue within a scene of 279 lines) and the language exuberantly 'jewelled', psychologically the dramatic pattern is very simple – basically a come/no situation, as may be judged from the above brief summary. The reader should bear in mind the great visual effect of this scene as Volpone is transformed from a bedridden *senex* into a resplendent gallant. In the texture of the dialogue there is little of the density that goes with inner conflict and sudden shifts of emotion in the two seduction scenes of *Measure for Measure* (see chapter 2). Volpone's speeches are parts of one long wooing aria, interrupted by the wholly different voice, tone, and rhythm of Celia. (It is surprising that, as far as I know, no attempt has been made so far to 'translate' the play into opera.) The dominant feature of Volpone's verse rhetoric is the 'hubristic hyperbole' which goes back to *Tamburlaine*; and as this style hardly varies, it should be sufficient to quote an extract – the exchange following Volpone's Catullian song to Celia:

VOLPONE: Why droops my Celia?
> Thou hast in place of a base husband, found
> A worthy lover: use thy fortune well,
> With secrecy, and pleasure. See, behold,
> What thou art queen of; not in expectation,
> As I feed others; but possessed, and crowned.
> See, here, a rope of pearl; and each, more orient
> Than that the brave Egyptian queen caroused:

> Dissolve, and drink 'em. See, a carbuncle,
> May put out both the eyes of our St. Mark;
> A diamant, would have bought Lollia Paulina,
> When she came in, like star-light, hid with jewels,
> That were the spoil of provinces; take these,
> And wear, and lose 'em: yet remains an ear-ring
> To purchase them again, and this whole state.
> A gem, but worth a private patrimony,
> Is nothing: we will eat such at a meal.
> The heads of parrots, tongues of nightingales,
> The brains of peacocks, and of ostriches
> Shall be our food: and, could we get the phoenix,
> Though nature lost her kind, she were our dish.
> CELIA: Good sir, these things might move a mind affected
> With such delights, but I, whose innocence
> Is all I can think wealthy, or worth th'enjoying,
> And which once lost, I have nought to lose beyond it,
> Cannot be taken with these sensual baits:
> If you have conscience –
> VOLPONE: 'Tis the beggar's virtue,
> If thou hast wisdom, hear me, Celia.
> Thy baths shall be the juice of July-flowers,
> Spirit of roses, and of violets,
> The milk of unicorns, and panthers' breath
> Gathered in bags, and mixed with Cretan wines.
> Our drink shall be prepared gold, and amber;
> Which we will take, until my roof whirl round
> With the vertigo: and my dwarf shall dance,
> My eunuch sing, my fool make up the antic.
> Whilst we, in changed shapes, act Ovid's tales,
> Thou, like Europa now, and I like Jove,
> Then I like Mars, and thou like Erycine,
> So, of the rest, till we have quite run through
> And wearied all the fables of the gods.

(3. 7. 185–225)

It is the sharp juxtaposition of attitudes and voices which create some of the effects of opera *buffo*. However, reader and audience are unlikely to experience instant comic release, for the swelling tirade of Marlovian rhetoric has a local effect of solemn incantation. It is mock-passionate; but it takes some time before the irony is fully felt. The stress must fall on the encyclopaedic naming, on the pedantic inventory behind the exotic nouns (out of manuals of jewellery and cookery). Once the ostentatious self-display, the linguistic hubris, is distinctly heard, it is clear that Volpone inflates his command of the dictionary beyond the bounds of any (probable or persuasive) erotic language. The verbal riches – like the objects they signify – expose the familiar hazards of over-advertising one's wares: somewhere, at some point in the flood of words, the listener will interpose a private pause, perhaps between 'the tongues of nightingales' and 'the brains of peacocks' – a dramatic pause, time enough for the Jonsonian subtext, which converts over-statement into a comedy of menace. A whole tradition of erotic poetry – the sensuality of things to promote the sensuality of persons – may well be evoked here; it ends by being 'debunked' into an auctioneer's catalogue. The verbal interaction with Celia is superbly controlled. It takes Celia's prudent reply (using the 'natural language' at its most conventional: 'Good sir, these things . . . but I, whose innocence is all . . . cannot be taken with these sensual baits') to alert the reader/audience to the extent of incongruity in the dialogue. Volpone's answer is, like that of a speech-machine that has been programmed with several sets of exotic substantives, and only such sets: an offer of *more* muchness. (Those baths, with 'The milk of unicorns, and panthers' breath'; the dwarf and the eunuch, attending all the sexual situations that Ovid's *Metamorphoses* can suggest by way of sublime 'porn'.) But the hubristic wit cannot out-wit, after all; rhetorical excess fails as a language of love/lust; verbal incontinence is countered by verbal primness (though Celia is capable of defensive rhetoric too, as in her next speech, lines 251–7). The grotesque mis-match between the two speakers underlines the element of parody in the whole duologue.

Whereas the very structure of the Shakespearian combat of wit, even the repartee of mocking in *Much Ado*, is participatory through the quick to-and-fro of the speakers' engagement, the structure of Jonsonian encounter advertises the distance of speaker from speaker. When, towards the end of the scene, Celia attempts to appeal to Volpone as a man reported 'virtuous', Volpone can only respond by expressing his alarm at his own reputation for impotence:

> Think me cold,
> Frozen, and impotent, and so report me?
> That I had Nestor's hernia, thou wouldst think.

(lines 260–3)

This 'absurd' speech with its synonymic triplets and the high-sounding bathos of 'Nestor's hernia', culminates in Volpone turning from rhapsody to rape. The attempt is discovered by the concealed Bonario, who interrupts grandiloquently, in lines which, in our theatre at least, are heard as the language of farce:

> Forbear, foul ravisher, libidinous swine,
> Free the forced lady, or thou diest, impostor.

> (lines 267–8)

We recognise the comic pattern of the plotter being hoisted with his own petard; his conspicuously masked language, too, has been unmasked.

In *The Alchemist* the wooing of Dol Common (disguised as a lord's sister) by Sir Epicure Mammon (mixing cupidity and lust in an over-reaching fantasy of gold and potency) is another extended parody of an amorous encounter. Here too, the wit is not in the exchanges themselves, but in the dramatic presentation of the couple's failure to dovetail in dialogue until, in their second scene, all sense is drowned in the pseudo-prophetic ravings of Dol. Mammon's attitude and verbal tone is given a kind of prologue – alerting the audience – in these fine mock-hubristic lines:

> She will feel gold, taste gold, hear gold, sleep gold:
> Nay, we will *concumbere* gold. I will be puissant,
> And mighty in my talk to her!

> (4. 1. 29–31)

The role-playing is more complex than in the Volpone–Celia encounter, as Mammon is essentially a dupe in the scene, and Dol the impostor; so Mammon is the victim of his own histrionic language of love, as elsewhere of his infatuation with the alchemical mumbo-jumbo. The combination of disguise and exuberant parody of love/lust might make one think of certain scenes in Shakespearian comedy, for instance of Bottom and Titania in the *Dream*; but Jonson's parody is more extreme, especially in language. (One can place it between Aristophanes and Genêt's *The Balcony* – with its fantasy language for role-enacting clients in the universal brothel.) The parody of amorous dialogue may be judged from this exchange (starting from Face's exit):

MAMMON: A certain touch, or air,
        That sparkles a divinity, beyond

144

An earthly beauty!
DOL: O, you play the courtier.
MAMMON: Good lady, gi' me leave –
DOL: In faith, I may not,
       To mock me, sir.
MAMMON: To burn i' this sweet flame:
       The Phoenix never knew a nobler death.
DOL: Nay, now you court the courtier: and destroy
       What you would build. This art, sir, i' your words,
       Calls your whole faith in question.
MAMMON: By my soul –
DOL: Nay, oaths are made o' the same air, sir.
MAMMON: Nature
       Never bestowed upon morality,
       A more unblamed, a more harmonious feature:
       She played the stepdame in all faces, else.
       Sweet madam, le' me be particular –
DOL: Particular, sir? I pray you, know your distance.

                                        (4. 1. 64–78)

Here the parody built into the duologue of seeming intimacy
acts as a sharply dramatic distancing device. At the same time,
the courting speeches are loaded with the specific parody of
courtly and Metaphysical conceits (as in 'The Phoenix never
knew a nobler death', with its possible echoes of both Shakespeare and Donne). The lover's oaths are exactly placed (and
interrupted by Dol) to allow Mammon to limber up for a more
extended hyperbolic speech; the interrupted lines, like the
pentameter broken by swear-words in an earlier quotation, produce excellent comic-colloquial dialogue, as distinct from tirades.
The speech beginning with Nature / Never, if properly attended
to, will advertise the counter-natural in Mammon's whole strategy of love – and speech-making. (The stress on the 'natural' as
an accepted standard, which is broken by the acquisitive drive,
was noted by L. C. Knights.)[48] After this distorted colloquy, the
mock-encounter of Dol and Mammon is gradually intensified to
the full Marlovian 'word music' (as in *Volpone*) but here based on a
glutton's food-guide:

       We'll therefore go with all, my girl, and live
       In a free state; where we will eat our mullets,
       Soused in high-country wines, sup pheasants' eggs,
       And have our cockles, boiled in silver shells,
       Our shrimps to swim again, as when they lived,

In a rare butter, made of dolphin's milk [. . .]

(4. 1. 155–60)

To such incantation there is no answer from Dol, as the duologue is interrupted by Face. It, or rather its babel-haunted version, is resumed three scenes further on:

[Enter] DOL, MAMMON

DOL: For, after Alexander's death – In her fit of talking
MAMMON: Good lady –
DOL: That Perdiccas, and Antigonus were slain,
    The two that stood, Seleuc', and Ptolomee –
MAMMON: Madam.
DOL: Made up the two legs, and the fourth Beast.
    That was Gog-north, and Egypt-south: which after
    Was called Gog-iron-leg, and South-iron-leg –
MAMMON: Sweet madam.
DOL: And last Gog-dust, and Egypt-dust, which fall
    In the last link of the fourth chain. And these
    By stars in story, which none see, or look at –
MAMMON: What shall I do?
DOL: For, as he says, except
    We call the Rabbins, and the heathen Greeks –
MAMMON: Dear lady.
DOL: To come from Salem, and from Athens,
    And teach the people of Great Britain –

[Enter FACE]

FACE: What's the matter, sir?
DOL: To speak the tongue of Eber, and Javan –
MAMMON: She's in her fit.
DOL: We shall know nothing –
FACE: Death, sir,
    We are undone.
DOL: Where, then, a learned linguist
    Shall see the ancient used communion
    Of vowels, and consonants –
FACE: My master will hear!
DOL: A wisdom, which Pythagoras held most high –
MAMMON: Sweet honourable lady.
DOL: To comprise
    All sounds of voices, in few marks of letters –
FACE: Nay, you must never hope to lay her now.

They speak together

DOL:	FACE:
And so we may arrive by	How did you put her into't?
Talmud skill,	MAMMON: Alas I talked
And profane Greek, to	Of a fifth monarchy I
raise the building up	would erect,

Of Heber's house, against
        The Ismaelite,
King of Togarmah, and his
        habergeons
Brimstony, blue, and fiery;
        and the force
Of King Abaddon, and the
        Beast of Cittim:
Which Rabbi David
        Kimchi, Onkelos,
And Aben-Ezra do
        interpret Rome.

With the philosopher's
        stone (by chance) and she
Falls on the other four,
        straight. FACE: Out of
           Broughton!
I told you so. 'Slid stop
    her mouth.   MAMMON: Is't
           best?
FACE:
    She'll never leave else.
    If the old man hear her,
    We are but faeces, ashes.
SUBTLE:[*within*] What's to do
           there?
FACE:
    O, we are lost. Now she
        hears him, she is quiet.

Upon SUBTLE's *entry they disperse*

(4. 5. 1–32)

It is characteristic of Jonson to let a relatively light parody of
courtship culminate in a parody of all language ('a learned linguist / Shall see the ancient used communion / Of vowels and
consonants'): Dol raving under the hubbub of three other speakers (another operatic composition); an intimate encounter reduced to cacophonous brawling; and the words to mere verbal
noise. Jonson transforms the scraps and fragments of biblical
exegesis, with those high-sounding Hebrew names straight from
Broughton's *A Concent of Scriptures* (1590), into mock-ritual. In
this dramatic incantation the dangerous instability of language as
communication can be heard bursting from its frame of neo-
classical decorum and satire. Here, as nowhere before, dialogue
is made to dislocate itself.

Jonson has never gone further in demonstrating that out-
witting wit, in excess, ends in linguistic madness – the ultimate
derangement of co-operative dialogue. (But for the language-
obsessed dramatist to create such madness is 'divine frenzy':
'you were mad when you writt your *Fox*, and madder when you
writt your *Alchymist*', wrote one of Jonson's 'sons'.)[49] Only the
puppets of the later *Bartholomew Fair* (1614) parody the very
potentials of stage dialogue so savagely, through the simpler art
of direct burlesque and crude texture. In the following brief
extract from 5. 3 Leatherhead is the puppet master, Pythias and

Damon are just two of his puppets and Cokes is a member of the
stage audience:

PYTHIAS: You lie like a rogue
LEATHERHEAD: Do I lie like a rogue?
PYTHIAS: A pimp and a scab.
LEATHERHEAD: A pimp and a scab!
      I say, between you, you have both but one drab.
DAMON: You lie again.
LEATHERHEAD: Like a rogue again!
PYTHIAS: And you are a pimp again, he says.
DAMON: 'And a scab again'
COKES: And a scab again, he says.

This dialogue of automata is played at the centre of the whirling and pig-loving fair: a street theatre where every encounter is
either a 'show' or a 'showing off', the bandying of words between
fools, hypocrites and rogues. It plainly exhibits the fragile
clockwork mechanism of question-and-answer: an insult, a question repeating the insult, an insult to out-bid the previous one, in
turn repeated by the puppet-master's exclamation, and so on,
with variations on the theme to keep the 'conversation' going.
For good measure, the puppet-master's own voice is heard commenting on his ventriloquist voices; and an inane spectator
keeps interrupting. Such is stage dialogue, its structure and clichés – the raw constituents ('foul' like Yeats's 'rag-and-bone shop
of the heart'). The contemporary reader may be reminded of
sequences in Eliot's *Sweeney Agonistes* or Ionesco's *The Bald Prima
Donna* in this early exposure of the emptiness – the witless wit – of
'talking'.

In the prose comedy *Epicoene, or The Silent Woman* (1609) the
theatrical emphasis is placed, for the greater part of the play, on
the parodox indicated by the subtitle – a supposedly silent
character in a gallery of speech-exhibitionists, male and female.
The first encounter between Morose and Epicoene is the only
scene in Jonson's hyper-garrulous comic drama where the out-
witting consists of saying nothing, or next to nothing in an
almost inaudible voice, in reply to the questioner. Morose (who
sums up his attitude to dialogue thus: 'all discourses but my
own afflict me' 2. 1. 3) begins the cross-examination of 'the silent
woman':

MOROSE: Can you speak, lady.
EPICOENE: Judge you, forsooth.   *She speaks softly.*
MOROSE: What say you, lady? Speak out, I beseech you.
EPICOENE: Judge you, forsooth.

(2. 5. 33–6)

Morose responds with a long, jubilantly congratulatory speech on the lady's 'divine softness', ironically regretting only that this marvellous gift of minimal speech might not enable the lady to shine with 'pleasant and witty conferences, pretty girds, scoffs, and dalliance', so much to be desired in a courtly man's 'bed-phere'. In a question-sentence that is more than a hundred words long (balanced cadences in a fine tirade), Morose asks whether the silent woman might really be expected to resist the courtly attractions of 'quickness of wit', for instance in 'amorous discourse':

> and do you alone so much differ from all them that what they
> (with so much circumstance) affect and toil for, to seem learn'd,
> to seem judicious, to seem sharp and conceited [witty], you can
> bury in yourself with silence, and rather trust your graces to the
> fair conscience of virtue than to the world's or your own procla-
> mation?

EPICOENE: I should be sorry else.
MOROSE: What say you, lady? Good lady, speak out.
EPICOENE: I should be sorry, else.
MOROSE: That sorrow doth fill me with gladness! Oh, Morose, thou art
happy above mankind! Pray that thou mayest contain thyself. I
will only put her to it once more, and it shall be with the utmost
touch and test of their sex.

(2. 5. 53–66)

So the catechism continues, to Morose's complete satisfaction: another long self-congratulatory tirade ends in full soliloquy ('Oh my felicity. How I shall be reveng'd . . .'). In the first encounter, the noise and speech-phobia of Morose has been outwitted by Epicoene's strategy of minimal speech (with Truewit's prompting 'wit' behind her); and it is appropriate that in the folly of his isolation Morose should reveal (to the audience) his futile desire to use his marriage to the silent woman as a means to revenge. The fullness of detail in that speech (the hated nephew's knighthood 'shall be the tenth name in the bond, to take up the commodity of pipkins and stone jugs') amounts to a grotesque parody of the private mind's voice: monologue as a vehicle of monomania. In the second encounter (3. 5), the Jonsonian plot brings, along with the moral, a linguistic revenge. The automaton-like (i.e. dehumanised) silent woman suddenly asserts herself and, in defending her right to receive visitors, bursts into a hyper-articulate and alliterative torrent of words:

EPICOENE: [. . .] Shall I have a barricado made against my friends, to be barr'd of any pleasure they can bring in to me with honourable visitation?
MOROSE: Oh Amazonian impudence!

Beyond the germinal feminist comedy (within the anti-feminine tone of the play), we recognise the full parody of the conversational framework in its reversal: the passive speaker turns tyrannous, and the tyrannically dominant speaker is reduced to vexed lamentation. However, at this point Jonson shifts the weight of linguistic satire away from the Morose–Epicoene encounter, to our partial disappointment, I think. Truewit takes over to torment Morose directly with a grotesque catalogue of what might be done to revenge the barber who has schemed against him. In a later scene (5. 3) Truewit arranges the prolonged verbal torture of Morose by a mock-divine and a mock-lawyer (Otter and Cutbeard in disguise), who expound the *duodecim impedimenta* that might warrant divorce: a superb burlesque litany (in Latin, out of Thomas Aquinas) culminating in a judicial debate on the husband's degree of impotence, simulated or manifest. The comedy of language then shifts to the comedy of sex (and it has been argued that the deviation from the norms of oral communication is inseparably linked to deviation from the norms of manliness).[50]

In the present context we should recall features of the witty dialogue in *The Silent Woman* which at least foreshadow the social world and the wit of Restoration Comedy. It is not surprising that *The Silent Woman* was regarded as a 'model' comedy by both Dryden and Congreve.[51] We saw one example in the Morose–Epicoene duologue: the would-be husband ironically quizzing his prim and silent wife-to-be: how can such a woman live up to the courtly expectations of 'quickness of wit'? The text of the play is shot through with little local debates on the uses of wit (a point that cannot be followed up in detail here). In the opening scene, 'wit' is brought into the foreground as its own subject: debated by Clerimont and Truewit (whose very names anticipate the names of Restoration Wits) in conversational badinage, unusually light in texture for Jonson. Clerimont declares that a preoccupation with morality can only damage wit: 'Foh, thou hast read Plutarch's Morals now . . . 'fore God, 'twill spoil thy wit utterly' (1. 1. 59–67). This opposition – 'moral' versus 'witty' – is still being voiced near the end of the play, once more by Clerimont: 'Faith, now we are in private, let's wanton it a little and talk waggishly' (5. 1. 24–5). That tone we recognise: it is to be heard again and again, in Restoration Comedy, and beyond it in Wilde and Coward. The comparison is right, as long as we keep it in proportion. Dryden implied that Truewit was too much of a scholar, 'with an allay of pedantry'. Barish defined the right balance: 'Truewit's cavalier tone, his urbane interest in mistresses and social trifling, contribute much to the manner of his Restoration descendants, but the latter have a way of licking their lips over a good antithesis that would have spelled affectation in Jonson.'[52] Apart from genteel, anti-serious wit, Jonson also introduces samples of pseudo-wit: the dialogue of chattering and backbiting characters: Amorous La Foole (styled a 'windfucker'), John Daw ('a mere talking mole'), and the Ladies Collegiate (who will test a candidate's wit before admission to membership). Their vain affectations of speech anticipate the ladies of preciosity in Molière (*Les Précieuses ridicules*), while the subject of their talk gives a foretaste of the lechery of Lady Fidget's coterie in Wycherley's *The Country Wife*.

Jonson's strongest link with Shakespearian comedy is not in the texture of wit in the dialogue, where punctilious decorum and the thrust of parody often work against the playful and sympathetic exchange of wit. The link is in the gargantuan linguistic appetite, feeding on all kinds of speech: the demotic word-noises of the market-place, the verbal vanities of the erudite and, above all, the jargon of charlatans. All that speech-food gives energy to the parodic wit that controls the dialogue. Jonson's link with the dialogue of the more limited Restoration Comedy is most marked in the 'easy' and 'pliant' conversation – and the advent of tittle-tattle – just noted in *The Silent Woman*. One may support that link by recalling that Jonson himself seems to have brought nearer the concepts of a 'comedy of humours' and a 'comedy of manners' in a late critical text, in the Folio edition of *Every Man in His Humour* (1616), which offers a revised definition of *humour*: 'It is a gentleman-like monster, bred, in the speciall gallantrie of our time, by affectation; and fed by folly.'[53] If Jonson's dialogue receives and magnifies the speech of the out-witting or out-witted monster, the dialogue of Restoration Comedy begins to register, more minutely, the wit of special gallantry, affectation, folly.

4. The 'in-wit' of Restoration Comedy

The uses of wit are both narrower and more central in the dialogue of Restoration Comedy than in any other mode of comedy before and after its efflorescence. Narrower, for gone is the playful generosity and metaphorical force of Shakespeare's love-wit, and gone the hyperbolic exuberance and moral clarity of Jonson's out-witting. More central, for wit in the new age signifies both a key value and a key style – not to say a totem in the self-consciously courtly and anti-puritanical culture of the period.[54] Wit is what a new hedonistic and genteel élite sets against earnestness and even seriousness, especially in love relationship; and wit is what is expected from all *talk*, so that rare is the character who is not a would-be wit. Never before, not in Jonson, not in Molière, has drama spawned such a gallery of strainers after wit, the False Wits epitomised by names like Sir Fopling Flutter, Sparkish, Witwoud and the rest. The status symbol of the age itself is wit. Repartee, as Dryden said, has become '*the very soul of conversation*'; and conversation the pivot of social life. 'What indeed can any one mean, when he speaks of a fine gentleman, but one who is qualified in conversation, to please the best company of either sex?'[55] Harcourt in Wycherley's *The Country Wife* (1. 1. 197–9) sees even the love-chase as a means to an end: 'if [mistresses] are used discreetly, you are the fitter for conversation by 'em'. The dialogue of comedy absorbs the 'talk of the town', not just of the court (Etherege must have done a certain amount of eavesdropping on promenades in St James's Park), and the new conversational prose often has a distinctly mimetic ring about it. That much can be said, provided we allow for the patterning and heightening of wit: recalling Congreve's justification of larger-than-life characters and language in *Concerning Humour in Comedy* (1695): 'I believe if a Poet should steal a Dialogue of any length, from the *Extempore* Discourse of the two Wittiest Men upon Earth, he would find the Scene but coldly receiv'd by the Town.'[56]

The new conversational wit-combat uses a prose language that is at once plainer and more analytical than anything that has gone before. That is what one would expect from the first post-Newtonian age, with its sceptical outlook and rational stylistic aims. Nurtured by the Royal Society, these aims included: 'to return back to the primitive purity and shortness' (bringing into a degree of stylistic fellowship scientists, puritans, and sensualists); and *'a close, naked, natural way of speaking* . . . bringing all things as near to the Mathematical plainness as they can . . . preferring the language of Artisans, Countrymen, and Merchants, before that of Wits and Scholars'. (Thomas Sprat, *The History of the Royal Society of London* (1667), emphasis added.)[57] But since when, one may ask, is wit all that mathematical or plain? One answer, based on N. N. Holland's context in *The First Modern Comedies*, would connect three levels – philosophical, relational and stylistic. The new 'mathematical' world view – which absorbed Newton, with chunks of Cartesian as well as empiricist metaphysics – disseminated a scepticism concerning all 'appearances' or secondary qualities based on sense impressions. The outer universe had become, in Whitehead's words, 'soundless, scentless, colourless'; and the social/personal world relative and insecure. So, in relationship, the spectacle of 'mere appearances' cast doubt on any possibility of knowing the 'true self' and other minds. This reinforced the growing mania for concealment and disguise in every way: in role-playing, double dealing, and dissembling talk.[58] It also reinforced hedonism. Against the emptiness of spatio-temporal relations, the characters of Restoration Comedy play out social/sexual/verbal games – hardly ever in full personal relationship. Wit offers, at least, the precarious appearance of gaiety between fits of passion and petulance: a surface dialogue which both softens and energises the 'love-chase'. The mythic/-metaphoric resonances of Renaissance wit (of both Shakespeare and Jonson) give way to a dialogue of lightly rational similitudes (a more linear, or 'metonymic' language in Roman Jakobson's sense). A narrower wit, but not a single style, and not monotonous (as L. C. Knights argued).[59]

The combat of wit itself is relatively off-centre and unstable – with shifting values and styles – in Restoration Comedy. Even in Etherege's *The Man of Mode* and in Congreve's *The Way of the World* (our key examples) we find, in comparison with *Much Ado about Nothing*, a less fully structured and less finely textured wit-combat.

Moreover, much of the wit in Restoration Comedy is not a combat of wit (as defined earlier), but something different: the cackling verbal self-display of False Wits (usually linguistic satire, as in Jonson) or else the not all that witty banter of sensual couples. Congreve probably had the most stable sense of distinction between True Wit (the expression of character) and False Wit (affectation) – a follower of Jonson in this respect. But this conception of wit itself can tilt the centre of comedy towards a sincere/ sympathetic couple and their plain dialogue, surrounded by the verbal filigree of false wits. *The Double Dealer* (1694), Congreve's second comedy, may well illustrate the difficulty of finding a norm for 'true' lovers and 'true' wit in the Restoration world of dissembling or affected wit. The central couple, Mellefont and Cynthia, is not so much gay and witty as sincere and serious; and around them twitter and twirl an assortment of foolish couples, including would-be wits like Brisk, 'a pert coxcomb', and Lady Froth, lover of the Muses. (The parody of the literati is, by the way, an interesting aspect of affected wit in this comedy.) In the following encounter Brisk is 'surprised' by Lady Froth who has overheard him sighing her name amid carefully rehearsed gestures of amorous play-acting (he declines to rehearse his speech as well, 'for witty Men, like rich Fellows, are always ready for all Expences'):

BRISK: But did I really name my Lady Froth?
LADY FROTH: Three times aloud, as I love Letters – But did you talk of Love? O Parnassus! Who would have thought Mr. Brisk could have been in Love, ha, ha, ha. O Heav'ns I thought you cou'd have no Mistress but the Nine Muses.
BRISK: No more I have I'gad, for I adore 'em all in your Ladyship – Let me perish, I don't know whether to be splenatick, or airy upon't; the Deuce take me if I can tell whether I am glad or sorry that your Ladyship has made the Discovery.
LADY FROTH: O be merry by all means – Prince Volscius in Love! Ha, ha, ha.[60]
BRISK: O barbarous, to turn me into Ridicule! Yet, ha, ha, ha. The Deuce take me, I can't help laughing my self, ha, ha, ha; yet by Heav'ns I have a violent Passion for your Ladyship, seriously.
LADY FROTH: Seriously? Ha, ha, ha.
BRISK: Seriously, ha, ha, ha. Gad I have, for all I laugh.
LADY FROTH: Ha, ha, ha! What d'ye think I laugh at? Ha, ha, ha.
BRISK: Me I'gad, ha, ha.
LADY FROTH: No the Deuce take me if I don't laugh at my self; for hang me if I have not a violent Passion for Mr. Brisk, ha, ha, ha.

BRISK: Seriously?
LADY FROTH: Seriously, ha, ha, ha.
BRISK: That's well enough; let me perish, ha, ha, ha. O miraculous, what a happy Discovery. Ah my dear charming Lady Froth!
LADY FROTH: Oh my adored Mr. Brisk!

Embrace.
(4. 6. 27–60)

This broadly operatic parody of posturing romantic attitudes – with laughter arias for 'serious passion' – speaks for itself both on the page and in performance (as in the National Theatre production, 1978–9). The parody is broad, clearly targeted, and comparable to other parodied encounters between would-be lovers and would-be wits in this play. Even so, Congreve saw fit to underline the norm by making Cynthia the mouthpiece for reflections which 'place' Fool-wit for the audience. In an earlier scene (3. 12) Cynthia is given a soliloquy to muse ironically upon the self-styled witty talk of the Froths and Brisk: 'Why should I call 'em Fools? The World thinks better of 'em; for these have Quality and Education, Wit and Fine Conversation, are receiv'd and admired by the World – If not, they like to admire themselves.' Cynthia becomes the non-comic heroine of the comedy, judging practically the whole 'scene' enacted around her. It is not then surprising that she speaks with perceptive irony about the *risky* certainty of a love encounter through sympathy, instead of indulging in the predominant relationship of the love-chase (with its thrilling insecurity and wit-combat):

CYNTHIA: I'll lay my life it will never be a Match.
MELLEFONT: What?
CYNTHIA: Between you and me.
MELLEFONT: Why so?
CYNTHIA: My mind gives me it won't – because we are both willing; we each of us strive to reach the Goal, and hinder one another in the Race; I swear it never does well when the Parties are so agreed – For when People walk Hand in Hand, there's neither overtaking nor meeting: We Hunt in Couples where we both pursue the same Game, but forget one another; and 'tis because we are so near that we don't think of coming together.[61]
(4. 1. 8–20)

This seems more introspective, more self-conscious than anything in earlier Restoration Comedy – or for that matter in Shakespearian comedy. It may even seem modern to us: its language of

155

self-critical awareness, in the midst of illusionist games, fore-shadows a dramatic world like Schnitzler's Vienna. Cynthia's quiet, analytical wit is, clearly, being exercised at the expense of wit in its dangerous sense – repartee, banter, wordplay and the rest. And there is no 'combat' here at all; the couple almost agree to 'steal out of the house this very Moment and marry one another' – a relatively uninteresting proposition for the fourth act of a Restoration comedy. In perspective, we know that Congreve is moving towards 'sincerity' – that difficult value in a culture of wit (a point to return to). Locally, we have a duologue that is, in its structure, syntax, rhythm, and vocabulary, the language of authentic encounter. From the simple question-and-answer of genuine inquiry ('What?' / 'Between you and me.' / 'Why so?') to the muted wit of Cynthia's cadenced speech, the speakers are engaged in exploring each other's thoughts. They 'correspond'.

Like blatant self-display and sincere communication, the directly sexual encounter is not particularly conducive to witty dialogue. In Etherege's *The Man of Mode* (1675–6), 4. 2, the scene that opens with the valet tying up bed linen, Dorimant and Bellinda talk thus to one another in their intimate farewell:

DORIMANT: What does that sigh mean?
BELLINDA: Can you be so unkind to ask me? – well –
Sighs
            Were it to do again –
DORIMANT: We should do it, should we not?
BELLINDA: I think we should: the wickeder man you to make me love so
           well – will you be discreet now?
DORIMANT: I will –
BELLINDA: You cannot.
DORIMANT: Never doubt it.
BELLINDA: I will not expect it.
DORIMANT: You do me wrong.[62]

(4. 2. 10–19)

And so on, with variations, for another thirty-two lines. Clearly *what* is being said here matters minimally; the speeches are contrived – an early use of naturalistic subtext – to give the actors a chance to convey the *how* of the couple's speech, in shared verbal rhythms of post-coital lingering. It is 'intimate' in the modern, almost cinematic sense, and justifies one's view of Etherege as the real master of casual conversational nuances throughout *The Man of Mode*. But the couple is having an *im*personal relationship in a language of languid non-wit. It is the exact opposite of the old language of wooing in wit-combat. *That* language Dorimant, the reformed rake-hero, has to re-learn – together with its strategy of feigned detachment and concealed love – when challenged by Harriet, who is accomplished in using her wit both as a verbal shield and as a lure.

In the openly sexual encounter Dorimant (whose Don Juanism was based on the real-life pursuits of Rochester) can afford *not* to resort to wit. It is enough for him to talk in a relaxed twosome: that mixture of bland speech and knowing tone which has become modish, once more, in our own permissive society. (His other style is a brutal language of abuse for the discarded mistress, Loveit.) It is only when Dorimant rediscovers the love-chase – where the would-be lovers are 'on level' as consciously self-concealing antagonists – that he rediscovers the old mode of the combat of wit. Dorimant's wooing of Harriet has *some* of the elements of the Shakespearian combat, the Beatrice and Benedick pattern of genuine love growing under the disguise of wit. But, before we look at a sample of their dialogue, we must recall the essential difference: Dorimant remains a predatory rake-hero throughout the comedy; and Harriet also has about her something rapacious, the country girl who can use her superior beauty and wit to out-wit her two rivals ruthlessly. A degree of self-interest, commercial advantage (Harriet has a fortune), and sheer malice is present in the realistic/experiential world of Etherege;[63] Shakespeare, we recall, removed comparable elements of bitter conflict from the world of the combative lovers to the subplot in *As You Like It* and *Much Ado*. The degree of conflict – the latent hostility – is immediately apparent in the first encounter of Dorimant and Harriet: where the couple engage in a verbal battle over quite elaborate metaphors of playing/gambling as a cover for the stakes in their sex-duel:

DORIMANT: I have been us'd to deep Play, but I can make one at small Game, when I like my Gamester well.
HARRIET: And be so unconcern'd you'l ha' no pleasure in't.
DORIMANT: Where there is a considerable sum to be won, the hope of drawing people in, makes every trifle considerable.
HARRIET: The sordidness of mens natures I know makes 'em willing to flatter and comply with the Rich, though they are sure never to be better for 'em.
DORIMANT: 'Tis in their power to do us good, and we despair not but at some time they may be willing.

HARRIET: To men who have far'd in this Town like you, 'twould be a great Mortification to live on hope; could you keep a Lent for a Mistriss?
DORIMANT: In expectation of a Happy Easter, and though time be very precious, think forty daies well lost, to gain your Favour.

(3. 3. 74–83)

This last phrase, the direct confessional utterance, is too unwitty for the witty Harriet, and she immediately calls her escort to walk away from Dorimant (in the Mall). However, the Restoration audience probably needed that direct and personal 'to gain your Favour' as a clue to the emotional ambivalence of the dialogue; just as Etherege found it necessary to 'frame' the whole exchange with Harriet's aside confessing her tender feelings for Dorimant: 'I feel [as great] a change within; but he shall never know it' (line 66). Otherwise the evasiveness of the combative couple might evade immediate comprehension. Such a dialogue sequence is, at any rate, more indirect and subtle than are the famous *double entendres* of the 'china scene' in *The Country Wife*, 4. 3; but then Etherege has moved quite a long way from Wycherley towards modernity, towards verbal games as 'territorial' testing (something now found in Pinter's erotic plays, e.g. in *The Collection*). The self-conscious play-acting needs pointing by the actors' tone and gesture: 'I can make one at small Game, when I like my Gamester well' is a species of verbal ogling; a somewhat crude variation on the theme of the 'coy mistress' attended by the patient cavalier. It is the texture of the dialogue that dictates such erotic-histrionic gestures. The syntax and rhythm (especially in the second exchange with its subordinate clauses and balanced cadences) is 'polite' without lightness. The absence of 'I' and 'you' pronouns (in several exchanges) and Dorimant's sententious rejoinders, further empty the duologue of personal dynamism, let alone tonal warmth. The vocabulary has a cumulative chill: not only through the keywords on gambling, winning and losing, but in the associated words indicating negative social/sexual states and attitudes: 'sordidness', 'flatter and comply', 'power', 'despair' and so on. No doubt, such lines *can* still be spoken in a light tone, but hardly with gaiety; and the contrary tone of measured hostility must be observed.

The whole context of the Dorimant and Harriet relationship confirms that their encounters are the kind of contest for 'favours' where every smile or pleasant word has to be fought for and is grudgingly given. Given, not in the 'merry skirmish' mood of *Love's Labour's Lost* and *Much Ado*, but with an underlying sense that every smile/look/pleasant word represents personal capital, to be invested with conscious calculation and heavily ironic detachment. Harriet, who is intelligently aware of the social rules of the game invented to let her male partner dominate, is determined to out-wit Dorimant's rake-wit: so every line she speaks is a way of scoring or scorning, to compel his surrender. Thus in their second encounter (4. 1. 110ff) Harriet justifies her 'demure curt'sy' and her look of scorn, which hurt Dorimant's vanity, by claiming for it 'nature' not just 'art', feeling not just dissimulation (though we know she is dissembling):

DORIMANT: Where had you all that scorn, and coldness in your look?
HARRIET: From nature Sir, pardon my want of art: I have not learnt the softnesses and languishings which now in faces are so much in fashion.

When Dorimant attempts to answer this 'sentimentally' by complimenting Harriet on the 'sweetness' of her face, Harriet snubs him, and a sustained combat of wit ensues over the gift of smiles. Harriet's wit gets more and more combative; Dorimant lapses into pleading ('Put on a gentle smile', line 127) and then into another aside on his undeclared love: 'I love her, and dare not let her know it . . . I fear sh'as an ascendant o're me and may revenge the wrongs I have done her sex' (lines 146–8). That aside may serve as an epitome of the dark emotions under the urbanity of 'in-wit'; Dorimant's melodramatic but justified fear of sexual revenge. It ushers in a duologue of anti-love; that is, a seemingly casual use of the word 'love' by Dorimant, prompts Harriet to combat love's language and gestures in a row of satirical sallies:

DORIMANT: Is the name of love so frightful that you dare not stand it?
HARRIET: 'Twill do little execution out of your mouth on me I am sure.
DORIMANT: It has been fatal –
HARRIET: To some easy Women, but we are not all born to one destiny, I was inform'd you use to laugh at Love, and not make it.
DORIMANT: The time has been, but now I must speak –
HARRIET: If it be on that Idle subject, I will put on my serious look, turn my head carelessly from you, drop my lip, let my Eye-lids fall, and hang half o're my Eyes – Thus while you buz a speech of an hour long in my ear, and I answer never a word! why do you not begin?

(4. 1. 159–69)

Clearly, this amounts to a taboo on tenderness; and a witty taboo on 'the true voice of feeling' in conversation. It is the Restoration equivalent of the parody of sonneteering and Petrarchan love-declaration in Shakespearian comedy (quite different from the later radical/Romantic taboo, where authentic love is unspeakable, as in Blake's 'Never seek to tell thy love'). But here, too, the Etherege duologue has a modern ring about it, with its self-conscious and style-conscious conflict over every inch of verbal territory. The gradual surrender of the rake ('male chauvinist') is marked by his incapacity to finish his increasingly un-witty sentences. To the end of the play Harriet remains the dominant speaker, the actress who holds the stage *within* the relationship ('my eyes – Thus'), and the superior wit. One of her last lines mimics and mocks not only the cries of the country, but also Dorimant's love-vow (and the prospect of Dorimant exchanging town for country in homage to Harriet): 'Methinks I hear the fateful noise of Rooks already – Kaw, Kaw, Kaw – There's music in the worst cry of London. My Dill and Cowcumbers to pickle' (5. 2. 414ff).[64]

Tone, values, phrasing (as in the last quotation) all remind us how essentially metropolitan is the wit of Restoration Comedy. The witty couple of Congreve's *The Way of the World* (1700) is, in this respect, in a direct line from Etherege's *The Man of Mode* (to be traced back to Dryden's *Secret Love* (1667)). Their combat is a form of pre-marital bargaining, a sex-duel for (aristocratic) equality. But the wit-combat in Congreve undergoes a further change, a culmination that is also an attenuation. For a start, the plot-dictated posture and strategy of the lovers, Mirabell and Millamant, is *less* combative: Mirabell is presented as a rake essentially reformed *before* the action of the play, while Dorimant's still dangerous sexual rapacity is being visibly and audibly tamed as part of the action in *The Man of Mode*; further, Millamant's wit does not have quite the sharp personal effrontery, nor the colloquial bite, of Harriet. *The Way of the World* enacts a love-game as distinct from a love-war. Though the latent aggression is there (and one particular production stressed the fortune-hunting greed of Mirabell and the 'dainty praying mantis' in Millamant),[65] the mellowing of wit seems to be the tonal norm. Such a reading fits the known tendency, in the last decade of the seventeenth century, for comedy to begin to move from cynical/neutral to sympathetic values. (The next stage is the exemplary/sentimental comedy, between Collier's puritanical attack on Restoration Comedy in his *Short View of the Profaneness and Immorality of the English Stage* (1968) and Steele's theory and practice of the 'weeping comedy' in *The Spectator*, no. 65 (1711) and in *The Conscious Lovers* (1722)).[66] Congreve himself moved towards values like 'sincerity' and 'integrity': seen in Mirabell, 'a Wit of the age of sense and sensibility. His predominant characteristic as a Truewit is his judgement rather than his fancy, and he is more addicted to *sententiae* than to similitudes' (to quote the somewhat overstated view of Fujimura).[67] Certainly Congreve took great care to distinguish between the quiet, meditative, non-ostentatious 'true wit' of Mirabell (as in the first encounter with Millamant in act two, see below), and the similitude-hunting, ostentatiously 'false wit' of Witwoud (in the scene immediately preceding the duologue).

Moreover, Congreve committed himself, in his Dedication, to something like a doctrine of purity in wit: by taking Terence (not Plautus), 'the most correct writer in the world', as his model in comedy: 'The purity of his Stile, and delicacy of his Turns, and the Justness of his characters.' Such qualities of style in dialogue had been nourished in Terence by: 'the Freedom of Conversation, which was permitted him with Lelius and Scipio, two of the greatest and most polite Men of his Age. And indeed, *the Privilege of such a Conversation*, is the only certain means of attaining to the *Perfection of Dialogue*' (emphasis added).[68] This interesting short manifesto on the conversational basis of dialogue should not be set aside just because Congreve used it, through comparing his own situation to that of Terence, to flatter the conversational art of his patron, the Earl of Montague; nor need the doctrine of the New Criticism on the 'intentional fallacy' make us ignore all authorial statements. For Congreve's intentions are written into the text:

MILLAMANT: I please myself; besides, sometimes to converse with fools is for my health.
MIRABELL: Your health! Is there a worse disease than the conversation of fools?
MILLAMANT: Yes, the vapours; fools are physic for it next to assafoetida.

MIRABELL: You are not in a course of fools?

MILLAMANT: Mirabell, if you persist in this offensive freedom, you'll displease me. I think I must resolve after all not to have you – we shan't agree.

MIRABELL: Not in our physic, it may be.

MILLAMANT: And yet our distemper in all likelihood will be the same; for we shall be sick of one another. I shan't endure to be reprimanded nor instructed; 'tis so dull to act always by advice, and so tedious to be told of one's faults: I can't bear it. Well, I won't have you, Mirabell. I'm resolved – I think – you may go. Ha, ha, ha! What would you give, that you could help loving me?

MIRABELL: I would give something that you did not know I could not help it.

MILLAMANT: Come, don't look grave then. Well, what do you say to me?

MIRABELL: I say that a man may as soon make a friend by his wit, or a fortune by his honesty, as win a woman with plain dealing and sincerity.

MILLAMANT: Sententious Mirabell! Prithee don't look with that violent and inflexible wise face, like Solomon at the dividing of the child in an old tapestry hanging.

MIRABELL: You are merry, madam, but I would persuade you for one moment to be serious.

MILLAMANT: What, with that face? No, if you keep your countenance, 'tis impossible I should hold mine. Well, after all, there is something very moving in a love-sick face – ha, ha, ha! – well I won't laugh; don't be peevish. Heigh-ho! Now I'll be melancholy, as melancholy as a watch-light. Well, Mirabell, if ever you will win me, woo me now. Nay, if you are so tedious, fare you well; I see they are walking away.

(2. 1. 393–427)

This duologue enacts a lovers' quarrel – that much is plain at once; but is it a combat of wit? It opens with a tussle of a conversation about conversation with fools (a variant of the witty discussion of wit itself in *Much Ado*). Mirabell is at first mildly witty ('You are not in a course of fools?') but then expresses a genuine grievance in fairly solemn language. (In the preceding group dialogue Millamant gloats ironically over the pain she has caused Mirabell by denying him a 'private audience'.) One might suppose the quarrel to belong to the convention we have been tracing, witty and combative. Yet, for a start, we notice how deliberately the 'grave' and 'sententious' and (by self-implication) 'plain-dealing' and 'sincere' Mirabell is opposed to the 'merry' Millamant. This may be an ingenious theatrical invention, exploiting the comedy of ill-temper for those who are watching Mirabell in good spirits (Millamant and the audience). However, it is not a dovetailing duet of wit. For Millamant herself is not all that witty here. She too lapses from the one witty repartee of the opening ('Yes, the vapours . . .') into at least mock-solemn dicta about their relationship ('And yet our distemper in all likelihood will be the same; for we shall be sick of one another'); and this line of attack soon gives way to the 'meant' language of the contrary woman ('I shan't endure to be reprimanded nor instructed'). This mild Shrew-posture may be situationally comic, but the language does not strike us as scintillating. As the scene develops, there are some Shakespearian echoes, notably Millamant's Rosalind-like challenge: 'Well, Mirabell, if ever you will win me, woo me now.' Even though one should not measure Congreve against the heights of Shakespearian comedy, it is clear that the challenge to 'woo' is not particularly wittily placed: it does not provoke a repartee (except perhaps in the form of a grimace or a gesture of disdain from Mirabell). What is more, situationally, there does not happen to be any wooing going on – either in disguise or in the guise of a witty skirmish. It is, again, a quarrel of engaged lovers: their courtship is too advanced for the insecurities and ambivalences that energise the wit-combat of *Much Ado* (with hostility over past misadventure in love written into the dialogue). This couple cannot become too intimate or 'serious' – in the manner of the Cynthia–Mellefont duologue in *The Double Dealer* – if it is to remain witty. Yet in their first duologue Mirabell and Millamant do talk to each other as if their relationship could be taken for granted – quite confidentially. 'And yet our distemper in all likelihood will be the same; for we shall be sick of one another' – is speculating on the dis-ease *within* the known relationship; it is assumed to have a future that is being somewhat threatened. And one exchange at least is strikingly inward and analytic:

MILLAMANT: What would you give, that you could help loving me?
MIRABELL: I would give something that you did not know I could not help it.

Mirabell is being at least as 'sincere' and perceptive and introspective as Cynthia in that other duologue from *The Double Dealer*; and it goes well beyond wit, which tends not to thrive on too much introspection. In short, Congreve, in modifying the combat of wit, creates quite a new type of dialogue, quite a strange blend of verbal styles. It might be said that that is the whole point of using and modifying a convention – a new blend of styles. That is so, but Congreve's blend is – within the context of wit-combat – precarious. Only the momentum of the acted encounter and, above all, the tonal/histrionic values of the lines keep up the impression of wit at all. The duologue is also structurally precarious for too much seems to depend on one scene: there is only this one sustained exchange and the 'proviso-scene' in act four. There are no intervening duologues between Mirabell and Millamant: there is no 'fall–rise' or other pattern to offer a dramatic pivot for the wit-in-love dialogue. Congreve has, then, compressed or telescoped the combat of wit into a measured scenic and verbal space.

All this is part of what one means by finding the wit-combat somewhat diminished in *The Way of the World* – more so than might be expected from general memory. That does not mean that memory is necessarily wrong, for I think that memory tends to crystallise around Congreve's theatrical tonalities in the texture of the dialogue and around the 'proviso-scene'. The tonal nuances are part of Congreve's art of miming conversation in such a way that it *advertises itself* as a style, an audible stylisation of the stress pattern, the shifts and intonations, of talk. What is new here, is the extent to which the dialogue depends on the delivery of the lines – on the speaking voice of the actor and, above all, the actress. We have here an eminently histrionic dialogue. More precisely, a dialogue for male/female voices written in an age that seems to have congratulated itself on the discovery of sexual differences, including the vocal organs, as well as on the replacement of the Elizabethan boy actor with illustrious prima donnas, like Congreve's Mrs Bracegirdle. The strong opposition of male/female tonalities is fairly constantly marked in the dialogue, intended to 'fascinate' the histrionic spectator. Millamant's lines are style-marked or cued for the 'feminine tone': 'Well, I won't have you, Mirabell. I'm resolved – I think – you may go. Ha, ha, ha' – where the punctuation, marking a coy pause or a provocatively hesitant resoluteness, is probably the most important 'sign' in the text of the dialogue. The tones also demand gestures, as in 'Sententious Mirabell!' – accompanied by something like Millamant waving her fan at Mirabell. Such tonal/histrionic effects *sound* witty even in lines not semantically witty.

Wit, on every level, in the best-known 'proviso-scene' of all (in act four), delightfully confirms that Congreve tends to compensate locally for a certain weakness in his overall use of the wit-combat convention. It helps to set this final duologue (as Kenneth Muir has done) against Dryden rather than Shakespeare; and to stress that Congreve is at his best in using a minor convention (the 'proviso-scene' is one, a convention-within-the convention of the full wit-combat). The comparison further illustrates Congreve's consummate skill in creating tonal nuances:

MILLAMANT: Ah, I'll never marry, unless I am first made sure of my will and pleasure.
MIRABELL: Would you have'em both before marriage, or will you be contented with the first now, and stay for the other till after grace?
MILLAMANT: Ah, don't be impertinent. My dear Liberty, shall I leave thee? My faithful Solitude, my darling Contemplation, must I bid you then Adieu? Ay-h adieu – My Morning Thoughts, agreeable Wakings, indolent Slumbers, all ye *douceurs*, ye *Someils du Matin*, adieu? I can't do't, 'tis more than impossible – Positively Mirabell, I'll lye a-bed in a Morning as long as I please.
MIRABELL: Then I'll get up in a Morning as early as I please.
MILLAMANT: Ah! Idle Creature, get up when you will – And d'ye hear, I won't be call'd Names after I'm Marry'd; positively I won't be call'd Names.
MIRABELL: Names!
MILLAMANT: Ay, as Wife, Spouse, my Dear, Joy, Jewel, Love, Sweetheart, and the rest of that nauseous Cant, in which Men and their Wives are so fulsomly familiar – I shall never bear that – Good Mirabell don't let us be familiar or fond, nor kiss before Folks, like my Lady Fadler and Sir Francis . . . Let us never Visit together, nor go to a Play together, but let us be very strange and well bred: Let us be as strange as if we had been marry'd a great while; and as well bred as if we were not marry'd at all.
(4. 1. 152–71; 4. 5 in World's Classics edn)

Set this extract against a representative duologue from Dryden's 'proviso-scene' in *Secret Love*:

CELADON: One thing let us be sure to agree on, that is, never to be jealous.

FLORIMEL: No; but e'en love one another as long as we can; and confess the truth when we can love no longer.
CELADON: When I have been at play, you shall never ask me what money I have lost.
FLORIMEL: When I have been abroad, you shall never inquire who treated me.
CELADON: Item, I will have the liberty to sleep all night, without your interrupting my repose for any evil design whatsoever.
FLORIMEL: Item, Then you shall bid me good-night before you sleep . . .

One can only agree with Kenneth Muir on the 'enormous superiority' of Congreve's dialogue. 'Dryden's lines are generalised, and they could have been spoken by almost any lovers on the verge of matrimony between 1660 and 1710; Congreve's are all perfectly in character, rich in detail, and continuously witty.'[69] One should add that the miming of 'the Freedom of Conversation' in an attempted 'Perfection of Dialogue' is once more a prominent feature in this exchange. Over and above *what* is being said (the endless fascination of marriage only on condition that . . .) *how* it is being said is vital. Witness the sudden switch from the evocative/wordly/socially-priviledged/ironic-rhetorical ('agreeable Wakings, indolent Slumbers, all ye *douceurs*, ye *Someils du Matin*, adieu') to the abruptly colloquial ('I can't do't . . .'); then the pseudo-rhyme of the 'turns' ('as I please / as I please' and 'Names / Names', backed up by the little dictionary of synonyms for 'wife'). All these are woven into the pattern of wit.

The Mirabell–Millamant duologues are the last of their kind. The fullness of the wit-combat – the collision and gradual maturing of the gaily interlocked courting couple, sustained throughout by a comedic structure – was not to be resuscitated. After Congreve, echoes and fragments of it make their way into playtexts – in Sheridan, Wilde, even in Shaw – but that is an art of allusion, of pastiche. The witty sex-duel then becomes a recognised 'old style', amusing partly because it recalls for the reader or audience those particular coded literary/theatrical resonances. The old wit-combat can still be used – a comedy of manners transformed into a comedy of mannerism – to re-enact (as in late Pinter) a familiar performance from the museum of the theatre.

4 The confessional duologue from Ibsen to Albee*

In Ibsen's later drama the dialogue of personal encounter, whereby two characters compel essential self-disclosures from one another through interlinked sessions of talk, reaches a new intensity and dimension. The duologue becomes central to the structure of action and develops unique features of style. As a general statement this may sound familiar, especially to the Ibsen critic, although there have been few studies of the dialogue, especially of the duologue, so far as I know.[1] The achievements of Ibsen's dialogue tend to be taken for granted, or else minimised, partly through hindsight gained from post-Ibsen drama which used, developed and conventionalised the once innovatory features of that dialogue. It had become the dominant mode of dialogue in naturalistic drama, which many later modern dramatists found it necessary to react against: to dislocate, or push towards a minimal and more implicit dialogue. If, however, our approach is from the past, through a quick 'retrospective method' – which should be acceptable in the Ibsen world – the innovatory force of Ibsen's duologues can be clearly seen.

In Sophoclean drama the relentless, ultimately destructive, quest for truth becomes a principle of action: Oedipus, for example, threatens the old Herdsman with torture for failing to disclose what he knows about the past (the guilt-laden origins of Oedipus himself). Question and answer interlock in a terrible inquisition until the Herdsman, aware that he is being asked 'to speak what is dreaded' (τῷ δεινῷ λέγειν, *Oedipus Rex*, line 1169) is gradually, line-by-line in the formal exchanges of stichomythia, forced to disclose the truth. But in this dialogue of confession the structure of action is almost everything, and the inward, psychological pattern is secondary. The inquisitorial exchange forces Oedipus to discover the *facts* of his origin and unconscious incest; his inward experiences are summed up in a four-line quasi-monologue; while the Herdsman's 'inner truth', the pain he finds in telling, is, as it were, a by-product of the exchange.

The central scenes of Shakespeare's major tragedies do embody the conscious self-expression of interacting characters, in full poetic complexity. Yet the great duologues of love (in *Romeo and Juliet* and in *Antony and Cleopatra*) and those of seduction and antagonism (in *Macbeth*, *Othello* and *Measure for Measure*) remain firmly action-centred and, despite their subtle psychology, are not primarily intended to enact a terrible process of mutual self-revelation through dialogue. The nearest approach to a confessional duologue in Shakespeare can be seen in the paradoxically distant intimacy of Hamlet and Horatio. Hamlet does reveal himself to Horatio, the 'just' man who is not 'passion's slave' (*Hamlet*, 3. 2. 60–72), bringing to the dialogue an integrity of self-expression and a naturalness of language otherwise only found in some of his soliloquies. But the duologue remains one-sided, Hamlet-dominated; Horatio remains relatively self-effacing and laconic, in keeping with the social convention between friends distanced by rank and the dramatic convention of the confidant.[2] In short, we are several stages from the sustained dual intimacy of the duologue in late Ibsen.

In Racine's purest tragedies, as in *Phèdre*, the action is centred on a series of confessions and revelations, reached tremblingly, through hints and indirections, which anticipate Ibsen and later drama. Nevertheless, even the most intimate confessional duologues of Phèdre retain a sublimity of expression which is at the opposite pole from 'the genuine, plain language spoken in real life' (Ibsen's conversational model for the communication of deeply felt experience). The degree of stylisation, or incantation, found in Racine as it were shields the characters from full person-to-person encounter. A tragic character like Phèdre is isolated in the midst of felt eloquence that only *seems* shared, by her confidante as well as by her potential lover, in a confessional duologue. The formal exchange of speeches gives rise to a *dialogue solitaire*.[3]

2.

This brief backward glance may help us to define Ibsen's duologues by underlining the elements of traditional drama that have been 'made new' and extended in *Rosmersholm* and the late plays. The Sophoclean quest for truth has been turned inward; and the confessional inwardness found in Hamlet speaking to Horatio, or Phèdre speaking to Oenone and Hippolyte, is converted into a full encounter of two interacting characters: a duologue fully expressing both duality and mutuality; Rosmer *and* Rebekka. These authentic duologues are then made central to the structure of action in an unprecedented way: they provide the most intense episodes while the plot around them – the intrigue of politics, the world of Kroll and Mortensgard – becomes a kind of carpentry for essences, or else a catalyst releasing self-revelation. The choice of a conversational model for deeper communication – something different from the 'imitation' of ordinary conversation, as we shall see – is a first, and precarious, attempt at expressing personal obsession, fantasy, dream and other fragments of the haunted mind, within the linguistic limits of standard speech. So transparent is such a conversational dialogue that the audience *seems* to recognise a replay of 'the way we talk', hardly aware of the degree of 'shaping'. In sum, the existential and structural heightening of the duologue coincides with a certain stylistic lowering (a seeming destylisation) of the language of personal encounter. Such a conjunction, of psychological complexity and linguistic transparency, was hardly possible before Ibsen. And soon after Ibsen (and after Strindberg and Chekhov) an increased self-consciousness, concerning both the inner mind and dramatic language itself, made the intimate duologue much more precarious. It is fortunate, in more than one sense, that *Rosmersholm* was a text for Freud and not the other way round; for the pre-Freudian and pre-modernist mode of Ibsen's duologues goes with a certain robustly 'naive' language (in Schiller's approving sense). In the further complexities of self and style in later European drama, characters, to adapt Judge Brack, don't *say* such things any longer.

In keeping with Ibsen's privileged status as a robust innovator in the first phase of modern drama, we repeatedly find, in the central duologues, that even the tentative, indirect, language of self-revelation is placed in a robust structure, like an intimate picture in a conspicuously gilded frame. There is a tension between the firm structure of dialogue and its delicate texture, corresponding to a tension between explicit and implicit speech,

between emphatic and groping self-expression. Take a para-
digm-like example from a late play. In *Little Eyolf* (1894) Allmers
returns from the mountains bearing within him the memory of
some great, self-transforming experience. He hints at it early in
the play and, under the pressure of questions from both Rita and
Asta, his half-estranged wife and his supposed half-sister, he
gradually unveils part of his experience, after these preliminaries:

RITA: *(exclaiming)* You've been through something while you were away.
　　　Don't say you haven't. Because I can see by the look of you.
ALLMERS: *(shaking his head)* Nothing at all – outwardly. But –
RITA: *(excitedly)* But – ?
ALLMERS: But inwardly – there's certainly been a minor revolution.
RITA: Good heavens!
ALLMERS: *(soothing her and patting her hand)* Only to the good, Rita, my
　　　dear. You can rest assured of that.
RITA: *(sitting on the sofa)* Now you must tell us about this at once. All about
　　　it!
ALLMERS: *(turning to Asta)* Yes, let us sit down too. Then I'll try and tell
　　　you. As best I can. *(He sits on the sofa beside Rita. Asta pulls a chair
　　　across and sits near him. There is a moment's pause.)*
RITA: *(looking at him unexpectedly)* Well, now – ? . . .

(pp. 227–8)

And so on, through further preliminaries, which Allmers himself
calls a 'sort of introduction', until the subject of Allmers' metamorphosis up in the mountains (which makes him put the crip-
pled child Eyolf in the centre of his life instead of the great book
on 'Human Responsibility') is broached. There is a further, more
inward, almost numinous, experience hidden within the confessed metamorphosis; but the revelation of that inner core of
experience is postponed until near the end of the play (where it is
given such significance, by both the frame and the emphatic
speech, that it seems to 'outshadow' the more direct action of
Eyolf's death, and the painful discoveries of Asta and Allmers
concerning their unfulfillable relationship). In a full confessional
duologue with Rita this strange experience, outside the actional
but within the thematic pattern of the play, is communicated by
Allmers (in an image that recalls the meeting with the Strange
Passenger in the fifth act of *Peer Gynt*): 'It seemed as though death
and I were going along like two good travelling companions'
(p. 278). But before we reach this inner core of the confession, we

witness once more the ritual of preliminaries, the attention-raising hints, which cease to be hints through repetition; and there, again, the solemn command to sit – on the bench by the summerhouse, as earlier on the sofa – is twice repeated. The frame for the confessional is a signalling pattern, a sustained ritual.

But is it not perverse, it may be objected, to point to the frame – functional and empty as it may seem – when it is the core of the duologue, the experience conveyed, that matters? My point is that this ritual of preliminaries in the confessional duologue is both typical (it keeps re-appearing) and significant. Structurally, Ibsen needs the confessional prologue to carry transition, suspense and warning signals to the audience; existentially, it marks the first steps in a descent towards deeper communion, the tremor before the taboo on speech is broken; linguistically, it marks the importance of 'naturalness' – people hesitate, repeat themselves, and go on hinting until their hints become explicit. (In later drama hints give way to subtler evasion or else to cruder attack.)

The explicitness of this groping towards an increasingly inward and authentic duologue can be traced back, briefly, to the well-made-play's 'visible' carpentry in the early plays. Bernick's confession of his guilt, in the final 'truth-telling' scene of *Pillars of Society* (1877) has about it an actor-politician's address to a stage audience. Although ostensibly he is responding to the pressures of a duologue with Lona, the woman who embodies his conscience, the confessional speech itself is external, morally ambiguous, and cliché-ridden. The dialogue of the famous 'discussion' that brings to an end *A Doll's House* (1879) with Nora's declaration of new-found independence, is essentially the climax of the play's argument, not a fully personal encounter. This is repeatedly confirmed in performance. The final exchanges between Nora and Torvald (as Raymond Williams judged) do not represent a 'living confrontation between actual people, but are rather straight, single declaration'. Torvald's questions are 'rhetorical questions and could, essentially, be all spoken by Nora herself'.[4] Nora's transformation springs from what she has just witnessed (her husband's totally disillusioning, self-centred response to their mutual crisis) and this transformation takes place in her mind, in the *silence* before she sits down, and bids Torvald to sit down, to communicate her resolution. The ensuing debate-duologue clarifies her new state of mind but does not itself transact the change, or change the speakers through what is being said.

The duologues in *Ghosts* (1881) are much more complex. Those between Mrs Alving and Oswald certainly have a far greater emotional intensity than those between her and Pastor Manders (where the confessional urge is damped by the Pastor's willed conventional language, so that the repressed passion of one-time potential lovers is barely allowed to resonate – as it does in the key duologues of later plays). Moreover, the duologues of mother and son are spaced out and structured with great mastery: from Oswald's first and partial revelation of his illness in act two (where the ritual frame, the verbal preliminaries and the sofa, become an essential antidote to the horror), to Mrs Alving's counter-confession, prompted by Oswald's ghost-laden talk of joy, *livsglede*, and interrupted by Pastor Manders on the threshold of disclosure:

MRS ALVING: *(who has been listening eagerly, rises, her eyes big with thought and says)* Now I see the connection.
OSWALD: What is it you see?
MRS ALVING: I see it now for the first time. And now I can speak.

(p. 154)

The careful preparation and underlining – signalling listen, an important disclosure is about to be made – becomes an element in the play's suspense, further enhanced when Mrs Alving's counter-confession is interrupted by Pastor Manders and postponed until act three. At that point, the painful insight into the *sammenheng*, the connection (the recognition that Oswald's father was driven into dissipation by a conventional and repressive marriage) is mixed up with the revelation that Regina is the illegitimate offspring of that dissipation. Regina is present, the duologue between mother and son is thereby extended; but though this fits in well with Ibsen's dramatic scheme, and further underlines the terrible irony of inheritance (Oswald's shattered hope to find in Regina a nurse-wife), it also smacks of well-made-play intrigue. The full authenticity of encounter is recaptured only in the final duologue, where Oswald reveals the imminent symptoms of syphilis (not named) and begs his mother to accept the task of administering a mercy-killing drug when the time is ripe. (This dialogue clearly breaks a long-held social and personal taboo; the son is allowed to demand from his mother a sacrifice for which there seems no precedent in drama before Ibsen. We need to recapture the terror of such taboo-breaking utterance, reflected in the otherwise so absurdly hostile reactions to the play a hundred years ago. At all events, that taboo is a good deal nearer to our own sensibility than, let us say, Antigone's horror at finding her brother lying unburied.)

The final duologue of *Ghosts* is so extreme and so compressed that it takes the speakers beyond the personal, in the sense of the individually personal as explored in later Ibsen duologues. What mother and son say to one another moves towards the elemental. Oswald tells of inexorable facts; Mrs Alving is faced with an unbearable dilemma, not worked out within the play; beyond that, the play points to a trans-personal situation, the emblematic mother–son relationship, a profane *pietà*, as in a demythologised morality play. Within that frame there is no outlet, no 'leisure', for full and mutual self-recognition, leading to self-transformation, as later in *Rosmersholm*. The language itself has something elemental and emblematic about it:

OSWALD: Well then, it's you that must come to the rescue, mother.
MRS ALVING: *(screams aloud)* I!
OSWALD: Who is nearer to it than you?
MRS ALVING: I! your mother!
OSWALD: For that very reason.
MRS ALVING: I, who gave you life!
OSWALD: I never asked you for life.

(p. 168)

Here the verbal exchange, with its semblance of argument and simple rhetoric (the 'I' calls), becomes a primary dialogue – a notation for cries. It can be seen as one of the first attempts, within naturalism, to make characters in intimate encounter speak 'the unspeakable'; and it anticipates the inarticulacy of broken speech and screams in later modern drama.[5] And when Oswald collapses, the duologue, and with it the play, ends, appropriately, with fragmented speech, repetitions, whispers and cries.

The duologues of *Rosmersholm* (1886), as already suggested, extend and deepen the functions of the intimate duologue significantly. The final confessional duologue between Rosmer and

Rebekka is unique: through it a sustained duel of opposed temperaments and values reaches a climax – vision and voice in unison in a duet of self-transformation. Ibsen has succeeded in returning the theatre to the interaction of two inwardly linked minds, without that final immobility of near-solipsism which in the last plays, especially in *John Gabriel Borkman*, turns dialogue at times into double monologue. In keeping with this happy paradox of inward interaction through words, Ibsen avoids excessive reliance on the relatively static device of introspection, or on the relatively novelistic device (as Szondi argued)[6] of retrospection. The words are still exploratory, testing a new experiment in living now (however burdened by the 'death-instinct'); and testing also the validity of *what* is being said by *how* it is being said. For these two, authentic action can only issue from authentic verbal exchange.

The language of this concluding dialectic of two minds is, correspondingly, at once compressed and fluid, carefully shaped and natural (by which I mean something distinct from raw naturalistic language in drama).[7] The final duologue is made up of an inner series of circling confessions akin to the movement of the outer series of confessions in the play (which cannot be traced in detail here): circling towards the centre of 'truth' from the circumference of evasion and half-admission. The outer series of confessions passes from the tense intimate duologue of Rosmer and Rebekka at the end of act two (including the ambivalent rejection of Rosmer's offer of marriage which aroused Freud's interest)[8] to the compulsive, but only half-true disclosure of her manipulative role in driving Beata to suicide, in the confession made to Rosmer in the presence of Kroll (as catalyst and domestic chorus) at the end of act three. The threads of intrigue and hidden passion are inextricably woven together in this pattern – in a dual style of declaratory statement and cryptic suggestion. The two threads and the two ways of speaking come together in the final duologue, in which the opening 'circle' presents estranged friends on the threshold of separation circling *away* from the intimate centre they had reached earlier (in the act two duologue just mentioned). The intimate form, *du*, remains, but otherwise the opening is a verbal game bent on evading the confessional urge ('My dear, don't let's talk about that now' p. 105). Then, with a sudden reversal, in response to Rosmer's self-doubt and charge of lying,

Rebekka chooses the present moment to grope her way towards a key confession:

ROSMER: Have you still more to confess?
REBEKKA: I still have the main thing.
ROSMER: What 'main' thing?
REBEKKA: The thing you've never guessed. The thing that gives light and
       shade to everything else.

(p. 106)

until, with pauses, further circling, and broken speech, Rebekka reaches the next circle: 'There came over me . . . this wild, uncontrollable passion.' The rhythm of utterance, at once urgent and hesitant, is to re-create for the audience, if only for a moment, the voice of the old, pre-Rosmer and pre-conversion Rebekka: which might have been an ecstatic voice urging Rosmer on and on (as Hilde Wangel drives her Master Builder up and up the tower) in a duologue of spiritual temptation with erotic undertones. Yet, with a total irony of situation and language, Rebekka now renews the taboo on fulfilled love and adapts to (in the bio-psychological sense) the grave and sublimated language of Rosmer and the Rosmer world: 'Peace of mind came down over me – like the stillness on the mountain-cliffs at home' (p. 108). The exchange of words amounts to full exchange of values and attitudes: Rebekka as convert to the puritanism of the Rosmer world, speaks in an 'ennobled' language.

Full communication – communion – is, even at this stage, inhibited, because Rebekka cannot bring herself to confess her fear of what happened in her past (the wholly unnamed fear of unconscious incest with her father) while Rosmer cannot overcome his self-doubt, or his doubting of Rebekka. And so, the next circle of confession enacts, in an authentic language, their distrust of the words they *had* spoken to one another, and of the words being spoken *now*. For Rebekka's former confession of duplicity has cast doubt on her new confession of fidelity. How can words alone 'verify' untested feelings, be made the evidence of things not seen? We have here a version of the Shakespearian tension between appearance and reality, which includes a tension between specious and trustworthy rhetoric:

REBEKKA: *(wringing her hands)* Oh, this murdering doubt! John – John!
ROSMER: Yes, it's terrible, my dear, isn't it? But I can't help it. I shall never
       be able to free myself from the doubt. Never know for certain
       that I have your love, whole and unflawed.

REBEKKA: But isn't there anything in the depth of your mind that assures
you that a change has come over me? And that the change has
come through you – through you alone?

ROSMER: Ah, my dear, I don't believe any longer in my power to change
people. I don't believe in myself in any way any more. I don't
believe in myself or in you.

REBEKKA: *(looking gloomily at him)* Then how are you to live your life?

ROSMER: That's what I don't know myself. I can't imagine. I don't see
that I *can* live it out. And I don't know, what's more, of anything
in the world it would be worth while to live for.

REBEKKA: Oh, life – it has a way of renewing itself.

(p. 111)

The more one attends to this exchange – in reading and in performance – the more authentic does the expression of Rebekka's
assurance of change, *forvandling*, as well as the countering fear
and doubt of Rosmer seem. The language of the dialogue itself,
authenticates the felt truth of what is being spoken: its spareness
or 'purity of diction', its quiet rhythm carried structurally by the
dovetailing of exclamation-question-declaration-question, by the
repetition of keywords (*live/life*) and by the crescendo of Rosmer's
haunted negatives: 'I don't believe . . . I don't believe in myself
. . . I don't believe in myself or in you. I can't imagine . . . I don't
see that I *can* live it out. And I don't know, what's more . . .' These
confessional utterances are, as it were, self-confirming – for the
audience.

But for the speakers themselves, words alone are no longer
certain good. So in the final circle, following the ironic counterpoint of Brendel's interruption, the duologue uses its own authenticity to show that the issue between Rosmer and Rebekka,
given their state of transformation *and* arrest, cannot be settled by
words, by confessional talk:

ROSMER: I will believe you on your bare word, this time too.

REBEKKA: Just words, John . . . How can you believe me on my bare word
after today?

(pp. 116–17)

The integrity of what has been spoken can only be tested by the
double suicide into which Rosmer, with self-confessed fascination of the horrible, tempts Rebekka with his challenges: 'You
draw back. You dare not do – what *she* dared' (p. 116). It is a brief
dialogue of temptation, which may seem an ironic reversal of

roles (since Rebekka was cast for the role of temptress in the play's retrospective action) and which completes the reversal of values (from passion to self-transcending death, *eros* into *thanatos*). The tension of the dialogue, actional and verbal, still testing alternatives, still open, probing and groping, is sustained to the end – where the ritual marriage vow brings a quiet consummation. That final sharing of values – 'For nu er vi ett' 'Now we are one' – is inseparable, as John Northam has shown,[9] from a *shared style*. The dualism of opposed personalities and worlds leads to oneness; the duologue ends by confirming the unison of speakers in the silence of extinction.

If in *Rosmersholm* the duologue remains throughout active and transformational – the words are the vehicles of subtle interaction between the speakers, here and now – in *John Gabriel Borkman* (1896) we have an early example in modern drama of a kind of post-actional dialogue. The three protagonists (anticipating from the start the 'one dead man and two shadows' of the end) are so to speak made to stand still on a platform or within a series of dramatic tableaux – to share a series of backward-looking confrontations, recognitions (of loss and betrayal) and a final epiphany (Borkman's vision). The whole play can be said to be constructed around the major duologues. Some of them, like the act-long re-encounter between the two sisters, are so long and sustained that one of the first things the director of the Norwegian television film of the play did was to reconstruct the duologues, interweaving those of acts one and two.[10] (For a duologue of that length and that degree of stylisation may seem, to a contemporary television audience, as much a theatrical construct as the monologue.) Structurally, the duologue is, then, more central than before; linguistically it is sparer – in the first three acts at times even stiff and static – until, in the final act, it modulates into the richly metaphoric language of Borkman's vision, stretching beyond personal dialogue, which may be said to lose the name of 'spoken action'. At first sight the act one duologue of the two sisters, Mrs Borkman and Ella Rentheim, seems particularly stiff and colourless: carrying a load of expository material (concerning Borkman's bankruptcy and present death-in-life) and the slow first round of the battle over the possession of Erhart (thematically important, but, in my view, less charged with felt life than are the past griefs of the protagonists).

But the dialogue gains tension through some built-in indirections which delay confessions otherwise imminent. Such indirections, or seeming impediments to full utterance, represent the formal social code of the speakers: they must sound polite, must seem circumspect (to one another and the audience) in their emotional brutality. For example, the 'unspeakable' is skirted thus:

MRS BORKMAN: *(provocatively)* I used those eight years, you see – while I had him under my eye.
ELLA RENTHEIM: *(controlling herself)* What did you say to Erhart about me? Is it anything you can tell me?
MRS BORKMAN: Oh yes, certainly.
ELLA RENTHEIM: Then do so, please.
MRS BORKMAN: I only told him what's true.
ELLA RENTHEIM: Well? (p. 302)

This use of words in a cat-and-mouse game (which depends on performance for full effect, and which seems to lose a good deal in translation) foreshadows the future dialogue of fierce evasion, within a subtext of banalities charged with emotion (as in Pinter). By contrast, the duologue between Ella and Borkman in act two is turned, from seemingly static retrospection into the mutual recognition of their potential love, lost in a pattern of repression:[11]

ELLA RENTHEIM: *(breathless)* Was that how it was with you then?
BORKMAN: I rather think it was.
ELLA RENTHEIM: That *I* was the dearest thing you had?
BORKMAN: Yes; something like that comes back to me.
(p. 330)

The rise in emotion (here indicated by the stage direction *breathless*) is partly a matter of context and cumulative pressure, but partly carried by this natural-seeming exchange whereby Borkman's almost casual admission of past love is matched by Ella's incredulous and painful discovery (soon to become rhetorically explicit).

But it is the transmuted duologue of Ella and Borkman in the final act that calls for further comment. For here we have, first of all, a remarkable correspondence between the structural, the scenic and the verbal transcendence of naturalism at one and the same time: as the backward-moving action suddenly turns to the future; and as those two move from the claustrophobic bourgeois parlour into a scenography of snow (which Edvard Munch called 'the most powerful winter landscape in Scandinavian art'),[12] their dialogue itself is freed from their constrained social and stylistic code – the spare and stiff language of encounter. Moreover, this metaphoric language is not wholly dependent on visual effects. (I myself recall a radio performance where the *alternate* symbolic landscapes of snow-and-ice and Rosmer's invisible kingdom – of mines and factories, and of death – were clearly counterpointed by words alone. And I am not quite sure how much is gained from seeing the new-fallen snow, etc., for the essential thing to be communicated is Borkman bursting out into the chilling clearness of winter air.)

The enrichment of the dialogue – expressing Borkman's personal vision through the imagery of that power-haunted *paysage intérieur* –is significant. But in the course of becoming rich and strange, the duologue, as interaction, also suffers a sea-change:

BORKMAN: . . . Ella! Do you see the mountain-ranges *there*, far away? One behind another. They rise up. They tower. *That* is my deep, unending, inexhaustible kingdom!

ELLA RENTHEIM: Yes, John, but there's a freezing breath coming from that kingdom!

BORKMAN: That breath is like the breath of life to me. That breath comes to me like a greeting from imprisoned spirits. I can see them, the millions in bondage . . . (*With outstretched hands.*) But I will whisper it to you here in the stillness of the night. I love you, where you lie as though dead in the depth and in the dark! I love you, you treasures that crave for life – with all the shining gifts of power and glory that you bring. I love, love, love you!

ELLA RENTHEIM: (*in silent, but rising emotion*) Yes, your love is still down there, John.

(p. 368)

This should be played and read, with the kind of pause that allows full realisation of the poignant irony: Borkman's vision is, from the point of view of relationship, a megalomaniac's final evasion of full encounter. As he turns from addressing Ella to declaring love to the mountains and their mines (strongly marked in the original by the untranslatable pronoun shift from *du* to the formal *jer* and *eder*), Borkman lets the intimate duologue swell into his self-obsessed monologue. The frame of the duologue is

179

kept at this stage only by Ella (who still desires intimate encounter) – the whole transition masterfully controlled by Ibsen. It remains to be noted that the texture of Borkman's speech is also ambivalent: it is both genuine self-expression and a piece of poetic property, an attack of bombast. It is one of the rare instances, in the prose plays, where Ibsen departs from what Knudsen called 'the idiomatic authenticity of the whole movement of speech' where 'the syntax had to ring true'.[13] It is, in short, an excursion into prose poetry, as distinct from the image-laden but spare poetry-of-the-theatre in *Rosmersholm*. It is a linguistic change appropriate to the change from dialogue as transformation to dialogue as epilogue: a final metamorphosis and recognition that is only partially embodied in an encounter of two minds in duologue. Ibsen is here creating a new mode of dialogue which, beyond its local interest, anticipates a future and problematic development: one speaker's 'excess' of speech, within dialogue, may become parodic (as in Gaev's address to the bookcase in the first act of *The Cherry Orchard*) or a symptom of dislocation, isolating speaker from speaker (ultimately the dialogue of Beckett's *pseudocouples*). Thus Ibsen opens up a new dimension of experience and expression – which is also a 'problem of style' – breaking the mould of strictly naturalistic dialogue in Borkman's epiphanic yet egocentric duologue.

3.

The confessional duologue has remained a central structural element in many forms of naturalistic drama for a remarkably long period of time, against the pressure of other modes, including patterns of dislocation in relationship and dialogue. O'Neill in his late plays – especially in *Long Day's Journey into Night* and in *Hughie*, the one-act play that is a virtual parable on the human need for self-disclosure – returned to the naturalistic duologue in search of both existential and verbal authenticity. Placed in the context of O'Neill's total work, and in the larger context of modern drama, O'Neill's late plays may seem 'backward-looking'. At the same time they point, over and above their intrinsic interest, to a recurrent mode of relationship and language;[14] O'Neill's rediscovery of this mode may indicate that we are dealing with a peculiarly stubborn, and, in our culture, still necessary structure.

In his ambitious expressionistic plays of the twenties, O'Neill attempted to go beyond interpersonal dialogue altogether: as in the rhythmic (poetic prose) monologues of Paddy and Yank in *The Hairy Ape* (1921) and in the elaborate 'thought asides' of *Strange Interlude* (1928–9), a version of 'audible thinking' where the characters reveal their unspoken responses, somewhat lacking in pressure and economy, saying little that could not be conveyed by subtly coded dialogue.[15] Then in *Mourning Becomes Electra* (1932–3), heightened prose dialogue is intended to absorb both the echoes of the Greek myth and the recognitions of the Freudian psyche. Viewed from a superficial version of avant-gardism, O'Neill's late return to 'mere' naturalism – to a dialogue of speech-in-character which is highly idiosyncratic – might seem a 'rearguard' action. Yet O'Neill was embarking on an adventurous new synthesis of styles, creating, in *Long Day's Journey*, a mode of dialogue flexible enough to express the interaction of four characters, through their memories and fantasies, in a language at once fluid and controlled, patterned yet spontaneous-seeming. Jean Chothia, who has illuminated this development in *Forging a Language*, notes that even in the expressionist plays O'Neill 'constantly veered towards sets and situations in which the familiar and human, as opposed to the remote or metaphysical, could be recreated and explored'.[16] The late plays mark then a mature efflorescence of O'Neill's special gifts for personal idiom in 'the vernacular', and for embodying personal encounter in dialogue.

The semblance of a certain stylistic anachronism in O'Neill's dramatic dialogue and play-form was highlighted, at the time of the first performance of *Long Day's Journey* (some fifteen years later than its date of composition in 1940–1) by the wider public's almost simultaneous discovery of Beckett's *Waiting for Godot* and Brecht's *Mother Courage* and the parable plays. Such a juxtaposition of three major modes of drama amounted to a critical windfall, for it sharpened our awareness of three distinct avenues of innovation within the 'imaginary museum' of the contemporary theatre. One of the more lasting critical insights of that direct experience in comparative drama was the acceptance of 'the line from Ibsen' – in O'Neill and in other dramatists[17] – as a continuing dramatic form and language. The 'conversational' mode of dialogue had retained its own validity and its own vitality, alongside the epic and the absurd theatre; all three modes offered immense potentialities – generative styles – for the future of drama. A play like *Long Day's Journey* demonstrated the value of an artistically renewed naturalism: the dialogue had to be moulded 'out of' familiar speech rhythms (in this instance out of the idiomatic speech of general American, with a partial use of Broadway slang) by a dramatist driven to write 'out of' the intolerable network of intimate family relationships. O'Neill had chosen the obsessions and torments of the nuclear family as his dramatic territory; both Brecht and Beckett had, on different ideological and artistic grounds, avoided it. In the context of post-Ibsen drama the family had come to signify – as in *Long Day's Journey* – a family of ghosts familiar to a whole culture: a community of isolates, a condition of separateness within inseparability. What is redemptive – it is difficult to avoid the loaded word – within such a tragic vision of destructive relationship is the urge towards 'truth-telling': the dialogue creates the conditions that allow the gradual emergence 'into the light' of suppressed knowledge, taboo subjects and dark family secrets. The sincerity of such revelations can only be made felt – as in Ibsen's major prose tragedies – through a language that *sounds like* the authentic 'dialect of the tribe': this family, this character, this tone, this kind of angry retort or sudden bid for reconciliation. In short, the 'natural' language of the dialogue is not just a medium but a value-carrying message – it is to guarantee or verify for the audience the 'genuineness' of the exchanges, of the in-fighting and the shared mutilations of personality.[18] And the structure of the dialogue must make it seem 'natural' that members of the family should be driven towards unmasking and self-disclosure. Although the overall structure of *Long Day's Journey* has a less relentlessly interactive logic than have comparable Ibsen plays, *Ghosts, Rosmersholm, Hedda Gabler* (at times the play seems to open up with Chekhovian flashes of incongruity and good humour) the axis of the dialogue remains the 'truth-seeking urge'. A kind of archaeological digging up of the characters' past provides much of the stuff of the dialogue, and its climaxes lead – with minimal direct action other than compulsive talking – to a series of self-disclosures, confessions.

The final act of *Long Day's Journey* is constructed to elicit – or provoke – just such a series of intimate confessions in two long duologues. That structuring around duologues is itself remark-able, for O'Neill had considerable skill in creating *group* dialogue: *The Iceman Cometh* is among the four or five most memorable plays ever scored for a large, many voiced-group, with precise dialects and idiolects. The two 'night-long' duologues crystallise out of a possible quartet of voices (Tyrone and Edmund, father and young-er son, followed by Edmund and Jamie, the older son, with Mary, the mother, cut off from the dialogue by her narcotised private world). What is being revealed is so intense and intimate that it can only be spoken 'naturally' between *two* characters. Nevertheless, the duologue-centred structure does not suffice for O'Neill, even though the emotional pressure is intensified through Mary's relapse into drug-addiction and Edmund's newly diagnosed consumption. He finds it necessary to create an even more palpable naturalistic release for the long speeches of self-revelation ('the terrible necessity of self-revelation', in Henry James's words) – drink. Drink must flow before the talk – to give an edge to the bitterness, and to provide the theatrical/natural occasions for slurred speech and drunken gesture. The dual advantage of the right measure of drunkenness as a confessional stimulant is made explicit by Jamie: next time he 'might not be drunk enough to tell you the truth. So got to tell you now'; and what he is about to tell his brother is 'Not drunken bull, but "in vino veritas" stuff. You better take it seriously' (p. 145). This is not only 'in character' for Jamie (though Tyrone and Edmund have also been spending the night drinking heavily) but also advertises the veracity – and the verisimilitude – of the confession to the audience. The word 'confession' is itself used by Jamie in a precise enough sense, coming from the descendant of Irish Cath-olics, to justify inflicting a terrible self-revelation on his younger brother. 'Feel better now. Gone to confession. Know you absolve me, don't you, Kid? You understand. You're a damned fine Kid' (p. 147).

Another device to create linguistic familiarity (probably over-familiarity, recalling the random confessions of a passenger in the railway compartment) can be seen in the explicit preambles and apologies offered around the confessional act: 'I've never admit-ted this to anyone before' (p. 130); 'maybe I shouldn't have told you' (Tyrone to Edmund, p. 132); 'You have just told me some high spots in your memories. Want to hear mine?' (Edmund to

Tyrone, p. 134). Such remarks constitute a formal communicative frame, which we recognise from Ibsen.[19] The over-explicit grounding of the major confessions between members of the Tyrone family must have been judged artistically necessary by O'Neill; yet *what* the characters say is not 'unspeakable'. Only Jamie's confession of deep jealousy towards his younger brother reveals an emotion, a degree of malice, normally difficult to divulge; Tyrone's remembrance of his wasted artistic talent, and Edmund's two speeches on his moments of inwardly discovered meaning, in the fog, and at sea, are not in themselves 'taboo' subjects (though alienation between the speakers must first be transformed into a degree of tenderness before such experiences can be voiced at all). It would seem more likely that the build-up of naturalistic probability is due to the speech-style that O'Neill reserves for the confessing character: long set speeches in heightened prose or, as with Jamie, the slangy, idiosyncratic tirade. Such heightened speech-making might jar on an audience that has been cued to a fairly strict type of naturalistic speech by the greater part of the playtext. In the preceding three acts the three male members of the family speak in relatively short, conversational 'turns', and with a fair degree of emotional restraint, trying to keep the tone of talk casual and low-keyed. (Only Mary's speech shows – under the impact of nervous anxiety and her gradual relapse into a drugged state – early symptoms of a pathological use of language: the syntax and rhythm vary from over-intense to languid, a good example of stylistic 'foregrounding'.)

The long duologue between Tyrone and Edmund fluctuates, from their opening exchange, between the admitted need for companionship and communication (the symbiotic dependence of the speakers on one another to ward off loneliness and anxiety) and angry bursts of accusation and counter-accusation. Most of the dialogue is dynamic, with sudden shifts of mood and tone, and a fair degree of equilibrium in the speech-ration of the speakers. But as Edmund charges his father with miserliness in a crescendo of bitterly ironic remarks, the balance of the dialogue is itself disturbed: giving way to a series of intense longer speeches, with Tyrone becoming the dominant speaker over a considerable stretch of playing time (nearly seven pages of text, pp. 126–33).[20] Driven by a sense of unadmitted guilt, Tyrone begins to exploit his own histrionic gifts, his habit of speech-making, his trained voice, his 'scornfully superior' tone (stage direction, p. 127), as a defensive weapon – obvious, but effective in its way. The whole sequence resembles a monologue – the would-be Shakespearian rhetoric of self-dramatisation: a poor man's Othello-speech, from a character who had seen himself as born to act Othello. Edmund's 'turns' are seen as mere interjections, disrupting Tyrone's torrent of words. One of the first exchanges – ostensibly a 'normal' or fully coherent communicative canter – makes it clear that Tyrone will not listen, will not allow himself to be deflected from his verbal parade:

TYRONE: (. . .) (*Abruptly his tone becomes scornfully superior*) You said you realised what I'd been up against as a boy. The hell you do! How could you? You'd everything – nurses, schools, college, though you didn't stay there. You've had food, clothing. Oh, I know you had a fling of hard work with your back and hands, a bit of being homeless and penniless in a foreign land, and I respect you for it. But it was a game of romance and adventure to you. It was play.

EDMUND: (*dully sarcastic*) Yes, particularly the time I tried to commit suicide at Jimmie the Priest's, and almost did.

TYRONE: You weren't in your right mind. No son of mine would ever – You were drunk.

EDMUND: I was stone cold sober. That was the trouble. I'd stopped to think too long.

TYRONE: Don't start your drunken atheist morbidness again! I don't care to listen. I was trying to make plain to you – (*Scornfully*) What do you know of the value of the dollar? When I was ten my father deserted my mother and went back to Ireland to die. Which he did soon enough, and deserved to, and I hope he's roasting in hell. He mistook rat poison for flour, or sugar, or something. There was gossip it wasn't by mistake but that's a lie. No one in my family ever –

EDMUND: My bet is, it wasn't by mistake.

TYRONE: More morbidness! Your brother put that in your head. The worst he can suspect is the only truth for him. But never mind.

(pp. 127–8)

As a dialogue of evasion this is cruder, more explicit, than Chekhov, but it precisely mimes the dismissal of one speaker by the other. The world, the ethos, of Edmund's short speeches (what he says about the suicide attempts, his own and that of Tyrone's father) are ruled out, as some kind of foul, breaking the rules of the verbal game as played by the principal speaker. Yet the interruptions strengthen the dialogue; Edmund's personal tone is prompted by the confessional mode and is offered in communicative trust; and Tyrone's rejoinders, though brusque and 'inauthentic' are a response of sorts. The two are engaged in án interactive duologue. Tyrone's refusal to enter into full, reciprocal communication – to respond 'in kind' to Edmund's attempt to deepen the conversation through *his* participation – is a symptom of the family's general refusal to listen to each other: any utterance that threatens the precarious family truce, is 'not heard', or is reduced by euphemism and mendacious domestic diplomacy. One of the functions of language is then to negate reality ('*No* son of mine would *ever'*, echoed a minute later by '*No one* in my family *ever* – '). The topic of suicide – presumably a recurrent thought for Edmund now faced with possibly incurable illness – is then dismissed, so that Tyrone can devote his considerable vocal resources to the consolations of past suffering and failure. Within the limits of 'natural' egocentricity, Tyrone nevertheless offers a genuine confession – that is, he can move from ordinary self-defence (from the charge of being a miser) to a genuine attempt at recalling how his essential goals as a young actor came to be blighted:

TYRONE: Yes, maybe life overdid the lesson for me, and made a dollar worth too much, and the time came when that mistake ruined my career as a fine actor. (*Sadly*) I've never admitted this to anyone before, lad, but tonight I'm so heartsick I feel at the end of everything, and what's the use of fake pride and pretence. That God-damned play I bought for a song and made such a great success in – a great money success – it ruined me with its promise of an easy fortune. I didn't want to do anything else, and by the time I woke up to the fact I'd become a slave to the damned thing and did try other plays, it was too late. They had identified me with that one part, and didn't want me in anything else. They were right, too. I'd lost the great talent I once had through years of easy repetition, never learning a new part, never really working hard. Thirty-five to forty thousand dollars net profit a season like snapping your fingers! It was too great a temptation. Yet before I bought the damned thing I was considered one of the three or four young actors with the greatest artistic promise in America. I'd worked like hell. I'd left a good job as a machinist to take supers' parts because I loved the theatre. I was wild with ambition. I read all the plays ever written. I studied Shakespeare as you'd study the Bible. I educated myself. I got rid of an Irish brogue you could cut with a knife. I loved Shakespeare. I would have acted in any of his plays for nothing, for the joy of being alive in his great poetry. And I acted well in him. I felt inspired by him. I could have been a great Shakespearean actor, if I'd kept on. I know that! In 1874 when Edwin Booth came to the theatre in Chicago where I was leading man, I played Cassius to his Brutus one night, Brutus to his Cassius the next, Othello to his Iago, and so on. The first night I played Othello, he said to our manager, 'That young man is playing Othello better than I ever did!' . . . (*Bitterly*). What the hell was it I wanted to buy, I wonder, that was worth – Well, no matter. It's a late day for regrets. (*He glances vaguely at his cards.*) My play, isn't it?

EDMUND: (*moved, stares at his father with understanding – slowly*). I'm glad you've told me this, Papa. I know you a lot better now.

TYRONE: (*with a loose, twisted smile*). Maybe I shouldn't have told you. Maybe you'll only feel more contempt for me. And it's a poor way to convince you of the value of a dollar. (*Then as if this phrase automatically aroused an habitual association in his mind, he glances up at the chandelier disapprovingly.*) The glare from those extra lights hurts my eyes. You don't mind if I turn them out, do you? We don't need them, and there's no use making the Electric Company rich.

EDMUND: (*controlling a wild impulse to laugh – agreeably*). No, sure not. Turn them out.

(pp. 130–2)

The frame of the duologue counterpoints the dominant monologue of Tyrone. There is a masterly transition, first from self-obsessed brooding on the past to direct address of the partner in present talk and card-playing: 'Well, no matter. It's a late day for regrets. My play, isn't it?' – with the ambiguity of 'play',[21] an unforced yet telling epitome of Tyrone's descent from 'high' to 'low' play. Edmund's response marks the point where he becomes a fully responsive partner in the dialogue; and the insight and emotion expressed ('I know you a lot better now') is a justification of dialogue as an agent of personal maturation. The phrasing of Edmund's short speech may seem raw, to an audience no longer used to such explicitness in intimate emotion, but it is counter-balanced by the irony of Tyrone's return to penny-pinching: 'The glare from those extra lights hurts my eyes.' Tyrone's own speech is that rare thing – a spontaneous artifice that blends the rhythms of the histrionic player and the suffering man. There is considerable variation in syntax and rhythm: moving from the emphatic opening ('That God-damned play I bought for a song . . . it ruined me with its promise of an easy fortune') to the hammering home of the short 'I'-centred sentences, with their cadenced parallelism, a veritable litany. That grammar of regret, the past conditional, encapsulates the imaginary past: 'I *could have been* a Shakespearean actor if I'd kept on.' In the rhetoric we recognise the character 'who sees himself in a dramatic light' (Eliot's example is Othello: 'And say, besides – that in Aleppo once . . .').[22] It is a rhetoric especially appropriate to an actor engaged in his 'presentation of self' to a one-man audience (and beyond it to the audience proper).

Tyrone's self-indulgent confession at least enables Edmund to respond in a new and intimate way – a response in kind, in full use of the occasion for confessional disclosure. It is as different from Tyrone's confession in its texture as it is in the values it conveys: the inward discovery of a moment of ecstatic freedom against a permanent sense of estrangement from the world (clearly connected with the youthful Edmund's cult of Nietzsche and with the quotations, woven into 'his' text, from Baudelaire, Swinburne and Dowson). In a long reverie, teetering on the edge of purple prose and poeticism, Edmund speaks his own role-playing speech, which becomes integrated into the give-and-take of a confessional duologue. (Our extract is preceded by thirty-six lines of Edmund's speech):

> And several other times in my life, when I was swimming far out, or lying alone on a beach, I have had the same experience. Became the sun, the hot sand, green seaweed anchored to a rock, swaying in the tide. Like a saint's vision of beatitude. Like the veil of things as they seem drawn back by an unseen hand. For a second you see – and seeing the secret, are the secret. For a second there is meaning! Then the hand lets the veil fall and you are alone, lost in the fog again, and you stumble on toward nowhere, for no good reason! (*He grins wryly.*) It was a great mistake, my being born a man, I would have been much more successful as a sea-gull or a fish. As it is, I will always be a stranger who never feels at home, who does not really want and is not really wanted, who can never belong, who must always be a little in love with death!
>
> TYRONE: (*stares at him – impressed*). Yes, there's the makings of a poet in you all right. (*Then protesting uneasily.*) But that's morbid craziness about not being wanted and loving death.
>
> EDMUND: (*sardonically*). The *makings* of a poet. No, I'm afraid I'm like the guy who is always panhandling for a smoke. He hasn't even got the makings. He's got only the habit. I couldn't touch what I

tried to tell you just now. I just stammered. That's the best I'll
ever do. I mean, if I live. Well, it will be faithful realism, at least.
Stammering is the native eloquence of us fog people.

(pp. 134–5)

The confession communicates the discovery of existential
meaning in the moment – 'the spots of time' of Wordsworth, the
'epiphany' of Joyce. It is an attempt to pass beyond the speaking
'I' to the impersonal vision of the would-be poet. The authenticity of the experience is weakened by utterances that sound like
intrusive authorial comment. Yet they might well be taken as 'in
character', the self-conscious young writer's need to underline
what is being said – twice: 'Like a saint's vision of beatitude. Like
the veil of things as they seem drawn back by an unseen hand.'
The total effect is that 'Edmund's reverie with its plain-speaking
coda makes us conscious not only of his inarticulacy but of his
pain at being unable to articulate his deeply felt experience.'[23] In
any case, the integration of the speech into the exchanges of the
dialogue – as Edmund confesses his failure as a poet in response
to Tyrone's genuine but naive praise – transforms the lyric moment into dramatic verbal interaction.

Jamie's entrance (referred to at the end of Edmund's speech)
opens the transition to the older brother's confession, a simpler
experience yet a harder one to speak of: the consuming jealousy
that led to a sympathetic attempt at 'derangement' (the decadent
fin-de-siècle postures translated into 'hick town' slang):

JAMIE: Nix, Kid! You listen! Did it on purpose to make a bum of you. Or
part of me did. A big part. That part that's been dead so long.
That hates life. My putting you wise so you'd learn from my
mistakes. Believed that myself at times, but it's a fake. Made my
mistakes look good. Made getting drunk romantic. Made
whores fascinating vampires instead of poor, stupid, diseased
slobs they really are. Made fun of work as sucker's game. Never
wanted you succeed and make me look even worse by
comparison. Wanted you to fail. Always jealous of you. Mama's baby, Papa's pet! (*He stares at Edmund with increasing enmity.*) And it was your being born that started Mama on dope. I
know that's not your fault, but all the same, God damn you, I
can't help hating your guts – !
EDMUND: (*almost frightenedly*). Jamie! Cut it out! You're crazy!
JAMIE: But don't get wrong idea, Kid. I love you more than I hate you. My
saying what I'm telling you now proves it. I run the risk you'll

189

hate me – and you're all I've got left. But I didn't mean to tell you that last stuff – go that far back. Don't know what made me. What I wanted to say is . . .

(p. 146)

The bravura speech goes on (for some thirty-three lines), with further interruptions from Edmund – mere interjections, not full responses, in keeping with the 'unspeakability' of Jamie's confession.

The three types of confession – first, the father's extroverted remembrance of past failure, then the younger son's reverie (the difficult expression of inwardness), and, finally, the older son's brusque self-denigration – offer authentic varieties of personal experience. Each confession is spoken within the cumulative dialogue (context) of the family's habitual recrimination and defensiveness, yet each becomes an instrument of insight and sympathy. Each is supported by an appropriate speech-style for the particular confessing character, so that, in the overall design, a counterpoint of languages is created (what I have called counterspeech).[24] The impulse to soliloquise with limitless abandon – the familiar risk of the confessional situation – is counterbalanced by a clear interactive frame; the confessional duologues culminate in Mary's final monologue (outside our present concern): self-enclosed, drug-ridden, overheard by the family yet beyond any possible response, any dialogue with another person.

The obsessive intimacies of family life within a densely structured dramatic situation – retrospective yet cruelly actual and reciprocal – engender an archetypal dialogue of confessions. By contrast, O'Neill's one-act play *Hughie* (1941)[25] dramatises a seemingly casual yet compulsive need for confessional talk – the attempt to provoke some kind of consolatory response from a stranger, in what looks like an accidental encounter in limbo. The scene is set in the lobby of a seedy West Side hotel in the New York of 1928; the compulsive talker or monologuist is Erie Smith, a 'small-fry gambler and horse-player' (stage direction, p. 9) whose luck seems to have deserted him since the death of Hughie, the night clerk; the listener, or the victim of Erie's stream of self-boosting anecdotes, is the new night clerk, Charlie Hughes, whom Erie tries to substitute, like a dummy, for the dead confidant. Across a gulf of incongruously insular private worlds and indifferent non-hearing (Erie is only interested in himself, Charlie is tired and 'far away') a little drama concerning dialogue itself is being enacted. It is the solipsistic territory often claimed by non-naturalistic drama (from late Strindberg to Beckett) but O'Neill writes a scrupulously authentic-sounding 'typical' language for the two speakers: Erie, as dominant speaker, is made to exult in a rich Broadway slang full of gambling and betting terms, intended to give 'the type's enduring lingo, and not use stuff current only in 1928' (Letter to Nathan, 6. 19. 1942).[26] The situation is unfolded indirectly but with precision, so that the audience can concentrate on the mode of speech rather than on the minimal 'story' (for the reader O'Neill supplies extensive stage directions, resembling the 'thought asides' of *Strange Interlude*, considerably shortened in the extract quoted). About half-way through the short play (about forty-five minutes of playing time) 'the dialogue of the deaf' crystallises around Erie's doomed attempt to interest the night clerk in the good old days when Hughie was still around to be nightly impressed by the grandeur that was Erie (but not allowed to become too intimate):

ERIE: (*He pauses confidentially*). I switched the subject on Hughie, see, on purpose. He never did beef about his wife again. (*He gives a forced chuckle.*) Believe me, pal. I can stop guys that start telling me their family troubles!

NIGHT CLERK: [A long stage direction indicates his absence of mind.] Ha-ha! That's a good one, Erie. That's the best I've heard in a long time!

ERIE: (*for a moment is so hurt and depressed he hasn't the spirit to make a sarcastic crack. He stares at the floor, twirling his room key – to himself*). Jesus, this sure is a dead dump. About as homy as the Morgue. (*He glances up at the clock.*) Gettin' late. Better beat it up to my cell and grab some shut-eye. (*He makes a move to detach himself from the desk, but fails, and remains wearily glued to it. His eyes prowl the lobby and finally come to rest on the Clerk's glistening, sallow face. He summons up strength for a withering crack.*) Why didn't you tell me you was deaf, buddy? I know guys is sensitive about them little afflictions, but I'll keep it confidential.

(*But the Clerk's mind has rushed out to follow the siren-wail of a fire-engine. 'A fireman's life must be exciting . . .'*)

Take my tip, pal, and don't never try to buy from a dope-pedlar. He'll tell you you had enough already.

(*The Clerk's mind continues its dialogue with the fireman . . .*)

Well, me for the hay. (*But he can't dislodge himself – then dully – *)

191

Christ, it's lonely. I wish Hughie was here. By God, if he was,
I'd tell him a tale that'd make his eyes pop! The bigger the story
the harder he'd fall. But he was that kind of sap. He thought
gambling was romantic. I guess he saw me like a sort of dream
guy, the sort of guy he'd like to be if he could take a chance.

(pp. 28–30)

Erie's speech goes on for over fifty lines of reminiscence and
rumination until he interrupts himself with a challenge to the
night porter ('Ain't it the truth, Charlie?' p. 31), hoping to be
reassured by his admiring audience, playing the role of the
'dream guy' once more. But the night clerk has ceased to listen,
awkwardly stammering: 'Truth? I'm afraid I didn't get – what's
the truth?'; so Erie's speech-drug fails on this occasion, and he
is forced to fall back on talking interminably 'aloud to himself,
without hope of a listener' (stage direction, p. 32). At one point in
the would-be duologue the tragi-comic speaker/listener relationship is varied: the night clerk suddenly rouses himself to a speech
that has, within his speech-level, a touch of groping eloquence –
sufficient to startle and deflate Erie once more, as his own speech-
dominance is being undermined and a gulf of 'alien standpoints'
is suggested:

ERIE: But Hughie's better off, at that, being dead. He's got all the luck. He
needn't do no worryin' now. He's out of the racket. I mean,
the whole goddamned racket. I mean life.
NIGHT CLERK: (*kicked out of his dream – with detached, pleasant acquiescence*).
Yes, it is a goddamned racket when you stop to think, isn't it,
492? But we might as well make the best of it, because – Well,
you can't burn it all down, can you? There's too much steel and
stone. There'd always be something left to start it going again.
ERIE: (*scowls bewilderedly*). Say, what is this? What the hell you talkin'
about?
NIGHT CLERK: (*at a loss – in much confusion*). Why, to be frank, I really don't
– Just something that came into my head.
ERIE: (*bitingly, but showing he is comforted at having made some sort of
contact*). Get it out of your head quick, Charlie, or some guys in
uniform will walk in here with a butterfly-net and catch you.
(*He changes the subject – earnestly.*) Listen, pal . . .

(pp. 35–6)

We do not need O'Neill's stage directions to realise that what is
being dramatised in the non-matching exchanges between Erie
and the Night Clerk is the sense of the former's virtual self-
annihilation that follows from the failure of conversational turns.

Erie's chosen partner fails to 'deliver': to give proper attention, i.e. total attention. The Night Clerk fails to 'tune in', responds in the wrong key.

Simple as these effects may look on the page – especially when compared with the dialogue of non-coherence in the theatre of the absurd – the text precisely embodies a little cycle of despair and aggression through the stops and accelerations of the dialogue. The topics of talk – the 'issues' – barely impinge on the speakers, who are guided by no motive, no interactive need, other than the compulsion to talk: Erie's need to be able to float with a new buoyancy on the crests of talk. It is, however, very much a text for performance (as shown in the revival of the play at the National Theatre):[27] the lines yield a rich variety of highly flavoured speech tones[28] and the inflation and deflation of Erie's ego calls for an exact language of posture and gesture. The carefully controlled naturalism of the one-act play has a human and stylistic authenticity: the dialogue reaches the edge of (but does not go over into) dislocation of speech. Though the naturalistic value of spontaneity – the illusion that the character doesn't know what he is going to say until he has heard himself speak – is driven towards unpredictability of speech, O'Neill does *not* seek an audience that is forced to include itself in Erie's moment of existential and linguistic bewilderment. A safe spectatorial distance reassures us through the sheer familiarity of two deaf conversationalists. Even so, there is enough pressure towards parallel monologues, in and behind this potential duologue, to link it with certain dialogue patterns in the theatre language of the more naturalistically conceived of Pinter's plays (e.g. *The Caretaker*) and especially with a one-act play by Albee, *The Zoo Story*, by chance almost contemporary with *Hughie*.

4.

Albee's *The Zoo Story* begins with a seemingly casual encounter between two strangers, between the feverish outsider Jerry and the pipe-smoking conformist Peter, in Central Park on a Sunday afternoon of the New York summer; it ends with suicide–murder. The active talker Jerry dies impaled on the knife he himself had forced on his more passive partner in conversation. If *Hughie* dramatised the absolute human need for talk as a partial escape from total loneliness, *The Zoo Story* makes the dialogue itself an instrument of destruction within a parable on total isolation ('no contact possible to flesh' through words alone). The dramatic situation is, then, at once more random-seeming and patterned, more 'extreme', than in *Hughie*. Jerry is seeking not just a partner, an interlocutor, a sympathetic listener; he has, it becomes gradually clear, a strategy of 'systematic derangement' intended to compel something like total attention – deeper communion – from his victim in conversation. Such a dialogue can only be doomed to failure: the complacency of the listener is no sooner dented, to some extent, than the challenger's despair and verbal violence is intensified. Jerry desires fullness of human contact through dialogue in a situation which, within the norms of Western society, especially for 'talking to strangers', can only offer partial, and finally alienating, attempts at communication. (The liberating or redemptive possibilities of Jerry's verbal onslaught cannot, in the structure of the play, be glimpsed by Peter before the violent climax.)

Even such a brief account of the dramatic situation will suggest some affinity with the solipsistic breakdown of language in absurd drama. Albee himself may have encouraged being placed in this way at one time (Martin Esslin included the play in his well-known anthology *Absurd Drama*)[29] by seemingly identifying himself with the new dramatic mode: 'The Theatre of the Absurd . . . facing as it does man's condition as it is, is the Realistic theatre of our time.'[30] However, the dialogue of *The Zoo Story* is best seen as a cross-breeding of naturalistic and absurdist elements, with the former dominant (which is one reason why the study of this one-act duologue is placed at the end of this chapter). It is a transitional play. The truth-telling urge of the confessional duologue, as we have known it from Ibsen on, gives way to Jerry's desperate urgency to talk at/to/with/for and past a relatively uncomprehending listener, a failing confidant. Conversational sallies ascend, through stages controlled by the inner pressure of Jerry's pathological need, to elaborate story-telling and finally to a verbal duel which leads to murder. The pattern of the dialogue follows a 'method of indirection'[31] – as we shall see – but this is something different from the mannerist dislocations in much Absurd drama. The syntax, the rhythm, and the vocabulary remain close to colloquial American speech or, as in the long narrative speeches of

Jerry, have a rounded literary articulateness. In the final sequence there are also immediately recognisable biblical allusions
and phrasing: 'I came unto you . . . and you have comforted me.'
The language is not itself the object of distortion; as in classical
naturalism, the devices of distortion and fragmentation in the
dialogue reflect the communicative needs of a distorted mind –
Jerry's needs. The peculiarities of his speech are 'in character',
and they dictate the compulsive non-logic of his conversation.
Meanwhile the audience is given clear signals to indicate what is
going on in terms of verbal interaction. It becomes gradually clear
that there is a systematic madness in the method Jerry uses to
unsettle and unseat Peter: tactically intensifying the verbal pressure from random remarks to the final torrent of abuse. The
cumulative dialogue is 'plotted' towards an almost Aristotelian
peripety.

The first stage seems a simple enough verbal encounter between two unlike strangers – Jerry is eager to talk while Peter is
'anxious to get back to his reading' (stage direction):

JERRY: (*stands for a few seconds, looking at Peter, who finally looks up again,
    puzzled*) Do you mind if we talk?
PETER: (*obviously minding*) Why . . . no, no.
JERRY: Yes you do; you do.
PETER: (*puts his book down, his pipe out and away, smiling*). No, really; I
    don't mind.
JERRY: Yes you do.
PETER: (*finally decided*) No; I don't mind at all, really.

(p. 160)

This ordinary ritual of verbal fencing goes on, until Jerry decides
to deflect it and so 'defamiliarises' the dialogue:

JERRY: You're married!
PETER: (*with pleased emphasis*) Why, certainly.
JERRY: It isn't a law, for God's sake.
PETER: No . . . no, of course not.
JERRY: And you have a wife.
PETER: (*bewildered by the seeming lack of communication*) Yes!

(p. 160)

And so on, mixing catechism and comic cross-talk, to elicit simple
personal confessions from Peter. Jerry comments on his method
with naive-seeming directness:

195

JERRY: Do you mind if I ask you questions?

PETER: Oh, not really.

JERRY: I'll tell you why I do it; I don't talk to many people – except to say like: give me a beer, or where's the john, or what time does the feature go on, or keep your hands to yourself, buddy. You know – things like that.

PETER: I must say I don't . . .

JERRY: But every once in a while I like to talk to somebody, really *talk*; like to get to know somebody, know all about him.

PETER: (*lightly laughing, still a little uncomfortable*) And am I the guinea-pig for today?

(pp. 161–2)

The way is now open to a full questionnaire – but even here the dialogue is much nearer to everyday conversation than are the cross-examination rituals in absurd drama (in Ionesco's *The Lesson* or in Pinter's *The Dumb Waiter*). The built-in repetitions, clichés and remarks that work like asides ('Wait until you see the expression on *his* face' p. 163) inform the audience though they disconcert – and disconnect Peter as listener. Having elicited a few direct answers from Peter, Jerry proceeds to start telling his long-winded and oblique stories, dominated by 'The Story of Jerry and the Dog!' The story-within-the play is central to the structure of the one-act play – and so to its interpretation; but here it concerns us only as a parallel to the pathos of failed communication which is about to be replayed in the dialogue: 'Don't you see? A person has to have some way of dealing with SOMETHING. If not with people . . . SOMETHING. With a bed, with a cockroach, with a mirror . . . no, that's too hard, that's one of the last steps' (p. 175).

It is too hard to deal with a mirror partly because it would perpetuate the monologue. Jerry wants to try dealing with people, one person; so it is essential for him to provoke a response, for instance a comment on his story from Peter (who is, we learn early in the dialogue, a publisher). But Peter cannot or does not want to respond. The non-response looks like a failure of sympathy, a habitual detachment, as Jerry's dog story, a personalised kind of 'shaggy dog story', is not difficult to follow, only difficult to 'allow' – for it points back to the desperate plight of the speaker:

(*Jerry is animated but Peter is disturbed.*)

JERRY: Oh, come on now, Peter; tell me what you think.

PETER: (*numb*) I . . . don't understand what . . . I don't think I . . . (*now almost tearfully*) Why did you tell me all of this?
JERRY: Why not?
PETER: I DON'T UNDERSTAND!
JERRY: (*furious, but whispering*) That's a lie.
PETER: No. No, it's not.
JERRY: (*quietly*) I tried to explain it to you as I went along, I went slowly; it all has to do with . . .
PETER: I DON'T WANT TO HEAR ANY MORE. I don't understand you, or your landlady, or her dog . . .

(p. 177)

Peter goes on to apologise and placate – very much the Everyman of our time, making a habit of both indifference and feigned conversational correctness. But by now it is too late, from Jerry's point of view; accompanied by a crescendo of physical attacks – tickling, pushing Peter almost off the bench, and drawing a knife – he escalates his verbal abuse until the climax of suicide–murder is accomplished. Only at that point – at the point of self-immolation – does it become clear to Peter, and to the audience, that 'not understanding' and 'not wanting to hear any more' constitute stages in a tragic failure of encounter. This final sequence of the duologue introduces a broken requiem, in which 'Oh my God' is restored from near-swearing to an echoing of its sacramental meaning in Jerry's howl and in Peter's supplication. Though probably not as effective as intended by Albee (it has a palpable staginess, and has the feel of being superadded to the rest of the playtext) at least it directs attention back to the whole duologue. We then see Jerry's desperate bid for 'a communion with something beyond the self'[33] – as a significant failure. It amounts to a parable on dialogue, in the transition between two modes of modern drama.

5 Duologues of isolation : towards verbal games*

1.

The confessional duologue has become pivotal in the structure of major plays from Ibsen on; but the growing centrality of the duologue in later modern drama often goes with the dissolution of the 'stable ego' of characters, and tends to replace the interactive speakers with voices calling out in isolation.

At first the dialogue between two centrally placed characters (interacting and exchanging their inner worlds in a kind of verbal osmosis) seems impelled by the 'truth-seeking urge' within a robust dramatic structure; such a structure assumes that the truth about this or that character, about their past, about their subtle, deliberately concealed experiences, their barely speakable interrelationship, may be unmasked through the mutual recognitions of talking. Then the truth shall set the speakers free – a form of dramatic logotherapy, the search for meaning revealed partly through speech.[1] Further, not only is the duologue often structually central in major, full-length plays with a whole gallery of characters, but the period of late naturalism – starting with Strindberg's *Miss Julie* (1888) – also sees the rise of the chamber play, with its small-scale cast. Such plays often crystallise around the verbal conflict of *two* antagonistic characters, as if what constituted the central scenes in the old tragedy had become the play itself. This new form of micro-play often presents a microcosmic allegory, from Strindberg to Beckett's *Happy Days*, Ionesco's *The Chairs*, Genêt's *The Maids* and Mrozek's *Exiles*.

The growing significance of the duologue – as a controlling scene or else as the substance of the shorter play – may well be seen as part of a general evolution in the new economy of dramatic form, and the performance economics of the new type of intimate theatre: Antoine's Théâtre Libre, the Freie Bühne in Berlin, The Independent Theatre in London, the Intimate Theatre

in Stockholm and so on. There must have occurred a simultaneous shift in sensibility – a shift of interest to the nuances of
individual personality and to the small-scale dynamics of collision between paired individuals. Such a shift corresponds to the
growing obsession with psychology and the dominance of the
'individualistic' middle-class audience – the relative social isolation of the bourgeois theatre. Historically, it is difficult to imagine
a duologue-centred play at any time earlier than the late nine-
teenth century. The multiple perspective and the chorus-like
ensemble of a large number of *dramatis personae* had seemed as
essential to the structure of a play in and since the Renaissance, as
the 'large canvas' (idiosyncratic as well as typical characters,
fictional worlds and languages) seemed essential to the development of the realistic novel. But beginning with Ibsen – as we
have seen in *Rosmersholm* and *John Gabriel Borkman* – the intimate
duologue attains a fullness and a passionate intensity: it becomes
both structurally dominant and verbally subtle. That it was a
relatively new mode of play-construction can be seen from the
characteristic grumble of a critic like Archer, the champion of
pure or dogmatic naturalism in the theatre; it is on record that
Archer read *The Master Builder* 'with a sinking heart as he saw
how *so much of the play seemed to be a mere duologue,* with Solness-
Hilde-Solness-Hilde endlessly repeated'.[2] At the other end of our
time-span, we recall how a contemporary Norwegian television
producer felt he had to scissor the duologues in *John Gabriel
Borkman* for fear of tiring his mass audience, no longer used to
sitting through attentively as two souls try to work out their
salvation in the leisured agony of their verbal confrontation.[3]

Once two characters are placed in sharp focus – their corner of
the world a microcosm, isolated from the dialogue of the group –
the way is open to further isolation, probing the abyss that may
separate one speaker from the other. Intensified 'individuation'
opens the way towards separate existence, amounting to divorce
(humanly and verbally) of those whom dialogue has joined together. We have seen how, in the final scene of *John Gabriel
Borkman*, the egomaniac Borkman is addressing the ore in the
mountains – no longer the person, the lover, supposedly being
addressed. In the final scene of Strindberg's *Ghost Sonata* the
Hyacinth Girl and the Student rapidly move through the stages of
diminishing communication as they wilt, in dream-like

acceleration, from the consecration of a kind of marriage to the dissolution of their fragile union. From Strindberg to Beckett this or that mode of distortion thrusts the once robust confessional duologue more and more towards a dialogue of solipsists, or the parallel monologues of a tangentially connected pair. We then reach a situation that was first defined as early as 1909 by the young Lukács: 'the new drama has no confidantes, and this is a symptom that life has robbed man of his faith that he can understand another man. . .Men become simply incapable of expressing the truly essential in them and what truly directs their actions; even should they in rare moments find words to fit the inexpressible, these words will at any rate go unheard past the spirits of others, or reach them with meaning transformed.'[4]

It is such a (gradual) dissolution in relationship that lies behind the various kinds of verbal dislocation, the incantation, the unspoken, the minimal speech, the inarticulate and the inexpressible, in Maeterlinck, Chekhov and Strindberg. (To connect that inwardness and fragmentation with Symbolism, as I have once done,[5] is to give only one context – that of the musicalisation of language in post-Wagnerian Europe. These mutations in the texture of dialogue are inseparably connected with the transformations in relationship, as experienced and perceived, in the first phases of aestheticism.)

The dissolution of relationship goes with something like a 'principle of uncertainty' concerning the truth of reality that any communication – any verbal interaction and exchange of values – can establish between two characters.[6] The boundaries of fantasy and reality, mask and face, past and present, begin to get blurred and become indistinguishable – as in hallucination and dream. By now we are so used to this ambiguity – it has become an obligatory doctrine among contemporaries of Pinter – that anyone reading a statement about the 'fluctuating interplay of truth and fiction' is likely to nod (either in agreement or in sleep). Yet, surely, it is among *the* major changes of sensibility in our culture. Most early naturalistic drama – like Greek and Renaissance drama before it – was written out of an implicit assumption that the 'truth' can be 'unmasked' – however circuitously, and at whatever cost to the protagonists and their community: the hidden cause of evil in Thebes is uncovered through Oedipus's relentless and self-destructive quest; the 'equivocation of the fiend' may destroy Macbeth, but it does not undermine the audience's hierarchy of values, the hard-earned sanity of distinguishing between the 'real' and the 'hallucinatory'. In *Rosmersholm*, with all its complexities, Ibsen still used a structure of cumulative dialogue that leads to Rebekka's final confession: 'the whole truth' revealed, paid for by sacrificial suicide. Ambiguity in a character's motive and utterance – like disguise, dissembling, 'smiling villainy' and all the countless strategies of human camouflage – was, until our own time, always presented within a solider framework that allowed the audience – and usually the protagonists themselves – to reach a point of final discovery. (The concept of recognition, *anagnorisis*, includes the discovery of 'truth'.)[7]

The merging of fantasy and reality in the dialogue of personal encounter is, then, one of the Copernican revolutions of modern drama. One reads: 'Time and space do not exist; on a slight groundwork of reality, imagination spins and weaves new patterns made up of memories, experiences, unfettered fancies, absurdities and improvisations' (Author's Note to *A Dream Play, Ett drömspel* (1902)).[8] If one reads this statement quickly, one is likely to nod. But supposing one reads slowly and repeatedly: 'Time and space do not exist. . .' 'Time and space do not exist. . .' How many of us *live* by such a belief or perception, even today? (except at the 'still point of the turning world', in mystical experience or in Buddhist meditation). The new structures of ambiguity were much more far-reaching than was the Renaissance tension between appearance and reality. Even dream-states are firmly placed, with all their shifts of identity, within the multiple perspective of *A Midsummer Night's Dream* and in Calderón's *La Vida es sueño* (*Life is a Dream, c.*1638). Dream, or hallucination, had always been one perspective among many. But now uncertainties of time, space and identity were to envelop the whole play and offer metaphors for man's condition, dealing with universals rather than with one plane of action. Strindberg himself tended to report as fact what we know must have been hallucination – like making love to his wife (separated from him by seven hundred miles).[9] From Strindberg on, through Pirandello to Pinter, any dialogue written from some doctrine holding that the true relations within a relationship *cannot* be verified, exhibits the symptoms of flux or diminished coherence.[10]

It will be part of my later argument that this shift in the modes of personal exchange eventually led to a new mannerism in the texture of dialogue. Mannerist styles tend to be hyper-elaborate, and highly marked or 'defamiliarised': in dialogue the verbal windows of inter-action give way to interreflecting mirrors. However, the late natu-ralism of Ibsen, Chekhov and Strindberg (who coined the term neo-naturalism for his own dramatic art) was not mannerist in this precise sense: it had little 'systematic derangement' of the language spoken by the characters. The conversational framework of ques-tion-and-answer – the coherence of the dialogue – remained rela-tively stable. And the texture of the dialogue, the speech-style of the characters in unstable and even in hallucinatory states, remained surprisingly close to everyday speech, and its 'flat banality'. But the relatively mimetic dialogue was then reconstructed towards a richly implicit total playtext: the verbal and non-verbal image-clustering of Ibsen, the orchestrated subtext of Chekhov, 'the second unspoken dialogue' of Maeterlinck, the allusive language of *The Ghost Sonata* where, in Strindberg's own words, 'people talk in semi-tones, in muted voices, and one is ashamed of being human'.[11] In sum, the shift in sensibility – in the value system of dialogue – was, in the first phase of modernist drama, more revolutionary than any changes in the structure and in the texture of dialogue. Interaction between the characters diminishes and begins to dissolve; and the characters themselves begin to 'split, double and multiply; they evaporate, crystallise, scatter and converge' (Strindberg, 1902).[12] But the gram-mar and idiom of dissolving identity and relationship remained, predominantly, in a 'steady state' in late and post-naturalist drama: the characters *talked about* or tried to express, even explain, their own dissolution. In short, the characters were still speaking 'in character' to some extent, like the Student in *Ghost Sonata* and The Father in *Six Characters*, in their self-conscious ways. The pressure towards a more abstract type of dialogue – moving 'beyond' charac-ter, towards an interchangeable language rather than a language of exchanges – was gradual.

2.

One of the first plays where the gradual change in patterns of dialogue can be rewardingly observed is Ibsen's *The Master Builder* (1892). The extent to which the duologues of Solness and

Hilde are structurally central, and quantitatively dominant, in this play, is truly remarkable. (No wonder Archer responded with a 'sinking heart' at first, coming from the balanced architectonics of the early and middle plays of Ibsen.) It is not too much to say that the whole play is a scaffolding to allow its central experience – the psychic infection resulting from the encounter of two compulsive fantasists – as much play-room as possible. Long 'operatic duets' luxuriate within an ostensibly still naturalistic dialogue. The two protagonists are in the forefront throughout the three acts of rise-and-fall: we watch their self-intoxication as they talk, exchanging vague memories and desires. These become potent and obsessive, through hints and relentless questioning around events or potentialities: did Solness kiss the teenage Hilde (ten years earlier) after he had climbed the church tower? (act one); obsessions breed further obsessions, artistic and erotic potentialities, in endlessly spiralling talk, in exchanged images (act two); and lead to the fatal attempt to re-enact the tower-climbing in a rapture of daring and fear (act three). Such an emotional pattern can only be communicated through a *precise ambivalence* in the dialogue – the blurring of what is and what is not 'verifiable', statement and suggestion, experience and longing. The speakers are in the grip of their own authentic (that is, not deliberately 'make-believe') games-playing: they do not yet play verbal games of the self-conscious and style-conscious kind (as in the fragile mannerist dialogue of late-modernist drama).

Their exchange of images – of the tower, and later of *their* 'castle in the air', their *luftslott* – are not mere 'wordplay' but a change in the inner experience of the characters. They correspond through their symbolic images. 'The signs are there in the language, in the way *they can share those images* without the need of explanation' (emphasis added).[13] They reach a deepening inward communion, which includes complexity, while they keep up, across a precise distance, a verbal dance, as measured as an encounter in Racine. The young girl and the ageing and, it is hinted, impotent man, establish an intense verbal intimacy, they excite and hypnotise each other; yet they never even use the *you familiar* – unlike Rosmer and Rebekka who address one another as *Du* – and their physical posture in relation to one another remains reticent. All the emotion is conveyed by words and changes of facial expression.

The feel of this precarious kind of verbal interaction can be caught in the first encounter, in which Hilde attempts to reconstruct what she claims had taken place between them ten years earlier – a kiss Solness claims to have forgotten. Hilde has been trying to elicit some kind of commitment from Solness to a shared 'remembrance of things past'; her strategy mixes teasing and investigative pressure – ideally played by an actress who can combine the roles of Ellida Wangel (*The Lady from the Sea*) and Rebekka:

SOLNESS: What in the world did I do next?

HILDE: Yes, that's just what I was waiting for – for you to have forgotten that too! I should have thought one couldn't help remembering a thing like that.

SOLNESS: Yes, well, just start me going and then perhaps – Well?

HILDE: (*looking steadily at him*) You came and kissed me, Mr Solness.

SOLNESS: (*with open mouth, getting up from his chair*) Did I?

HILDE: Oh yes, you did. You took me in both arms and bent me over backward and kissed me. Many, many times.

SOLNESS: Why, my dear Miss Wangel –!

HILDE: (*getting up*) You're never going to deny it?

SOLNESS: Yes I certainly *am* going to deny it!

HILDE: (*looking scornfully at him*) Very well.

(*She turns and goes slowly across to the stove and remains standing close beside it, motionless, with her back turned and her hands behind her. There is a short pause.*)

SOLNESS: (*going cautiously up behind her*) Miss Wangel –?

(*Hilde is silent and does not move.*) Don't stand there like a statue. All this, that you said, it must be something you've dreamt. (*He puts his hand on her arm.*) Now listen – (*Hilde makes an impatient movement with her arm. Solness speaks as though an idea had occurred suddenly to him.*) Unless –! Wait a moment –! There's something here that goes deeper, you'll find. (*Hilde does not move, Solness speaks quietly but emphatically.*) I must have *thought* all this. I must have *willed* it. Have *wished* for it. Have *wanted* it. And so –. Wouldn't that be the explanation? (*Hilde is still silent. Solness speaks impatiently.*) Oh very well, damn it all, – then I *did* it, I suppose!

HILDE: (*turning her head a little, but not looking at him*) Then you admit it now?

SOLNESS: Yes. Anything you like.

HILDE: That you put your arms round me?

SOLNESS: Oh, yes!

HILDE: And bent me over backward?

SOLNESS: A long way back.

HILDE: And kissed me?

SOLNESS: Yes, I did.
HILDE: Many times?
SOLNESS: As many as ever you like.
HILDE: (*turning suddenly towards him, with the dancing and happy expression in her eyes again*) There, you see; I managed to get it out of you in the end!

(pp. 149–50, note the pattern
of Hilde's four long silences
while Solness speculates about
the 'reality' of the kiss)

Question and answer still interlock here, in the relentlessly coherent way we find elsewhere in Ibsen's confessional duologues. But the 'truth issue' is *not* settled by the verbal exchange – merely suspended (a willing suspension of disbelief on the part of Solness) for the time being. So coherence of 'manner' carries a growing ambiguity of 'matter'. At the same time a psychic tension is being built up. This can only be inadequately conveyed by a short dialogue extract, as the mutual play-enchantment of this couple needs the 'long run' of intensifying exchanges Ibsen had written for them. It also requires performance, perhaps more than any other late Ibsen play, to convey the gradual intoxication through banal words – as the voices gain tension, at once miming and counterpointing each other. And each voice has at least two tones here: Hilde combines the naive and the knowing, the child-like and the *femme fatale* (the exotic allure of the girl from 'the Far North'); while Solness shifts from the ironic ('Yes I certainly *am* going to deny it') to the inward ('I must have *thought* all this') and back again to the, now less assured, ironic tone. The double voice corresponds to the sense of a double presence – that of a scared old man and that of a callow youth (the duality once perfected by Olivier) in Solness's 'presentation of self'.

All the most intense scenes of *The Master Builder* turn on, are structurally made to revolve around, ambivalent images: images of obsessive fantasy which generate a potential reality. If in act one the language of encounter is dominated by those images (the tower-climbing, the remembered kiss) which conjure up the incantation of the past, then acts two and three metamorphose those images by projecting them into the present moment and into the action desired in the imminent future. So those images are fuel: a speech–energy that overheats the speakers as they move from a fantasy past, into a fantasy still to be enacted. Hilde wrests her 'kingdom' from Solness: the two of them build their 'castle in the air' – through words alone at first. The exchanges are intensified by the uncertainties, the multiple possibilities – evoked and feared as they are being named, and the names are exchanged. The energy of these exchanges is finally sufficient to drive Solness up the tower he had actualy built; the dialogue works 'magically' – or toxically – as in the temptation scene of *Othello*. The careful Ibsenite scaffolding – the exposition and rather ponderous context-building of the 'public' dialogue – increasingly gives way to the 'private' and fragmented duet of two identities merging through their talk.

It amounts to a new texture of dialogue, within the older, more solid scene-building structure of Ibsen's naturalism: an experiment in 'troll-language' within the bourgeois conversation. The old structure still has elements of the confessional framing we have noted before[14] (for example, Solness exclaiming 'For now at last I've got someone I can talk to!' leading, with the assurance or banality of a domesticated ritual to: 'Come here and let's sit down, Hilde. Sit here on the sofa, – so that you have the garden to look at' (pp. 167–8)). The new texture of dialogue has a feverish movement about it, with Solness and Hilde completing each other's phrases, with sudden shifts of mood and tone:

SOLNESS: In the sagas there are tales of Vikings who sailed to foreign lands and killed men –
HILDE: And carried off women –
SOLNESS: – and kept them captive –
HILDE: – took them home with their ships –
SOLNESS: – and treated them like – like the worst of trolls.
HILDE: (*looking straight before her with half-veiled eyes*) I think *that* must have been exciting.

(p. 179)

Here the eroticism is, in context, still half-consciously expressed, as Hilde's eyes are *half-veiled*; and the exchanges should be spoken in half-tones. Ibsen is exploiting the felicitous half-awareness of pre-Freudian characters – and audiences. The Viking exchange is followed by a kind of fugue of more lyrical – but still ambivalent – images: Solness compares Hilde to 'a wild bird of the woods', then modifies the image to 'a bird of prey', which she accepts and plays with.

Opaque, half-verbal or sub-verbal peaks of communication

occur in the final act, as when Solness is trying to probe Hilde's conversation with his dark wronged wife Aline, and Hilde responds with a crescendo of silences:

SOLNESS: (*after a short pause*) Did you talk to her long?
HILDE: (*stands motionless and doesn't answer*).
SOLNESS: Long, I'm asking?
HILDE: (*silent as before*).
SOLNESS: What did she talk about, Hilde?
HILDE: (*still silent*).
SOLNESS: Poor Aline! I suppose it was about the little boys.
HILDE: (*a nervous shudder runs through her; then she nods quickly once or twice*).

> (p. 193, 'her' and 'she' refer to Solness's wife)

A little later, in the same duologue, Ibsen makes Hilde answer a question about her home '*as if half-asleep*' – three times – and then in a trance-like state (corresponding to the 'half-veiled eyes' and the 'unfathomable expression in her eyes' (pp. 195–7)). Ibsen has developed a dynamic notation for sudden transitions of mood in his stage directions, to give a fully theatrical (visible, audible, tactile) embodiment to his experiment in dialogue: a dialogue where 'less is more'. After Hilde's silences in half-sleep, for example, the motif of the castle is introduced by her – now sitting up, 'full of life. Her eyes have again their happy, dancing expression.' The castle image is intensified in a later sequence, in another verbal fugue – a kind of rapture in fantasy (Solness 'becoming more and more alive'). And after a carefully placed interruption (the entrance of Ragnar, followed by Mrs Solness and Dr Herdal: the chorus for the tower-climbing) comes another castle-building duet, with its broken, dovetailing phrases, and its contagious image-swapping. The sequence of duologues reaches its climax (pp. 203–7), the direct prelude to the catastrophe.

Ibsen knew he was drawing on the power of direct experience in portraying not just the reality/fantasy play of emotions, but the precarious fluctuations of gesture, mood and language that carry the rhythms of 'enchantment'. He may not have known that in trying to do justice to that pattern of experience he took the art of writing dialogue several steps further – working with devices also worked on, in different ways, by Chekhov and Strindberg (and in his late music dramas, by Wagner). It is a language for dream-state encounters, half-tones for half-true (or 'unverifiable') disclosures between two speakers fascinated by each other's latency and ambiguity.

3.

In his late, 'post-Inferno' plays, Strindberg dissolved what was left of the solid structure of interactive dialogue. The language of the chamber play *The Ghost Sonata* (1907) might well seem disconnected if we came to it straight from the over-determined 'logic of conversation' in much of Ibsen's *Ghosts* (1881); more relentlessly than *The Master Builder*, it fuses past and present, 'reality' and 'fantasy' in a turning kaleidoscope of verbal patterns. It is well known that Strindberg developed what can only be called a radical concept of dialogue much earlier, at least as early as the writing of *Miss Julie* (1888):

> Finally the dialogue. Here I have somewhat broken with tradition by not making my characters catechists who sit asking stupid questions in order to evoke some witty retort. I have avoided the symmetrical, mathematically structured dialogue of the type favoured in France, and have allowed their minds to work irregularly, as people's do in real life, when, in conversation, no subject is fully exhausted, but one mind discovers in another a cog which has a chance to change. Consequently, *the dialogue, too, wanders, providing itself in the opening scenes with matter which is later taken up, worked upon, repeated, extended and added to, like the theme in a musical composition.*
> (From Strindberg's Preface to Miss Julie, emphasis added)[15]

In practice, the fluid and often hyper-naturalistic dialogue of *Miss Julie* remained in many respects 'catechismic' and logically balanced; even the 'dream-swapping' duologue (when Julie and Jean, the aristocratic girl who lures the self-assertive valet into a sexual relationship, exchange pointedly matching images of tree-climbing, she falling back, he reaching the top branch) has a marked coherence and symmetry. It makes use of the idea of dream-talk, but it is not talk 'out of' a dream.[16] The idea of letting thoughts be transmuted by dream, and of constructing dialogue by analogy with 'a musical composition' (see also Introduction, pp. 6–7) was tried out more fully only in the late plays, in and after *A Dream Play* (1902). Then the deranged fluidity aims at embodying the surreal, but, in the nature of that plane, often suggests disembodied speakers. Nevertheless, in the shifting fantasmagoria of *The Ghost Sonata* there remain several sequences of sustained dialogue which may well sound conversational enough; these include centrally placed duologues of intimate encounter, discovery and recognition.

First, the exploratory duologue between the Old Man and the Student in the opening scene; then the macabre purgatorial duologues between the Old Man and the Mummy, and between the Old Man and the Colonel at the inquisitorial 'ghost supper'; and finally the musicalised love-and-death duet of the Student and the Daughter in the fading ecstasy of the Hyacinth Room. All these duologues deliberately suggest a 'conversation of ghosts': they are full of sudden shifts of topic and perspective, fragmented, falling away from the 'old style', from the referential and expository functions of dialogue before Strindberg. A certain language-weariness is also explicitly invoked (one of the early examples in drama of the symbolist attack on the inadequacy of language, from Mallarmé to Hofmannstahl). For example, towards the end of the ghost supper – before the Old Man destroys the Colonel and the Mummy destroys the Old Man, by words alone – there is one more attempt at keeping the party talk going:

COLONEL: Shall we talk, then?
OLD MAN: (*slowly and with pauses*). About the weather, which we know? Ask after each other's health? We know that, too. I prefer silence. Then one can hear thoughts, and see the past. Silence hides nothing. Words conceal. I read the other day that differences of language arose through the need of primitive peoples to keep their tribal secrets private. Languages are cyphers; it's only a question of finding the key;

(p. 179)

The language-motif is one that is likely to be perceived by any reader or spectator (not just by those obsessed by language) and is likely to be perceived as linking up with other speeches on the destructive power of speech. The participants at the ghost supper come to grief when their crimes are named; and in the final scene the Student speaks of a parallel event of verbal exposure when, through talking and telling, his father had 'stripped the company naked'. Consequently, in this play speech is feared as much as other agents of destruction (the demonic cook, for instance); even the Student and the Daughter (the innocent couple in a world of total corruption) are in mortal danger of dying of their dialogue:

DAUGHTER: Don't tell me. If you do, I shall die.
STUDENT: I must, or I shall die.

(p. 188)

No wonder their exchanges hover between 'telling' and the fear of telling, in motive; between love and the death of love, in subject; while in style, they hover between direct personal declaration and a lyricism that moves beyond personal speech – to a prose litany, to incantation, prayer and song, in the final movement of the play.

When we look at the actual structure and texture of the dialogue we make a surprising discovery: it is much more stable and 'normal' than we might expect from the dislocations of time and action, the blurred perspectives and the sudden shifts of identity. The opening duologue between the Old Man and the Student, and the two monologues of the ghost supper, have quite a regular 'conversational framework' with proper questions and answers probing uncertainties of fact and event, in a language that shows no sign of distortion. If anything, it moves towards the brevity of telephone conversations as Strindberg must have intended:[17]

STUDENT: It's strange how a story can exist in two such different versions.
OLD MAN: You think I'm not telling you the truth.
STUDENT: What else am I to think? My father never lied?
OLD MAN: True, true. One's father never lies. But I am a father, too; so –
STUDENT: What are you trying to tell me?
OLD MAN: I saved your father from complete destitution. . .

(p. 160)

So we have here a clear and natural dialogue concerning two opposed versions of a story from the past, which neither the Student nor the audience has *any* means of verifying, distinguishing from lie or fantasy. In the next scene even the Mummy, abandoning her parrot-voice as she emerges from her surreal cupboard, starts speaking *in an ordinary human voice* (stage direction) and speaks in a language of 'ordinary human' recognition, regrets, and threats:

MUMMY: (*in an ordinary human voice*) Is it Jacob?
OLD MAN: My name *is* Jacob –
MUMMY: (*with emotion*) And my name is Amelia.
OLD MAN: No, no, no! Oh, Lord Jesus –
MUMMY: This is how I look now. Yes. And I used to look like that. One

lives and learns. I stay in the cupboard mostly, to avoid seeing people – and being seen. What are you looking for in here, Jacob?
OLD MAN: My child. Our child.
MUMMY: She's sitting over there.
OLD MAN: Where?
MUMMY: There. In the hyacinth room.

(p. 174)

Quite a co-operative 'logic of conversation' for a conversation of ghosts; at all events, a good deal nearer to Strindberg's own naturalistic plays than to the ghosts in Beckett's *Play* (to bring in a synchronic comparison and mark the contrast with the complex verbal texture of later modernist drama).[18] For most of the dislocations of *The Ghost Sonata*, uncanny and powerful as they may be, especially in a rare good performance, depend either on conceptual dislocations ('I stay in the cupboard mostly' says the old woman) or on visual effects – the ravages of her face and body in contrast with the figure embodied in the statue ('This is how I look now. Yes, and I used to look like this'). In short, the strange transformations of theatrical action and space–time are not yet worked out, or are only germinally worked out, at the level of verbal texture in the dialogue.

In the haunting but imperfectly achieved final duologue, between the Student and the Daughter, something else happens: the dialogue compresses a whole cycle of relationship – love, marriage, decline and death – within the cycle of one sustained encounter.[19] The speakers grow and fade, undergo corruption 'unto death', but their transformations are signalled by their dialogue, not enacted through it. At first, the lyrical love-duet reaches towards full intimacy in the student's meditation on the roots, the stalk, the six-headed petals of the hyacinth – an image of the world:[20]

DAUGHTER: Who first imagined this vision?
STUDENT: You.
DAUGHTER: You.
STUDENT: You and I together. We have given birth to a vision. We are wed.
DAUGHTER: Not yet.
STUDENT: What remains?
DAUGHTER: The waiting, the trials, the patience.
STUDENT: Good! Try me. (*Pause*)

(p. 184)

But the mention of the negative states of marriage – of being itself – is enough to cast upon the couple's exchanges a chill, 'the pale cast of thought'; this poignant transformation itself is embodied in the dialogue. And the irruption of love-destroying consciousness is theatrically reinforced by the irruption of the demon-cook followed by the Daughter's litany of chores in that doomed household:

STUDENT: Sing to me!
DAUGHTER: Wait! First the toil, the toil of holding the dirt of life at bay.

(p. 186)

The mood of the dialogue is utterly changed, but not the mode. They go on talking, in the same way, until the Student's monologue (concerning his father's destructive speech already mentioned) and his lyrical address to the universe – turning away from the lover, evoking Christ's descent into hell, calling on the Saviour of the World. The Daughter shudders, crumples up and dies; and the scene ends with the Student's prayer and song. An attempt at choric – and religiose – universality has taken the place of the incomplete and imcompletable personal duologue.

It could be said that fragmentation and fade-out is the appropriate dialogue for a relationship that breaks down in mid-talk, and fades out with the fading of the hyacinth room. The whole decaying social and personal world is, in dramatic imagery and evocation, its proper context. It might be further argued that the attempt to restore the chorus and open up drama to the universe (aided by the harp's strings, a white light, the moaning heard from behind the screen, and the appearance of Böcklin's painting of the Island of the Dead) is a particularly appropriate way to end this scene. If so, the duologue is not only innovative but also achieved in the Wagnerian conclusion. But it is more likely, in my view, that a point has been reached in the dissolution of relationship – and in the parallel dissolution of interactive and personal dialogue – for which Strindberg was not yet 'ready' in terms of construction and verbal texture. Like several leading dramatists across two later generations – including Pirandello and O'Neill, Sartre and Camus – he brought radically new perceptions about relationship into an innovatory play-form, but did not fully translate his new vision and form into a corresponding 'theatre of language'. The transformations of character and dramatic world are running ahead of the transformations enacted in and through the dialogue.

The dialogue of Strindberg's late plays did achieve a texture not found, not needed, in the earlier naturalistic plays (with their strife of wills): 'a language for togetherness'. As Inga-Stina Ewbank pointed out, the duologue between the Student and the Daughter in *The Ghost Sonata* (in the exchanges over the symbolism of the hyacinth) amounts to an affinity, 'their speech-patterns interweave, to the point where their thoughts fuse'.[21] O'Neill had earlier celebrated in *The Ghost Sonata* the end of 'the family Kodak', of naturalism and the advent of 'some yet unrealised region where our souls, maddened by loneliness and the ignoble articulateness of flesh, are slowly evolving their *new language of kinship*'.[22] There is something appropriately paradoxical in singling out a language of 'togetherness' or 'kinship' in dialogue just at the point where dialogue no longer embodies 'solid character' in fullness of interaction. Through fusion, the speakers seem to be becoming interchangeable in their mode of speech.

4.

Thus we come to the dialogue of the *pseudocouple*,[23] one of Beckett's supreme theatrical inventions (forty years or so after *The Ghost Sonata*, which may well have influenced Beckett's drama). In the present context we shall be attending to the language of togetherness or kinship in Beckett's dialogue for inseparable pairs (Vladimir and Estragon, Hamm and Clov) more than to features of dissolution. The language of cyclic run-down has been over-stressed by me in another context, to the diminishment of the dialogue itself.[24]

It was not an arbitrary point of view, for one way of reading Beckett's drama is still to note its emergence out of an endlessly spiralling monologue towards diminishing speech: the escape of *dramatis personae* out of their total isolation into a dialogue more or less reluctantly accepted by them, to pass the time. It is also the escape of their author from the solipsism of his fiction: 'In the last book, *L'Innomable*, there's complete disintegration. No "I", no "have", no "being". No nominative, no accusative, no verb. There's no way to go on.'[25] Out of that fiction without personal pronouns, without deictics – whose absence is a mark of pathology, of madness, said Roman Jakobson concerning the later poetry of Hölderlin[26] – the way out was the theatre: where dialogue is all but inescapable, with its active grammar of personal pronouns and 'having' and 'being'.

Since the inner development of Beckett's later drama itself follows a move towards monologue and rhythmic abstraction, it is possible to understate his success in making the soliloquisers engage in endless quasi-encounters – in dialogue – in the early work, in *Waiting for Godot* and *Endgame*. The later work, from *Krapp's Last Tape* to *Not I* and *Rockaby* (1981) is then seen as both typical and creatively fascinating in its elimination of dialogue. And, with a certain flair for perceiving general patterns for modern drama, it is then tempting to juxtapose three generations of ghost dialogue: Ibsen's ghosts talk in inexorable logic; Strindberg's ghosts coalesce over the heady scent of the hyacinth; while the three poor ghosts of Beckett's *Play* chatter rhythmically and in utter isolation, each in a separate urn – out of each other's earshot, not understood, on first hearing, by the audience. For in *Play* 'there is no attempt to communicate, no semblance of intentional verbal contact between the three characters, but rather three separate monologues controlled by the moving spotlight. . .The spotlight provokes language as an inquisitor, but it does not mean that it is demanding answers or even communication.'[27] Dialogue then finally gives way to patterned dramatic speech of various modes, as Beckett himself pointed out to Martin Esslin: 'The text fell into three parts: *Chorus* (all characters speaking simultaneously); *Narration* (in which the characters talk about the events which led to the catastrophe); and *Meditation* (in which they reflect on their state of being endlessly suspended in limbo).' The repetition of these three parts demands a complex arithmetic of rhythmic variation, Beckett explained, in which 'each subsection is both faster and softer than the preceding one. If the speed of the first Chorus is 1 and its volume 1, then the speed of the first Narration must be 1 plus 5% and its volume 1 minus 5%. The speed of the following segment, the first Meditation, must then be (1 plus 5%) plus 5%, and its volume (1 minus 5%) minus 5%.' And so on, the text to go on *ad infinitum*.[28]

From this drive towards linguistic abstraction, towards rhythmic and semantic acceleration to the point of depersonalised speech, we return to the duologue of the pseudocouples. The new context may enable us to rediscover Beckett's mastery of the precarious, semi-personal duologue: the pivotal unit in the structure of the two early and major plays. And the new context may also redirect our attention to certain clear and simple features of Beckett's dialogue, which tended to be overlooked in the stress put on verbal ingenuity, on allusiveness and literary echoes, metaphysical clowning, rhythmic and imagistic repetition, in short – density of texture. We may rediscover the extent to which the would-be dialogue creates a residual language of encounter: the miming of conversational gestures between *personae* who begin to interact *as* persons.

In *Waiting for Godot*, Vladimir and Estragon can be seen as a symbiotic couple, in tragi-comically precarious relationship, akin to marriage or close friendship: at once essential and frustrating, an inseparable union marked by bouts of separation and threats of leaving. Apart from the ambivalence of their emotional relationship (which is hardly a problem for reader, audience, or critic) there is the uncertainty of their functional relationship, their degree of fusion or separate identity (which still is a critical problem). Are they to be regarded as split-off fragments of one psyche, as semi-persons or non-persons with virtually anonymous and interchangeable roles? ('The various figures which [Beckett] puts on stage are not really persons but figures in the inner world.')[29] Or do their differences outweigh their resemblances: Vladimir 'more intelligent, sensitive, analytical, articulate', and so on, while Estragon is 'the more spontaneous animal, instinctual, sulky, childish, lethargic, egotistic', and so on. Whatever the emphasis – and it may be a question of alternate focus seen through bifocal lenses – this couple does interact through words: the dialogue embodies the shifts and the comic pains of relationship. That shifting and many-faceted dialogue, ranges from the distinct, light shaping of popular drama – *commedia dell' arte* and music hall cross-talk – to the more literary stichomythia (as in the oft-quoted fine lyrical sequence on the dead voices: 'Rather they whisper. / They rustle. / They murmur. / They rustle' (pp. 62–3)) and 'flyting', the exchange of abuse (as in the bout that begins with 'Ceremonious ape!' and ends, in ultimate insult, with 'Crritic!' (p. 75)).

The seeming stasis of 'endless' talk gains its energy from the

existential/verbal need summed up in the exchange that introduces the 'dead voices' sequence:

ESTRAGON: In the meantime let's try and converse calmly, since we're
　　　incapable of keeping silent.
VLADIMIR: You're right, we're inexhaustible.

(p. 62)

The self-conscious talk about talk signals a *need for conversation*.
It is built into the text, and dramatised with a light touch, a
semblance of naturalness. It runs through the whole text, epitomised by Vladimir's early appeal: 'Come on, Gogo, return the ball,
can't you, once in a way?' It is present in act one, in those little
turns criss-crossing Vladimir's telling of the story of the second
thief who was saved, through Vladimir's refusal to hear either the
dream or the joke Estragon wants to tell, followed by:

ESTRAGON: (*gently*). You wanted to speak to me? (*Silence. Estragon takes a
　　　step forward.*) You had something to say to me? (*Silence. Another
　　　step forward.*) Didi. . .
VLADIMIR: (*without turning*). I've nothing to say to you.

(p. 16)

The quiet personal encounter is followed by an embrace, a recoil
(from Vladimir's garlic breath) and the talk of the satisfactions of
hanging, with an attendant erection, as an alternative to conversation. In act two it becomes more difficult to sustain this germi-
nation of talk out of empty time, so the 'meta-talk' becomes more
anguished:

ESTRAGON: Don't touch me! Don't question me! Don't speak to me! Stay
　　　with me!
VLADIMIR: Did I ever leave you?

(p. 58, opening sequence)

Long silence.

VLADIMIR: Say something!
ESTRAGON: I'm trying.

Long silence.

VLADIMIR: (*in anguish*). Say anything at all!
ESTRAGON: What do we do now?

(p. 63, after the 'dead voices' sequence)

ESTRAGON: That's the idea, let's contradict each other.
VLADIMIR: Impossible.

VLADIMIR: Thinking is not the worst.
ESTRAGON: Perhaps not. But at least there's that.

VLADIMIR: That what?
ESTRAGON: That's the idea, let's ask each other questions.

(p. 64)

There are other exchanges of this kind, all marked by *personal need and concern* on the relational level, and by a pleasing sense of *co-operative verbal games* on the linguistic level. These essential features of Beckett's dialogue (more strongly felt in full context and in performance) seem to me to distinguish this dialogue quite sharply from the mannerist and parodic language of Pinter and Stoppard, which will be discussed later. It is not simply that Beckett 'came first' and that comparable types of dialogue in later drama (especially in *Rosencrantz and Guildenstern are Dead* and *No Man's Land*) echo the rhythms of Beckett in recognisable pastiche. More important, the tragi-comic sense suffuses the dialogue: painfully and playfully embodying a never-ending encounter. The quasi-persons of the endless duet attempt to 'make words' as others might 'make love'. The physical and psychic contrast between the two speakers finds some counterpart in their speech-styles: Vladimir is given to monologues, to abstract musings and vocabulary, and tends to take the initiative in eliciting memories, recognitions, brief spells of hoping, from Estragon. In performance, even the more interchangeable 'turns' – stichomythia and cross-talk – can be finely tuned into a duet of voices; distinct tones – the merry lamenting Gogo versus the melancholy consoling Didi – resonate with the clash of attitudes.

The dialogue of *Endgame* is also illuminated by the present context. There, too, the elements of personal concern and need, and the felt tension of residual interaction through words, are marked (again more strongly than I once thought, and again to be distinguished from mannerist dialogue). Much of the play is structured around personal duologues: after a brief prologue, a long duet for Clov and Hamm (pp. 13–18), briefly joined by Nagg; a sustained and incantatory duologue for Nagg and Nell (pp. 18–22) and a second long duologue for Hamm and Clov (pp. 22–34), including two solo flourishes for Hamm, and broken by a short recitative for Hamm and Nagg. And in these duologues the sense of relationship – father/son, master/servant etc. – is poignantly personal and immediate: a feature of the text that much critical commentary, with its over-interpretation of the philosophical 'meaning' of the play, has managed to obscure. Yet

217

Beckett wanted an 'extreme simplicity of dramatic situation and issues' whose verbal texture yields 'fundamental sounds' (a simplicity we have to recapture in performance).[30] The dialogue of *Endgame* has a greater degree of abstraction than that of *Godot* and is suffused with tragic echoes – the mood of Racine's 'majestic sadness' within a mode of residual tragedy.

The tragic tonalities often involve intimately personal exchanges (a kind of caring, parodied by a weary contempt for the person being cared for):

HAMM: Did you ever see my eyes?
CLOV: No.
HAMM: Did you never have the curiosity, while I was sleeping, to take off
    my glasses and look at my eyes?
CLOV: Pulling back the lids? (*Pause*). No.

And again, still in the opening duologue:

HAMM: You don't love me.
CLOV: No.
HAMM: You loved me once.
CLOVE: Once!
HAMM: I've made you suffer too much. (*Pause*). Haven't I!
CLOV: It's not that.
HAMM: (*shocked*). I haven't made you suffer too much?
CLOV: Yes!
HAMM: (*relieved*). Ah you gave me a fright!

(pp. 13–14)

These bare exchanges directly interrelate the speakers, and contribute to their situation of 'inseparability' which is elsewhere dramatised by Clov's inability to leave Hamm (however ambiguously, and for whatever ignoble reasons of dependence). Even if the dialogue keeps veering away from a 'tender display of emotion' (as has been argued)[31] it does remain personal. The calculated sadism of a reply like Clov's 'Pulling back the lids?' or Hamm's darkly histrionic 'I haven't made you suffer too much?' are part of the dialogue – well within the personal question-answer framework.

The miming of a personal duet also frames the less personal – speculative and metaphysical – exchanges:

HAMM: Clov!
CLOV: (*impatiently*). What is it?
HAMM: We're not beginning to ... to ... mean something?

218

CLOV: Mean something! You and I, mean something! (*Brief laugh*). Ah,
    that's a good one!
HAMM: I wonder. (. . .)

(pp. 26–7)

That poignantly ironic 'You and I' is the quintessential mode of
dialogue – it transforms a 'thought' into a 'relationship', a metaphysical question into a rhetorical question, which calls for, and
gets, some sort of answer. The duologues of Hamm and Clov are
conspiciously rich in a constant wheeling of personal pronouns
(deictics); Hamm's incessant 'you' addresses are especially
marked. Recently a dialogue sequence from *Endgame* was quoted
to show the significant difference between 'history' (*histoire*, narrative that can tell a story without relying on 'you' and 'I') and
'discourse' (*discours*, made up of the exchange of speaker and
hearer within a dramatic 'here-and-now').[32]

More playfully, the text of *Endgame* itself draws attention to its
dialogue-centredness:

CLOV: I'll leave you.
HAMM: No!
CLOV: What is there to keep me here?
HAMM: The dialogue. (*Pause*). I've got on with my story. (*Pause.*) I've got
    on with it well. (*Pause. Irritably.*) Ask me where I've got to.

(p. 39)

And there follows a sustained 'canter' where Clov as stooge has
to revitalise the dialogue, and incidentally Hamm's flagging interest in the story he is working on, through enacting the role of
the questioner. It is an elicited dialogue – or the artifice of the
play-language exposed in a 'meta-language', as befits Beckett's
'meta-theatre'. It is, no doubt, a style-conscious verbal texture.
And yet, even here, the sequence flows out of a brief
personal/existential exchange ('I'll leave you.' 'No') which links
up with one of the central motifs of the play. And the verbal game
concerning dialogue/story/dialogue likewise remains integrated
in the whole text – points back to the cumulative dialogue of the
total text at several recurrent points:

CLOV: Do you see how it [the story] goes on.
HAMM: More or less.
CLOV: Will it not soon be the end?
HAMM: I'm afraid it will.

CLOV: Pah! You'll make up another.
HAMM: I don't know. (*Pause.*) I feel rather drained. (*Pause.*) The prolonged creative effort. (. . .)

(p. 41)

The coherence of the overall structure – its connectedness locally
and across the whole playtext – appears to be supported by the
recurrent simplicity, or purity, of speech – both syntax and vocabulary. Action and feeling are distanced but not 'killed' at any
point. The disruptions and manipulations . . . in the exchange
and inter-relationship between the utterances of two characters'
are present, but do not threaten to dislocate. Locally and cumulatively the duet-like dialogue sequences are 'signifying' and 'doing' and 'playing' with talk – as was argued by Dina Scherzer[33] –
through a meaningful enactment of the strategies of talk. And
that achievement remains even though Beckett chose to abandon
this particular mode of play-language, moving towards monologue and soliloquy, in complex patterns – as Ruby Cohn
showed[34] – in a related series of short plays and playlets. He may
thus have reversed the general evolution of drama, by turning
the 'dramatic' back into the 'lyric' mode, or into the fragmented
solo 'epic'. Whatever the final judgement on that, in the beginning was the dialogue – in the two duologue-centred plays.

5. Mannerist dialogue in Pinter's later plays

The parodox of Pinter's dialogue has always been that while it is
much nearer to one line of naturalism (the subtle line from
Chekhov) than anything in Beckett, the overall *shaping* of the
dialogue tends to foreground what sounds non-natural, what
dislocates encounter and verbal exchange. Perhaps the nearer the
texture of a particular pattern of dialogue seems to come to the
syntax and rhythm of everyday speech, the more audible becomes every 'deviation' – idiom focussed into idiocy, the question-
and-answer framework blurred into linguistic shadow-boxing,
the verbal exchanges turning (turning as we listen) into verbal
games people play. We can use quite a traditional and precise
term for a language that excels in playing internal variations on
its own verbal themes – *mannerism*.[35] My view is that in the later
plays of Pinter mannerist aspects of dialogue become more
marked and more arbitrary and, correspondingly, the emotional

force of interaction between the speakers in personal encounter tends to get attenuated.[36]

In a play like *The Caretaker* (admittedly the most 'mimetic' of all of Pinter's plays) one can trace an inner connection between all the main features of the play and, especially, between the language and the action. There is a central focus on interacting characters within an almost classically precise plot-situation, which the exchanges of dialogue, even at their most implicit, help to create. In the sequence of duologues (between three variously paired characters) which make up much of the play, most dislocations of encounter between the two speakers are made felt and illuminated by the dialogue itself. For example, Aston's long and moving monologue at the end of act two (in which he, in a beautifully coherent broken speech, tells how he was forced to undergo electric shock treatment) is so placed as to make it clear that he is disconnecting himself from Davies, who sits through the speech in stubborn isolation. That is the overall effect – a long speech seemingly released by, and addressed to, another person, who is supposed to be a sympathetic listener but who is 'disconnected' from the speaker; and the speaker is then left 'talking to himself' or the void. Locally, the effect is strengthened by the poignant realisation that Aston once saw himself as something of a 'communicator': 'But they always used to listen. I thought . . . they understood what I said. I mean I used to talk to them. I talked too much. That was my mistake' (p. 54). The cumulative local effect is then reinforced, early in act three, by Davies's angry lament to Aston's brother Mick:

> Couple of week ago . . . he sat there, he give me a long chat . . . about a couple of week ago. A long chat he give me. Since then he ain't said hardly a word. He went on talking there . . . I don't know what he was . . . he wasn't looking at me, he wasn't talking to me, he don't care about me. He was talking to himself! That's all he worries about . . . I mean we don't have any conversation, you see? You can't live in the same room with someone who . . . who don't have any conversation with you.
>
> (p. 63)

The final paranoid repetitions about the missed conversation (as much 'in character' as the rough grammar and the ordinary idiomatic repetitions: 'Couple of week ago' . . . 'about a couple of week ago') bring home to the audience the peculiar ironies of this particular human and linguistic suffering. Similarly, the bravura speech by Mick in act three, spun out of an interior decorator's catalogue by day-dreaming and or sadism, remains an integral part of the cumulative dialogue – though it has a mannerist texture. Apart from being an effective language of theatrical fantasy (one thinks of Jonson's hyperbolic fantasists) it does suggest for Mick the role of the trickster, who is beginning to play an elaborate game of verbal torture with Davies, the tramp. Elements of the early speech are later taken into the 'duologue of revenge' where Mick consolidates his triumph over Davies, helping to annihilate the tramp's status in the house:

DAVIES: What do you mean?

MICK: Well, you say you're an interior decorator, you'd better be a good one.

DAVIES: A what?

MICK: What do you mean, a what? A decorator. An interior decorator.

DAVIES: Me? What do you mean? I never touched that. I never been that.

MICK: You've never what?

DAVIES: No, no, not me, man. I'm not an interior decorator. I been too busy. Too many other things to do, you see. But I . . . but I could always turn my hand to most things . . . give me . . . give me a bit of time to pick it up.

MICK: I don't want you to pick it up. I want a first-class experienced interior decorator. I thought you were one.

DAVIES: Me? Now wait a minute – wait a minute – you got the wrong man.

MICK: How could I have the wrong man? You're the only man I've spoken to. You're the only man I've told, about my dreams, about my deepest wishes, you're the only one I've told, and I only told you because I understood you were an experienced first-class professional interior and exterior decorator.

DAVIES: Now look here –

MICK: You mean you wouldn't know how to fit teal-blue, copper and parchment linoleum squares and have those colours re-echoed in the walls?

DAVIES: Now, look here, where'd you get –?

MICK: You wouldn't be able to decorate out a table in afromosia teak veneer, an armchair in oatmeal tweed and a beech frame settee with a woven sea-grass seat?

DAVIES: I never said that!

MICK: Christ! I must have been under a false impression!

(pp. 71–2)

Already in *The Homecoming* similar bravura speeches – especially the pimp-talk of Lenny – are more arbitrarily used; and by the

time we get to *No Man's Land*, Briggs's verbal labyrinth of Bolsover Street (in act two) is severed from interactive speakers, and
indulgently mannerist. The distinction between integral and arbitrary uses of mannerist dialogue can be clearly seen, if we
contrast Pinter's handling of the duologue in *Old Times* (1971) and
in *No Man's Land* (1975). I hope this brief contrasted study will
contribute to an understanding of mannerism in the contemporary theatre.

The second act of *Old Times* opens with elements of a conventional farce, in the bedroom. Anna (the intrusive and enigmatic
friend of the wife, Kate) and Deeley (the insecurely combative
husband) are engaged in verbal games while Kate has a luxurious
bath. The first verbal game concerns Deeley's claim that he can
remember an occasion, a party, twenty years earlier, when he
spent some time gazing at Anna's stockinged thighs, she being
aware of his 'gaze'. At this stage Anna neither confirms nor
disconfirms her awareness of that gaze, of that indirect erotic link
in the remote past. The second verbal game concerns Kate's bath,
or rather ways of drying her, with a proper division of labour
between husband and friend:

DEELEY: Of course she's so totally incompetent at drying herself prop-
erly, did you find that? She gives herself a really good *scrub*, but
can she with the same efficiency give herself an equally good
rub? I have found, in my experience of her, that this is not in fact
the case. You'll always find a few odd unexpected unwanted
cheeky globules dripping about.
ANNA: Why don't you dry her yourself?
DEELEY: Would you recommend that?
ANNA: You'd do it properly.
DEELEY: In her bath towel?
ANNA: How out?
DEELEY: How out?
ANNA: How could you dry her out? Out of her bath towel?
DEELEY: I don't know.
ANNA: Well, dry her yourself, in her bath towel.

(*Pause*)
(pp. 54–5)

In the next three rounds, marked by pauses, Deeley first pro-
poses that Anna would do it 'properly'; then suggests that they
should do it together, with powder; and finally he resumes
responsibility for the act ('After all, I am her husband. But you can
supervise the whole thing').

The surface banalities of this exchange are theatrical on the level of immediate impact in that they 'intrigue' the 'knowing' audience: those boldly timid flights of sensuous fantasy around the act of drying Kate's body, the local savour of *scrub* against *rub* (to be spoken with emphasis) of 'unwanted cheeky globules dripping about', and of that loop in the conversation which allows us to inspect the preposition 'out'. (While this is a recurrent stylistic trick in Pinter, it is, in this instance, in keeping with Anna's old-world pedantry, with her use of words like 'lest' and 'gaze' – also underlined in the dialogue – and her genteel clichés hoarded from the post-war years.) Structurally, the scene is so placed that it sharpens awareness of a verbal *combat*, increasingly hostile, over the possession of Kate's past and present, real-or-imagined, identity. The rest of the act gradually intensifies this verbal combat until (only a few minutes of playing time from the end) it modulates into a chilling re-enactment of a trauma suffered in the past, in Kate's spare final monologue which releases some pent-up psychic horror in the fantasy image of Anne's corpse in the shared room:

> You stuck in your grin. I looked for tears but could see none. Your pupils weren't in your eyes. Your bones were breaking through your face. But all was serene. There was no suffering. It had all happened elsewhere.

(p. 72)

To Kate's long speech there is no answer other than the mime that re-enacts the combat of the three figures, and leaves them stranded in frozen postures after the husband's sobbing has stopped.

There can be no answer either to certain 'truth-test' questions imported from naturalistic drama – questions concerning the old-time conflict 'behind' the macabre metaphor of the corpse, for example. Pinter writes consistently within his own 'principle of unverifiability'.[37] *Old Times* offers no built-in distinctions between levels of 'reality' and 'fantasy', in action or dialogue; its plot-structure is more implicit than in any of the previous major plays, and the verbal texture is now primary (as in *Landscape* and *Silence*[38]) with a patterned collection of vague memories and arbitrary assertions. Nevertheless, this mannerist texture is still relatively firm in structure. The verbal exchanges form units which 'add up', move towards a significant catastrophe which mimes a tragic recognition. Many of the exchanges can be seen as verbal combats, a generic blend between the old comedy of manners (Wilde's Gwendolen and Cecily quarreling over lumps of sugar) and Pinter's own earlier comedies of menace (Ben and Gus in tense argument over the idiom 'light the kettle'). I would call it a comedy of mannerism. It dramatises the playfully noncommittal and indefinitely 'stretchable' word-games that cluster around memory and desire, and the ambiguities of mere potentiality.

No Man's Land (1975) takes the comedy of mannerism further, within a looser and more static structure. The juxtaposition of Spooner, the seedy would-be poet, and Hirst, the man of letters in prosperous decline, creates a collision of self-consciously *literary* styles from the start. Spooner's orotund, at once narcissistic and fulsome speech-making seems to parody a whole set of verbal postures and impostures, taking in its stride a gallery of pastiche voices (from generalised Georgian to precise Prufrock).

In the opening encounter his long speeches flow and intrude like lava into the rock-like taciturnity of the host – the nearest thing to direct linguistic satire in Pinter (with a clearly defined modern Grub Street milieu, the poetaster of Chalk Farm creeping up to Hampstead). However, at a certain point in act one (p. 29) Hirst, in response to Spooner's claim that 'We share something. A memory of the bucolic life', waxes eloquent, speaks of the 'village church [where] the beams are hung with garlands, in honour of young women of the parish, reputed to have died virgin' and of garlands for all who died unmarried. Spooner is emboldened, probes into his host's past, his married life, in a sequence of mannered insinuations:

SPOONER: I would say, albeit on a brief acquaintance, that you lack the essential quality of manliness, which is to put your money where your mouth is, to pick up a pintpot and know it to be a pintpot, and knowing it to be a pintpot, to declare it as a pintpot, and to stay faithful to that pintpot as though you had given birth to it out of your own arse.
You lack that capability, in my view. . . .
I offer myself to you as a friend. Think before you speak. For this proposition, after thought, will I assure you be seen to be carte blanche, open sesame and worthy the tender, for it is an expression of a quite unique generosity and I make it knowingly.
HIRST: *attempts to move, stops, grips the cabinet.*
Remember this. You've lost your wife of hazel hue, you've lost her and what can you do, she will no more come back to you, with a tillifola tillifola tillifoladi-foladi-foloo.

HIRST: No.
> *[Pause]*
> No man's land . . . does not move . . . or change . . . or grow
> old . . . remains . . . forever . . . icy . . . silent.
> [Here a series of carefully graded stage directions indicate
> Hirst's fall, and he crawls out of the room.]
SPOONER: I have known this before. The exit through the door, by way of
> belly and floor.

(pp. 32–4)

It might be said that this dialogue 'mimes' the interaction of host
and visiting parasite, and offers an effective counterpoint between Spooner's ornate invective and Hirst's reflective poetic
words. At the same time, attention is increasingly held – even in a
performance where Gielgud and Richardson provided the virtuoso speaking the text calls for – by the collage of pastiche styles:
Spooner's 'tilifola' echolalia and internal rhyming ('hue/do/
you/foloo' and the distinctly Eliotic 'I have known this before/
door/floor') act as a kind of verbal sandwich for Hirst's speech,
with its Beckett-like fragmentation and lyricism underlining the
play's title – its stasis.

Such effects are repeated and elaborated, without verbal
interaction, in act two. The bravura speech on Bolsover Street
(pp. 62–3) (an intricate one-way system with no exit that is too
obviously made to 'stand for' Life At A Dead End) is typical both in
its stylistic exhibitionism and its structural obliqueness (it is part
of the verbal fencing between Spooner and Briggs, one of Hirst's
retainers, a rather faint echo of Pinter's earlier comedy of menace). The long-sustained 'spoof' meeting between Spooner and
Hirst (pp. 68–79) is a particularly good example of a further
elaboration in a comedy of mannerism. The sequence begins with
a duologue wholly patterned out of the clichés of pre-war upper-
class speech, compressed Coward. Hirst opens this verbal game
with a monologue made up of non-stop lines and questions that
might have been one half of a conversation at a reunion of old
acquaintances – with a parody of empty reminiscence, complete
with a high frequency of name-dropping (Oxford, resonant 'U'
surnames, Lord's in '39, famous names in cricket, afternoon tea
in Dorchester with the polite seduction of Emily, Spooner's al-
leged wife, over buttered scones, Wiltshire cream, crumpets and
strawberries). The counter-game is a duet which begins with the
clipped exchanges of cartoon clubland:
HIRST: You did say you had a good war, didn't you?

226

SPOONER: A rather good one, yes.

and (over a full scene that is parasitical on the old comedy of manner squabbles over who seduced whom on what occasion and with what degree of treachery to friendship) gradually modulates back to Spooner's classically cadenced verbal attacks:

> It is you who behaved unnaturally and scandalously, to the woman who was joined to me in God.

and is answered by Hirst's role-parrotting protestations:

> I, sir? Unnaturally? Scandalously?

The long verbal exchange ends with another fragmented monologue by Hirst, including his wittily phrased nostalgia for a vanished age ('In my day nobody changed. A man was.') and an evocation of the family photograph album.

The pastiche dialogue does not – despite or because of the style-conscious ingenuity –rise to a re-enactment of the pressures of experience, real or imagined (as in *Old Times* or the small-scale *Landscape*). The reliance on Beckett pastiche – with occasional direct quotations and echoes – tends to diminish rather than support the imagery or impotence, sterility and stasis – the implied 'no man's land' theme. Direct allusion to a contemporary dramatist's language is, indeed, one of the riskiest features of systematic mannerism; in this instance, it calls for comparisons with *Endgame* in the informed section of the audience (and in this play Pinter does not approximate either Beckett's anguish or the incantatory rhythmic power of *Endgame* or *Play*). This raises the general problem of literary allusiveness in drama, as opposed to direct quotation in naturalism and parodic theatricality. In this particular play one of the problems is that the literary allusiveness is spread out among at least three of the characters (Spooner and Hirst share the recognisable Beckett echoes, and Briggs has read Newman).[39] All three are literary and highly literate gentlemen, no doubt. But does not mannerism end by the manner tending to remain the same – even in the hands of a master of counterpoint like Pinter – irrespective of the matter, the speaker and the situation?

6. Universal parody in Stoppard

Stoppard's plays, particularly *Rosencrantz and Guildenstern are Dead* (1967) and *Travesties* (1974) fully exploit the potentialities of parodic theatricality. The host-plays – *Hamlet* and *The Importance of Being Earnest* – nourish and control the new meta-plays in all their elements: the old texts provide not so much a target for direct parody as a frame of action, a myth (story universally known); residual cartoon-like characters; and a genre with the appropriate dramatic language. The borrowed amalgam is then inventively modified, and made to absorb layer upon layer of newly created parodic text. In this sense Stoppard's parody transcends all the known limits of dramatic burlesque (the simple Gilbertian and the richly polyphonic Elizabethan) and pervades practically the whole texture of the play. It is a theatricality that tends to become universally parodic. At its best it embodies and celebrates what Jonas Barish once called the 'theatrical theatre, as distinct from the anti-theatrical theatre of Stanislavski and Beckett'.[40] It is also a post-modern theatricality whose robust appetite has consumed portions of Pirandello and Beckett; their anguished questioning has been transformed into an exuberant advertisement for philosophical and linguistic relativity. The serious parody is not hampered by a dominant ideology or style; as in Joyce (whom I called the indirect master of parodic theatricality before Stoppard directly dramatised Joyce in *Travesties*)[41] almost *any* gesture and language may serve. The relativist interplay of languages, within rapidly shifting stage perspectives, explores analogues of man's basic uncertainty.

Rosencrantz and Guildenstern are Dead manages to exploit some of the built-in theatrical overtones of *Hamlet* (the play's concern with acting, and the play-life metaphor)[42] but the text of the host-play is not directly burlesqued. It is not Shakespeare's tragic vision and language that is the target of parody. Passages from *Hamlet*, more or less intact (the commissioning of the two attendants and their first meeting with the Prince; Claudius's 'Love, his affections . . .' speech; and the order to seek Hamlet after he has killed Polonius)[43] are quoted – in a new frame. It is this new meta-text, with the omissions and intermissions appropriate to the fragmented perspective of the two cue-less would-be performers, that casts a parodic light back on the old text itself. (In my view the omissions end by demythologising the tragic sense of life in a way comparable to broad burlesque, but that is another point.)

For his own dialogue Stoppard does not resort to pastiche

Shakespeare. He writes an exploratory dialogue in a collage of styles for the two attendants and the Player, marked by a short staccato form of stichomythia with echoes of *Waiting for Godot*. And this dialogue encircles the host-play, probes it and swallows it. As befits parodic art – which self-consciously displays the codes of style it is discarding – the dialogue points to itself: tells of its failure to sustain structured action and laments its own decay. More than once Aristotelian principles are evoked with ironic nostalgia (in a situation where the 'story' cannot cohere, and all the mirrors reflect further mirrors):

ROS.: I want a good story, with a beginning, middle and end.
PLAYER: (*to Guil.*): And you?
GUIL.: I'd prefer art to mirror life, if it's all the same to you.
PLAYER: It's all the same to me, sir.

(p. 59, also p. 58)

And more than once, the duologue of the two attendants ruefully explores the dislocations of question-and-answer:

ROS.: I remember when there were no questions.
GUIL.: There were always questions. To exchange one set for another is
           no great matter.
ROS.: Answers, yes. There were answers to everything.
GUIL.: You've forgotten.

(p. 28; see also: pp. 29–30, 33, 40)

The loss of connection – between question and answer – is linked with Hamlet's ambiguities and evasions, and the corresponding growth of uncertainty in the asymptotically groping minds of Rosencrantz and Guildenstern. Dislocation is mimed by mannered verbal games which, though they seem to be the weakest features of the play, are partly justified as a serious parody of the speakers' own fall from dialogue:

GUIL.: I'll hie you home and –
ROS.: – out of my head –
GUIL.: – dry you high and –
ROS.: (*cracking high*) over my step over my head body! – I tell you it's all
           stopping to a death, it's boding to a depth, stepping to a head,
           it's all heading to a dead stop.

(p. 27; see also p. 89)

As Bigsby points out, 'their loss of control is mirrored in a fragmentation of language'.[44] To that extent, the parody of dialogue is, here, mimetic.

However, the dialogue of language games (which may have links with Wittgenstein's *Investigations*, and with the fashion for aleatory art through the repeated metaphor of coin-tossing) at no point seems to centre or even settle on personal exchange proper. The play's own ideal dialogue is the question-question-question-question model (all answers replaced by questions) as in the question set (p. 31) that follows the rapid elimination of statement, repetition, grunts, synonyms, and rhetoric – all are 'fouls' in that round of the game-like duet.

Stoppard's verbal pyrotechnics go with a distrust of interactive dialogue and it is interesting to note that he himself finds dialogue difficult to write. In an interview with Ronald Hayman he said (concerning *Jumpers*): 'In practice the monologues played themselves, and all the conventionally easy bits – the dialogue – were very difficult to get right.'[45] This is borne out by the genuine inventiveness of the endlessly racing philosophical monologue given to George Moore in *Jumpers* (no philosopher has ever been able to turn the paradox of Zeno's arrow into a parable for the theatre that works both as physical action and as metaphysical meditation) while the duologues between Moore and his wife Dotty barely manage to rise above the level of the literary charades to which they are addicted.

In *Travesties* – as the title promises – dialogue itself is travestied by the hyper-verbal duets in which the characters collide: collisions of pastiche. *Travesties* is not content to use Wilde pastiche as the 'new material' of its dialogue; it swallows up Joycean parody, Tzara's Dadaist language, Shakespeare fragments and Lenin's speeches (which remain immune to full parody). The ingenious double distancing whereby *The Importance of Being Earnest* is being performed, as it were, *in* the erratic or prismatic memory of Old Carr (who claims to have met Joyce, Tzara *and* Lenin when he was British Consul in Zurich) allows almost any shift and combination of style. Since Joyce and Tzara are thoroughly theatricalised as they appear on Carr's memory-screen *within* the rewritten framework of *The Importance*, the dialogue becomes a chain of parodic variations. For example, the Wildean comedy of manners is rapidly extended to a farcical duet on causality:

TZARA: Eating and drinking, as usual, I see, Henry? I have often observed that Stoical principles are more easily borne by those of Epicurean habits.

CARR: (*stiffly*) I believe it is done to drink a glass of hock and seltzer before luncheon, and it is well done to drink it well before luncheon. I took to drinking hock and seltzer for my nerves at a time when nerves were fashionable in good society. This season it is trenchfoot, but I drink it regardless because I feel much better after it.

TZARA: You might have felt much better anyway.

CARR: No, no – post hock, propter hock.

TZARA: But, my dear Henry, causality is no longer fashionable owing to the war.

CARR: How illogical, since the war itself had causes. I forget what they were, but it was in all the papers at the time. (. . .)

(p. 36)

And so on, to a debate on chance and Dada art (which starts off with Tzara saying 'Dada dada dada dada' thirty-five times in rapid succession) until, later in the same act, Tzara declares his love to the Gwendolen of the meta-play by drawing from a hat slips of paper with the cut-up words of 'Shall I compare thee . . .' (The 'found poem' is remarkably non-accidental, beginning with 'Darling. Shake thou thy gold buds'; and Dada is being further stabilised, or immunised, by the on-going comedy of manner framework – a point of some interest in judging the limitations of parody.)

It is only to be expected that when Joyce re-enters he should engage Tzara in a long duel of styles (pp. 56–63). Joyce uses, among other styles, his own 'Ithaca' catechism in cross-examining, in the role of Aunt Augusta, the upstart Tzara (whose aleatory art is the antithesis of Joyce's all-consuming structures). This combat of modernist wits concludes with a 'quiz' on the factions within Dada, Huelsenbeck's Communism, and Tzara's radical anti-creed demanding:

TZARA: The right to urinate in different colours.

JOYCE: Each person in different colours at different times, or different people in each colour all the time? Or everybody multi-coloured every time?

TZARA: It was more to make the point that making poetry should be as natural as making water –

JOYCE: God send you don't make them in the one hat.

(pp. 61–2)

This is too much for Tzara (stage direction) who proceeds to denounce Joyce with Jonsonian invective in the name of anti-art, calling vandals and desecrators 'to smash centuries of baroque subtlety'.

Seldom has the theatre been parodic to this extent: the primary parodies of Wilde and Joyce are further extended into an interlocking meta-parody. (The play opens with a prologue which replaces dialogue with a polyglot pot-pourri: Tzara reads from his collage poem, Lenin and Nadya exchange remarks in Russian, while Joyce dictates to Gwendolen a trilingual extract from 'The Oxen of the Sun' episode, which is itself a travesty of English prose styles.)[46] One might have thought all that was enough for one play, but we are treated to other sequences of pastiche dialogue: the first meeting between Joyce and Carr is transacted through the exchange of limericks (pp. 33–6); a combat between Carr and Cecily turns the titles of Gilbert and Sullivan operettas into invective (pp. 74–5); and the para-Wildean misunderstanding between Gwendolen and Cecily is argued out in sung rhyme in the manner of 'Mr Gallagher and Mr Shean' (pp. 90–3). While each of these scenes may be a minor *tour de force*, they are gratuitous and tend to 'divert' the audience to the point where the parody is felt to have no target left. But then, farcical exuberance celebrates excess, and parody goes on feeding on itself.

Having gone so far towards universal parody, Stoppard lets act two be dominated by the near-documentary Lenin scenes, which are deliberately excluded from the *Importance* scheme, 'for it would have been disastrous to Prismise and Chasublize the Lenins'.[47] The straightness of language and staging – Cecily's lecture on the origins of the revolution in the opening scene, and the dramatisation of Lenin's letters, telegrams and speeches towards the end – gives the voice of political revolution a hearing *outside* parody. Historically verifiable events further underpin that language, pitted against the doubly fictive languages of Joyce and Tzara, the voices of artistic revolution. Are the Lenin scenes then to be taken as the play's centre of gravity? If so, they should provide the kind of focus within parodic theatricality which Elizabethan drama offered. But such a view, though it might please the dogmatic Marxist–Leninist, would contradict the parodic structure and tone of the whole play, written from a thoroughly relativistic point-of-view (externally supported by Stoppard's view that a speech Joyce makes in defence of art 'is the most important speech in the play', and by his support for a liberal democratic society outside the theatre).[48] The play's curious tension between the 'baroque farce' of the hyper-parodic language and the 'authentic speeches' of Lenin need not have the effect of 'dislocating the play'.[49] But it certainly creates a collision of styles, a precarious collage dialogue.

The precariousness seems to go beyond this particular scene, and may well tell us something about the dialogue of parodic theatricality generally. For in a dialogue of interreflecting parodies anything quoted, or seemingly anchored in reality, is likely to get engulfed. There can be no spokesman (not Lenin, not Joyce), for the multiple perspective has no centre. The speakers are voices which get 'mixed' in the multi-vocal wit machine. The delights of such a pan-parodic theatre have a clear enough contemporary appeal: relativism; the theatre breeding theatre; language playing upon language (post-Einstein, post-Pirandello and post-Wittgenstein). The question is whether such a fully parodic theatricality can find room for anything so grave as a centre of gravity.

6 The impersonal/personal duologue from Brecht to Shepard*

1.

We have seen how the gradual diminishment of interaction between speakers more or less 'unverifiable' – in terms of identity, situation and then in terms of speech – has led to unstable and mannerist types of dialogue. The dissolution of 'those whom dialogue has joined together' can lead to a kind of internal depersonalisation – a duologue of semi-persons and *pseudocouples*. The contrary direction, in the broad theatricality of epic and popular drama, may go with a kind of external depersonalisation – a duologue of non-intimate, partial encounters. The actual forms taken by the dialogue of personal encounter in and after Brecht are, however, richly varied and many-faceted.

It is only when we turn to Brecht's theatre (especially the late parable plays) that certain key questions, present in this study from the start, become fully pressing – with the pressure of an ongoing and contemporary question. To ask: what is happening in the dialogue of Brecht's theatre? (a deliberately anti-individualistic and anti-illusionist theatre) is to ask again: what is the role of dialogue within the total play-language (including chorus, song, set speeches etc.)? And again: what is the role of the personal duologue within the group dialogue? Does an overall dramatic structure – with an outward-directed ideology and a choric/narrative concept of language – end by excluding the element of personal exchange from the dialogue? Or is there a constant need and function for a dialogue of (two) *dramatis personae* who exchange values and speech-styles which are uniquely theirs?

These questions compel a brief return to the Greeks, to Shakespeare and to one direction in modernist drama, for there is a line

234

that runs from Aeschylus to Brecht. We have seen how the plot-centred structure of Greek tragedy made Kierkegaard, among others, set the ancients and the moderns in direct opposition – precisely from the point of view of dialogue.[1] While Greek tragedy did not develop 'the dialogue to the point of exhaustive reflection, so that everything is absorbed in it', in modern tragedy (here including Shakespeare) the action '*can* be exhaustively represented in situation and dialogue'. Kierkegaard can hardly be blamed for failing to foresee the advent of the Brechtian theatre; in other respects his dictum still has critical force. Several studies of Greek drama have put the stress on the impersonality – or on the stereotyped symmetry – of the dialogue. Aeschylus can be seen, from one point of view, as the most Brechtian among the Greeks: writing political/religious drama for the whole *polis*, centred on the chorus, that vehicle of vision or communal 'teach-in'. But in Sophocles the concern with personal vision and personal idiom in speech is marked and recurrent. And in the highly dialectical Euripides (who had diluted the purity of the Dionysiac chorus with the pale cast of Socratic dialogue, as Nietzsche charged) the clash of ideologies is often inseparable from a clash of personal attitudes and voices – witness Orestes and Electra 'debating' the murder of their mother (*Electra*, 967–82, pp. 88–102, esp. 98ff). In short, even though the dialogue often is a secondary element, in contrast to the chorus, in the mythic/epic theatre of the Greeks, our study points to the essential function of that dialogue: discovery and recognition in a unique personal encounter at the centre of the play, which transforms the situation, and sometimes the language, of the speakers.

In Shakespearian tragedy, and, to a lesser extent, in comedy, the personal duologue is often pivotal, 'embodying the principles of growth and change' through the interaction of the protagonists. (The total subversion of Othello's mind and language through Iago's early form of verbal brain-washing is only the most fully developed type of transformational duologue.) This does not mean that we can fully understand the love-duets of Romeo and Juliet unless we attend to the speeches of the Verona market place (Mercutio, the Nurse, the verbal fencing of the two warring households); or that we can fully enjoy the wit-combat, from *Love's Labour's Lost* to *Much Ado About Nothing* unless we attend to the elaborate verbal dance of the whole group around the principal 'combatants'. But it is the chronicle-based histories (not studied in this book) which are, clearly, the generic forerunners of Brecht's epic theatre. With their broad patterns of narrative and ritual speech, the histories leave less room for the duologue of personal encounter than any of the tragedies. Yet in *Richard II* the personal duologue is part of the total play-language (duologues between Richard and Bolingbroke, between Gaunt and the Duchess of Gloucester, and between Richard and his queen) in a structure of action which is shaped towards tragedy. And even the more broadly based epic structures of the two parts of *Henry IV* and *Henry V* present, as part of the counterpoint, personal duologues – usually in scenes that are Shakespeare's own invention, like the scenes of jubilant, if make-believe, intimacy between Prince Henry, Falstaff and the other boon companions at the Boar's Head (whose talk has a generous sprinkling of mutual 'thou' addresses), and the famous wooing scene between King Henry and the daughter of the French king. It is not surprising that Auerbach chose the intimate-sounding conversation between Prince Henry and Poins (in 2 *Henry IV*, 2. 2) to show that Shakespeare refused the separation of high and low levels of style.[2] One might as well say that Shakespeare refused the separation of the impersonal and personal modes of dialogue.

From Racine to Ibsen and beyond, the dominant structure of drama *was* the kind of close structure that Brecht defined, negatively, as 'dramatic', and which Szondi considered the pure dialogue-centred model of dramatic form.[3] Within that dramatic structure the personal or confidential duologue became significant and central. Brecht was opposed to all that, but his epic theatre was not the only or the first type of counter-theatre, reacting against the mimetic dialogue within a closed and intimate structure. Nietzsche was among the first who hoped to revive the chorus, its ritual and mythic power set against the all-too-human dialogue of naturalism: 'The introduction of the chorus is the decisive step whereby we declare war, openly and honestly, on all Naturalism in art.' (*Die Geburt der Tragödie*, 1872.)[4] The urge to remythologise the structure and language of drama was the explicit conception behind, and the essential innovation within, Eliot's *Murder in the Cathedral*, with its careful orchestration of a version of the Aeschylean chorus; and in that play the dialogue is predominantly impersonal, Thomas Becket is distanced from the other speakers, even from the shadowy Tempters (who might be said to emanate from his own mind, as inner voices).

The Brechtian epic theatre has proved itself more vital, and more lastingly influential, than the ritualistic drama of Eliot and others, as an anti-illusionist mode. It developed a form of secular-mythic openness – and a tough but stylised choric speech – which had no need to fall back on a theatre of priests. But how much room did that theatre leave for the dialogue of personal encounter?

Brecht provides his own context for the study of dramatic dialogue in a supposedly 'anti-dramatic' theatre. Though he wrote little on language and dialogue specifically, his general theory of the epic theatre, and the implicit testimony of the plays themselves, spell out a new attitude to dialogue. The central ideas of epic theatre have, in a sense, become too famous, so that Brecht's working hypotheses and workshop poetics are in danger of being reduced to catchwords (the 'alienation effect', etc.). The opposition of 'epic' and 'dramatic' is, however, central to the study of dialogue, as it is to all aspects of theatre. Brecht's well-known early formulation of the opposition between the two types of theatre (the Aristotelian and the epic) is thoroughly and propagandistically dualistic:[5]

The 'Dramatic' Theatre:	The Epic Theatre:
the stage embodies a sequence of events	*the stage narrates the sequence*
involves the spectator in an action and uses up his energy, his will to action	makes him an observer but awakes his energy
allows him feelings	demands decisions
communicates experiences	*communicates pieces of knowledge*
spectator is brought into an action	*is placed in front of an action*
is plied with suggestion	*with arguments*
sensations are preserved	till they become insights
man is given as a known quantity	man an object of investigation
man unalterable	alterable and altering
tense interest in the outcome	tense interest in what happens
one scene exists for another	*each scene exists for itself*
linear course of events	*curved course of events*
natura non facit saltus	*facit saltus*
the world is what it is	the world is what it is becoming
	(emphasis added)

237

If we reflect on those definitions that bear most directly on questions of dialogue (all the other items in the catalogue have *some* bearing on dialogue) we would expect to find a dramatist committed to a type of dialogue that aims at something like pure narrative (discourse) or else debate: 'the stage narrates the sequence'; 'communicates pieces of knowledge'; 'is placed in front of an action . . . with arguments . . . till they become objects'. All this in opposition to those keywords of naturalist and symbolist drama: embodying, communicating experience, suggestion, sensation, etc. A total commitment to Brecht's doctrine would result in a predominantly choric language or a dialogue so impersonal that it could no longer communicate personal experience, feeling, tension – in short relationship and personal encounter. But the doctrine is marked by certain internal oppositions (as befits a writer who believed in 'the dialectic') and is accompanied by certain important changes in practice (as befits a believer in historical change). If we attend to the dialogue of the parable plays especially – with a brief reminder of Brecht's evolution as a dramatist – we get quite a complex reading.

The position of the dramatist who claims to be anti-dramatic is paradoxical enough, for a start. But what exactly was it that Brecht wanted to reject? In the present context, the quickest answer might be: the line from Ibsen; the kind of confessional and 'infolding' dramatic dialogue that is the focus of the two preceding chapters. Brecht is, clearly, against both the structure and the language (as well the value system) of the Ibsenite dialogue, with its relentless psycho-logic and its illusionist urge to be faithful to the language actually spoken in real life. More than that, Brecht is opposed to the notion of Nature (and with it to 'natural language') as something ahistorical: it is not the vehicle of truth-telling, but the solace of the bourgeois audience.[6] Brecht does not want to imitate, but to inform; does not want to 'infold' but to unfold; does not want a psychological or symbolic but a historical and histrionic dialogue. All that would go against the dialogue of close structure and inwardness (as found in the confessional duologues of *Rosmersholm* and *John Gabriel Borkman*) with all that whirling retrospection, those nuances of introspection.

And yet, Brecht wanted to, and did, write dialogue that sounds *like* real speech, often embracing dialect and contemporary slang in his stylised shaping of language. He wanted a language of gesture–*gestus*–in a dialogue that could follow exactly *the attitude of the person speaking*. 'For language is theatrical in so far as it conveys the mutual attitude of the speakers.'[7] Above all, he wanted the colour, the swiftness, the savour, the punch, the humour and the sound of a certain kind of colloquial (or quasi-colloquial) speech. The frame of question-and-answer (which the subjective modernists from Strindberg on were attenuating or dissolving) was restored and relished both in itself and as a vehicle of dialectical thought. The cut-and-thrust of the 'turns' – the reply, the retort, the repartee, etc. – all these are inescapable in dialogue as dialectic. (It is worth recalling that in German, as in other languages, *Repliken* is a virtual synonym for dialogue.)

Brecht's literary eclecticism – ranging from Rimbaud to Kipling, from the popular ballad to the tender lyric – was unified by the theatricality of his dialogue. As John Willett put it, the many different stylistic influences all 'helped him to put his finger on the fundamental sense: they purified his language and showed him the practical and aesthetic value of saying just what one really means and no more'.[8] The phrase *purified his language*, with its symbolist connotations, may sound unexpected in the context of Brecht's theatre language. Yet it is apt: for Brecht did want to purify 'the dialect of the tribe' but in the opposite direction from the symbolists, away from a 'language within the language', and from speech of soul. The opposition to an etiolated kind of verbal purity went with an opposition to those aspects of relationship that are epitomised by the symbolist love of 'intimacy' and 'inwardness'.[9] Indeed, Brecht might seem to be even more opposed to subjective/symbolist than to naturalistic drama – the line from *The Ghost Sonata* to Beckett's *Play* and Pinter's *No Man's Land*. (It is on record that Brecht wanted to write an anti-*Godot*, a counter-play to *Waiting for Godot* before he died; we can imagine its thrust.)

On the map of modern drama, in its second greatest period of innovation, Brecht and Beckett stand as polar opposites, yet linked by their joint opposition to the structure of 'absolute' drama and its fully interpersonal dialogue. Our popular images keep them poles apart: Brecht taking up Galileo's fabled telescopes and focussing on the planet-wide dimensions of the world 'out there'; Beckett peering down some electro-microscope at the beautiful, deadly bacteria of the solipsistic self. Each of these perspectives goes with an anti-illusionist language. It has been argued (interestingly enough in contrasting Brecht with Pirandello who made theatre out of the painful fusion, or confusion, of 'reality' and 'illusion') that Brecht attempts to separate art/illusion from life/reality, and to show their non-fusion, the clear distance between them.[10] Yet perhaps only the mature Brecht managed to create a distanced dialogue which nevertheless operates on the level of personal exchange, with speech-in-character and 'felt life', in crucial scenes of the play.

Before looking at two mature parable plays, it is worth recalling the paradox of the early Brecht's hyper-subjective search for an 'objective' theatre. Before the epic theatre comes *Baal* and *In the Jungle of the Cities* with the isolation of the self, the near-impossibility of human communication, the uselessness of language as a vehicle of understanding and friendship. Baal is not just the *poète maudit* or the apostle of phallic narcissism (four decades before the rise of his Anglo-Saxon counterparts). He also exclaims: 'I'll make a new Adam, I'll have a go at the inner man'; and he escapes from dialogue into song, tirade and sexual intimacy. Even more interesting, in the present context, is the long-sustained duel of two men towards the end of *In the Jungle of the Cities* – between Shlink (getting old and ruthless in pursuit of companionship through money and conflict) and Garga (the younger man, in turn submissive and self-assertive, and finally abandoning his voracious benefactor to a lynching crowd). Their struggle, a metaphorical boxing match between two men, linked by latent homosexuality in a strife of 'styles' (anticipating Shepard's *The Tooth of Crime*) reaches a climax in the penultimate scene of the play. Huddled together in a tent by the gravel pits of Lake Michigan, these two talk about their failure to reach one another in a final and failing duologue. The scene has some of the effects of absurdist drama[11] except that the two characters are separate and distinct (no fusion towards a Beckettian *pseudocouple*) and the 'failure of language' is still explicit and rather wordy: Garga has rejected Shlink's love for him and then complacently rejects also the uses of language, of conversation; and Shlink, with growing despair over the division – the schizoid division, *Entzweiung*[12] – caused by their words, begins to doubt even the efficacy of carnal union (which he has been extolling as a primitive salvationist creed). Even conflict, enmity, can no longer connect them:

SHLINK: The endless isolation of man makes even of enmity an unattainable goal. Even with animals it is impossible to come to an understanding.

GARGA: Nor does speech help all that much.

SHLINK: I have watched animals. Love – warmth from bodily proximity – is our only grace in all the darkness. But the union of the organs is the only union, and it can never bridge the gap of speech.

(p. 61)

Those not familiar with the work of the early, pre-Marxist, Brecht might hardly recognise this encounter (with its stillness in the frenzied 'jungle', and the dialogue of two men at the point of breakdown) as 'Brechtian'. The Berliner Ensemble's programme note to their production of *The Jungle* included a comment which is part apology, part an attempt to see the dialogue in a Marxist light: the play is said to offer 'a critical attitude towards drama at a time when it is no longer possible [to use] a dramatic duel-dialogue in a totally alienated world'. Wherever that world, mythic or real, is located (in and beyond the capitalist world) it is clearly one that Brecht went on to reject: a world of failing language, where the speakers are split in a duologue of psychic dualism.

The didactic plays (*Lehrstücke*) of Brecht's middle period are largely impersonal, and even the great epic plays – *Mother Courage* and *Galileo* – have little dialogue centred on personal encounter. We remember those plays for their overall action, for their central stage metaphors (Mother Courage and her wagon, Galileo and his complacent eating, symbol of his seeming surrender) and perhaps for such speeches as Mother Courage congratulating Kattrin on her dumbness ('Be thankful you are dumb, you'll never contradict yourself') or for the proverb-contests in either play, and the fine set speeches, the argument and the polemics. But the parable plays have a different scale and artistic balance: mythic rather than historical, drawing on the simple artifice of folk art, the parable play can make use of heightened speech, expressive gesture, and a humane dialogue that is the vehicle of personal encounter in the midst of a mythic/choric total play-language.[13]

In *The Caucasian Chalk Circle* and in *The Good Woman of Setzuan* Brecht achieved a rare fusion of the personal and impersonal modes in dialogue – as in the whole structure of action. On the one hand, both plays have a tremendous sweep – large number of characters, rapid episodic action, movement, exotic scenography, masks, songs. Both create a sense of openness to the natural and cosmic world beyond the human scene of action: a river, cliffs, a glacier; the gods descending from the sky (as in *The Birds* of Aristophanes. The choral commentaries of the Singer and the Musician, and the songs of the characters themselves, frame and extend the action: scenes of turmoil, cruel war (*Chalk Circle*) and rapacious business (*Good Woman*). On the other hand, certain quiet scenes of encounter between couples, presented with the directness of naive art – the betrothal of Grusha and her soldier Simon, the sudden love of Shen Te and the pilot – become central in the epic structure and crystallise the exchange of values through the exchange of personal feeling.

The Caucasian Chalk Circle (if we may invert the chronology of composition for the instance)[14] has great simplicity within a multi-level design. It also offers a paradigm for the dialogue of personal encounter within the general upheaval of civil war and revolution. We may start with the 'wooing' encounter wherein the good soldier Simon Shashava opens up the possibilities of relationship with the simple-minded kitchen maid Grusha Vashnadze, in a courting strategy made up of impudence and genuine concern. Just before the Easter feast (which portends the fall of the Governor, in whose palace Grusha is employed) Simon sets to interrogating the girl:

SIMON: So the young lady has been down to the river again?
GRUSHA: Yes, at the poultry farm.
SIMON: Really? At the poultry farm, down by the river . . . not higher up maybe? Near those willows?
GRUSHA: I only go to the willows to wash the linen.
SIMON: (*insinuatingly*) Exactly.
GRUSHA: Exactly what?
SIMON: (*winking*) Exactly that.
GRUSHA: Why shouldn't I wash the linen by the willows?
SIMON: (*with exaggerated laughter*) Why shouldn't I wash the linen by the willows! That's good, really good!
GRUSHA: I don't understand the soldier. What's so good about it?
SIMON: (*slyly*) 'If something I know someone learns, she'll grow hot and cold by turns!'
GRUSHA: I don't know what I *could* learn about those willows.
SIMON: Not even if there were a bush opposite? And everything could be seen from it? Everything that goes on there when a certain person is – er – 'washing linen'?
GRUSHA: What *is* it that goes on? Won't the soldier say what he means and have done with it?

SIMON: Something goes on. And something can be seen.
GRUSHA: Could the soldier mean I put my toes in the water? When it was
    hot once in a while? There was nothing else.
SIMON: There were the toes. And more.
GRUSHA: More what? At most the foot?
SIMON: The foot. And a little more. (*He laughs heartily.*)
GRUSHA: (*angrily*) Simon Shashava, you ought to be ashamed of yourself!
    To sit in a bush on a hot day and wait till someone comes and
    dips her foot in the river! And I bet you bring a friend along too!
    (*She runs off.*)
SIMON: (*shouting after her*) I didn't bring any friend along!

It is a dialogue of polite third-person formalities (much more clearly marked in style in the German text: 'Und das Fräulein war also wieder einmal am Fluss? / Ich versteh den Herrn Soldat nicht') which becomes the vehicle for the exchange of Simon's personal ('bloody personal') questions and Grusha's simpleminded and finally protesting response. On that little climax the ceremonious tone is exchanged for the direct address, the 'you' familiar: 'Simon Chachava, du solltest dich schämen.' – 'Simon Shashava you ought to be ashamed of yourself!' The shift in modes of address is carried by a kind of leap into intimacy – the couple is launched from a casual into a committing encounter, all within the light folk art frame, part ritual, part improvisation in relationship.

The first encounter leads (still in the first act, called The Noble Child), to a duologue of betrothal, again blending the formal and the colloquial, the impersonal and the personal mode. With the fall of the city and the threat of chaos and violence, there is not a moment to be wasted for Simon to make his proposal to Grusha. Nevertheless, he speaks with catechismic circumlocutions: elaborately questioning his 'intended one', in keeping with the courtly peasant code he judges appropriate for the occasion:

SIMON: Since we're in a hurry we shouldn't quarrel. You need time for a
    good quarrel. May I ask if the young lady still has parents?
GRUSHA: No, only a brother.
SIMON: As time is short – the second question is this: Is the young lady as
    healthy as a fish in water?
GRUSHA: Maybe once in a while I have a pain in the right shoulder.
    Otherwise I'm strong enough for my job. No one has com-
    plained. So far.
SIMON: Everyone knows that. Even if it's Easter Sunday, and there's a

question who should run for the goose, she's the one. The third
question is this: Is the young lady impatient? Does she want
apples in winter?

GRUSHA: Impatient? No. But if a man goes to war without any reason and
no message arrives – that's bad.

SIMON: A message will come. And now the final question . . .

GRUSHA: Simon Shashava, I must go to the third courtyard and quick. My
answer is yes.

SIMON: (*very embarrassed*) Haste, they say, is the name of the wind that
blows down the scaffolding. But they also say: The rich don't
know what haste is. I'm from . . .

GRUSHA: Kutsk . . .

SIMON: So the young lady has already inquired about me? I'm healthy,
have no dependents, make ten piasters a month, as a paymas-
ter twenty piasters and I'm asking – very sincerely – for your
hand.

GRUSHA: Simon Shashava, it suits me well.

SIMON: (*taking from his neck a thin chain with a little cross on it*) My mother
gave me this cross, Grusha Vashnadze. The chain is silver.
Please wear it.

GRUSHA: Many thanks, Simon. (*He hangs it round her neck.*)

SIMON: It would be better for the young lady to go to the third courtyard
now. Or there will be difficulties. Anyway, I have to harness the
horses. The young lady will understand.

GRUSHA: Yes, Simon.

They stand undecided.

GRUSHA: Simon Shashava, I shall wait for you. (. . .)

(pp. 514–15)

The duologue has the feel of an authentic personal union. It is
neither sentimental nor individual – the folk art frame distances
or 'socialises' the quality of verbal exchanges. Yet each character
is 'characteristic' in speech: Grusha displaying the mixture of
patient responses suddenly cut short by a simplistic genius for
direct statement ('I must go . . . quick. My answer is yes' – to the
question not yet put); and Simon, switching from the humorous teasing speeches of the first encounter to the solemnities due
to the occasion. Brecht attached social value to this speech-style,
connecting Simon with the kind of thorough and thoughtful
speech that would endure: 'Simon has a bearing that marks his
self-esteem and dignity. No hasty, unconsidered sentence,
everything he says is thorough and carefully thought through.
He speaks so that even his grandchildren may one day receive
what he had once said, word for word.'[15]

One might say that each speaker is given a speech-style which is both typical and unique, social and personal. Such speech-styles have the quality of an engraved epigram and yet they are far from static – the dialogue becomes fully interactive. The emotion of the speakers is, however, not fully expressed; in a deliberate 'epic' device Brecht transfers the fuller expression of Grusha's emotion and commitment from the dialogue to the song she sings to Simon at the end of this betrothal scene. (The song, with its burden 'Ich werde warten auf dich unter den grünen Ulme.' 'I shall be waiting for you under the green elms' has echoes of a simple Soviet war song.) Taken as a whole, the internal distancing devices in this duologue still leave us with an encounter very much in 'the foreground'; the hard-edged language is the vehicle of personal values and expressions. We may see in this a paradox of *Verfremdung*/distancing – it is hard yet tender, distant yet 'here and now'. But then, one of the effects aimed at by Brecht has always been to make the ordinary seem extraordinary: to signal to the audience, for signal attention. Not empathy, but complete attention to what is being said and transacted, here and now.

In context, the betrothal duologue is only an episode within the superbly rendered general confusion of voices in the besieged palace – as the servants rush hither and thither, the governor's wife lingers over the brocaded dresses coveted for her flight, and Grusha picks up the bundle with the governor's baby, unable to resist 'the terrible temptation of goodness'. This needs to be recalled to see that Brecht has come near to the Shakespearian art of juxtaposing public and private, group and duet, impersonal and personal modes, in a unified play-language.

The Good Woman of Setzuan has comparable kinds of perfectly achieved personal encounter, in a naive art framework, between Shen Te, the poor generous girl, and Yang Sun, the would-be pilot, her lover and potential exploiter. The pattern of dialogue between these two is complicated by the doubling of 'the good woman' into the dangerously altruistic Shen Te and the protectively ruthless 'cousin' Shui Ta. A duologue conducted by a *Doppelgänger* with a 'third person' (forming a trio of voices) offers interesting modulations of speech-style. We have two contrasted ways of speaking, two voices: one soprano, as it were, for generous and life-affirming emotions; the other bass and guttural, for calculating constraints and rejections. These tonal differences clearly correspond to a clash between personal and impersonal modes of utterance in Brechtian dialogue.

The first encounter between Shen Te and Yang Sun is presented as a virtual saving of the despairing young man from suicide by hanging, through his reluctant listening to the young woman's simple conversational consolations. At one point (clearly a point of increasing attention by the pilot, in the pattern of being 'talked back into life') Yang Sun asks Shen Te to talk about herself. ('Sprich von Dir'.) The conversation rises and falls, reaches a degree of intimacy, until the young man, sceptically curious, asks for further supplies of talk:

YANG SUN: Go on talking. A voice is a voice.
SHEN TE: Once, when I was a little girl, I fell, with a load of brushwood. An old man picked me up. He gave me a penny too. Isn't it funny how people who don't have very much like to give some of it away? They must like to show what they can do, and how could they show it better than by being kind? Being wicked is just like being clumsy. When we sing a song, or build a machine, or plant some rice, we're being kind. You're kind.
YANG SUN: You make it sound easy.
SHEN TE: Oh, no. (*Little pause.*) Oh! A drop of rain!
YANG SUN: Where'd you feel it?
SHEN TE: Between the eyes.
YANG SUN: Near the right eye? Or the left?
SHEN TE: Near the left eye.
YANG SUN: Oh, good. (*He is getting sleepy.*) So you're through with men, eh?
SHEN TE: (*with a smile*) But I'm not bowlegged.
YANG SUN: Perhaps not.
SHEN TE: Definitely not.
         Pause.
YANG SUN: (*leaning wearily against the willow*) I haven't had a drop to drink all day, I haven't eaten anything for *two* days. I couldn't love you if I tried.
         Pause.
SHEN TE: I like it in the rain.

(pp. 436–7)

Only the full scene (with the visual effect of movement and gesture, perhaps the pilot's physical approach towards the girl as he smiles for the first time) can convey the full sense of transformation in this duologue. But our quiet extract shows how the little story told by Shen Te becomes shared and 'effective' through her successful attempt to personalise it ('Once when I was a little girl . . . You're kind') – letting the agency of dialogue end Yang Sun's suicidal isolation. The naive exchange over drops of rain then turns an everyday conversational transaction into felt interaction, marked by Yang Sun's new-found good humour and concern for another person.

Set against this the duologue between Shui Ta (the double) and the same young pilot in the scene (scene five) where he has begun to plot the financial exploitation of Shen Te:

SHUI TA: Two people can't travel for nothing.
YANG SUN: (*not giving* SHUI TA *a chance to answer*) I'm leaving *her* behind. No millstones round *my neck*!
SHUI TA: Oh.
YANG SUN: Don't look at me like that!
SHUI TA: How precisely is my cousin to live?
YANG SUN: Oh, you'll think of something.
SHUI TA: A small request, Mr Yang Sun. Leave the two hundred silver dollars here until you can show me two tickets for Peking.
YANG SUN: You learn to mind your own business, Mr Shui Ta.
SHUI TA: I'm afraid Miss Shen Te may not wish to sell the shop when she discovers that . . .
YANG SUN: You don't know women. She'll want to. Even then.
SHUI TA: (*a slight outburst*) She is a human being, sir! And not devoid of common sense!
YANG SUN: Shen Te is a woman: she *is* devoid of common sense. I only have to lay my hand on her shoulder, and church bells ring.
SHUI TA: (*with difficulty*) Mr Yang Sun!
YANG SUN: Mr Shui Whatever-it-is!
SHUI TA: My cousin is devoted to you . . . because . . .
YANG SUN: Because I have my hands on her breasts. Give me a cigar. (*He takes one for himself, stuffs a few more in his pocket, then changes his mind and takes the whole box.*) Tell her I'll marry her, then bring me the three hundred. Or let her bring it. One or the other. (*Exit.*)

(pp. 452–3, a free translation)

Within a parable play everything – all the details of situation and dialogue – acts as a local parable. The opposition between private feeling and public role, between love and ruthless conflict of interests, corresponds to the opposition of personal and de-personalised voices in the language of encounter. In the exchange between Yang Sun and Shen Te the full emotion is again left unspoken: it is carried by limited speech and completed by gesture – in this respect resembling the devices of a naturalistic subtext. However, the audience response will undoubtedly focus attention on the transference of emotion we witness in the first encounter: Shen Te transforming Yang Sun's suicidal despair into a muted and grudging acceptance of the 'real presence' of another person. In the second encounter Shui Ta's tough counter-voice is not only devoid of feeling; it borders on parody, as it turns a marriage proposal into a hard business proposition. All personal interaction is now displaced by mere transaction. Every word has an economic connotation, compulsion or restriction; here there is no exchange of values, only a haggling over exchange values: three hundred silver dollars for a (spurious) promise of marriage. The dialogue is alienated in the classic Hegelian–Marxist sense, as well as in the Brechtian sense of distancing, through the ventriloquist voices which cannot express 'the true voice of feeling' in relationship. By contrast Shen Te's speech is not alienated, only framed. Her dialogue with Yang Sun embodies an interchange of values and feelings; it is carried by two distinct voices, speech-styles.

It must be remembered, in conclusion, that the personal duologues, though set within the epic canvas, are quite centrally placed in the structure of each parable play. Moreover, they are not isolated episodes, but form one main strand in the multilayered structure of the whole action; related scenes, other duologues, follow from the ones discussed. In *Good Woman* there is a brisk courting dialogue immediately before the chaos of the non-wedding scene (scene five):

YANG: Can you sleep on a straw mattress the size of that book?
SHEN TE: The two of us?
YANG: The one of you.
SHEN TE: In that case, no.

Within a few scenes Yang Sun overhears Shen Te sobbing at the back of the shop (scene nine). Personal commitment has been tested, and found wanting, in the context of a mercenary society. In *The Caucasian Chalk Circle* the end of the feudal war brings the return of the soldier to confront – as in a folk tale, once more – the bride suspected of having been unfaithful to him: their sad, self-conscious exchanges, their hints and unsatisfactory attempts at clarification, offer another example of an 'as if' personal duologue. Then the testing of the relationship is carried over into the second part of the play which is dominated by the corrupt/just judge Azdak.

It must also be remembered that in performance the visual effects – gesture and movement – enhance the personal element, the intimate and semi-intimate tones, in the dialogue. It is difficult to stage Simon's teasing of Grusha without something like a knowing wink, a sly move forward, accompanying his respectably lewd laughter – taking liberties of gesture within the peasant formality. Again, it is hardly possible to look into someone's eyes, or to conduct a discussion over a girl's legs (whether bow-legged or not) without the theatre space between the two speakers becoming perceptibly less distant. Facial expressions are appropriate for these characters who, unlike the wicked Governor's wife or Shui Ta, do not wear masks. Verbal style, voice and gesture would be in concord in these duologues.

Thus, in counterpoint to, but still within, the framework of all the distancing devices – which include the overall theatricality, the didactic prologue in *The Caucasian Chalk Circle*, and the open-ended direct address to the audience in the epilogue of *Good Woman* – we are witnessing the unique dialogue of persons in significant relationship. Brecht has rediscovered the dialogue of personal encounter within the frame of a complex popular theatre.[16]

2. The duel of electronic words and music

The murderous duel of styles between two rock stars in Sam Shepard's *The Tooth of Crime* (1972) is among the most compelling verbal combats in contemporary drama. As dramatic encounter it seems rooted in pre-literary myth, enriched by various layers of modern American slang. The pattern of combat between the ageing star and his ruthless young challenger recalls the ritual murder of the aged priest-king by his young and magically resourceful successor, in Frazer's *The Golden Bough*. As a song contest it recalls *The Master Singers of Nuremberg*, with its promise of artistic triumph for the superior singer. The crescendo of insult-swapping, the exchange of abuse – which makes up significant sections of the playtext – is as old as the medieval 'flyting'; patterned invective is one way to energise the dialogue. These are valid cultural contexts, and it cannot be doubted that Shepard does aim at fusing the primitive and the contemporary. Yet from the standpoint of the play's hero or anti-hero, the

ruthlessly contemporary Crow, such connections with the past
have little or no meaning: he is unaware even of the origin of his
own 'style' in black soul music. His experienced opponent, Hoss,
gains his only success – in the second round of the contest – when
he exposes Crow's ignorance of his own stylistic roots. For someone so totally 'with it', mastered by the mastery of the present,
historical perspective has become irrelevant.[17]

The central duel between Hoss and Crow has several dimensions of interest in the present context. First, while the ruth-
lessness of the combat depersonalises the combatants, the sheer
intensity of their verbal tournament gives it the feel of a personal
encounter. Crow's superman posture enables him to expose
Hoss's vulnerable humanity – his age, his dependence on the
past, his failure to create a new style, his impotence. But even
Crow cannot entirely avoid 'speaking personally'. When one of
his questions is directly addressed to Hoss, as 'you' (instead of
being flung at him in a fusillade of short, sharp, yapping
impersonal remarks) Hoss at once responds with a counter-ques-
tion: 'There! Why'd you slip just then? Why'd you suddenly talk
like a person?' (p. 48).

The second special interest is the texture of the dialogue. It is
made up, in the course of a patterned battle of styles, of many
different kinds of language: cowboy talk; 1920s gangster talk;
the style of the delta blues singer, the voodoo man, and so on.
The main text itself ingeniously fuses slang taken from Westerns,
from gambling, car racing, rock music and astrology (the 'charts'
of the last two overlap comically, as they might in Jonson). Such a
collage of jargons may suggest that we are dealing with a play
where verbal pastiche is predominant – and that is so. However,
the total effect is not mannered or mannerist, for all the style-
samples are hammered into a new mode of interactive
dramatic dialogue. Speech and counter-speech are subordinated
to the ruthless confrontation between the two 'stars'; and the
verbal contest is energised and externalised by dramatic distancing.

In that respect the play is far removed from all the play-forms
and modes of dialogue of earlier drama (especially from Ibsen to
Pinter). Its affinity is with Brechtian theatre, even though Shepard does not aim at distancing in the sense of intellectual cool-
ness. The distancing is in the broad theatricality that places the

action firmly on stage, turning the characters into vocal super-stars, framing and parodying what is enacted and spoken. The dialogue refuses to suggest, or enter, inner states of being; there is no interaction between souls in strife, only a ruthless fight to the finish between two men. Such a fight was the main meta-phor for Brecht's *The Jungle of the Cities* (see above); and it is interesting to discover that Shepard – who considers Brecht as his favourite dramatist – sees the long bout between two men in *The Jungle* as 'metaphysical'.[18] What was a metaphor in Brecht's play becomes the substance of action in Shepard's *The Tooth of Crime*: the directly experienced American pop culture setting has en-abled the later dramatist to give an immediate physical and verbal concreteness to the raw fight of the two men over mastery of mind, body, word and song. The combat is the stuff of the dialogue itself.

Most of act two is taken up with successive rounds of the great battle of words between Hoss and Crow. (It is also a battle of music, of song and chanting and shouting – a dimension of the play that only performance or recording can do justice to.) The two men decide early on that their fight for supremacy is to be decided not by knives ('shivs') or a murderous car race, but by a contest of performing styles:

HOSS: Yeah, so this is how you play the game. A style match. I'm beginning to suss the mode. Very deadly but no show. Time is still down to the mark, kid. How's your feel for shivs anyway?
CROW: Breakdown lane. Side a' the road days.
HOSS: Yeah, well that's the way it's gonna to be. I ain't used a blade myself for over ten years. I reckon it's even longer for you. Maybe never.
    (*Hoss begins to switch into a kind of Cowboy–Western image.*)
    I reckon you ain't never even seen a knife. A pup like you. Up in Utah we'd use yer kind fer skunk bait and throw away the skunk.
CROW: Throwing to snake-eyes now Leathers. [the name given to Hoss by Crow]
HOSS: So you gambled your measly grub stake for a showdown with the champ. Ain't that pathetic. I said that before and I'll say it again. Pathetic.

(p. 49)

At this point 'Crow is getting nervous' (stage direction) for he has no really effective verbal weapon against that style – in effect an authentic 'old style', suggesting a code of values, integrity.

When, within minutes of play-time, Hoss shifts to 1920s gangster style, Crow at once feels more confident; and when Hoss resumes his own style, Crow responds by imitating Hoss's walk (a preliminary move in the 'take-over bid' for the older man's empire and stardom). The preliminary round seems to be won by Hoss, who does claim victory and goes on to insist on the presence of a referee for their main battle of words.

The audience, apart from needing time to adjust to the rapid shifts of style, is now prepared for a full-blown song contest or 'talking opera'. This term is the one Shepard himself uses in the long stage direction which specifies the use of a microphone by each contestant, and their mode of speech: 'They begin their assaults just talking the words in rhythmic patterns, sometimes going with the music, sometimes counterpointing it. As the round progresses the music builds with drums and piano coming in, maybe a rhythm guitar too. Their voices build so that sometimes they sing the words or shout. The words remain as intelligible as possible like a sort of talking opera.' Clearly, 'as intelligible as possible' is open to wide interpretation.[19] The ideal production would release the play's rhythmic power coupled with overall clarity of sense – comparable to that achieved in a good performance of Eliot's *Sweeney Agonistes*. Shepard's text is sufficiently controlled – articulately inarticulate – to enable the reader, and even more the audience, to respond at once to the essential idiom and rhythm of the duel.

The first round sees Crow get a flying start over Hoss by a kind of low litany of abuse, a crescendo of contempt:

CROW: Pants down. The moon show. Ass out of the window. Belt lash. Whip lash. Side slash to the kid with a lisp. The dumb kid. The loser. The runt. The mutt. The shame kid. Kid on his belly. Belly on the blacktop. Slide on the rooftop. Slide through the parkin' lot. Slide kid. Shame kid. Slide. Slide.

HOSS: Never catch me with beer in my hand. Never caught me with my pecker out. Never get caught. Never once. Never, never. Fast on the hoof. Fast on the roof. Fast through the still night. Faster than the headlight. Fast to the move.

CROW: Catch ya' outa' breath by the railroad track.

HOSS: Never got caught!

CROW: Catch ya' with your pants down. Whip ya' with a belt. Whup ya' up one side and down to the other. Whup ya' all night long. Whup ya to the train time. Leave ya' bleedin' and cryin' for Ma. All through the night. All through the night long. Shame on the

kid. Little dumb kid with a lisp in his mouth. Bleedin' up one
side and down to the other.

(pp. 54–5)

Hoss cannot 'answer' Crow's hammered terms of abuse with
anything either as copious or as inventive in 'style'. For Crow has
a certain aggressive originality *vis-à-vis* Hoss, who remains defensive and loses the round. No doubt there is not much that seems
original in the strategy of 'Shame on the kid' as such. But there is a
superior local power in Crow's oral violence: in the staccato
phrasing and the echoic sounds (whip lash and hissing), in the
repetition and acceleration of all those pounding insults, many of
them taken from the jargon of the rock loser: 'the runt', 'the
shame kid', etc.[20] It amounts to a new type of hard rock style, in
performance and speech, which threatens to diminish and engulf
the backward-looking Hoss (a kind of left-over Elvis Presley
performer). Hoss's main defence, in the second round, is to fall
back on the 'old style': he first talks like an ancient delta blues
singer and then as 'a menacing ancient spirit – a voodoo man'.
This gives him the initial confidence of being rooted in a world
superior in human and personal as well as in musical and linguistic terms:

HOSS: Ha! Yo lost dew claw. Extra weight. You ain't come inside the
    South. You ain't even opened the door. The brass band contain
    yo' world a million times over.
CROW: Electricity brought it home. Without juice you'd be long forgot.
HOSS: Who's doin' the rememberin'? The field opened up red in Georgia,
    South Carolina. A moan lasted years back then. The grey and
    blue went down like a harvest and what was left?
CROW: That scale hung itself short.

(p. 60)

In this round Crow is weakening: he can only appeal to the needs
of time present – the new styles of electric music – he does not
succeed in neutralising Hoss's 'old style' at this stage. Both quantitatively and qualitatively Crow ceases to be the dominant
speaker, for the duration of this round. His attack turns into
defence, the crescendo of free-flowing insults turns into a few
feeble one-sentence replies; the pounding rhythm and inventive slang lose their vigour. However, the referee (who seems
biased to the impartial audience, as well as to Hoss) only allows a
draw.

253

In the third round Crow counter-attacks, resuscitated by the violent staccato rhythms of a renewed catalogue of abuse. This speech-style, primitive and ritualised, not only gives him power but magically robs Hoss of his verbal resources, his faculty of effective answering. This time Crow's invective gets even more personal, hitting the older man 'below the belt', incapacitating him with a gipsy spell of belittling rhymes and chimes. Rough slang charges of impotence and failure have the effect of causing impotence and failure: 'Still gets a hard on but can't get it up . . . Can't get it together with chicks in the mag. Can't get it together for all of his tryin'. Can't get it together for fear that he's dyin'. Fear that he's crackin' busted in two. Busted in three parts. Busted in four. Busted and dyin' and cryin' for more'. This crippling incantation reduces Hoss to the loser portrayed, who can only utter short questions and exclamations of futile protest. The referee ignores Hoss's old-world appeals to fairness, and awards the round (and so the whole style-match) to the younger challenger. The catastrophe, if one may call it that, presents Hoss as a humble learner in the new singing school, trying to take over the language and gesture of his young master. The final duologue then has a pattern of attempted reconciliation, perhaps an attempt to move into a new style. But Hoss cannot come to terms with the new style, and cannot abandon the human and verbal virtues (which have become weaknesses) of his own old style: 'too much pity' and 'too much empathy', as Crow proclaims. So Hoss commits suicide on stage – in the old style; and the play ends with the unchallenged, and seemingly unchallengeable, triumph of the new style, devoid of wasteful pity and empathy.

The sustained style-match between the two rock star antagonists (*agonistes*) is Shepard's theatre metaphor, fully embodied in the text of the duologue. It is clear and simple and locally effective; and it would be a mistake to over-interpret it by making too much of its representative existential and social meaning. As in pop art, the surface is what matters most here: 'it's all there, there is nothing more', as Andy Warhol once said of his paintings.[21] Yet both the vitality and the vulgarity of that art can now be seen to mark a technological civilisation which is losing *both* its popular and its 'high' culture – still more American than European, carrying the risk of a contagious dehumanisation of language and thought. In Shepard's play we meet that stage of civilisation as a controlled voice in a still human and value-carrying dialogue. The magical overthrow of Hoss by words alone recalls the dialogue of incantation through which Macbeth loses his humanity and Othello his moral sanity. The dualism of two worlds coming into fatal collision in a duologue of speech-styles is, as this study testifies, a recurrent structure in traditional drama. What has changed – what is most marked, both humanly and stylistically, in the dialogue of the Shepard play – is the *degree* of impersonality. Crow can be seen as a self-styled super-person (that is, a non-person) who defeats what is left of the personal in the self-awareness and the 'style' of the older singer.

One is tempted to recall how, in the first stage of European drama, in the great recognition scene between Electra and Orestes, in Sophocles, the duologue seems to suspend all interest in external plot, in material circumstance, in revenge. All that seems to matter is the emotional response, the recognition by Electra of the 'innermost being' of her brother. 'The act of recognition becomes an act of grasping on the part of the soul, and the act of grasping into one's possession becomes a break-through from the image of a person that has been nursed in one's mind to the body of the person actually standing before one's eyes':[22]

ELECTRA: Voice have you come?
ORESTES: Hear it from no other voice.

A fusion of voices, of styles – 'innermost being' – that is one pole of dialogue, from the *Electra* of Sophocles to the final act of Ibsen's *Rosmersholm*. The other extreme pole may be found, for the time being, in this dialogue of the electronic age. There is a total antagonism of voices and styles; 'innermost being' becomes a term as quaint in this context as the phrase 'grasping . . . of the soul'. What is left to grasp is speech-styles *as* power or 'pure focus', enabling the winner to annihilate the loser's residual personality and language:

CROW: You wanna be like me now?
HOSS: Not exactly. Just help me into the style. I'll develop my own image.
　　　I'm an original man. A one and only. I just need some help.
CROW: But I beat you cold. I don't owe you nothin'.

(p. 64)

In so far as Crow's mastery of style can be articulated, he does make an attempt at teaching it to the defeated champion (in a speech that comes minutes after 'There's too much pity, man. Too much empathy.'):

> We gotta break yer patterns down, Leathers. Too many bad habits. Re-program the tapes. Now just relax. Start breathin' deep and slow. Empty your head. Shift your attention to immediate sounds. The floor. The space around you. The sound of your heart. Keep away from fantasy. Shake off the image. No pictures just pure focus. How does it feel?
>
> (p. 69)

Hoss feels 'just different' at first, then 'Trapped. Defeated. Shot down.' His suicide marks the final defeat of his relatively personal values and speech-style by the triumphantly depersonalised skills of the superstar. By way of compensation, the audience is challenged to *'shift attention to immediate sounds'* (stage direction). (In another context Beckett called his work 'a matter of fundamental sounds'.)[23] But the audience, permitted to listen to the duel of words with pity and empathy, may end by reflecting on the distance we have travelled from the recognition duologues of Orestes and Electra.

Notes

Introduction

1. In *Six Dramatists in Search of a Language* (Cambridge, 1975) I have included a select bibliography of studies in dramatic language (pp. 247–8), based on a survey of the then extant criticism of modern drama. In the early seventies three major studies of dramatic language were published coincidentally: John Russell Brown's *Theatre Language* (London, 1972), Ruby Cohn's *Dialogue in American Drama* (Bloomington, 1971), and Pierre Larthomas' *Le langage dramatique* (Paris, 1972). The only general work to appear since 1975 is Gareth Lloyd Evans, *The Language of Modern Drama* (London, 1977) reviewed by me in *Yearbook of English Studies*, 7 (1977), 351–2. Recent monographs with a language-centred approach include: Madelaine Doran, *Shakespeare's Dramatic Language: Essays* (Madison, Wisconsin, 1976); Jean Chothia, *Forging a Language, A Study in the Plays of Eugene O'Neill* (Cambridge, 1979); Ruby Cohn's new study of Beckett, *Just Play* (Princeton, 1980), Chs. 2–6; James Eliopulos, *The Language of Samuel Beckett's Plays* (The Hague, 1975); and Austin Quigley, *The Pinter Problem* (Princeton, 1975). Growing awareness of the role of language in drama is further reflected in a great variety of articles and essays (some of which are noted in the individual chapters). In this book I have tried to work out a new focus and method for the study of dramatic dialogue.
2. Especially in *Between Man and Man* (London, 1961), part 1 (originally *Zwiesprache*, 1929), and *I and Thou* (1923; rpt. Edinburgh, 1937), esp. pp. 3–18.
3. All types of non-dramatic dialogue – in philosophy, fiction, poetry, opera and film – had to be excluded from this study, though all these areas of interest were borne in mind. There is a very thorough two-volume study of philosophical and discursive dialogue: Rudolf Hirzel, *Der Dialog, ein literatur-historischer Versuch* (Leipzig, 1895). A good recent study of fictional dialogue is Norman Page, *Speech in the English Novel* (London, 1973).
4. See Aristotle, *Poetics* VI, 14 and XIX, 3; Lodovico Castelvetro, in *La Poetica di Aristotile volgarizzata* (1570) first developed a doctrine of consistently naturalistic language; François Hédélin, in *The Whole Art of the Stage* (London, 1684; reissued New York, 1968) stressed the primacy of dialogue since the dramatist can only speak through 'the mouth of his actors'. The Aristotelian approach is opposed by J. L.

Dramatic Dialogue

Styan in *Drama, Stage and Audience* (Cambridge, 1975), pp. 5–6, and it is used as a polar opposite of Artaud in Cohn, *American Drama*, pp. 3–7.

5. I am using the 7th edition (Frankfurt, 1970). What follows is my paraphrase, with translated extracts, of pp. 14–17. I am grateful to Professor Kurt Otten and Helga Wilderotter, both from Heidelberg, for discussing with me Szondi's approach and helping in the translation.

6. James Joyce, *A Portrait of the Artist as a Young Man* (London, 1916; rpt. 1956), p. 219.

7. John Russel Brown, *Shakespeare's Dramatic Style* (London, 1970); J. L. Styan, *The Elements of Drama* (Cambridge, 1960) and *Drama, Stage and Audience*. Ladislav Matejka and Irwin R. Titunik (eds.), *Semiotics of Art, Prague School Contributions* (Cambridge, Mass., 1976), esp. Jindrich Honzl, 'The hierarchy of dramatic devices' (1943), pp. 118–27 and Jiri Veltruský, 'Basic features of dramatic dialogue' (1942), pp. 128–33. Keir Elam, *The Semiotics of Theatre and Drama* (London, 1980) includes a full bibliography. Good introductory articles: Umberto Eco, 'Semiotics of theatrical performance' in *Drama Review*, 21, no. 1 (March 1977), 107–17; Tadeusz Kowzan, 'The sign in the theatre', *Diogenes*, 61 (1968), 52–80; Susan Bassnett-McGuire, 'An introduction to theatre semiotics' in *Theatre Quarterly*, x, 38 (1980).

8. Friedrich Nietzsche, *Die Geburt der Tragödie* (*The Birth of Tragedy*, 1872), quoted from Robert W. Corrigan (ed.), *Tragedy: Vision and Form* (San Francisco, 1965), pp. 443, 444, 448–9.

9. See A. C. H. Smith, *Orghast at Persepolis* (London, 1972).

10. In L. C. Knights, *Explorations* (Harmondsworth, 1964), p. 39.

11. B. L. Joseph, *Elizabethan Acting* (London, 1951), pp. 12–14. See also Ch. 2, pp. 77–8 below.

12. Erich Auerbach, *Mimesis, dargestellte Wirklichkeit in der Abendländischen Literatur* (Berne, 1946; English translation by W. R. Trask, Princeton, 1968), pp. 318, 312.

13. Northrop Frye, *Anatomy of Criticism* (Princeton, 1957; rpt. New York, 1965), p. 269.

14. Not only in the character-study-type criticism (Bradley) but also in theatre-centred criticism (Granville-Barker's *Prefaces*). See also notes 10 and 11, and Ch. 2 below.

15. See Ch. 2, section 2.

16. (1) Nils Erik Enkvist, in lectures and conversations (Cambridge, May 1980) and in 'Categories of situational context from the perspective of stylistics' in *Language Teaching and Linguistics: Abstracts*, vol. 13, no. 2 (April 1980), pp. 75–94. For the concept of the 'speech act' the best initial text is still J. L. Austin, *How to do Things with Words* (Oxford, 1962), lecture viii ff, and *Philosophical Papers* (Oxford, 1961; rpt. 1971), Ch. 10.

(2) For the relevance of the 'speech act' to theatrical performance see J. O. Urmson, 'Dramatic representation' in *Philosophical Quarterly*, 22, no. 89 (October 1972), 333–43.

258

(3) For discourse analysis see especially: Malcolm Coulthard, *An Introduction to Discourse Analysis* (London, 1977), and Deirdre Burton, *Dialogue and Discourse* (London, 1980). Burton's socio-linguistic study, which appeared after I had completed my own manuscript, draws a much more direct line from 'naturally occurring conversation' to dialogue in modern drama than I do.

17. Reprinted in P. Cole and J. L. Morgan (eds.), *Syntax and Semantics*, vol. 3 (New York, 1975), pp. 41–58, 45.
18. See my *Six Dramatists*, pp. 1ff.
19. See also sections 4 and 5 below and my 'Mimesis and the language of drama' in James Redmond (ed.), *Themes in Drama*, 3 (Cambridge, 1981), pp. 225–33.
20. John Russell Brown's *Shakespeare's Dramatic Style* is a notable exception.
21. Morris Weitz, *Hamlet and the Philosophy of Literary Criticism* (1964; rpt. London, 1965).
22. See my '*Endgame* – and the End of (a) Tragedy' in Stig Johannesson and Bjørn Tysdahl (eds.), *Proceedings of the First Nordic Conference of English Studies* (Oslo, 1980).
23. See Allan Rodway, *The Truths of Fiction* (London, 1970), Chs. 2, 8 and p. 124.
24. In *Contemporary Approaches to Ibsen*, 4 (Oslo, 1979), p. 21.
25. See Jonas Barish, 'Exhibitionism and the anti-theatrical prejudice', *ELH*, 36 (1969), 1–29.
26. Quoted in Cesare Molinari, *Theatre through the Ages* (London, 1975), pp. 231–6, 234. The middle style of middle-class values goes with a pressure towards complete authenticity. Thus Emilia Galotti can confide to her father that she is not afraid of the prince who may rape her, but of the pleasures by which she may be seduced.
27. Lionel Trilling, *Sincerity and Authenticity* (Oxford, 1972), esp. Chs. 5 and 6.
28. See Sigmund Freud on *Rosmersholm* in 'Some character-types met with in psychoanalytic work' (1916) published in *Psychological Works*, vol. 14 (1953) and reprinted in James MacFarlane (ed.), *Henrik Ibsen: A Critical Anthology* (Harmondsworth, 1970), pp. 392–400.
29. Maynard Mack, 'The Jacobean Shakespeare: some observations on the construction of the tragedies', in John Russell Brown and Bernard Harris (eds.), *Jacobean Theatre*, Stratford-upon-Avon Studies I (London, 1960; 1965), pp. 10–41, 19–20. See Ch. 2, pp. 85–6 below.
30. In K. Muir and S. Schoenbaum (eds.), *A New Companion to Shakespeare Studies* (Cambridge, 1971), p. 156.
31. See also Ch. 2, pp. 62–6, and note 4. One of the best statements on the gradual development towards the 'freedom of dialogue' in Shakespeare is in Percy Simpson's 'Shakespeare's versification', in *Studies in Elizabethan Drama* (Oxford, 1955), p. 88.
32. See *Six Dramatists*, pp. 236–7, and pp. 198–202 below for history.
33. *Endgame* (London, 1958), p. 45.
34. *Six Dramatists*, p. 154. By coincidence I saw, shortly after writing this,

Dramatic Dialogue

Ruby Cohn's discussion of 'monologue versus dialogue' (with reference to my own comments) in *Just Play*, pp. 64–6. Beckett's own direction of *Krapp's Last Tape* at the Young Vic in August 1980 seemed to bear out my reading.

Chapter 1: *The duologue of recognition in Greek tragedy*

* Unless otherwise stated the translated text is quoted from David Grene and Richmond Lattimore, *Greek Tragedies* (9 vols., Chicago and London, 1960), vols. 1–2. The text has been compared with numerous other translations and, above all, with the double-text editions in the Loeb Classical Library.
 1. The only works I found illuminating – on style and language rather than on dialogue itself – are: Anne Lebeck, *The Oresteia: A Study in Language and Structure* (Cambridge, Mass., 1971); F. R. Earp, *The Style of Sophocles* (Cambridge, 1944); and W. B. Stanford, *Aeschylus in his Style* (Dublin, 1942). Further direct commentaries on Greek dramatic dialogue are acknowledged on pp. 36 and 40–1 above. On the metres of Greek tragedy see H. Lloyd-Jones, *Introduction to the Agamemnon: A Translation with Commentary* (Englewood Cliffs, New Jersey, 1970), pp. xvii–xx.
 2. L. H. G. Greenwood, *Aspects of Euripidean Tragedy* (Cambridge, 1953), p. 139.
 3. For historical studies of the Greek theatre see Peter D. Arnott, *An Introduction to the Greek Theatre* (London, 1959; rpt. 1974), esp. Chs. 1 and 3; Lloyd-Jones, *Introduction to the Agamemnon*, pp. xiv–xvi; and Oliver Taplin, *Greek Tragedy in Action* (London, 1978). My personal visits to Athens, Delphi and Epidaurus proved invaluable.
 4. Reprinted in Arnold P. Hinchliffe (ed.), *Drama Criticism: Developments Since Ibsen* (London, 1979), pp. 35–9, 38.
 5. *Poetics* VI, 4–9 in S. H. Butcher, *Aristotle's Theory of Poetry and Fine Art* (London, 1907), pp. 24–7.
 6. John Gould, 'Dramatic character and "human intelligibility" in Greek tragedy', *Proceedings of the Cambridge Philological Society*, n.s. 24 (1978), 46, discussed in M. I. Finley, *The Idea of a Theatre: The Greek Experience* (British Museum Publications, 1980).
 7. Reprinted in Corrigan (ed.), *Tragedy: Vision and Form*, pp. 454–5.
 8. *Ibid.*
 9. The strongly ritualistic conception of Greek tragedy – that of Nietzsche, Gilbert Murray, the Cambridge anthropologists, Eliot and Francis Fergusson – was opposed by Gerald F. Else, *The Origin and Early Form of Greek Tragedy* (Cambridge, Mass., 1965) and others. See also my *Six Dramatists*, pp. 97–8 and notes 23 and 24.
10. It is a pre-classical language. Sophocles said that he had struggled through a period of imitating the pomposity of Aeschylus before achieving his own finished style; and in *The Frogs* of Aristophanes Euripides is made to attack the style of Aeschylus as obscure, non-

260

sensical, pretentious, bombastic, bewildering and tautological. See Stanford, *Aeschylus*, pp. 1–2.

11. H. D. F. Kitto, *Greek Tragedy: A Literary Study* (London, 1939; rpt. 1961), pp. 106–8, 108.

12. Lebeck, *Oresteia*, pp. 93–5, 110–14.

13. Auerbach, *Mimesis*, p. 46.

14. George Thompson, *Aeschylus: A study on the social origins of drama* (London, 1941; rpt. 1946), pp. 177–9. I doubt if many readers or spectators would find the dialogue at the crisis of the *Agamemnon* 'incongruous or even absurd'. As this scene will not be studied here, see for a good defence Hermann Gundert, 'Die Stichomythie zwischen Agamemnon und Klytaimestra' (Agam. 931–43), in Hildebrecht Hommel (ed.), *Wege zu Aischylos* (Darmstadt, 1974), pp. 217–31.

15. Albin Lesky, *Greek Tragedy* (London, 1938; rpt. 1965).

16. G. M. A. Grube, *The Drama of Euripides* (London, 1941; rpt. 1961).

17. This judgement is coloured by the Cambridge Theatre Company's production of the *Electra* of Euripides (Arts Theatre, Cambridge, 26 February–1 March 1980) directed by David Raeburn.

18. This order is also accepted by Kitto, *Greek Tragedy* and by Lloyd-Jones, *Introduction to the Agamemnon*, while Brian Vickers, in *Towards Greek Tragedy* (London, 1973), Ch. 3, argues for the order: Aeschylus, Euripides, Sophocles, followed by the *Orestes* of Euripides.

19. Earp, *Style of Sophocles*, pp. 135–6. On the simplicity of the Sophoclean language in the later plays: 'There are many lines in Sophocles which might, so far as the diction goes, occur in a prose writer . . . but we are not meant to feel, as we are with some modern writers, that is just how we would express ourselves' (p. 45). Cf. also the comparison between Sophocles and Shakespeare, both moving – with great individual differences – towards a simpler language, more action-related speeches, where 'the poetry seems to come by accident', in the later plays (pp. 163–4 and 173ff). Karl Reinhardt, *Sophocles* (1933; rpt. London, 1979), read after the completion of this chapter, confirms my reading of the Sophoclean vision of relationship. See esp. pp. 157–61.

20. Kitto, *Greek Tragedy*, p. 248.

21. *Ibid.*, Ch. 12. Contrast Grube who regards the *Electra* as Euripides' masterpiece as a 'drama of character', in *Drama of Euripides*, p. 314.

22. For the 'standard accent' see Kitto, *Greek Tragedy*, p. 269; see also Greenwood, *Euripidean Tragedy*, p. 13; for the style of Sophocles see preceding section, pp. 46–9 above.

23. In Vellacott (ed.), *Euripides: Medea and Other Plays* (Harmondsworth, 1963), p. 13.

24. In the phrasing of the synopsis of the Cambridge programme. See note 17.

25. Quoted from Euripides, *Electra*, Loeb Classical Library (London and Cambridge, Mass., 1912; rpt. 1965).

26. In Nietzsche's *The Birth of Tragedy* (1872), esp. section 9. See also the Introduction, p. 6 above.

Chapter 2: *Duologues of transformation in Shakespeare*

* The quotations are from the New Shakespeare (Cambridge).
1. See also Introduction, pp. 28–9 and Ch. 1, pp. 35–7 above for Coleridge and Kierkegaard on 'modern' tragedy and dialogue.
2. For a recent and illuminating essay on the question of speech-in-character versus choric speech see Nicholas Brooke, 'Language most shows a man . . .? Language and speaker in *Macbeth*', in Philip Edwards, Inga-Stina Ewbank and G. K. Hunter (eds.), *Shakespeare's Styles* (Cambridge, 1980), pp. 67–77.
3. Auerbach, *Mimesis*, p. 324.
4. Most studies of Shakespeare's verbal style show a surprising neglect of dialogue as a central focus of attention. See also Introduction, pp. 6–7 above.

   The references in this paragraph are, respectively: Wilhelm Franz, *Die Sprache Shakespeares in Vers und Prosa* (Halle on Saale, E. Germany, 1898–9; rpt. 1939), no. 717: 'Durch die freie Wortwahl war die Prägnanz des Ausdrucks in den unbeengten Wechsel von Rede und Gegenrede ein weiter Spielraum gegeben'; George Rylands, *Words and Poetry* (London, 1928), pp. 144–8; Simpson, *Studies in Elizabethan Drama*, p. 80; Frank Kermode (ed.), *The Tempest*, The Arden Shakespeare (London, 1954; rpt. 1965), pp. lxxxi, lxxix.
5. Shelley, *A Defence of Poetry* (1909), p. 134. Maurice Charney, 'Shakespeare's unpoetic poetry', in *Studies in English Literature, 1500–1900*, xiii (Houston, 1973), pp. 199–207. *Tolstoy on Shakespeare* (1907), pp. 43–4, quoted in Kenneth Muir (ed.), *King Lear*, The Arden Shakespeare (London, 1952; rpt. 1972), pp. xxiv–xxv.
6. These terms are fully discussed in my 'Natural, mannered, and parodic dialogue', *Yearbook of English Studies*, 9 (1979), 28–54.
7. 'The sociology of modern drama', reprinted in Eric Bentley (ed.), *The Theory of the Modern Stage* (Harmondsworth, 1968), pp. 423–50, 442.
8. L. C. Knights, 'An Approach to *Hamlet*', in *Some Shakespearean Themes and An Approach to Hamlet* (1959; rpt. Harmondsworth, 1966), pp. 193–6.
9. Lukács, 'Sociology of modern drama', p. 440.
10. I find myself in disagreement with M. M. Mahood: 'There is no one to share Hamlet's burden'; and on Horatio: 'the man who is not passion's slave is not one who can understand Hamlet's deepest disquiet', in *Shakespeare's Wordplay* (London, 1957), p. 118. The problem of incompletely reciprocal relationship is discussed by me below.
11. In the New Shakespeare edition (Cambridge, 1934; rpt. 1968), p. 197.
12. I have generally argued against B. L. Joseph's view that 'it does not matter' whether speeches are seen as dialogue, soliloquy or monologue. Introduction, p. 7 and note 13 below.
13. Joseph, *Elizabethan Acting*, pp. 124–3, 125. See also note 7.
14. See esp. Roman Jakobson and Lawrence G. Jones, *Shakespeare's Verbal Art in 'The Expense of Spirit'* (The Hague, 1970), pp. 10–32.
15. B. Ifor Evans, *The Language of Shakespeare's Plays* (London, 1952), p.

55. But see also Mahood considering the sonnet 'full of conceits and quibbles of the Religion of Love' in *Shakespeare's Wordplay*, p. 63.

16. T. S. Eliot, *On Poetry and Poets* (London, 1957), pp. 87–8.

17. The discussion of the wedding-night duologue was cut for reasons of economy.

18. Harley Granville-Barker, *Prefaces to Shakespeare*, second series (London, 1930), pp. 141–2, and M. C. Bradbrook, *The Living Monument* (Cambridge, 1976), p. 186.

19. John F. Danby, '*Antony and Cleopatra*: A Shakespearean adjustment', reprinted from *Poets on Fortune's Hill* (London, 1952), in Barbara Everett (ed.), *Antony and Cleopatra*, Signet Classics (New York, 1963; rpt. 1964), pp. 244–69, 252.

20. Raymond Williams, *Drama in Performance*, 'The New Thinker's Library' (London, 1968), pp. 53–79, 63.

21. *Prefaces*, ed. cit., note 13, p. 210. The discussion of the 'duplicated' duologues in the Alexandria scenes was cut for reasons of economy.

22. *The Tempest* is discussed in the final section, pp. 100–5. See also Kermode (ed.), *The Tempest*, pp. lxxvii–lxxxi, lxxix.

23. Mack, 'The Jacobean Shakespeare', pp. 10–41, 19–20.

24. *Ibid.*, p. 18.

25. Lady Macbeth's 'seductiveness' was strongly marked in the BBC 2 production of the opera (3 December 1977). Verdi also gives some tenderly 'seductive' tonality to Iago's baritone in the second act of *Otello*.

26. For the 'co-operative principle' in conversation see also Introduction, pp. 9–10. In *Shakespeare's Dramatic Language*, Madelaine Doran drew attention to Iago's favourite strategy of arguing from mere probability (rhetorical enthymeme) and through conditional and subjunctive (*if*) clauses (pp. 63–91).

27. Robert B. Heilman, *Magic in the Web: Action and Language in Othello* (1956), Ch. 1, section 2, reprinted in Laurence Lerner (ed.), *Shakespeare's Tragedies, An Anthology of Modern Criticism* (Harmondsworth, 1963), pp. 120–2, 121.

28. G. Wilson Knight, *The Wheel of Fire* (London, 1930; rpt. 1960), pp. 97–8.

29. See also Rosalind Miles, *The Problem of Measure for Measure, A Historical Investigation* (London, 1976), esp. Ch. 2, III.

30. Margaret Leighton found the exactly right tones in her recording of the part: The Shakespeare Recording Society, 1961.

31. William Empson, *The Structure of Complex Words* (London, 1952), p. 274.

32. See Enid Welsford, *The Court Masque* (Cambridge, 1927), pp. 335ff.

33. Preceded by the first encounter where Miranda takes Ferdinand for 'a thing divine' (1. 2. 410–506) and followed by the brief and strange 'showing' of Ferdinand and Miranda playing chess (5. 1. 174–7).

34. See Anne Barton, 'Leontes and the spider: language and speaker in Shakespeare's last plays' in Edwards *et al.* (eds.), *Shakespeare's Styles*.

35. Lecture on *The Tempest*, reprinted in Terence Hawkes (ed.), *Coleridge on Shakespeare* (Harmondsworth, 1969), pp. 220–40.
36. Essay on *The Tempest* (London, 1952) reprinted in Kenneth Muir (ed.), *Shakespeare, The Comedies: A Collection of Critical Essays* (New Jersey, 1965), pp. 164–75, 169. For a discussion of the 'anti-Miranda' critics see E. M. Tillyard, *Shakespeare's Last Plays* (London, 1938).
37. See Inga-Stina Ewbank, '"My name is Marina": the language of recognition', in Edwards *et al.* (eds.), *Shakespeare's Styles*, pp. 111–29.
38. Bradbrook, *Living Monument*, p. 215.
39. On the universal significance of the self-conscious rhetoric of 'rhetorical man' see Richard A. Lanham, *The Motives of Eloquence, Literary Rhetoric in the Renaissance* (New Haven and London, 1976), esp. Chs. 1, 2 and 6.
40. Anne Barton, 'Shakespeare and the limits of language' in *Shakespeare Survey*, 24 (1971), 19–30, 30.
41. Inga-Stina Ewbank, '"My name is Marina"', esp. pp. 128–9, 128.

Chapter 3: *The combat of wit*

* The quotations are from the New Shakespeare (Cambridge); The New Mermaids (London) for Jonson, except Regents Renaissance Drama Series (London) for *The Silent Woman*; editions for Restoration Comedy are specified in the relevant notes.
1. M. C. Bradbrook, 'Shakespeare the Jacobean dramatist' in Muir and Schoenbaum (eds.), *New Companion to Shakespeare Studies*, p. 156.
2. C. S. Lewis, *Studies in Words* (Cambridge, 1960), p. 97.
3. *Ibid.*, p. 101. Flecknoe warns that wit should not include these features, in *Discourse of the English Stage* (1664).
4. J. R. Mulryne, *Shakespeare: Much Ado About Nothing*, Studies in English Literature 16 (London, 1965), p. 11.
5. C. L. Barber, *Shakespeare's Festive Comedy* (Princeton, 1959), pp. 99–103, 10.
6. 'Old and New Comedy' in *Shakespeare Survey*, 22 (1960), 1–5.
7. Wylie Sypher, *The Meanings of Comedy* (New York, 1956), pp. 253–4.
8. See William G. Crane, *Wit and Rhetoric in the Renaissance* (New York, 1937), pp. 3–8, and my own references to shifting senses of wit, especially in the introductory paragraph, in discussing *Much Ado* and on Jonson, pp. 106, 126ff, 136ff.
9. *Much Ado About Nothing* (Cambridge, 1923), pp. xxi–xxii.
10. For example Lyly's *Love Metamorphosis* (1590) with its formal, antithetical, wit; a courtly courting game which is hardly comic:

    RAMIS: Dost thou disdaine Love and his lawes?
    NISA: I doe not disdaine that which I thinke is not,
        yet laugh at those that honour it if it be.

    For a fuller discussion see D. L. Stevenson, *The Love-Game Comedy* (New York, 1946), pp. 2–6.
11. See my 'Natural, mannered, and parodic dialogue', 28–54.

12. In *Critical Quarterly*, 9, no. 3 (Autumn 1967), 217–28, 220.
13. See Introduction, pp. 9–10.
14. See note 11 and pp. 66–75 above.
15. For example the stichomythia exchanges between Adriana and Luciana in *The Comedy of Errors*, 2. 1. 9–41, and Julia playing upon the Host's meanings in *The Two Gentlemen of Verona*, 4. 2 (after the song). See also M. C. Bradbrook, *The Growth and Structure of Elizabethan Comedy* (London, 1955; rpt. 1973), p. 51 on the 'quick, shallow dexterity' of wit in the early comedies; she also suggests that Petruchio's wooing is the comic counterpart of Richard III's wooing of Lady Anne.
16. The sun/moon dialogue can be contrasted with the wager scene and Kate's non-ironic submission speech on the obligations of the wife (5. 2. 136–79). See also Robert H. Heilman, Introduction to the Signet Classics edn of *The Taming of The Shrew* (New York, 1966), especially pp. xxxvii–xlii. Contrast 'The *Shrew*' in Charles Marowitz, *The Marowitz Shakespeare* (London, 1978), reviewed by me in *Shakespeare Quarterly*, 31, no. 3 (1980), 436–7.
17. The title page of the Quarto (1598) reads: '*A Pleasant Conceited Comedie* called *Loves Labors Lost*'. On the parody of mannerism within the playtext, see note 11.
18. M. C. Bradbrook, *Shakespeare and Elizabethan Poetry* (London, 1951), p. 215.
19. Berowne's 'sharp wit', as portrayed by Maria (2. 1. 40) may be contrasted with the almost hostile account of Berowne's wit given by Rosaline in her speech demanding penance (5. 2. 837).
20. The lines here given to Rosaline (as in the Folio) were assigned to Katharine in the Quarto, probably due to revision of a first draft which may have included a confusion of identity through masking – an idea used in the Muscovite scene. See Richard David in the Arden edn (London, 1951), Introduction, pp. xxi–xxiii, and Dover Wilson in the New Cambridge edn (2nd edn, 1962), pp. 120ff. I think Dover Wilson is mistaken in supposing that this dialogue sequence (which he places in brackets in the text) has been made superfluous by Shakespeare's revisions.
21. The style suggested may lump together, no doubt ironically, 'natural speech' and rustic/pastoral (to be parodied in the Silvius of *As You Like It*).
22. Discussion of the wit-combat in *A Midsummer Night's Dream* was cut for reasons of economy.
23. Stevenson, *Love-Game Comedy*, p. 198.
24. See also H. J. Oliver's Introduction to the New Penguin *As You Like It* (Harmondsworth, 1968), pp. 32–4.
25. In his interesting contrast between Shakespearian and Jonsonian irony Sackton understates the role of language in *As You Like It*. See Alexander H. Sackton, *Rhetoric as a Dramatic Language in Ben Jonson* (1948; rpt. London, 1967), p. 165. I make a distinction between sympathetic and pathological uses of linguistic satire/parody, but the

former (see Celia on Rosalind and Rosalind on Orlando) is still a language of wit.

26. Allan Rodway, *English Comedy* (London, 1975), p. 103.

27. See Angus McIntosh, '*As You Like It*: a grammatical clue to character' in *Review of English Literature*, 4, no. 2 (April 1963), 68–81, and note 1 for key references. But McIntosh limits himself to the Rosalind–Celia duologues.

28. See Ch. 5, section 4 and note 26 on dialogue and deictics.

29. It is possible to act Orlando as the dumb lover – Simon Callow's interpretation in the National Theatre production of July 1979.

30. Alexander Leggatt, *Shakespeare's Comedy of Love* (London, 1974), p. 205.

31. Jonas A. Barish, 'Pattern and purpose in the prose of *Much Ado About Nothing*', *Rice University Studies*, 60, no. 2 (1974). Other relevant studies of the prose style: William G. McCollom, 'The role of wit in *Much Ado . . .*', *Shakespeare Quarterly*, 19, no. 2 (1968), 165–74, and Brian Vickers, *The Artistry of Shakespeare's Prose* (London, 1968), esp. pp. 173–99. See also note 36.

32. Reprinted in Hawkes (ed.), *Coleridge on Shakespeare*, p. 115.

33. John Palmer, *Political and Comic Characters of Shakespeare* (London, 1962), Ch. 5., esp. pp. 480ff.

34. Cf. Lewis, *Studies in Words*, p. 97; McCollom, 'Role of wit', 165–74; and Crane, *Wit and Rhetoric*, pp. 3–8.

35. As in the RSC touring production, Autumn 1979, with Charlotte Cornwell as Beatrice and Kenneth Colley as Benedick.

36. This view is also held by David L. Stevenson; see esp. his Introduction to the Signet Classics edn of *Much Ado* (New York, 1964), pp. xxii–xxv, where he puts the stress on the 'mimetic', the 'actual' and the 'spontaneous' in the language used for the interchanges between the characters.

37. Bernard Shaw, *Our Theatres in the Nineties* (London, 1932), vol. 3, pp. 320–6, 323.

38. J. L. Styan, *Shakespeare's Stagecraft* (Cambridge, 1967).

39. See Jonas A. Barish, *Ben Jonson and the Language of Prose Comedy* (Cambridge, Mass., 1960), p. 296.

40. See p. 106 above.

41. Nevill Coghill, 'The basis of Shakespearean comedy' in Anne Ridler (ed.), *Shakespeare Criticism 1935–60* (London, 1963), p. 201.

42. Leo Salingar, '"Wit" in Jacobean Comedy', forthcoming, MS., pp. 1–15, 4.

43. Jean Vannier, 'Theatre of language', *Tulane Drama Review* (Spring 1963), 182, quoted and discussed by me in *Six Dramatists*, pp. 168–9. See also note 47.

44. L. C. Knights argued for this in *Drama and Society in the Age of Jonson* (London, 1937), pp. 194ff. His finding has been confirmed by the exhaustive linguistic study of Esko V. Pennanen in *Chapters on the Language in Ben Jonson's Dramatic Works* (Turku, 1951), pp. 200–1 (summary).

45. T. S. Eliot, 'Ben Jonson' (1919), quoted from *Elizabethan Dramatists* (London, 1962), p. 76. Barish stressed the unstable or Baroque element in Jonson's dramatic language; cf. my 'Natural, mannered, and parodic dialogue', 34–5.
46. Bradbrook, *Elizabethan Comedy*, p. 55.
47. Sackton, *Rhetoric in Ben Jonson*, p. 165.
48. In *Drama and Society*.
49. James Howell (one of Jonson's 'sons'), *Epistolae Ho-Elinae* (1645), quoted by Leo Salinger, 'Comic form in Ben Jonson' in Marie Axton and Raymond Williams (eds.), *English Drama: Forms and Development* (Cambridge, 1977), p. 49.
50. Terence Hawkes, *Shakespeare's Talking Animals* (London, 1973), esp. pp. 157–65.
51. See Dryden, *Of Dramatic Poesie*, ed. W. P. Ker (London, 1908), I, p. 83; and Congreve, 'Concerning Humour in Comedy' in *Comedies*, The World's Classics (London, 1925), pp. 5–6.
52. *Ben Jonson*, p. 296.
53. *Every Man in His Humour* (3. 4. 20–2) quoted in J. B. Bamborough, *Ben Jonson* (London, 1970), p. 32. In the Quarto version a humour is defined as 'a monster bred in a man by self love, and affectation, and fed by folly' (3. 1. 157–8). I have taken over part of Bamborough's interesting discussion of this point.
54. For an interesting account of the post-puritan context see Rodway, *English Comedy*, Ch. 7.
55. John Dennis, *Defence of Sir Fopling Flutter* (1722), quoted by P. A. W. Collins, 'Restoration Comedy' in Boris Ford (ed.), *From Dryden to Johnson*, The Pelican Guide to English Literature 4 (Harmondsworth, 1957), p. 163; pp. 160–5 is an excellent discussion of the context of wit. The fullest discussion of the history of the witty couple is John Harrington Smith, *The Gay Couple in Restoration Comedy* (Cambridge, Mass., 1948). L. C. Knights attacked Restoration wit as dull in his famous essay 'Restoration Comedy: The reality and the myth', *Scrutiny*, 6 (1937), 122–43, reprinted in *Explorations*, which started a critical debate on wit and, even more, on attitudes to sex. See F. W. Bateson, 'L. C. Knights and Restoration Comedy', *Essays in Criticism*, 7 (1957), 56–7, and John Wain, 'Restoration Comedy and its modern critics', reprinted in *Preliminary Essays* (London, 1957), pp. 1–35. I have deliberately postponed re-reading these essays until the completion of my study.
56. In William Congreve, *Comedies*, The World's Classics (London, 1925), p. 6.
57. In Joel E. Spingarn (ed.), *Critical Essays of the Seventeenth Century* (Oxford, 1908), vol. 2, pp. 112–19, 118.
58. N. N. Holland, *The First Modern Comedies: The significance of Etherege, Wycherley, and Congreve* (Bloomington, 1956), esp. Ch. 6. Although much of the book is contextual, it also argues for the study of language in Restoration Comedy: pp. 231ff.
59. In *Explorations*, esp. pp. 131–7. See also note 55.

60. 'Volscius in love' is a reference to Buckingham's *Rehearsal*, 3. 2. For convenience, I have kept the World's Classics edn scene division, though I agree with Peter Holland, *The Ornament of Action, Text and Performance in Restoration Comedy* (Cambridge, 1979), esp. Ch. 4, pp. 125–37, that the French-type division was the wrong model for Congreve's plays. For *The Way of the World*, which is more fully discussed, I use Brian Gibbons' New Mermaids edn (London, 1971), the text 'As it is Acted.'

61. This is the passage whose balance of vowel changes Bonamy Dobrée admired in the Introduction to World's Classics edn, p. 23. The 'vowel balance' or phonetic approach has, in my view, a limited value in the study of dramatic language.

62. Quotation from John Conaghan (ed.), *The Man of Mode*, The Fountainwell Drama Texts (Edinburgh, 1973).

63. See also two interesting discussions of this play: Wain, *Preliminary Essays*, pp. 1–35, 16; and Jocelyn Powell in *Restoration Theatre*, Stratford-upon-Avon Studies, 6 (London, 1965), Ch. 2, esp. pp. 58–69.

64. Earlier on (5. 2. 141–58) Dorimant has vowed to leave Hyde Park for Hampshire in a serious, un-witty but (for the audience) comic wooing exchange.

65. John Peters' review of the RSC production, *Sunday Times*, 29 January 1978.

66. See also Holland, *First Modern Comedies*, pp. 199–209, 201.

67. Thomas H. Fujimura, *The Restoration Comedy of Wit* (Princeton, 1952), quoted and discussed by Kenneth Muir in *The Comedy of Manners* (London, 1970), pp. 111–12.

68. World's Classics edn, pp. 337–8.

69. In *Restoration Theatre*, Ch. 10, pp. 234–5.

Chapter 4: *The confessional duologue from Ibsen to Albee*

*   The Ibsen quotations are from *The Master Builder and Other Plays*, translated by Una Ellis-Fermor, The Penguin Classics (Harmondsworth, 1958), except for *Ghosts* where the text is quoted from *Seven Famous Plays*, translated by William Archer (London, 1950). The original Norwegian text was studied for all the playtexts quoted. The O'Neill quotations are from *Long Day's Journey into Night* (London, 1956) and *Hughie* (London, 1962); those for Albee are from *The Zoo Story* in Martin Esslin (ed.), *Absurd Drama* (Harmondsworth, 1965). The sections on Ibsen in this chapter were offered as a paper at the Fourth International Ibsen Seminar, Skien, 1978, and reprinted in Daniel Haakonsen (ed.), *Contemporary Approaches to Ibsen*, 4 (Oslo, 1979), pp. 34–49.

1. Studies of Ibsen's dramatic language: Inga-Stina Ewbank, 'Ibsen's dramatic language as a link between his "realism"' and "symbolism"', and 'Ibsen and "the far more difficult art" of prose', respectively in *Contemporary Approaches to Ibsen*, 1 and 2 (Oslo, 1966 and 1971). Trygve Knudsen, 'Phases of style and language in the works of

Henrik Ibsen' in *Skrifttradisjon og litteraturmål*, Festskrift (Oslo, 1967), pp. 143–71. John Northam, *Ibsen, A Critical Study* (Cambridge, 1973) and 'A note on the language of *Rosmersholm*', *Ibsenårbok* (Oslo, 1977).

2. See Ch. 2, section 2.
3. Lucien Goldmann, *Racine* (Paris, 1956), pp. 26–7 (using a phrase borrowed by Lukács).
4. Raymond Williams, *Drama from Ibsen to Brecht* (London, 1968), p. 77.
5. See Inga-Stina Ewbank, 'Shakespeare, Ibsen and the unspeakable', Inaugural Lecture, Bedford College, London, 1975 and my *Six Dramatists*, pp. 23–5. For the ending of *Ghosts* see also Francis Fergusson, *The Idea of a Theater* (New York, 1954), pp. 158–74, 164 and Egil Törnquist in *Contemporary Approaches to Ibsen*, 4, pp. 50–61.
6. Peter Szondi, *Theorie des modernen dramas (1880–1950)* (Frankfurt, 1956), esp. pp. 22–31.
7. See also my 'Natural, mannered, and parodic dialogue', 28–54.
8. In 'Some character-types met with in psychoanalytic work' (1916) in James Stratchey (ed.), *Psychological Works*, vol. 14 (1953), reprinted in James McFarlane (ed.), *Henrik Ibsen*, Penguin Critical Anthologies (Harmondsworth, 1970), pp. 392–9.
9. In 'The language of *Rosmersholm*', pp. 209–15.
10. The film, directed by Per Bronken, was shown by Norwegian television (NRK) on 10 January 1978.
11. See also Ella's key phrase of Recognition: 'I've never really known till this evening what it was exactly that happened to me' (p. 331).
12. Michael Meyer, *Ibsen* (London, 1967; rpt. 1974), p. 783.
13. Knudsen, 'Style and language in Ibsen', p. 162.
14. Apart from books by Jean Chothia and Egil Törnquist (cited below), the following studies have some bearing on the study of O'Neill's dramatic language: Oscar Cargill, B. Fagin and W. Fisher (eds.), *O'Neill and his Plays: Four Decades of Criticism* (London, 1962), pp. 463–76; John Henry Raleigh, *O'Neill, the Man and his Works* (South Illinois, 1965); and Robert F. Whitman, 'O'Neill's search for a "language of the theatre"' in John Gassner (ed.), *O'Neill: A Collection of Critical Essays* (Englewood Cliffs, New Jersey, 1964) – more on dramatic theme than on dialogue.
15. See also Egil Törnquist, *A Drama of Souls: Studies in O'Neill's Super-Naturalistic Technique* (Uppsala, 1968), Ch. 5, esp. pp. 199–216 (interesting classification of types of soliloquy and monologue in relation to dialogue).
16. Chothia, *Forging a Language*, esp. Ch. 6 and Conclusion. I am indebted to this work for several insights.
17. See also Egil Törnquist, 'Ibsen and O'Neill: a study in influence', *Scandinavian Studies*, 37 (August 1965), 211–35. The discovery of O'Neill's late plays also coincided with the fame of Osborne's early plays.
18. See also my 'Natural, mannered, and parodic dialogue', 28–54 and Introduction, pp. 23–4 above.
19. See pp. 169–71 above.

20. Heavily cut in certain productions e.g. BBC Radio 3, 15 January 1970.
21. See also Cohn, *American Drama*, p. 50.
22. T. S. Eliot, '"Rhetoric" and Poetic Drama' (1919) in *Selected Essays*, 3rd edn (London, 1951), pp. 37–42. Eliot's comment on *Long Day's Journey* is worth recalling: 'one of the most moving plays he had ever seen', Cargill *et al.* (eds.), *O'Neill and his Plays*, p. 1.
23. Chothia, *Forging a Language*, p. 167.
24. See my 'Mimesis and the language of drama', pp. 225–33, esp. pp. 231–2 and Introduction, pp. 10–11 above.
25. *Hughie* is the only one-act play O'Neill completed in a planned series of seven or nine plays.
26. Quoted in Törnquist, *A Drama of Souls*, p. 186, note 4. The stage dialect of Erie was popularised by Damon Runyon. See also note 28 below.
27. The Cottesloe Theatre, February 1980.
28. The richness is partly in the slang containing, in Mencken's phrase, 'pungent humor and boldness of conceit'. See Chothia, *Forging a Language*, p. 120 and note 10.
29. *Absurd Drama*, esp. p. 22.
30. 'Which theatre is the Absurd one?', *New York Times*, 25 February 1962, in John Gassner, *Directions in Modern Theater and Drama* (New York, 1965), pp. 329–36, 334. See also C. W. E. Bigsby's argument for Albee's distinct vision in *Albee* (Edinburgh, 1969), pp. 18–20.
31. Ruby Cohn, *Edward Albee*, University of Minnesota Pamphlets on American Writers, 77 (Minneapolis, 1969), p. 6.
32. Charles R. Lyons, 'Two projections of the isolation of the human soul', *Drama Survey* (1965), pp. 121–38, 134.

Chapter 5: *Duologues of isolation: towards verbal games*

* The Ibsen quotations are from the Penguin Classics edition (see first note to Ch. 4); those from Strindberg are from *The Father, Miss Julie and The Ghost Sonata*, translated by Michael Meyer (London, 1976), except for quotations from the author's notes to *Miss Julie* and *A Dream Play*, which are from *Six Plays of Strindberg*, translated by Elizabeth Sprigge (New York, 1955). The Beckett quotations are from *Waiting for Godot* (London, 1956) and *Endgame* (London, 1958); Pinter quotations are from *The Caretaker*, 2nd edn (London, 1967), *Old Times* (London, 1971) and *No Man's Land* (London, 1975); those from Stoppard are from *Rosencrantz and Guildenstern are Dead* (London, 1967) and *Travesties* (London, 1974).
1. A method developed by Viktor E. Frankl, *The Doctor and the Soul: From Psychotherapy to Logotherapy* (1946; rpt. Harmondsworth, 1973).
2. Reprinted in James W. McFarlane (ed.), the Oxford *Ibsen*, vol. VIII, pp. 535–6.
3. Per Bronken. See Ch. 4, note 10.
4. Reprinted in Bentley (ed.). *Theory of the Modern Stage*, pp. 442–3. See also Ch. 2, note 7.

5. In *Six Dramatists*, pp. 22ff.
6. For Pinter on verification see note 37 below.
7. See also pp. 22–5 above: 'sincerity' and 'dissembling'.
8. *Six Plays of Strindberg*, p. 193.
9. Source: Michael Meyer, lecture given at The Royal Society of Literature, 20 March 1980.
10. For reasons of space and balance Pirandello's dialogue will not be discussed in this chapter. See my '*Six Characters*: Pirandello's last tape', *Modern Drama*, XII, 1 (1969), 1–9, which formed the basis of my inaugural lecture at the British Pirandello Society, Bristol, 1 March 1980.
11. Quoted in James McFarlane, 'Intimate Theatre: Maeterlinck to Strindberg' in Malcolm Bradbury and James McFarlane (eds.), *Modernism* (Harmondsworth, 1976), pp. 514–26, 525; a most illuminating chapter – including an indispensable section on Maeterlinck's 'second unspoken dialogue' – a term first used by Johannes Schlaf (1906).
12. Author's Note to *A Dream Play*.
13. See John Northam, 'Ibsen: Romantic, Realist or Symbolist?' in *Contemporary Approaches to Ibsen*, 3 (Oslo, 1977), pp. 155–62, 159.
14. See Ch. 4, pp. 169–71 above.
15. Strindberg, *The Father, Miss Julie and the Ghost Sonata*, translated by Michael Meyer, pp. 98–9.
16. *Ibid.*, p. 116.
17. Strindberg is probably the first dramatist to see the connection between the advent of the telephone and the needs of modern dialogue.
18. See below, esp. section 4, pp. 213–14.
19. See also Brian Rothwell, *Miss Julie and The Ghost Sonata*, Open University pamphlet (London, 1977), pp. 25–6.
20. The intimacy of the encounter is even more strongly marked in Swedish, with the use of the you familiar (Din):

    FRÖKEN: . . . Vilkens tanke var det?
    STUDENTEN: Din!
    FRÖKEN: Din!
    STUDENTEN: Vår! – vi har fött något tilsammens, vi äro vigda . . .

    (XLV, 198–9)

21. In Irene Scobie (ed.), *Essays on Swedish Literature: from 1880 to the Present Day* (Aberdeen, 1979), pp. 5–43, 39.
22. Quoted from Cargill *et al.* (eds.), *O'Neill and his Plays*, pp. 108–9. Emphasis added.
23. Beckett himself first used this term (*pseudocouple*) for the paired characters of his unpublished play *Eleuthéria*. See *En attendant Godot*, introduction by Colin Duckworth (London, 1966), p. xlvi.
24. See my '*Six Dramatists*', Ch. 4.
25. Quoted by John Fletcher, *The Novels of Samuel Beckett* (London, 1964), p. 194.

26. Conversation between Roman Jakobson and the author.
27. Beryl S. Fletcher *et al.*, *A Student's Guide to the Plays of Samuel Beckett* (London, 1978), pp. 173–4.
28. *Ibid.*, p. 172. Quoted from *Encounter*, September 1975.
29. Eva Metman, 'Reflections on Samuel Beckett's plays' (1960), quoted in Duckworth, *Godot*, pp. xcix–c. Ruby Cohn, Bernard Dukore and Martin Esslin are cited for similar viewpoints.
30. See Beckett's letter to Alan Schneider in Bell G. Chevigny (ed.), *Twentieth Century Interpretations of Endgame* (New Jersey, 1969), p. 12.
31. Eliopulos, *Language of Beckett's Plays*, p. 95.
32. Elam, *Semiotics of Theatre*, pp. 144–9.
33. Dina Scherzer, 'Beckett's *Endgame*, or what talk can do', *Modern Drama*, XXII, 3 (1979), 291–303.
34. See Cohn, *Just Play*, esp. pp. 58–75 (her comments on my discussion of 'semblance of dialogue'). See also Introduction, p. 31 and note 33. In another recent study, Ronald Hayman hears even in the dialogue of *Godot* 'the form and rhythm of internal monologue', *Theatre and Anti-Theatre* (London, 1979), p. 5.
35. For a fuller discussion of mimesis versus shaping in Pinter's earlier plays see *Six Dramatists*, pp. 21–2 and pp. 174–91; for the difference between the languages of Beckett (and Ionesco) and Pinter, see *ibid.*, pp. 168–74. For the context of mannerism from Elizabethan to post-modernist drama, see my 'Natural, mannered, and parodic dialogue', 28–54, where my study of late Pinter and Stoppard first appeared.
36. I go a long way with Austin E. Quigley's argument, in *The Pinter Problem*, in seeing language as interpersonal rather than referential, and wanting a synthesis of the 'what' and the 'how'. But the problem of mannerism does not vanish.
37. 'The desire for verification is understandable but cannot always be satisfied. There are no hard distinctions between what is real and what is unreal, nor between what is true and what is false.' Pinter's programme note on *The Room* and *The Dumb Waiter*, Royal Court Theatre, 8 March 1960.
38. *Six Dramatists*, pp. 189–90.
39. *No Man's Land*, SPOONER: 'A metaphor. Things are looking up' (p. 32). HIRST: 'Someone is doing me to death' (p. 46). 'I say to myself, I saw a body drowning. But I am mistaken. There is nothing there' (p. 95). Briggs speaks of 'A vast aboriginal financial calamity' (p. 61). For Pinter's debt to Beckett see also John Bush Jones, 'Stasis as structure in Pinter's *No Man's Land*', *Modern Drama*, XIX, 3 (1976), 291–304: an excellent discussion, but I differ in my evaluation.
40. Barish, 'Anti-theatrical prejudice', 28.
41. *Six Dramatists*, pp. 33–4 (a section written in 1969).
42. See also William Babula, 'The play-life metaphor in Shakespeare and Stoppard', *Modern Drama*, XV, 3 (1972), 279–81.
43. *Rosencrantz and Guildenstern are Dead*, respectively pp. 25–7, 37–8, 57 and 63.

44. C. W. E. Bigsby, *Tom Stoppard*, Writers and their Work, no. 250 (London, 1976), p. 13. I have quoted the same passage before, with a different gloss, in 'Old and new in London now', *Modern Drama*, XI, 4 (1969), 437–46.
45. Ronald Hayman, *Tom Stoppard* (London, 1977), p. 11. But why is dialogue 'conventionally easy', I wonder?
46. Richard Ellman, 'The Zealots of Zurich', *TLS*, 12 July 1974, p. 744.
47. Hayman, *Tom Stoppard*, p. 10.
48. *Ibid.*, p. 9, and Stoppard's review of Paul Johnson's *Enemies of Society*, 'But for the middle classes', *TLS*, 3 June 1977, p. 677. Stoppard argues that while in life truth and absolute morality need to be affirmed, art is not representational and cannot be true or false.
49. Bigsby, *Tom Stoppard*, pp. 26–7. Stoppard himself uses the phrase 'a complete dislocation of the play' in the final stage direction (i.e. in a different context) in *Travesties*, p. 97. On Stoppard's own ambivalent distinction between *theatricality* and a 'literary piece' (which he would like to write) see Hayman, *Tom Stoppard*, pp. 11–12. As is well known, Stoppard's two plays about dissidents, *Professional Foul* (London, 1977) and *Every Good Boy Deserves Favour* (London, 1977), are 'committed' plays, even though they remain fully playful. I would say they are *not* parodic in the sense here used. In private conversation, Stoppard agreed the later plays were different, but did not wish to discuss the difference.

Chapter 6: *The impersonal/personal duologue from Brecht to Shepard*

* The Brecht quotations are from *Seven Plays*, translated by Eric Bentley (New York, 1961). All translations were compared with the text in *Gessamelte Werke* (Frankfurt-on-Main, 1967), vols. 1, 2 and 7. The Sam Shepard quotations are from *The Tooth of Crime and Geography of a Horse Dreamer* (London, 1972; rpt. 1974).
1. See Ch. 1, pp. 36–7 and note 7.
2. Auerbach, *Mimesis*, Ch. 13. Other scenes referred to: 1 *Henry IV*, 1.2 and 2.4; *Henry V*, 5.2.
3. See Introduction, pp. 3–5 and note 5.
4. Quoted and discussed in my *Six Dramatists*, pp. 98ff.
5. In Notes to *The Mahagonny Opera* (1937). German text in *Gessamelte Werke*, vol. 7, pp. 1008–11; this translation by Eric Bentley.
6. Cf. Roland Barthes, 'The tasks of Brechtian criticism', *Theatre Quarterly*, IX, 33 (1979), 25–9, 28. The additional point on 'natural language' is my own.
7. John Willett, *The Theatre of Bertolt Brecht* (London, 1959), p. 98, quoting from Brecht's essay on work with Charles Laughton, 'Aufbau-einer Rolle-Galilei' (1958). See also *Gessamelte Werke*, vol. 7, pp. 1117–26.
8. *Ibid.*, p. 98.
9. See *Six Dramatists*, pp. 22–7, and Katharine Worth, 'Evolution of

European "drama of the interior": Maeterlinck, Wilde and Yeats', *Maske und Kothurnen*, 25, no. 2 (1979), 162–70.

10. Silvio Gaggi, 'Brecht, Pirandello, and two traditions of self-critical art', *Theatre Quarterly*, VIII, 32 (1978), 42–6.

11. It was the Berliner Ensemble production that first alerted me to the affinity between this duologue in *The Jungle* and certain scenes in Beckett. See also Lyons, 'Two projections', 121–38.

12. The German text is much more telling (e.g. Shlink's second speech): 'Aber die Vereinigung der Organe ist die einzige, sie überbrückt nicht die Entzweiung der Sprache' *Gessamelte Werke*, 1, pp. 185–92, 187.

13. The terms 'parable play' and 'epic play' overlap, and have been much disputed; Brecht himself kept changing his generic labels. He did at one point declare that *The Caucasian Chalk Circle* was not a parable (*Gessamelte Werke*, 17, p. 1205). See J. M. Ritchie, *Brecht: der Kaukasische Kreidekreis* (London, 1976), pp. 48–9, and R. Gaskell, *Drama and Reality* (London, 1972), pp. 139–46.

14. *The Caucasian Chalk Circle* written 1943–5, produced 1954; *The Good Woman of Setzuan* written 1938–42, produced 1943.

15. From Werner Hecht (ed.), *Materialen zu Brechts 'Der Kaukasische Kreidekreis'* (Frankfurt-on-Main, 1968), p. 70. My translation.

16. Part of this material was included in my paper given to the British Comparative Literature Association, University of Kent, Canterbury, December 1980.

17. See also Charles R. Bachman, 'Defusion of menace in the plays of Sam Shepard', *Modern Drama*, XIX, 4 (1976), 405–15, 411.

18. Sam Shepard, 'Metaphors, mad dogs and old time cowboys', Interview with the Editors and Kenneth Chubb, *Theatre Quarterly*, IV, 15 (1975), 3–24, 12. The first play Shepard says he has read was *Waiting for Godot*; otherwise he attributes his originality to ignorance about the theatre. Interview, p. 5.

19. Shepard discusses the relation between words and (rock) music in his *TQ* interview (n. 18), pp. 12–13.

20. Bruce W. Powe, '*The Tooth of Crime*: Sam Shepard's way with music', *Modern Drama*, XXIV, 1 (1981), 13–25, 22.

21. Catharine Hughes, *American Playwrights 1945–75* (London, 1976), pp. 72ff.

22. Reinhardt, *Sophocles*, pp. 159–60.

23. Samuel Beckett, Letter to Alan Schneider, 12 August 1957: 'My work is a matter of fundamental sounds (no joke intended) made as fully as possible, and I accept responsibility for nothing else.' (See Ch. 5, note 30).

Index

absurdist element: in Albee, 194,
  in early Brecht, 240
Aeschylus, 34, 235
  Agamemnon, 17, 37–8, 42
  The Libation Bearers, 30, 38–9, 42;
    Orestes–Electra duologue of
    recognition in, mythio-
    archetypal, tending to
    ritualistic, 44, 45–6, 61
Albee, Edward, *The Zoo Story*, 193–7
alienation in dialogue, 21–2, 248, *see
  also Othello*; Albee, *The Zoo Story*;
  Brecht, *In the Jungle of the Cities*
anti-verbal theatre, 5, 6
Archer, William, on *The Master
  Builder*, 199, 203
Aristophanes, *The Birds* parody of
  Euripides in *The Frogs* by, 51
Aristotle, *Poetics*, 3, 35
Arnold, Matthew, on the poetry of
  wit, 110
Arnott, P. D., *An Introduction to the
  Greek Theatre*, 260
Auerbach, E., *Mimesis*, 7, 39, 62, 236
Austin, J. L., *How to do Things with
  Words*, 258

Babula, W., 'The play-life metaphor
  in Shakespeare and Stoppard',
  273
Backman, C. R., 'Defusion of menace
  in the plays of Sam Shepard', 274
balance, in dialogue, 12–13
Bamborough, B., *Ben Jonson*, 267
Barber, C. L., *Shakespeare's Festive
  Comedy*, 107
Barish, J.: *Ben Jonson and the Language
  of Prose Comedy*, 266; *Exhibitionism
  and the Anti-Theatrical Prejudice*, 23,
  259; 'Pattern and purpose in the
  prose of *Much Ado about Nothing*',
  127

Barthes, R., 'The tasks of Brechtian
  criticism', 238, 273–4
Barton, Anne: 'Language and
  speaker in Shakespeare's last
  plays', 264; 'Shakespeare and the
  limits of language', 104, 264
Beckett, Samuel, 19, 20, 182, 213
  Eleutheria (unpublished), 272
  Endgame, 14, 15, 214, 217–20,
    227
  Happy Days, 33, 198
  Krapp's Last Tape, 31, 214, 240
  L'Innomable (novel), 213
  Not I, 30, 214
  Play, 211, 214, 227
  Rockaby, 214
  Waiting for Godot, 13, 108, 181,
    214, 215–17
Bigsby, C. W. E.: Albee, 270; *Tom
  Stoppard*, 229, 273
Bradbrook, M. C.: . . . *Elizabethan
  Comedy*, 137, 265; *The Living
  Monument*, 263, 264; *Shakespeare and
  Elizabethan Poetry*, 265;
  'Shakespeare the Jacobean
  dramatist', 106, 264
Brecht, Bertolt, 20, 29–30, 182, 236,
  237
  Baal, 240
  The Caucasian Chalk Circle, 30, 48,
    241–5
  Galileo, 241
  The Good Woman of Setzuan, 30,
    31, 241–2, 245–9
  In the Jungle of the Cities, 29–30,
    240, 251
  Mother Courage, 181, 241
Brooke, N., . . . 'Language and
  speaker in *Macbeth*', 262
Brown, J. Russell: *Shakespeare's
  Dramatic Style*, 258, 259; *Theatre
  Language*, 257

Buber, M. S., *Between Man and Man, I and Thou*, 3, 257
Büchner, Georg, *Woyzeck*, 18
Burton, Deirdre, *Dialogue and Discourse*, 259
Butcher, S. H., *Aristotle's Theory of Poetry and Fine Art*, 260

Calderón, Pedro, *La Vida es sueno*, 201
Castelvetro, Lodovico, *La Poetica di Aristotile volgarizzata* (1570), 257
Chaplin, Charlie, in *City Lights*, 107
character: put before plot in Shakespeare, after plot in Greek drama, 35, 62
Chekhov, Anton, 29, 200, 202, 207
  Cherry Orchard, 7, 17, 31, 180
  Three Sisters, 26
chorus, in Greek drama, 32–3, 34
  in Aeschylus, 45, 46
  Euripides and, 32, 235
  Nietzsche and, 236
chorus/spokesman: minor characters as, in Shakespeare, 69
Chothia, Jean, *Forging a Language*, 181, 257, 269, 270
clown-wit, 108, 111–12
Cocteau, Jean, 33
Coghill, N., 'Shakespearean comedy', 137
coherence, in dialogue, 16–19
Cohn, Ruby: *Dialogue in American Drama*, 257, 258; *Just Play*, 31, 220, 257, 260, 272; *Edward Albee*, 194, 270
Coleridge, S. T.: 'Greek Drama and Shakespeare's Drama', 13, 35, 39, 62
  on *Hamlet*, 68; *Much Ado about Nothing*, 127; *The Tempest*, 103
  on the 'shaping imagination', 12
Collier, Jeremy, *Short View of the Immorality and Profaneness of the English Stage* (1699), 161
'comic relief': early form of, in Euripides, 54
confessional duologue, *see under* duologue
Congreve, William, 23, 150
  Concerning Humour in Comedy, 152
  The Double Dealer, 154–6, 163

The Way of the World, 127, 153, 160–6
conversation: idea of dialogue as, 7–8, 10
  language of, in *Romeo and Juliet*, 78
  question and answer structure of, 7, 8ff
Coulthard, M., *An Introduction to Discourse Analysis*, 259
counter-speech, 10ff
Crane, W. C., *Wit and Rhetoric in the Renaissance*, 264, 266
crisis, dialogue of: in Racine and Ibsen, foreshadowed in Euripides, 43

Danby, J. F., 'Antony and Cleopatra: a Shakespearean Adjustment', 263
Daniel, Samuel, *Cleopatra* (1594), 81
David, Richard, introduction to *Love's Labour's Lost*, 265
Dennis, John, *Defence of Sir Fopling Flutter* (1722), 267
dialogue, 1–2
  of crisis, 43
  derivation of word, 2–3
  dislocation of, 17–18
  distancing in (Brecht), 245, 248, 249
  dramatic, 2, features of, 10–11
  includes total sign language, 5, is between 'music' and conversation, 5–8, imitates conversation in interactive structure, 8–9, 161
  interchange of values in, 19–21; sincerity and dissembling, 22–5; sympathy and alienation, 21–2; taboos, 25–6
  mannerist, 8, 202, 203; in Pinter's later plays, 220–7
  structure of, 11–12; balance and domination, 12–14; coherence 16–19; modes and moods, 14–16
  see also duologue
Dobrée, Bonamy, 268
  on *The Tempest*, 104
dominance, in dialogue, 13–14
Doran, Madelaine, *Shakespeare's Dramatic Language*, 257, 263
Dryden, John, 117, 152

on Ben Jonson, 139, 150, 151
Secret Love, 160, 165–6
duologue: combat of wit in, *see* wit
    confessional, 22; in Albee, 193–7;
        in Ibsen, 73, 168–72, (*Ghosts*)
        172–3, (*John Gabriel Borkman*)
        177–80, (*Rosmersholm*) 173–7; in
        O'Neill, 180–3, (*Hughie*) 190–3,
        (*Long Day's Journey*) 183–90; in
        Shakespeare, (*Hamlet*) 66–7,
        72–5, (*Othello*) 92
    functions of, 27–33
    impersonal/personal, 234–7; in
        Brecht, 237–42, (*Caucasian
        Chalk Circle*) 242–5, (*Good
        Woman of Setzuan*) 245–9; in
        Shepard (*The Tooth of Crime*),
        249–50
    of isolation, moving towards
        verbal games, 198–202; in
        Beckett, (*Endgame*) 217–20,
        (*Waiting for Godot*) 215–17; in
        Ibsen (*Master Builder*), 202–8;
        mannerist, in Pinter's later
        plays, 220–7; in Strindberg
        (*The Ghost Sonata*), 209–13;
        universal parody, in Stoppard,
        227–33
    of recognition, in Greek tragedy,
        36–44, 235; in Aeschylus, 44,
        45–6, 61; in Euripides, 44,
        51–60; in Sophocles, 44, 46–51,
        61
    of transformation, in
        Shakespeare, 62–3, 65–6, 85–6,
        (*Antony and Cleopatra*) 80–5,
        (*Hamlet*) 65–75, (*King Lear*)
        64–5, (*Macbeth*) 85–9, (*Measure
        for Measure*) 96–9, (*Othello*) 63,
        89–95, (*Romeo and Juliet*) 75–80,
        (*The Tempest*) 100–5

Eagleton, T., 'Language and Reality
    in *Twelfth Night*', 111
Earp, F. R., *The Style of Sophocles*, 49,
    240, 261
Elam, Keir, *The Semiotics of Theatre
    and Drama*, 258, 272
Eliopulos, J., *The Language of Samuel
    Beckett's Plays*, 257
Eliot, T. S.: 'Ben Jonson', 267
    Murder in the Cathedral, 32, 236–7
    Poetry and Drama, 78

On Poetry and Poets, 263
'"Rhetoric" and Poetic Drama',
    188, 270
Sweeney Agonistes, 148, 252
Ellman, R., 'The Zealots of Zurich',
    273
Else, G. F., *The Origin and Early Form
    of Greek Tragedy*, 260
Empson, W., *The Structure of Complex
    Words*, 263
Enkvist, N. E., on interactive
    linguistics, 9, 258
Esslin, M., *Absurd Drama*, 194
Etherege, George, *The Man of Mode*,
    152, 153, 156–60
euphuism: parody of, in wit-combat,
    110
Euripides, 15, 28
    chorus in, 32, 235
    Electra: Orestes–Electra duologue
        of recognition in, parodic-
        dialectical, speech beyond
        character, 44–5, 51–60, 61
    Iphigenia in Aulis, 43, 56
Evans, B. Ifor, *The Language of
    Shakespeare's Plays*, 263
Evans, G. Lloyd, *The Language of
    Modern Drama*, 257
Ewbank, Inga-Stina, 213, 269; '"My
    Name is Marina"', 264; *Shakespeare,
    Ibsen, and the Unspeakable*, 269

family, the nuclear: in post-Ibsen
    drama, 182
Fergusson, F., *The Idea of a Theater*,
    269
Finley, M. I., *The Idea of a Theatre: the
    Greek Experience*, 260
Flecknoe, Richard, *Discourse of the
    English Stage (1664)*, 264
Fletcher, B. S., et al., *A Student's
    Guide to the Plays of Samuel Beckett*,
    272
'flyting': in Beckett, 215
    in Elizabethan drama, 42
    in medieval Moralities, 13
    in Shepard, 249
folk-tale: formal semi-intimacy of
    dialogue in, 48
    in Brecht, 244–5
Ford, Boris (ed.), *From Dryden to
    Johnson*, 267

Ford, John, *'Tis Pity She's a Whore*, 26

Frankl, V. E., *The Doctor and the Soul*, 198, 271

Franz, W., *Die Sprache Shakespeare in Vers und Prosa*, 63, 262

Frazer, J. G., *The Golden Bough*, 249

Freud, S.: drama pre- and post-, 24, 56, 169, 206
    on Ibsen, 174, 259

Frye, Northrop: *Anatomy of Criticism*, 7, 258; 'Old and New Comedy', 107–8

Fujimura, T. H., *The Restoration Comedy of Wit*, 161

Gaggi, S., 'Brecht, Pirandello, and two traditions of self-critical art', 274

Gelber, Jack, *The Connection*, 16

Genet, Jean, *The Maids*, 198

genre: concepts of, and dialogue, 14–16

Goldmann, Lucien, *Racine*, 168, 269

Gould, John, 'Dramatic characters and "human intelligibility" in Greek drama', 260

Granville-Barker, H., *Prefaces to Shakespeare*, 263

Greek drama: dialogue and chorus in, 32, 34, 45, 46, 235
    duologue of recognition in, *see under* duologue

Greenwood, L. H. G., *Aspects of Euripidean Tragedy*, 40–1, 260, 261

Grice, H. P., *Logic and Conversation*, 9

Grube, G. M. A., *The Drama of Euripides*, 40, 261

Gundert, H., 'Die Stichomythie zwischen Agamemnon und Klytaimestra', 261

Haakonsen, D., 'existential' study of Ibsen by, 20

Handke, Peter, *Kaspar*, 7–8, 19, 31

Hawkes, T., *Shakespeare's Talking Animals*, 150, 267

Hayman, R.: *Theatre and Anti-Theatre*, 272; *Tom Stoppard*, 273

Hecht, W., *Materialen zu Brecht's 'Der Kaukasiche Kreidekreis'*, 274

Hédelin, François, *The Whole Art of the Stage* (1684), 257–8

Heilman, R.: *Action and Language in 'Othello'*, 95, 263; introduction to *The Taming of the Shrew*, 265

Hirzel, R., *Der Dialog*, 257

Hitler, A., speeches of, 90

Holland, N. N., *The First Modern Comedies*, 153, 268

Holland, Peter, *The Ornament of Action: Text and Performance in Restoration Comedy*, 268

Homer, *Odyssey*, 54

Howell, James, *Epistolae Ho-Elinae* (1645), 267

Hughes, Catherine, *American Playwrights 1945–75*, 274

hypocrite, originally meaning 'actor', 23

Ibsen, Henrik, 24, 51, 167, 168
    A Doll's House, 171
    Ghosts, 17, 172–3, 208
    John Gabriel Borkman, 13, 174, 177–80, 199
    Little Eyolf, 170
    The Master Builder, 24, 175, 199, 202–8
    Peer Gynt, 170
    Pillars of Society, 171
    Rosmersholm, 21, 25, 169, 173–7, 255

improvisatory theatre, 17

incest, in Sophocles, Ford, Ibsen, 25–6

incomprehension, tragedy of, 94, 99

Ionesco, E., *The Bald Prima Donna*, 19, 148
    The Chairs, 198
    The Lesson, 196

Jakobson, Roman, 214 (with L. C. Jones) *Shakespeare's Verbal Art*, 78, 263

James, Henry, on the 'terrible necessity of self-revelation', 183

jargons: collage of, in *The Tooth of Crime*, 250
    in Jonson, 139–41

Jones, J. Bush, 'Stasis and Structure in Pinter's *No Man's Land*', 272–3

Jonson, Ben, 13, 22
    Alchemist, 15, 94, 140–1, 144
    Bartholomew Fair, 147–8
    Epicoene or the Silent Woman, 148–51

Everyman in His Humour, 139, 151–2
Timber: Discoveries upon Men and Matter, 139
Volpone, 136, 141–6
wit (out-witting), in major comedies of, 107, 136–40
Joseph, B. L., *Elizabethan Acting*, 7, 77, 258, 262–3
Joyce, James: *Portrait of the Artist as a Young Man*, 4, 258
Ulysses, 53
and Stoppard, 228, 232–3

Kennedy, A. K.: '*Endgame* and the end of tragedy', 15, 259; 'Mimesis and the language of drama', 10, 259, 270; 'Natural, mannered, and parodic dialogue', 66, 262, 265, 269, 272; *Six Dramatists in Search of a Language*, 10, 257, 259, 260, 269, 272
Kermode, F., introduction to *The Tempest*, 63, 85
Kierkegaard, A., on Greek and modern tragedy, 36–7, 235
King Leir, The True Chronicle History of (16th century), 64
Kitto, H. D. F., *Greek Tragedy*, 38, 51, 261
Knight, G. Wilson, *The Wheel of Fire*, 263
Knights, L. C.; *An Approach to 'Hamlet'*, 68, 262; *Drama and Society in the Age of Jonson*, 138, 145, 267; *Explorations*, 6, 153, 258; 'Restoration Comedy: the reality and the myth', 267
Knudsen, T., on Ibsen's style and language, 269

language: anti-illusionist, of Brecht and Beckett, 239
musicalization of, 200
theatre of, 66, 212; created by Jonson, 139
Lanham, R. A., *The Motives of Eloquence: Literary Rhetoric in the Renaissance*, 264
Larthomas, P., *Le langage dramatique*, 257
Lebeck, Anne, *The Oresteia: a Study in Language and Structure*, 260, 261

Leggatt, A., *Shakespeare's Comedy of Love*, 125
Lesky, A., *Greek Tragedy*, 40, 261
Lenin, in Stoppard's *Travesties*, 230, 232
Lessing, G. E., plays of, 23
Lewis, C. S., *Studies in Words*, 106, 266
linguistics; concern of, with conversation, 9–10, 258–9
literary allusiveness, in Pinter's *No Man's Land*, 227
Lloyd-Jones, H., *Introduction to the Agamemnon*, 260, 261
Lukács, Georg, 'The sociology of modern drama', 67–8, 200
Lyly, John, *Love's Metamorphosis* (1590), 264–5
Lyons, C. R., 'Two projections on the isolation of the human soul', 270

McCollom, W. G., 'The role of wit in *Much Ado about Nothing*', 266
McIntosh, A., '*As You Like It*: a grammatical clue to character', 266
Mack, Maynard, 'The Jacobean Shakespeare', 85–6, 259, 263
Maeterlinck, M., 200, 202
Mahood, M. M., *Shakespeare's Wordplay*, 262, 263
mannerist dialogue, 8, 202, 203
in Pinter's later plays, 220–7
Marlowe, Christopher, *Tamburlaine*, 13
Marowitz, C., *The Marowitz Shakespeare*, 114, 265
meta-language, meta-theatre, 219; meta-plays, 228
Metman, E., 'Reflections on Samuel Beckett's plays', 272
Meyer, Michael, *Ibsen*, 269
Miles, Rosalind, *The Problem of 'Measure for Measure'*, 263
modes and moods in dialogue, 14–16
Molière, 107
Le Misanthrope, 25
Les Précieuses Ridicules, 151
monologues: parallel, 30, 31, 192, 200, 214
solipsistic, 30
Mozart, W. A., *Die Zauberflöte*, 104

Mrozek, Slawomir, *Exiles*, 198
Muir, Kenneth, *Restoration Theatre*, 165, 166
Mulryne, J. R., *Shakespeare: Much Ado about Nothing*, 264
'music', idea of dialogue as, 5–7

Newton, Isaac, 153
Nietzsche, F. W., *Die Geburt der Tragödie*, 6, 58, 59, 235, 236
Northam, John: 'Ibsen: Romantic, Realist or Symbolist?', 271; 'The language of *Rosmersholm*', 177; *Ibsen, A Critical Study*, 269

Oliver, H. J., introduction to *As You Like It*, 266
O'Neill, Eugene, 180–1, 213
    The Hairy Ape, 181
    Hughie, 33, 180, 190–3
    The Iceman Cometh, 183–90
    Long Day's Journey into Night, 180, 182
    Mourning Becomes Electra, 181
    Strange Interlude, 181, 191
Osborne, John, *Inadmissible Evidence*, 14

Page, Norman, *Speech in the English Novel*, 257
Palmer, John, *Political and Comic Characters of Shakespeare*, 127
parodic dialogue, 8, 15
    universal, in Stoppard, 227–33
Pennanen, E. V., . . . *Language in Ben Jonson's dramatic works*, 267
personality, subordinated in Greek tragedy, 35
Pinter, Harold, 18, 20, 217, 220–7
    The Birthday Party, 11
    The Caretaker, 14, 21, 221–2
    The Collection, 158
    The Dumb Waiter, 196
    The Homecoming, 222
    Landscape, 30, 227
    No Man's Land, 217, 222–3, 225–7, 272–3
    Old Times, 16, 223–5, 227
Pirandello, L., 240
    Each in his Own Way, 16

Six Characters in Search of an Author, 14, 202
plot: put before character in Greek drama, after character in Shakespeare, 35, 62
Powe, B. W., 'The Tooth of Crime: Sam Shepard's way to music', 274
Powell, Jocelyn, 'Restoration Theatre', 268
pseudocouple, term first used by Beckett, 272
    duologue of, 213
    and semi-persons, 234

Quigley, A. E., *The Pinter Problem*, 257, 272
Quiller-Couch, A. T., introduction to *Much Ado about Nothing*, 109–10

Racine, Jean, *Phèdre*, 73, 168
Raleigh, J. H., *O'Neill, the Man and his Works*, 269
recognition: concept of, includes discovery of 'truth', 201
    duologue of, in Greek tragedy, *see under* duologue
Reinhardt, K., *Sophocles*, 255, 261, 274
Renaissance drama, multiple vision of, 24
Restoration Comedy: in-wit of, 152–66
    Jonson's link with, 151
rhetoric, true and false, 22
riddles: stichomythia as vestiges of, 40 and *passim*
Ritchie, J. M., *Brecht: der Kaukasische Kreidekreis*, 274
Rodway, A.: *English Comedy*, 122, 137–8, 267; *The Truths of Fiction*, 259
Rothwell, B., *Miss Julie and The Ghost Sonata*, 271
Rylands, George, *Words and Poetry*, 63

Sackton, A., *Rhetoric as a Dramatic Language in Ben Jonson*, 140, 266
Salingar, L.: 'Comic form in Ben Jonson', 267; '"Wit" in Jacobean Comedy', 266
Scherzer, Dina, 'Beckett's *Endgame*', 220

Schiller, J. C. F. von, 169
semiotics, Prague school of, 5, 58
Shakespeare, W.: comedies of,
  compared with Jonson's, 137–8
  duologue in: combat of wit,
    108–12; of transformation,
    62–3, 65–6, 85–6
  histories by, as forerunners of
    Brecht's epic theatre, 236
  progression towards
    speech-rhythms in, 29, 261
  stichomythia in, 64, 71, 82
Shakespeare, W., plays of:
  Antony and Cleopatra, 21, 80–5
  As You Like It, 121–6, 157
  Comedy of Errors, 113, 265
  Hamlet, 15, 18, 22, 32, 65–75,
    168, 228
  Henry IV (1), 108, 236
  Henry IV (2), 236
  Henry V, 236
  King Lear, 22, 49, 64–5
  Love's Labour's Lost, 30, 107, 108,
    114–20, 159, 265
  Macbeth, 85–9
  Measure for Measure, 96–9
  Midsummer Night's Dream, 13, 42,
    108, 201
  Much Ado about Nothing, 27, 32,
    101, 108, 126–36, 157, 159, 163
  Othello, 19, 22, 66, 89–95, 235
  Pericles, 104
  Richard II, 236
  Richard III, 13, 64
  Romeo and Juliet, 32, 64, 75–80
  Taming of the Shrew, 112–14, 265
  Tempest, 100–5
  Twelfth Night, 108, 111–12
  Two Gentlemen of Verona, 113, 265
Shaw, G. B.: *Our Theatres in the
  Nineties*, 266
  Pygmalion, 26
Shelley, P. B.: *The Cenci*, 26
  A Defence of Poetry, 65, 262
Shepard, Sam, *The Tooth of Crime*,
  240, 249–56
Simpson, Percy, *Shakespeare
  Versification*, 63, 259
sincerity, in dialogue, 22–5
Smith, A. C. H., *Orghast at Persepolis*,
  6, 258
Smith, J. Harrington, *The Gay Couple
  in Restoration Comedy*, 267

social/cultural context, of a system of
  values, 20ff, *see also* taboos
soliloquy, Elizabethan convention of
  and modern drama, 32–3, *see also*
  monologues
Sophocles, 28, 34, 261
  Antigone, 7, 42–3
  Electra: Orestes–Electra duologue
    of recognition in,
    dramatic–personal, tending to
    conversational (speech in
    character), 44, 46–51, 52, 61,
    235, 255
  Oedipus Rex, 25–6, 167–8
speech, interplay between different
  modes of ('polyphony'), 27, *see also*
  counter-speech
Sprat, Thomas, *The History of the
  Royal Society of London* (1667), 153
Stanford, W. B., *Aeschylus in his
  Style*, 260, 261
Steele, Richard: *The Conscious Lovers*
  (1722), 161
  on the 'weeping comedy', 161
Stevenson, D. L.: introduction to
  Much Ado about Nothing, 266; *The
  Love–Game Comedy*, 109, 120, 265
stichomythia: in Greek plays, 8, 13,
  16–17, 28, 39–43, 158, 167
  in Beckett, 215
  in Shakespeare, 64, 71, 82
Stoppard, T., 217
  Every Good Boy Deserves Favour,
    273
  Jumpers, 230
  Professional Foul, 273
  *Rosenkrantz and Guildenstern are
    Dead*, 217, 227, 228–9
  Travesties, 217, 230–3
Strindberg, August, 51, 80, 207
  A Dream Play, 201, 202, 208
  The Father, 13
  The Ghost Sonata, 13, 24, 104,
    199–200, 202, 209–13
  Miss Julie, 198, 208
  The Stranger, 13–14
structure: before character, in Greek
  concept of tragedy, 35
  of dialogue, 11–19
Styan, J. L.: *Drama, Stage, and
  Audience*, 5, 258; *The Elements of
  Drama*, 258; *Shakespeare's Stagecraft*,
  133

symbolist drama, 239
sympathy: flow of, in dialogue, 21
Sypher, Wylie, *The Meanings of Comedy*, 108
Szondi, Peter, *Theorie des modernen dramas*, 3–4, 174, 236, 258

taboos: breaking of, by Ibsen, 172–3
Elizabethan, on girl taking initiative in confession of love, 79
Restoration, on tenderness and 'true voice of feeling', 160
in system of values, 20, 25–6
Taplin, O., *Greek Tragedy in Action*, 260
telephone in modern drama, Strindberg and, 210, 271
Terence, 'the most correct writer in the world' (Congreve), 161
texture of dialogue, as micro-structure, 12
theatre: anti-verbal, 5, 6
Aristotelian 'dramatic' v. Brechtian epic, 237–8
improvisatory, 17
theatres, Greek, 34–5
theatrical, use of word, 23
Thompson, George, *Aeschylus: a Study on the Social Origins of Drama*, 40, 261
'thou', use of: in Brecht (*Caucasian Chalk Circle*), 243
in Ibsen (*Rosmersholm*), 179; absence in (*The Master Builder*), 203
in Shakespeare (*As You Like It*), 124; (*Hamlet*), 71–2, (histories), 236; (*Much Ado about Nothing*), 135
in Strindberg (*Ghost Sonata*), 211, 271
Tillyard, E. M., *Shakespeare's Last Plays*, 264
Tolstoy, N., on Shakespeare, 262
Törnquist, E.: in *Contemporary Approaches to Ibsen*, 269; *A Drama of Souls: Studies in O'Neill's Supernaturalistic Technique*, 269, 270; Ibsen and O'Neill, 270
Trilling, L., *Sincerity and Authenticity*, 24

truth: fluctuating interplay of fiction and, 200
in Ibsen, 171–8
in O'Neill, 182–90
quest for, in early naturalistic drama, 167, 200–1

Urmson, J. O., 259

values: interchange of, in dialogue, 19–26
Vannier, Jean, 'Theatre of language', 139, 266
Vellacott, P., 55–6
verbal games, in *Endgame*, 219, and *Waiting for Godot*, 217
in Pinter, 220–7
in Stoppard, 227–33
Verdi G.: *Macbeth*, 87
Otello, 263
verifiability; 272, *see also* truth
Vickers, B.: *The Artistry of Shakespeare's Prose*, 266; *Towards Greek Tragedy*, 261

Wagner, Richard, 6, 207, 249
Wain, John: 'Restoration Comedy and its modern critics', 267
Webster, John, *The White Devil*, 90
Weitz, M., *Hamlet and the Philosophy of Literary Criticism*, 15
Welsford, E., *The Court Masque*, 263
Wesker, Arnold, 23
Wilde, Oscar, 27, 228, 230
The Importance of Being Earnest, 225
Willett, John, *The Theatre of Bertolt Brecht*, 239, 274
Williams, Raymond: *Drama from Ibsen to Brecht*, 171; *Drama in Performance*, 82, 263
Williams, Tennessee, 23
Wilson, J. Dover: introduction to *Hamlet*, 72; introduction to *Love's Labour's Lost*, 265
wit: the combat of, 106–9; in-wit of Restoration Comedy, 152–66; love-wit, in Shakespeare's comedy of courtship, 109–31; out-witting,

in Jonson's major comedies, 136–52
    sympathetic or alienating, 23
    true and false, 154, 161
Wittgenstein, L., *Philosophical
  Investigations*, 230

Worth, K., 'Evolution of the
  European "drama of the interior"',
  239, 274
Wycherley, William, *The Country
  Wife*, 151, 152, 158